ROADS
TO
CENTER PLACE

A Cultural Atlas
of Chaco Canyon
and the Anasazi

Kathryn Gabriel

Johnson Books: Boulder

For my husband, David Loving
In memory of Ed Pino of Zia Pueblo

Cover design by Molly Davis
Cover photo by Michael Mouchette
Photographs by the author unless otherwise noted
Drawings by W.J. Underwood unless otherwise noted

Library of Congress Cataloging-in-Publication Data

Gabriel, Kathryn.
   Roads to center place: a cultural atlas of Chaco Canyon and the Anasazi /
Kathryn Gabriel. — 1st ed.
      p. cm.
   Includes bibliographic references and index.
   ISBN 1-55566-079-7
   1. Pueblo Indians—Roads. 2. Pueblo Indians—Astronomy. 3. Pueblo
Indians—Antiquities. 4. Chaco Canyon (N.M.)—Antiquities. 5. Southwest,
New—Antiquities. I. Title.
E99.P9G32   1991   91-12348
388.1'09789'82—dc20   CIP

Printed in the United States of America by
Johnson Publishing Company
1880 South 57th Court
Boulder, Colorado 80301

CONTENTS

Acknowledgments

Much appreciation to John Roney, Myrna Fink, and Alan Hoffmeister of the Bureau of Land Management for their generous assistance with materials. Without them, this book would not have been possible. Special thanks to Thomas W. Windes and Frances Joan Mathien of the National Park Service; to David E. Doyel for technical advice; to my editor Rebecca Herr for keeping me honest; and to Alice and Robert Gabriel and Sharon Niederman for their support.

INTRODUCTION
THE CENTER PLACE

In the beginning, the Grandmother, Spider Woman, created the world, the sun, the stars, and the People. She coaxed First People to climb the bough ladder from the underworld through the *sipapu*, the gateway, to come out standing and admire her good work. Then she told First People to find the *itiwanna*, the center place. Reclining on the ground, she rested her head on Serpent Hill and stretched her extremities equidistance to the four horizons, making her heart the center place. The canyon became her birth canal through which were born the clans who served her. Their majestic great houses were built along her spinal cord. Her arteries became their holy roads. The rain that fell on the crops planted in her womb proved the right actions and good thoughts of the First People. All traveled to the place of emergence to build sacred houses with the clans. Such was the *ianyi*, the power of Center Place.

Within the human cortex crouches an impulse to build something huge. Anthropologists call that sudden urge, when acted upon, a florescence, but it is not as mundane as that. From indigenous villages and their connecting trade arteries have grown colossal monuments with paved limbs stretching across whole continents. We stand in awe of the vault in sophistication, the grace with which the architecture was constructed, the sheer tonnage of earth and stone. We are incredulous of the human capability to perform such a feat at any other time but the present. Yet the quickening has occurred more than once a millennium, and it hasn't been limited to race by geography, as if building on a grand scale is a biological tropism.

That sudden urge was acted upon more than a thousand years

Deep ruts in this aerial view of Pueblo Bonito (top left) and Chetro Ketl (center), Chaco Canyon, may have been prehistoric roads. (Photo by Charles A. Lindberg, 1929; courtesy School of American Research Collections in the Museum of New Mexico. Negative 130206.)

ago in Chaco Canyon (A.D. 900–1130) in what is now northwestern New Mexico. About a thousand years after they first appeared in the archaeological record, the Anasazi began transforming their round pit homes into ceremonial chambers and their square storage rooms into complex structures, some of which were aligned with the cardinal directions and the solstices.

The principal great house, Pueblo Bonito, underwent construction and modification for three centuries. Within that period, eight other multistoried buildings with up to seven hundred rooms were built within the canyon, all with the same planned symmetry, massive core-veneer masonry, and numerous ceremonial chambers called great kivas. Another 150 Bonito-style structures, referred to as outlying communities, sprang up across the Colorado Plateau, which encompasses New Mexico, Arizona, Utah, and Colorado—an area of more than 100,000 square miles.

Within that area, the Anasazi also built an elaborate road system that collectively amounted to a potential of 1,500 miles, most of which, some say, connected to Chaco Canyon. Although the Anasazi possessed neither the wheel nor any beast of burden (for neither would survive the terrain), their roads were highly engineered. The paved, curbed roads maintained a constant thirty feet in width. They were artificially laid out in a preconceived route, adhering to some prime directive for linearity—the roads did not veer around hills or cliffs but rather cut through them or were built over them. Obstacles were negotiated with scaffolding, ramps, causeways, or rock-cut steps. Periodically, a roadside shrine or "herradura" was built into a widened part of the road where the view is particularly breathtaking. Some roads run parallel to each other for two-lane traffic.

These roads were not for casual use. Little evidence of roadside camping was found, and the roadside platforms and towers seem to serve no practical function. The roads did not grow from trade routes, which normally follow the path of least resistance around geological obstacles. The Anasazi roads to Chaco Canyon were deliberately engineered at the expense of an enormous amount of human labor, as were the great houses, and were built, curiously

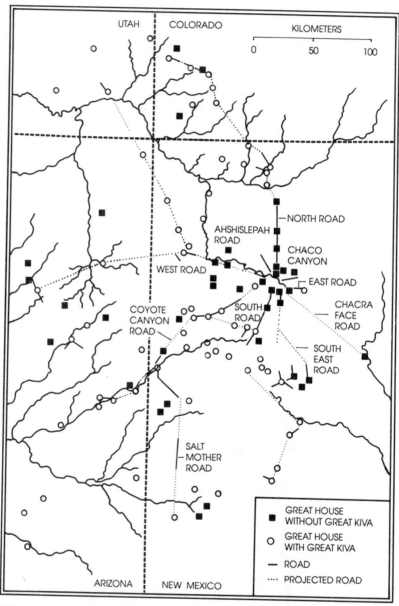

Most archaeologists believe that by A.D. 1050 as many as seven major prehistoric roads led to Chaco Canyon. New road segments continue to emerge as research continues. Segments in Colorado, Utah, and Arizona were connected to Chaco Canyon by the author for emphasis, although they do not appear in typical schemes of projected roads.

enough, during dry years, if our dating is accurate, when energy should have been conserved for survival.

The Chacoan roads are probably the best documented of all the pre-Columbian road systems. The roads have been known since their discovery a century ago, and nearly two hundred miles of road have been documented in the past fifteen years by a handful of archaeologists, universities, and agencies. Archaeologists have postulated as many as seven roads out of Chaco Canyon by connecting road fragments and outliers to the canyon. This reasoning was left over from the theory that Chaco Canyon was the administrative or political hub of an empire that thrived on a redistribution system. It seemed plausible that the roads would lead to that hub for the purpose of transporting goods, connecting communities, and moving great numbers of people.

Although the debate continues, many archaeologists now believe that Chaco Canyon was the ceremonial nexus for the outlying communities. Supporting evidence for this theory includes extensive religious architecture in the canyon, along with a dearth of burials (with the exception of a few high status burials), intermittent consumption of huge amounts of food at the great houses, and large-scale breakage of ceramic vessels. It appears that wor-

As many as 150 great houses (also called public houses) sprung up across the Colorado Plateau, characterized by similar features at Pueblo Bonito at the heart of the system in Chaco Canyon. (Photo by Michael Mouchette.)

shippers bearing pottery and gifts of food came to the canyon on the roads periodically for ceremony.

Only two and possibly three roads, however, have been confirmed as contiguous roads. The vast majority of the known roads are in the immediate Chaco Canyon area or emanate directly from Chacoan outliers, but have no obvious destination and do not necessarily connect with other houses. Furthermore, as the roads approach outlying structures, their surfaces are often more pronounced and the stairways, ramps, and berms are more numerous and elaborate. These roads, which seem more like malls, are direct extensions of the great houses themselves, perhaps designed for cosmological emphasis, a show of power, or pure aesthetics. Some road fragments do connect to important resources while others head off in the direction of neighboring towns.

By the mid-twelfth century, Chaco Canyon lay suddenly deserted. The roads appear to have been ritually closed, the important chambers of the great houses dismantled and burned. Many of the distant great houses were left to the elements, unvisited and unmolested. The Navajo living in the area today regard the roads as evil and dark. After all, the Navajo considered the *Anaasa'zi'* to be the "ancient enemy."

The Navajo, who are not descendants of the Anasazi, nevertheless inherited the great houses and the roads after the Chacoans abandoned them, and today, they continue to harbor myths about them. Navajos refer to the roads as tunnels where legendary figures hid from *Ye'iitsoh* (Big Monster). Some archaeologists refer to the roads as ceremonial ways, while others say that their nonutilitarian purpose, supplemented with other evidence, suggests that they are "monuments to social organization," projects much like the pyramids or standing stone formations. Much as they do in Mesoamerican societies contemporary with the Anasazi, the road fragments may reflect an insatiable appetite for order, by underscoring a cardinal direction or an astronomical alignment.

We can only impose our loose interpretation of eclectic Pueblo belief on the actions of their predecessors, the Anasazi, as I did in the first paragraph of this introduction. Generally speaking, in the

Many of the Chacoan roads, called "ceremonial ways," led to shrine-crowned buttes such as Fajada Butte (left) at the mouth of the canyon. The roads may have also aided travelers in navigating the vastness of the San Juan Basin. (Photo by Michael Mouchette.)

Pueblo view, a cardinal direction is linked to a season; above is the present physical plane, below is the underworld where everything is opposite to the above. The center place is the pueblo— and the individual. To the Pueblo, a road is a kind of altar, a channel for the life's breath, and to travel the straight road to the center place is to strive for equilibrium.

In those terms, and in the context of the Anasazi, the word "atlas" takes on new meaning. *Roads to Center Place: A Cultural Atlas of Chaco Canyon and the Anasazi* is more than a guide to road corridors and archaeological features, it is a map to a lifeway.

Older than the Mesas:
Ancient Roads and Trails

From a secular, cost-benefit perspective, it is difficult to imagine how a society such as that of the Anasazi could justify the construction of hundreds of miles of wide surfaced avenues during a drought. Our present concept of "roads" cannot be applied to a pre-Columbian New World context. In our contemporary society, a road is considered to be a route of overland communication between established communities. Roads tend to be reminders of political power and are connectors of political entities. But the road is a five-thousand-year-old product of evolution, manifested in different forms.

From neolithic hunting paths and intertribal trails emerged intercontinental trade routes and imperial highways that held vast empires intact. To understand the ceremonial ways of the Anasazi in the greater San Juan Basin, we must first walk a few miles on the roads of other ancient cultures.

Old World Roads

"Now the Carthaginians are said to have been the first to pave roads with stones," writes an early scholar. "Afterwards the Romans laid them out over almost the whole world, for directness of journey, and to prevent the populace from being workless." Our contemporary notion of the road comes from the Romans, but they weren't the first to construct roads. Road engineering dates as far back as the third millennium B.C. In that time period, the towns in the Indus Valley had brick-paved streets, understreet drainage, and curved street corners for wheeled carriages.

During the next great period of Indian civilization, Mauryan rulers from the fourth to the second centuries B.C. built a royal road through the imperial capital of Pataliputra. From the Indian route books, the Greek philosopher Eratosthenes (who accurately estimated the circumference of the earth) calculated the length of this great road to be 16,000 Greek *stadia* or 2,600 miles.

Other ancient roads have been found such as the one constructed by the Assyrian road engineers. The *ummani*, or pioneer corps of the army of the Tiglath Pilesar I, cut a road through the mountain ranges to the north of Mesopotamia as the king pursued his enemies about 1,100 years before Christ.

Some roads of the ancient empires served a more ecclesiastical purpose. A processional way around the Dharmarajika stupa at Tsila in ancient India was made from lime and sand mortar in which were set colorful shells in geometric patterns. Ceremonial ways have been recorded in the Assyrian empire from the tenth century on. The road of the kings at Nineveh, built in the reign of Sanherib (c. 700 B.C.) was ninety feet wide. The Egyptians built immense causeways to accommodate the building blocks used in the construction of the pyramids, and later the placement of the statues of gods.

The ancient road system of China was to southeast Asia what the Roman roads were to western Europe. The imperial roads were about two thousand miles in length, and were connected with a vast length of earthen roads and bridle tracks. Many of them were broad, well built, and paved with massive slabs of stone. Steep mountain walls were ascended with stone steps broad enough to oblige a mule. Tunnels cut through the crests of the ranges shortened the climb. Maintenance of these roads was provided through a land tax, but the stones made travel so miserable that most taxpayers stuck to the beaten paths.

Chinese roads tended to follow a straight line for a distance on the plains, and are conveniently sinuous on the slope of a hill. The bends in Chinese roads were incorporated, according to legend, out of the necessity to dodge evil spirits, although the explanation may have been adapted to the practical need to avoid certain political turfs.

When the Romans conquered Syria, they were given access to the world of the Orient and its luxuries. Rome and Chang-an became connected by a trade route, the final stage of China's silk trade system. By the first century B.C., Chinese silk was common among rich courtiers of the Persian empire. Caravans shuttled along the long and arduous road between Susa and Chang-an, exchanging gold and horses for silk. Major trading contacts with Europe began about that period as well.

The Roman roads served salt trade and the military, beginning in 312 B.C. when Appius Claudius persuaded the senate to build a 130-mile avenue from Rome to the recently won city of Capua, so important for its coastal salt pans. The Romans may have borrowed the concept of the road from the Carthaginians' stone-paved roads built to accommodate the wheeled chariot, but the tomb-lined Via Appia is heralded as an engineering marvel built on a firm foundation for heavy travel and water drainage. Rome's

The ruined Cluniac priory, founded in 1090 by William de Wareness in Castle Acre, Norfolk, England, sits on a Roman road called Peddars Way. The native road was of little strategic importance, but the Romans invested a great deal of time and effort in turning this trail into a well-built trade route that included a 16-foot causeway and reached widths of 45 feet.

tentacles spread from this first road construction project throughout Europe, North Africa, and the Middle East, an estimated length of 53,000 miles.

Roman roads enabled a legion to quickly reach any point threatened by attack or rebellion. Their main purpose, however, was not for conquest but for administration. The roads were engineered to radiate from Rome to the outermost parts of the Empire. These radial roads had many branches, connected by a network of minor crossroads. They united the subjects of the most distant provinces by an easy and familiar intercourse. In addition to the official and military traffic, the roads were largely used by civilians, who traveled to Rome to attend musical and athletic events, to teach or be taught, and to maintain the colonial missions sent out by the church. The Roman Empire would not have been possible without its system of well-built roads.

Participation in the construction of roads reinforces social values and is an end in itself. This sentiment was echoed by J.W. Gregory in 1938 in *The Story of the Road*: ". . . the Romans did the same throughout all the World, to make the Roads straight, and to keep the Multitude out of Idleness." Romans had large supplies of slave labor to draw on, and many miles were built by soldiers as well, sometimes to avoid disciplinary problems.

From the Romans and the Indians, we inherited such roadside attractions as guardhouses and staging posts, bed and breakfasts, and *itinerarii* or guidebooks. Roman roads also reflected the distinction between the *viæ praetoriæ*, state-owned roads maintained by a state-paid bureaucrat, and the *viæ rusticæ*, built and maintained by private individuals or townships.

Pre-Columbian Trails

What is remarkable is the proliferation of sophisticated roadways among the traditional routes of communication and exchange scattered across the Western Hemisphere. To appreciate the full scale of the road monuments, it is important to distinguish them from trails or paths.

The major distinction between roads and trails is made with respect to two attributes: width and degree of construction. In general, trails are no more than a couple feet wide, while roads vary from a few feet to up to sixty feet wide. The consistently greater width of formalized roads is due to more extensive construction. A road is cleared and graded, sometimes paved with materials, and is either elevated like a causeway or is level with the ground.

Colleen Marguerite Beck, who has provided the most thorough research on Peruvian roads to date, made this distinction between roads and trails in 1979: "Paths are geomorphic, following a route that is the easiest, most direct way between two geographical points . . . paths conform to the natural surface of the land and do not involve planned alteration of the course . . . the path is caused by the friction of feet on the earth." The only labor investment in a path, she says, is in deciding the easiest course.

In contrast, prehistoric Peruvian roads, and pre-Columbian roads in general, may be geomorphic on occasion, but to a much more limited extent than paths, and involve a considerable labor investment, including surveying, engineering, and construction. "Thus a road is planned and built, whereas a path is the result of wear," Beck writes.

Trails tend to serve no other purpose than to get from one point to the next in the most expedient manner, their course marked by generations of use. Of trails in New Mexico, the host to Chaco Canyon, G. Thompson, in an 1879 survey of the "interior tribes of the west" for the U.S. government, wrote:

> Their trails are remarkable extending as they do in a straight line from one pueblo to another, and even traced from ruin to ruin. These deeply worn paths, even on the rocks, passing without swerving to right or left, over valley, plain, or ascent of mesa—as though the trail was older than the mesas, or before the canyons gnawed into the plateaus by erosion, had reached their pathway— speak more powerfully than all else of how old a people they are.

Trails have been discovered all over California. Many of the trails were wide and worn a couple feet deep from long use and therefore could be traced long after the Indians abandoned the paths. Wailaki trails in California progressed in straight lines without going around mountains in the way. Sometimes the Wailaki had trails that went to look-out stations at the highest part of the mountains, perhaps to observe the movements of enemies. Similarly, "Miwok trails were usually airplane in their directness, running up hill and down dale without zigzags or detours," writes an explorer.

"Myriads of Indian trails crisscrossed each other in the valleys [of] California," writes another explorer. "Early travelers were often confused by the multitude of choices; they needed and used Indian guides to show the correct paths."

Trails in Arizona and Nevada share the same characteristics and cultural association as those in California. The widths of these trails ranged from 12 inches upward and rarely exceeded 20 inches. In some areas the trail was cut through boulders. As rocks were pushed aside, a slight ridge or berm was formed by clearing the rock debris to either side.

A favorite Sunday adventure for many New Mexicans is to visit the ruins at Bandelier National Monument and climb the spindly ladders and trails hugging the sides of the volcanic cliffs in the footsteps of the Anasazi. Visitors can ascend ladders and rock climbways of carved out footholds and handholds to reach Ceremonial Cave 150 feet above the canyon floor. At Tsankawi, a ruin in a detached section of Bandelier, a circular route runs through the prehistoric village. The path visitors follow is in many places the original trail. Centuries of treading have worn ankle-deep ruts in the rock.

Trails in New Mexico have long been observed and commented on as side-bars to reports on archaeological sites. Early archaeologists discovered trails while excavating ruins and tried to distinguish between native Pueblo and Navajo trails. Edgar Hewett, an early prominent Chacoan archaeologist, made the following entry in 1909:

> One must climb to the mesa top by the old Navajo trail south of the Rito, follow this a mile or two toward the mountains, and then descend by an ancient rock trail into the gorge at the site of the old Tyuonyi villages [at Bandelier National Monument]. Another ancient trail enters the canyon from the north.

John P. Harrington, another archaeologist, stumbled across the same roads, saying that knowledge about the ancient trails is surprisingly difficult to get, which seems to be true across the board for all North American trails. While some of the trails he mentioned in 1916 are major links covering long distances, including "the old and still well-worn trail to the Ute Indian country," most appear to be short connections between nearby pueblos. A third archaeologist, William Boone Douglas, in 1917, mentioned trails "leading up the mesas and along the ridges." A fairly clear distinction seems apparent between shorter "use trails" and longer trails, which in many cases seemed planned.

Frank Hamilton Cushing, in his research on Zuñi traditions, said that an old trail connected some of the abandoned pueblos with the source of salt at Zuñi Salt Lake. In 1896, he wrote:

> Not only did a trail (used for such long ages that I have found it brokenly traceable for hundreds of miles) lead down from the clifftown country to this broad valley to the Lake of Salt, but also there have been found in nearly all the cliff dwellings of the Mancos and San Juan section, whence this trail descends, salt in the characteristic kernels and colors found in this same source of the Zuñi supply.

Indian trails in the Eastern United States possessed the same sort of characteristics. The width of trails, according to William E. Myer, in 1928, varied depending on the vegetation and terrain of the area crossed:

> In the wooded or mountainous regions of the central southern United States, the Indians were forced to go in single file and the paths were usually from 18 to 24 inches in width. On the open grassy prairies of the Middle West, however, where there were no special obstacles, they proceeded en masse in such formation as suited their pleasure, and thus often made wide trails.

Rest Stops and Trail Markers

Adding to the mystery of the Anasazi roadways are the accompanying circular rock shrines, called *herraduras*, which are often found at subtle changes in road direction, and elevated room-

This large "Bonito Cairn," on the edge of West Mesa overlooking the Chaco Wash and Escavada Wash junction, was built in Bonito-style masonry. It is typical of trailside cairns of most Native Americans. Some cairns seen near Anasazi roads today were built by Navajo who reused the roads. (Photo courtesy National Park Service.)

blocks called *avanzadas*. These structures show no signs of practical use. The forerunners of these structures may have been the typical features of aboriginal trails. Cairns, low circular piles of stones seldom exceeding a meter in height or diameter, are a world-wide phenomenon. They are sometimes found at forks in the trail, while larger ones appear at passes. Trails of the Yurok in California were marked by piles of twigs or cairns of stone sometimes accumulated in heaps several feet high. It is said that every Indian passing by deposited a twig or rock on the pile.

One section of trail in California contained sixty-four cairns of differing sizes, the largest being two to three feet high with a base diameter of four feet. Occasionally, the cairns reached substantial proportions. At the apex of the Mopi Pass in the Turtle Mountains of San Bernardino County, three identical cairns grew so large that they eventually coalesced into one, weighing an estimated three tons.

An account of Shoshone trails in Nevada by ethnologist W.J. Hoffman in 1878 suggests that the act of building such features

along trails indicates that the trails were formalized and not expected to change:

The Indians who occupy small patches of soil for permanent en-
campments are in the habit of selecting suitable places along the
foot-trails for gathering the fruit of this tree [piñon] and storing it
for future use, as well as for such of the tribe as may be unable to
reach camp, or in want of food. All the Shoshones in the southern
interior of Nevada provide for one another in this manner.

Their mode of doing so is in this wise: a number of stones are
collected, each of them from one-half to one cubic foot in bulk,
which are arranged in the shape of a circle having a diameter of
from two to four feet. When fruit is abundant (which happens
once in three years in respective localities), it is collected and
piled into this circle, covered over with sticks and leaves, and finally a layer of earth, so as to secure them from rodents and
birds. Still, the former more frequently discover these deposits
than the benighted warrior for whom they are intended.

The Shoshones do not know of any circles connected with religious or burial ceremonies. Circles of similar construction [are]
sometimes found upon elevated points of land, where they are located as a post from which a good view of the surrounding country can be obtained.

In Colorado, heavy vegetation hampers the tracking of aboriginal roads. In 1878, William Byers wrote the following account on
an area above the timberline:

At Boulder Pass, 55 miles west of Denver, an old trail or trace led
where a wagon road is now built. It passes at 11,600 feet above sea
level, and traverses at that height a plateau above timber line for
about 20 miles further south on the same range, but of still greater
length, is a similar pass, by a transverse ridge, but of still greater
length above timber line. Here is an old roadway which has evidently borne infinite travel of some kind. At intervals along it are
circular works, apparently for protection or hiding places.

Stone heaps, equivalent to the cairns found widely in the West,
have been found along the trails in Ohio and reputedly had prehistoric burials beneath them.

Shrines and sleeping circles (rock circles possibly used for
overnight lodging) have even been found on the trails around

Paquime, a village at Casas Grandes in northern Mexico that is twenty-seven times larger than Pueblo Bonito. Casas Grandes is believed to have been on a trading circuit with Pueblo Bonito. The Malpais trails form a network that connects waterhole to waterhole, and reaches in all directions toward the dunes and in the deserts beyond the Sierra. A system of signal towers alongside the roads were used for widespread smoke or fire communication. The road passed nearby shrines and sleeping circles. Heavily varnished flakes and tools may occasionally be found on these abandoned trail sections.

Roadside features in the Southwest are analogous to those in China, Tibet, and Peru. At the summit of a high pass in China and Tibet, each traveler adds to the cairn a stone slab which is often engraved with the Buddhist prayer, "Om mane padme, hom."

An early twentieth century scholar, E.G. Squier, thought the road system of China and Tibet to be adopted in Peru. Of the Inca roads he wrote:

All these passes over the mountains are marked by huge piles of stone raised like the cairns of Scotland and Wales, by the contributions of a single stone from each traveller as an offering to the spirit of the mountains, and as an invocation for their aid in sustaining the fatigues of travel. These great stone heaps still exist, and will remain to the end of time, monuments marking ever the routes of travel in the days of the Incas.

The stone heaps and cairns and shrines and circles could have served a more practical use as trail markers, mile markers, or survey aids. Practicality is often consecrated. Regardless of their origin, the stone configurations may have guaranteed protection.

Rights of asylum, enforced by superstition, were assumed by many travelers on primitive roads. The aborigines in Australia traveled safely on intertribal tracks protected by fetishes. In medieval times, pilgrims and crusaders were safeguarded by religious sentiment. Roads were often placed under "The King's Peace," as in the case of four Roman roads by decree of Edward the Confessor, which did little, however, to protect later travelers from highwaymen. A note on "The Sacred Road" of Herodotus of early classical times states, "Wayfarers on the road were under the God's protection. . . . This was the route of the sacred embassies to Delphi; by it Apollo himself went." The fact that the Navajo believed the ancient ones were protected from monsters when they traveled on the Chacoan roads suggests that they may have been protected by rights of asylum.

Ancient roads were not the next logical step after trails in the evolution of transportation. Trails were invented the first time a hominid followed the same route to the next camp more than once. Roads in wheelless societies were an expression of so much more than mere travel.

High Roads of the Pre-Columbian World

Primitive societies do not build roads, though they may have trails and paths. The construction of roads implies a centralized government that exercises influence over an area of greater extent than the roads themselves. This entity must have the power to command labor to build roads, technical experts to supervise the work force, and a level of technology competent to survey and undertake construction.

In Mexico, the best documented prehistoric roads are those surrounding the Chalchihuites site of La Quemada in Zacatecas. Currently, an estimated 102 miles of pre-Conquest roadways dating to A.D. 700 to 900 have been mapped and have been noted and commented upon since the first half of the nineteenth century. The roads were constructed above the ground surface so that two parallel rows of stone are constructed in a straight line to the desired height and width. The area between was then filled with rubble and capped with flagstones. Archaeologist Charles Trombold, who recently redated La Quemada to A.D. 600 to 800, said the roads were built to emphasize political power.

Of the Mesoamerican and South American systems, the Inca roads are said to be the most similar to those of Chaco in construction technique, patterning of associated architecture, and roadbed dimensions.

Chavín de Huantar was a religious center that held sway over a thousand square miles of modern Peru from 850 B.C. to about A.D. 200. The ancestors of the Inca emperors, the Chavín, among other subcultures, may have built some of the original roads the Inca later used to keep a 35,000-square-mile empire intact during the twelfth century A.D.

The superhighways of the Inca provided the cohesion for an empire stretched across three distinct regions: the Andean highlands, the tropical rain forest, and the desert coastal strip. The royal road along the spine of the Andes ran 3,450 miles from the Columbia-Ecuador border to Central Chile, and is said to be the longest trunk road in the world prior to the nineteenth century. It was linked by lateral roads to the 2,500-mile-long coastal highway like rungs of a ladder.

The system included intermittently paved roads up to twenty-four feet wide, tunnels, bridges, and stepped pathways cut into rock. Mountains were traversed with long stairways that ascended hundreds of feet in some places. Rivers were crossed with rope bridges or cantilevered arches of large slabs of stone.

The roads were built, with citizenry labor, for the purpose of administration and dispatching military units with haste, and used to tax the same citizens who built them. Clinging to the precipitous edges of gorges, teetering across rope bridges hundreds of feet above raging rivers, or sprinting along an arid plateau, the traffic was by foot or by llama. As in other pre-Columbian civilizations, the wheeled vehicle did not exist and so most of the roads were almost entirely unpaved with the exception of approaches to important towns.

Nevertheless, the roads were engineered. Causeways were built and cliffs cut away in order to maintain a basic width of twenty-four feet throughout the entire 2,500 miles of coastal highway. An important aspect of the Inca roads is the existence of parallel roads, used exclusively and contemporaneously by different portions of the population.

Because of the arid climate of coastal Peru, much of the roads have been preserved. Archaeologists have used these roads as models of how the Chacoan roads may have looked. This is not to suggest that the Chacoan roads are an offspring of the Peruvian roads or that the roads served the same purposes. But climate and terrain along the coastal section necessitated the same kind of construction the Anasazi used. Both roads were cleared, graded, lined with walls, and exhibit features which were elevated above the surrounding terrain.

Like the Chacoan roads, the Peruvian roads have roadside attractions. Beck notes that several types of architectural remains are associated with the roads: *huacas* (presumably administrative structures), isolated settlements with attached structures, isolated structures with single or multiple rooms, and windbreaks, which are similar in shape to the herraduras found on Chacoan roads.

Although the characteristics of the Chacoan roads may resemble those of the Peruvian roads, their purpose may be more closely aligned with the Maya roads.

The Maya civilization flourished for more than three and a half millennia; its Classic period (A.D. 300 to 900) was six centuries long. The Maya controlled a territory of some 125,000 square miles, encompassing the present-day Central American countries of western Honduras, El Salvador, Guatemala, and Belize, the Mexican states of Tabasco and Chiapas, and the entire Yucatan peninsula. These accomplished mathematicians, astronomers, architects, historians, and engineers built some sixty vast architectural complexes studded with palaces and pyramids.

Stories of the ancient roads show up in the accounts of the Spanish who came to the New World in the fourteenth century. On his way from Cahabon to Bacalar, Father Joseph Delgado was caught by "*los enemigos Ingleses*," an English pirate and renegade colony entrenched at Belize. They left the pious and pitiful padre in his underwear, and he groped along to the Bacalar by following the ancient road through the swamps.

While the Mesoamerican and Maya roads differ from those of the Chaco area in that they are paved, above-ground causeways rather than below-grade sunken avenues, they share the attributes of extreme linearity, the existence of parallel routes, true constructed surfaces, intensive formalization near monuments, and road-side structures in high places.

The Maya roads are said to exceed any contemporary road in Europe. "Indeed, it was not until the Lancaster Turnpike was opened in 1792 that any other American road equalled the Maya highways," says one Maya scholar.

The Maya *sacbe** (literally, "white road") runs so straight that not a single one curves. At Cobá, a causeway was built just so that two sacbes, running parallel to each other a few dozen yards apart, would not have to sacrifice linearity to Lake Macanxoc. By bending the road even slightly, the expensive water-bound structure could have been avoided. "Where Maya planning and Nature come into conflict, Nature usually loses out," as the saying goes.

A typical example of this near-obsession with geometric engineering is the sacbe between Yaxuná and Cobá. Thomas Gann was one of the first researchers to identify roads in the Maya area and in 1925, he described that stretch as probably one of the most remarkable roads ever constructed. "It was convex, being higher in the centre than either side, and ran, as far as we followed it, straight as an arrow and almost flat as a rule," Gann wrote.

The great elevated road, or causeway, is more than sixty-three miles long, thirty-two feet wide, from two to eight feet high. The sides were built of great blocks of cut stone, many weighing hundreds of pounds. The central part was filled in with unhewn blocks of limestone, and the top was covered with rubble, which was cemented over. This is the longest road to have been explored and is one of sixteen roads originating at Cobá, representing one of the most extensive systems known at any Maya city. The road includes seven straight-line segments varying only a few degrees in their bearings. The road between Aké and Izamal includes two straight segments thirty-two kilometers long.

Maya architecture gave way to an ostentatious show of power. The rulers of Tikal, the most powerful of all Maya cities, reigned for

---

*The plural of sacbe in Yucatecan Maya is sacbeob. For the sake of simplicity, the plural of sacbe will be the anglicized sacbes throughout this book.

nine hundred years. Temples I and II of the Great Plaza face each other on the plaza, the center of monuments and palatial buildings. Connecting the Great Plaza with outlying temples are four broad, raised causeways, one of them at times as wide as 190 feet.

Moreover, Maya architecture, for the most part, was oriented toward astronomical events along the horizon. These events were incorporated into complex calendric systems and recorded, at certain intervals, on stelae as they were believed to have related to Maya elite, although there are no direct references to sightings.

Examples of archaeoastronomy in Maya architecture are infinite. The so-called Group E structures at Uaxactún, Guatemala, represent the prototype of a series of sun watcher's stations found in that region. The classic example of Maya geoastronomy in architecture is the Caracol tower at Chichén Itzá in Yucatán. This round observatory features horizontal sight tubes directed to positions of astronomical significance. The stairways are oriented to the cardinals. Meanwhile, there is some evidence that the Maya roads may have also been assigned geometrical orientations.

Axial symmetries as emphasized by roads are common in pre-Columbian New World architecture. The streets of the Teotihuacán-influenced cities among the Maya ruins tend to be oriented toward astronomical events. The main avenue of Teotihuacán near Mexico City, later called the Street of the Dead by the Aztecs, is oriented on a north-south axis 15° 28' east of north. The street originates from the Pyramid of the Moon and crosses the entrance of the Pyramid of the Sun, which faces west toward the sacred mountain, Cerro Colorado, and to the point on the horizon where the Pleiades star cluster set around May 18, A.D. 150. The heliacal rising of the Pleiades was observed among many ancient civilizations and apparently duly recorded by ancient astronomers to fix civil, religious, and agricultural dates in the year. The appearance of the star cluster on the horizon announced the beginning of the day when the sun cast no shadows at high noon.

Dwarfing the great houses in northern New Mexico and rivaling the pyramids of Mesoamerica are the earthworks of the eastern United States. There, extensively engineered mounds incorporating formal below-grade roads may date to as early as 1000 B.C., although the Poverty Point culture in the Lower Mississippi Valley of Louisiana built the earliest known road in North America around 1500 B.C. Monks Mound at Cahokia, near present-day St. Louis, had a 1,037-foot by 790-foot base, rose four successive terraces 100 meters high, and contained an estimated 805,839 cubic yards of dirt.

The peak of development at Cahokia coincides with development at Chaco Canyon (A.D. 900 to 1150). More a pyramid than a pile of earth, Monks Mound had manicured surfaces and steep ramps allowing access to tiered platforms. As an urban center, as many as thirteen thousand residential units may have surrounded the central temple and plaza complex.

These earthworks, built along the Mississippi, appear to have been connected by a regional road system. Aerial photographs identify the Natchitoches Traces connecting Cahokia with settlements in Louisiana. Even at Cahokia there existed a "Woodhenge" observatory and north-south and east-west axes.

The architects of Chaco Canyon were no exception to the New World tendency to orient their buildings to reflect the cosmos. Quite a number of great houses in the canyon exhibit a north-south axis while others appear to be oriented to the matrixes of the solstices and, possibly, to lunar standstills. Moreover, the north-south axis seems to be emphasized by the Great North Road, which heads due north from Pueblo Alto for 50 kilometers. Pueblo Alto is a great house on the northern mesa of the canyon and also exhibits a north-south alignment. Clearly, the Chacoans, like other high civilizations of the New World, were familiar with the rudiments of astronomy.

Whenever civil and ecclesiastical powers were synonymous, roads served as sacred monuments while legitimizing a political geography. But while the roads of the ancient empires of the Far East were built to honor immortal kings, roads in the New World may have defined a sacred cosmological order. In this hemisphere, many roads can be seen as direct extensions of monumental architecture. As architecture themselves, roads are elements of complex citadels that functioned as centers of religious and administrative power.

Interpreting the Roads

In 1777, Bernardo de Miera y Pacheco, a mapmaker, surveyed the northern reaches of the New World for the king of Spain with an eye on areas suitable for colonization. Miera often came upon the ruins of prehistoric Indians and took the opportunity to comment on them in his reports. One entry included the Aztec Ruins on the junction of the River of Nabajoo (San Juan) and Las Animas where there "still remain in those meadows vestiges of irrigation ditches, ruins of many large and ancient settlements of Indians, and furnaces [kivas] where apparently they smelted metals." Miera was not the last to strain his interpretations through his own cultural screen.

Nor was Miera the last to mistake roads for irrigation ditches. Although subsequent Spanish and American explorers stumbled into the Chaco area from time to time, observations of Anasazi roads, erroneously identified or otherwise, were another century coming. Because the San Juan Basin was not seriously explored by the Spanish or Mexican governments, it is not surprising that road segments were not recognized and reported until American surveying parties began to seriously push into the basin.

Canals, Logging Roads, and Ceremonial Ways

The first reference to a Chacoan road may have been made by Professor Oscar Loew, a member of the Lt. Wheeler Geographical Survey, who in 1874 observed "traces of a former road to Abi-

Many early observers mistook the prehistoric roads for canals. This low-sun-angle photo shows a prehistoric canal near Kin Bineola. Note how much more sinuous the canal is compared to the sheer linearity of most Anasazi roads. (Photo courtesy Bureau of Land Management.)

quiu [New Mexico] sixty miles off." Loew mistakenly identified the nearby ruin as Pueblo Bonito, but it was in fact Pueblo Pintado, seventeen miles east of Pueblo Bonito. The road, however, may have been an historical Navajo trail. The following year, Lieutenant C.C. Morrison, a member of the Sixth Cavalry accompanying the same survey team, also visited the Chaco area. He corrected Loew's misnaming of Pueblo Pintado. He also mistook a dam for a road near Kin Klizhin, six and a half miles southwest of Pueblo Bonito.

William Henry Jackson, a photographer with the Geological and Geographical Survey of the Territories, entered the canyon on the heels of Loew and Morrison in 1877 and remapped all of the survey work to date. Jackson named after himself one of several stairways he discovered in the craggy cliffs behind Chetro Ketl and Pueblo Bonito. These stairways were integral aspects of the intracanyon road system. Nevertheless, the bulk of the roads remained hidden.

S.J. Holsinger, who served as special agent for the Government

Land Office to investigate the Hyde Exploring Expedition at Pueblo Bonito in 1901, and who could recognize an Anasazi road for what it was, nevertheless interpreted the South Road from Kin Ya'a as a canal. "The vestige of two large reservoirs [great kivas] and a huge canal [the west fork of the South Road]...now 20 feet on the bottom, passes within a few yards of the Ruins [Kin Ya'a]."

Holsinger correctly identified several other roads around Pueblo Alto on the north rim of Chaco Canyon and Kin Ya'a in the southern periphery of the Chaco region. He probably received most of his information from Chacoan pioneers Richard and Marietta Wetherill, who led the Hyde Exploring Expedition and began initial excavations in the canyon in 1896.

No one thought much about the roads until Neil Judd helped set up the National Geographic Expedition's field operations in the canyon in 1921. Judd interviewed Navajos whose ancestors had moved into Chaco Canyon after the Anasazi vacated the premises, and who may have had some sort of cultural memory of what the roads were. One informant told Judd that a particular cut through a hill in South Gap must have been a wagon road, or perhaps a canal.

Judd didn't accept the informant's story. He noticed pathways leading from one great house to another, and that one road in particular might have been used for logging. Whatever their purpose, he was impressed:

> Jackson's stairway is one of the best, but what was its purpose? The diverse "roads" are equally beyond convincing explanation. . . . Each was a prodigious undertaking of which the Late Bonitians or their contemporaries were thoroughly capable but each remains a mystery.

Judd called the roads "ceremonial ways," perhaps after the term "chantways" crudely translated from a Navajo word meaning ceremonial song, dance, and origin legend. But Judd never quite reconciled the obvious utilitarian purposes of some roads.

Economic interpretations were applied to the roads early on. In 1901, a photograph appeared in Museum of New Mexico's *El Palacio* magazine with the following caption: "Ancient Road Near

National Geographic Expedition leader, Neil Judd, marveled at Jackson Stairs at the head of a rincon behind Chetro Ketl. William Henry Jackson discovered these stairs and the prodigious undertaking of the roads. (Photo by R. Gwinn Vivian, courtesy BLM.)

Aztec, New Mexico: The road is perhaps thirty feet wide, its sides being marked with pebbles and boulders. . . . It was used in hauling stone from a quarry two miles over the hill."

Edgar Hewett, head of the School of American Research, which excavated Chetro Ketl, also must have believed that the roads were tied to a New World economy. He would take his students for walks in the 1920s and 1930s along the roads and would even say that someday the roads linking Chaco to Mexico would be found.

Following the work of Judd and Hewett in the 1920s, most subsequent research in the canyon was carried out by the University of New Mexico (UNM) field school program (also headed by Hewett) and the National Park Service (NPS). The UNM field school was confined primarily to small village sites, and the NPS projects were mostly oriented to salvage or ruin-stabilization. Emphasis on exploration of the large Chacoan towns, so prevalent in the previous four decades, was reduced substantially, with the result that investigations neglected some of the attending features. Water control devices, roads, and neighboring communities, all recognized in the 1920s and early 1930s as a part of Chacoan prehistory, were essentially forgotten, or in some cases were denied as ever having existed. For example, Donald Brand said there was "neither evidence or need for such an assumption" that irrigation ditches were used in Chaco Canyon.

The focus in Chacoan archaeology shifted again in the 1950s and early 1960s as a result of research conducted by Gordon Vivian, whose work had a direct bearing on future investigations of the Chacoan roads.

But the canal interpretation persisted.

In the late 1940s, Vivian noticed what he called lineaments in aerial photographs of Chaco Canyon taken ten years earlier by the Soil Conservation Service and believed them to be part of an extensive water control system. His son, Gwinn Vivian, interpreted the stairways around Chaco Canyon as "pour-off" structures included in the Anasazi's water works system. In 1967, Gwinn Vivian and Robert Buettner excavated a portion of "Canal 3" between Pueblo Alto and Chetro Ketl and found not a canal but a broad roadway carved into rock and lined by masonry walls. The realization that the canals were in fact roads led to a survey of the canyon defining six road systems.

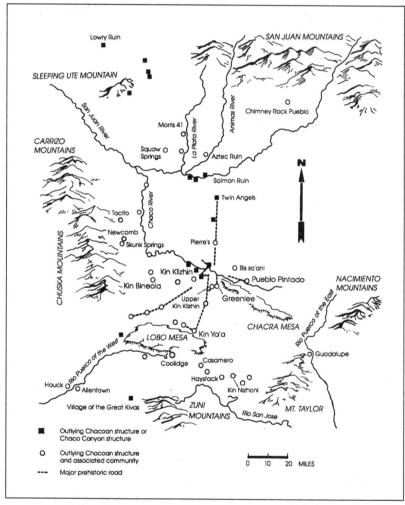

Chaco culture was seen as a "redistribution system" in the early 1970s, in which food and other resources were brought into the canyon by way of the roads and redistributed among low-productivity outliers. Later archaeologists suggested that "everything was going into the canyon and nothing was coming out." The map shows the major outliers thought to be involved in the system, as well as the only confirmed major roads.

Soon after Vivian and Buettner began their 1970 roadway survey, the National Park Service, along with the University of New Mexico, began its major long-term research in Chaco Canyon in 1971. The NPS/UNM Chaco Research Project chose Pueblo Alto as the focus of the study because of its association with the roads. At the same time, an Eastern University of New Mexico group began excavating Salmon Ruin just beyond the end of Pueblo Alto's North Road, and eventually took on the road as well. Both projects sought to acquire new aerial photography and techniques for studying the roads.

At about this time, geologist Thomas R. Lyons, of the New Mexico Archaeological Center (later called the NPS/UNM Chaco Center), began experimenting with remote sensing, a complex analysis of various types of aerial photography, to identify man-made and natural phenomena. Lyons used closed-circuit television systems to analyze black-on-white, color, and infrared imagery. An edge enhancer was used to accentuate lines that appeared in existing aerial photographs. Obscure or hazy lines such as walls of a ruin, edges of a prehistoric road, or a low rock outcrop would stand out sharply on the television screen with the help of the enhancer. The density-slicing monitor was used to transmit to the

Modern road in Chaco Canyon, with Pueblo Bonito (upper left) and Pueblo del Arroyo (upper right). (Photo by Robert Gabriel.)

television screen an image in which each color represented a distinctive part of the landscape, such as rock, soil, flora, or water. By changing the colors, a given feature could be made to contrast with its surroundings, thus allowing more accurate definition. These systems were instrumental in plotting the extent of the Chaco road system.

The energy crisis of the late 1970s did more to expand the known perimeters of Anasazi occupation in the Chaco region than any other research project to date. The Four Corners region is rich in coal, natural gas, and uranium. Approximately 75,000 acres of public, private, and Native American lands contained 3.52 billion tons of coal. The ruins were threatened by proposals to recover those resources. Sponsored by industry, archaeologists urgently inventoried thousands of acres of archaeological remains.

These projects, particularly one sponsored by the Public Service Company of New Mexico (PNM), broadened the Anasazi horizons by discovering a countless number of great houses scattered across the landscape. The roads were perhaps the most important but least understood archaeological features outside of Chaco Canyon.

By the 1980s, the Bureau of Land Management (BLM) was brought in to balance the need to preserve antiquity with the energy needs of modern society. BLM conducted a massive survey of the roads incorporating a multidisciplinary team of individuals who had experience studying prehistoric roads. Apart from determining where road preservation might conflict with potential coal mining areas, the project was charged with verifying the roads, compiling a documentary history of their study, and developing techniques for identification and documentation.

John Stein, a BLM road investigator, wrote in *El Palacio* magazine:

A major concern of BLM was the lack of information about the physical character and location of individual road segments. Many of the roads were known only from aerial photography. Some were—and still are—hypothetical. Some archaeologists challenged the existence of the road system, claiming that the peculiar linearities represented fence lines, geologic anomalies, or historic wagon roads. Others were comfortable with the existence of roads but felt they had irretrievably vanished and would not be amenable to terrestrial documentation.

In the summer of 1981 through the fall of 1982, the BLM team confirmed what most field researchers already knew: an extensive, constructed road system emanated from Chaco Canyon. The report, however, stated that although the investigations immeasurably increased knowledge of the roads, the actual extent of the network remained "fragmentary."

The BLM kept a conservative profile in its first report, which came out in 1983. A degree of engineering did indeed go into the layout of the roads, the report said. But the methodology and the amount of labor that went into the roads was not understood. Although the report acknowledged that some of the great houses and roads were built for Bonito-phase activities (from Chaco's classic period, A.D. 900 to 1130), it also noted that, in some instances, the road-related structures were built before the roads. The factors that controlled the alignment of the roads and their association with the great houses, the signaling stations, and the shrines were not understood.

According to the concluding notes of the report, the function of the roads was still unclear:

> There is no question that most of the roads connected Chacoan great houses, but for what purpose? Although a variety of functions possibly served by the roads have been postulated, including communication of construction materials, transport of trade goods of other types (e.g., turquoise, shell, lithic materials) the fact remains that with the exception of ceramics, no durable artifacts have yet been found on the roads that provide an indication of transport of specific items. This lack of durable items may suggest transport of perishable goods, although this must remain in the realm of intuition and speculation.
>
> Other aspects of the Chacoan roads remain enigmatic. The relatively sudden appearance of formalized roads has no known explanation as of the present, nor does their equally rapid disfunction. Cessation of construction and maintenance of the roads in the Basin is clearly related to the demise of the Bonito Phase; material

culture on the roads suggests that the roads were seldom utilized by post-Bonito phase occupants of the basin floor.

This BLM statement was issued in 1983; the second report came out in 1987. The BLM project marked the end of a decade of massive Chaco Canyon investigations. The only other large-scale field excavation and survey project was conducted at Pueblo Alto by the National Park Service/University of New Mexico Chaco Research project, which began work in 1975 and ended it in 1979; that report, however, didn't come out for another eight years. Other reports on the entire NPS/UNM project, which began in 1971, are still in the writing. Archaeologists are just now catching up with the hiatus in field work. But the archaeological work of the 1970s was breathless: the discovery of each new road and outlying great house community must have been like laying down railroad track as the train puffed along behind the workers.

The discovery of four hundred miles of road, which increased the potential collective mileage to fifteen hundred miles, brought archaeologists out of the dark trench the canyon had become. More outliers were discovered—as many as one hundred great houses over an area of 150,000 to 300,000 square kilometers. The roadways raised more questions about the Chaco Canyon picture that archaeologists had been steadily creating before it was learned just how big the picture really was. Their thinking had to be adjusted to accommodate the new information.

In the 1983 BLM report, Gwinn Vivian said the interpretation of Chacoan roads and the road network closely followed two very different interpretations of the Chaco culture itself. Some held that it evolved in response to changing environmental conditions, while others believed that it was influenced by Mesoamerican traders. Both of these explanations had been proposed before the roads data became available. Both were based on economic schemes and more specifically the transportation of goods.

In keeping with the idea that the Chaco culture fluoresced on its own, Thomas Lyons and Robert Hitchcock, the masterminds of the remote sensing techniques used in finding the roads in the early 1970s, came up with a new theory that would encompass the outliers and the roads. The theory, known as the "redistribu-tion system" theory, was embraced by James Judge, who became director of the NPS/UNM Chaco Center in 1974. The theory fit in with the new ecology of the 1970s: the study of how seemingly separate entities related to each other. In this view, the system re-lied on an elite in Chaco Canyon who administered the redistribu-tion of goods and food among the outliers in an attempt to com-pensate for the effects of sporadic rainfall across the San Juan Basin. The roads kept the system—goods and labor—flowing in and out of the canyon like feedback lines on an electronic circuit.

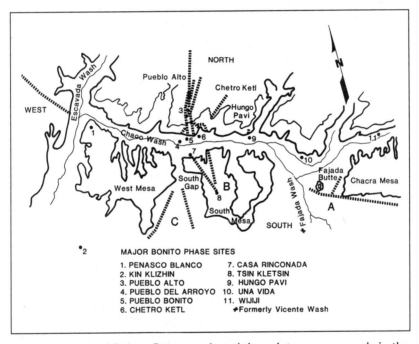

MAJOR BONITO PHASE SITES

1. PENASCO BLANCO	7. CASA RINCONADA
2. KIN KLIZHIN	8. TSIN KLETSIN
3. PUEBLO ALTO	9. HUNGO PAVI
4. PUEBLO DEL ARROYO	10. UNA VIDA
5. PUEBLO BONITO	11. WIJIJI
6. CHETRO KETL	✦Formerly Vicente Wash

Gwinn Vivian and Robert Buettner plotted these intracanyon roads in the early 1970s. The East Division Road (Pueblo Pintado to Chaco Canyon) is not shown. (Photo courtesy BLM.)

Chaco as a Cultural Ecosystem

The San Juan Basin is a shallow bowl where air tends to stagnate and become either colder or warmer than air that would flow in and out of the basin more freely. Chaco Canyon acts like a basin drain, drawing in cold air from the side canyons in the winter. In the summer, the canyon can sometimes feel like a suffocating oven. Between 1941 and 1970, temperatures in Chaco averaged 50°F, with highs of 73°F in July and lows of 29°F in January. Extremes have ranged from -38°F in the winter to above 100°F in the summer.

Although we cannot be certain what prehistoric conditions were like, we can be fairly sure that farming, particularly for maize, was a high-risk venture in Chaco. Severe late spring and early fall frosts are common in Chaco and the San Juan Basin. A frost-free period of about 120 days is often considered necessary for the growth of corn. Recent estimates of frost-free days in one part of the canyon have ranged between 126 days and 150 to 160 days—enough to grow corn—while estimates in another part of the same canyon dropped to as low as 100 frost-free days. Historically, the Navajo practiced horticulture with mixed success in the canyon and occasionally suffered regional crop losses because of frosts. Farming on the mesa tops might have been preferable, but water, which washed down the canyon when it did rain, would have been scarce in those regions.

Thus the absence of reliable surface water, very low annual rainfall that varied from region to region, extreme temperatures, and a very short growing season combined to make Chaco Canyon a poor place for growing one's own food. The lack of wood resources made Chaco a poor location for building the heavily over-timbered structures that characterized the Chaco climax, and sparse fuel wood resources made Chaco an unlikely place to spend winters. Sandstone, a good building material, was the only resource offered in abundance and it was thoroughly exploited for building. A redistribution system—or the cultural ecosystem as James Judge called it—might have made the place inhabitable.

From the perspective of the Chaco-centric archaeologist, the roads appeared to begin at Chaco, placing Chaco at the center of a network. This, of course, was based on the assumption that such a network would have a center. This led to the belief that the roads were built to accommodate a complex cultural ecosystem that redistributed goods from areas of high productivity to areas of low productivity. Although climatic conditions across the San Juan Basin were always marginal, they fluctuated from place to place and from year to year. Some areas received just enough rainfall to sustain a small crop. The fortunate towns outside the canyon that had bumper crops theoretically brought the surplus food into the canyon, where it was stored in the canyon's warehouses—possibly the great kivas—and then redistributed to areas affected by famine. It was also proposed that the outliers must have provided the labor for the great houses inside the canyon. Thus, the redistribution system is accountable for Chaco Canyon's boom town growth.

In her 1980 thesis, Margaret Senter Obenauf argued that the prehistoric roads were obviously built through the cooperation among many of the towns that relied on a common purpose and some form of organization at a supracommunity level. The presence of a transportation network indicated that there must have been other kinds of ties—social, religious, and economic—which were promoted by the roadways.

Those ties may have been established in the San Juan Basin as early as Basketmaker III to Pueblo I times (A.D. 500 to 700). Highly mobile, these groups developed strong kinship ties with groups outside the canyon and an equally strong system of exchange that would have eased fluctuations in crop yield during dry times.

By the late ninth century the population of the San Juan Basin increased to the point that the Anasazi had to stay put in order to protect their territories. At this time the reciprocal exchange routes would have become more formalized and the nature of the exchange would have changed, shifting from reciprocity between kin to reciprocity between towns or even regional areas. Because of its early ability to produce agricultural surpluses through floodwater irrigation, its central location, Chaco Canyon, emerged as the economic, administrative, and ceremonial center of this budding redistribution network and the system supported the administrators and craft specialists living inside the canyon. (The extent of the turquoise cottage industry in the canyon has only recently been discovered. See Chapter Ten for more information about turquoise and also about other more recent theories on leadership and power in Chaco Canyon.)

During dry years in the canyon proper, the situation was reversed, with food coming from those living in high diversity, high rainfall areas on the periphery or the Chaco "halo," a term coined by archaeologist David Doyel.

The Chacoan economic system proposed by James Judge in the 1970s was fully operational by A.D. 1020. The roadway network played many important roles in the ecosystem, the most important of which was the transportation of goods into the canyon. But just what kinds of goods were transported was never determined. Obenauf, now an archaeologist with BLM, analyzed this aspect of road economics in her 1980 thesis, described in the following paragraphs.

Without roads, the transport of surplus food to a central location, and subsequent distribution to outlying areas, would have expended a considerable amount of energy—more calories than the food itself afforded. Of the crops grown by the Chacoans, dried and shelled corn and dried beans would have been the most profitable agricultural product transported over the distances. Piñon nuts from the outliers near mountain areas would have also made for a profitable cargo.

The roads would have expedited the rapid transport of perishable foods such as game from the mountains. With the large population believed to exist in the canyon by archaeologists in the mid-seventies (estimates range from 1,000 to as high as 10,000 per great house), the game in the vicinity would have been seriously depleted. Since there was no evidence that the Chacoans raised domestic animals for their meat (turkeys were found at Pueblo Alto although they were not necessarily raised for food), large game may have been brought in over long distances.

The large ponderosa pine roofing vegas so prevalent in the Bonito-phase towns were not available near the center of the system and so were transported on the roads. Some theorize that the Chacoans deforested the immediate canyon area, making the import of timber mandatory. Furthermore, it has also been postulated that the Chacoans over-farmed the area, thereby draining the local water tables and causing erosion, which would have also necessitated the redistribution system.

A considerable amount of broken vessels lined the north road, particularly whitejars used to carry water. The jars were either used to carry other goods, or they were the cargo themselves.

According to the ecosystem model, roads were crucial to the development of social integration. With participants spread across hundreds of square miles, the roads underscored social, economic, and ceremonial links between Chaco Canyon and the outliers and among the outliers themselves. Intercommunity cooperation was necessary to build the roads. They provided quicker communication between the outliers, and promoted social travel, trade, and the exchange of news and information. Since the roads were engineered for their visibility, Obenauf suggested that the roads were part of a line-of-sight communication system which included tower kivas and some shrines.

The Chacoan Outliers of the Redistribution System

What of the outlying towns at the other end of the roads? Concurrent with major excavation projects at Chaco Canyon proper and the discovery of the extensiveness of the roads was a survey of the outliers led by Michael Marshall in 1979. The survey was sponsored by the Public Service Company of New Mexico (PNM), which had a coal burning plant and mining interests in the area. The objective was to identify Chacoan outliers, discover their common attributes, and nominate them to the National Register of Historic Places.

In order to distinguish the extracanyon ruins as bona fide outliers, some concrete evidence was needed to show a family resemblance at least in architectural style. Marshall found that, and much more. The PNM-funded team (see bibliography for names) confirmed the existence of a redistribution system and emphasized that it was an egalitarian one.

The authors of the PNM report defined a Chacoan outlier as a constellation of small masonry unit houses clustered about one or more public buildings and great kivas, usually situated on a mesa or in the middle of a plain. In most cases, such buildings were associated with a prehistoric roadway.

Public buildings of the Bonito Phase ranged in size from ten to one hundred rooms and were usually multistoried and terraced. The buildings were thought to be pre-planned because there was no evidence of additions or expansions. Kivas in Chaco Canyon were usually subterranean circular rooms, but in the outliers, the circular rooms were built above ground and set in large square or rectangular rooms within the buildings themselves. Hence the term "blocked-in kiva" was coined.

In comparison to the surrounding village houses, the public houses often contained extra-large rooms with high ceilings. Elevated kivas and tower kivas were built into or situated along the back or in the north section of the block. Large plazas were often built adjacent to the house and were enclosed by either a massive masonry wall or a tier of single-story rooms. Embedded in the plazas are one or more underground kivas.

The prehistoric roadways often entered a community from various directions, passing near or proceeding directly to (or projecting from) the public houses. Rounding out the Chacoan community were prehistoric irrigation facilities such as main channels, laterals with gates, and dams; reservoirs were occasionally found in nearby farmlands.

The PNM team also found sites along the roads which did not have a great kiva, such as Kutz Canyon, Halfway House, Pierre's Site, Upper Kin Klizhin, and Greenlee's Site. These sites were smaller than other Bonito public houses and were away from good farmland, which suggested to Marshall that the sites had a function which did not require a kiva, or that they might have been built by a different group of people.

The fact that the outliers had such architectural elements as a public house and a great kiva proved to Marshall that each outlier was autonomous and not colonized by a Chacoan elite. More likely, productivity and alliances on the fringes of the Chacoan sphere led to impressive developments in the outlying areas. Yet these autonomous units cooperated with each other in an exchange system.

The architecture of the outliers accommodated a cooperative system. Surplus grain may have been stored in the larger rooms of the public houses to enable the farmers to survive three-year dry cycles. The core-veneer masonry may have helped to keep the rodents out, especially if the grain was parched and then sealed in large culinary vessels. Vents near the ceilings provided air circulation to eliminate destructive molds, fungi, or insect larvae. Raised doorsills prevented the escape of heavy cool air.

"The fact that the peripheral Chacoan communities are on good productive soils, while the central complex is not, further strengthens the conclusion that Chaco Canyon was a regional exchange center that could not support itself locally," Marshall and the other PNM authors wrote. "The Chacoan system may have been close to becoming organized like some agricultural societies in Mesoamerica." Kenneth Hirth, in an *American Antiquity* paper, "Interregional Trade and the Formation of Prehistoric Gateway Communities," was quoted for emphasis:

> The emergence of stratified societies with perpetual leadership appears to have been closely related to control over production and redistribution of resources. In Mesoamerica, we find an early stimulus for trade in the differential distribution of key resources and the unpredictability of maize yields. In areas such as the Central Mexican highlands, the juxtaposition of a number of distinct ecological zones stimulated regional symbiosis that provided a strong economic basis for later state level society.

Problems with the Redistribution System

In 1983, James Judge presented a paper at a seminar on Dynamics of Southwestern Prehistory held in Santa Fe, New Mexico, in which he reinvented the cultural ecosystem model and redistribution system. He argued that if the Anasazi had practiced redistribution, there would have been noticeable holes in the stores in Chaco. This was not the case. Goods and food were being stock-piled in the Chacoan warehouses. Frances Joan Mathien, a long-time Chaco archaeologist with the National Park Service, ex-pressed it best: "It seems everything goes into the canyon and nothing goes out." Later Michael Marshall was to note that "most goods flowed into Chaco Canyon for use by resident populations with little movement of goods back to the outliers."

In a lecture given at the University of New Mexico in 1987, Judge said that the overkill of construction in Chaco Canyon dur-ing times of drought disproved the redistribution system. The first rule of anthropology, Judge told the audience, is that a society that can control water can control people and thereby organize a complex society. The Anasazi engineered irrigation systems and devices for catching run-off and for the first 130 years of the flo-rescence, this may have sufficed. During the 900s, when the Cha-coans began building their great houses, the canyon was even wetter than today.

But the social complexity of Chaco Canyon seems to have been driven by the very lack of water, because the society reached its peak during drought. Remember these dates, because they often show up in many of the theories concerning the use of the roads. The first drought was between A.D. 1030 and 1048. This was fol-lowed by a period of average rainfall. A second drought took place from approximately A.D. 1081 through 1099. The turn of the century brought thirty years of good rainfall followed by a twenty-five-year drought that led to a major abandonment of the canyon by A.D. 1150. The canyon was reoccupied after A.D. 1180 by a group some still refer to as Mesa Verdeans because of their non-Chacoan ceramic and architectural style. They left the canyon in the mid-1200s, during another drought.

Coinciding with these dates are periods of interesting building spurts. Judge said the driest years were marked with a "frenzied building intensity," equal to more than 55,000 man-hours a year during the peak after A.D. 1100. The frenzied building activity is indicated by start-up projects never completed. The mood of the times seems to have been compounded by a tendency to over-build, as shown by the oversized great houses and the compulsive attention to masonry that was plastered with mud, never to be admired until centuries later when erosion revealed its beauty.

Chacoans began their great house land development in the early 900s with the construction of Pueblo Bonito, Penasco Blanco, and Una Vida. Planning is indicated by the existence of similar large multistoried floor plans and circular pit structures in the plaza that are lined with large ramadas, or porched work areas and storage rooms. These buildings were situated strategically among small house communities near major drainage systems.

Not much happened by way of canyon development until after A.D. 1030. Construction began on Chetro Ketl, a one-story holdover from the 900s. This project began in A.D. 1038, ending in 1054. Pueblo Bonito was given additions, and Pueblo Alto was built on the northern mesa of Chaco Canyon above the two (A.D. 1040).

Of special significance is that construction on the roads began around A.D. 1050—during the height of the eighteen-year drought. Judge believed that the roads were extended into the region around A.D. 1080, during the next drought.

The next period of construction, from A.D. 1050 to 1075, was not as eventful. The great houses continued to be modified during this period, and construction steadily increased every year. The only great house begun during this period was Pueblo del Arroyo.

After A.D. 1075, the building program hit an all-time high. Six major construction projects were carried out. The east and west wings were added to Pueblo Bonito, a three-story row of storage rooms was built to the rear of Penasco Blanco, the north and south wings were added to Pueblo del Arroyo, and Wijiji was constructed.

Many of the outliers were also built during the eleventh century: outliers in the southern periphery were built in the first half of the century, while the northern outliers were built toward the twelfth century.

Much more was going on in Chaco Canyon than merely administering the distribution of emergency rations. The fact that more than two hundred thousand trees were hauled into the canyon over forty to seventy miles for the construction of the Chacoan great houses seemed to many scholars a poor investment of energy, especially during drought. This was not an efficient use of a redistribution system.

In the 1983 BLM report, Gwinn Vivian cautioned against irrevocably accepting an economic explanation for the Chacoan roads. "Some roads are difficult to explain within the economic context," he said. For example, the volume of traffic would never have reached proportions requiring the construction of the double and quadruple roads to the north and south of Chaco Canyon. Similarly it is unclear what economic advantages would have been gained by routing five separate roads south from Pueblo Alto to points in the canyon bottom less than a kilometer away, not to mention the elaborate and numerous ramps and rock-cut stairways along these routes. Nor has the standard Chacoan road width of thirty feet been shown to have any economic benefits.

The redistribution system theory died when the dust from the last round of archaeological surveys and excavations settled and the reports came out. The cultural ecosystem model has stayed intact and ceremony has replaced redistribution as the central force driving the Chacoan economy.

The abundance of religious architecture such as the great kivas in the canyon (eighteen were found in all) suggested to many that Chaco Canyon was a ceremonial center. Other indicators included the large cache of Chaco black-on-white cylinder jars, the green and scarlet macaws, the large quantities of turquoise, and the cache of painted wood found in the canyon, all of which may have served religious purposes. Furthermore, the findings of the Pueblo Alto excavations revealed evidence of road control and the fact that the great houses had a generally low population with intermittent periods of overflowing population. Perhaps the roads accommodated a system in which the people flocked to Chaco Canyon as pilgrims bearing offerings and volunteering to build and took nothing home but a bolstered faith. The research project at Pueblo Alto revealed more in the drama of the roads.

A Ruin with a View

For more than a century, the Navajo have been telling explorers about a notorious gambler named Noqoilpi, or "Always Wins," who lived in Chaco Canyon nearly a thousand years ago, gaming for property, wives, and great houses. He forced the Chacoans to build great villages, an arena, and a race track for his games. His greed led to the downfall of the civilization in the canyon.

Although different versions place the gambler at different great houses, Thomas C. Windes, author of the four-volume report on Pueblo Alto, the final major research push in Chaco Canyon, believes Noqoilpi lived in the Pueblo Alto complex on the northern mesa of the canyon. Pueblo Alto would have been a strategic home for such an opportunist.

The Pueblo Alto Complex

Pueblo Alto sits on a turnpike of roads which connect Chetro Ketl and Pueblo Bonito in downtown Chaco Canyon to important urban centers north of the San Juan River. The complex, which lacks the distinguishing great kiva/small house units of a classic Chacoan residence, appears to serve no other function than the roads. Roads actually pierce the walls of Pueblo Alto. A more detailed description of the roads in the Pueblo Alto vicinity are included in the Anasazi Atlas in Chapter Twelve.

Pueblo Alto commands a panoramic view of the entire San Juan

Basin in all directions. From Pueblo Alto, one can see Huerfano Peak north along the Great North Road and Tsin Kletzin, a similar road-related complex on the south side of the canyon, as well as several outlier communities to the north and east. Turning 360 degrees, one can view the San Juan and La Plata Mountains to the north, the Chuska Mountains to the west, along with Ford Butte and Shiprock. Hosta Butte is to the southeast, and Mt. Taylor and the Jemez Mountains are to the southwest. From here messages could have easily been relayed from pinnacle shrine to shrine on into Colorado, Arizona, and Zuñi country to the south. The concave earth and sky form a bowl and all the geographical gouges seem to empty into Chaco Canyon. Here Chaco Canyon looks like the crossroads of the cosmos—the Center Place for opportunists and spirit dancers alike.

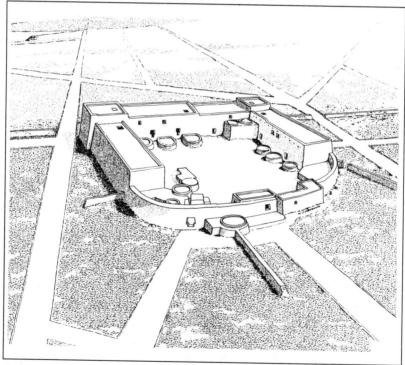

Pueblo Alto was positioned strategically to intercept traffic coming into Chaco Canyon from the north and east. Note in the artist's rendition how pedestrians were received directly into the great house.

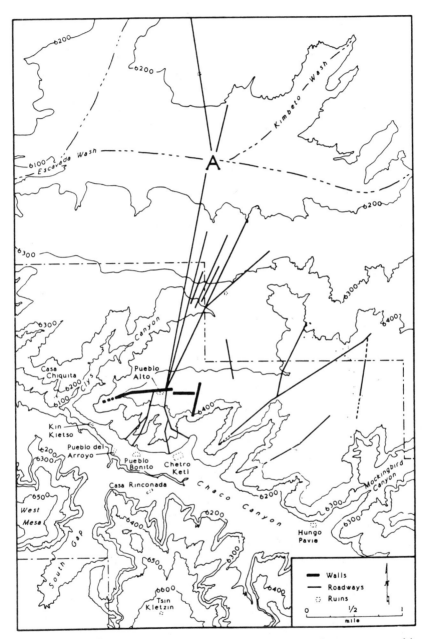

This map plots the wall and some of the road segments that converge with Pueblo Alto. (Map courtesy National Park Service.)

Unlike other initial great houses built in the canyon during the Bonito phase, Pueblo Alto was not positioned to take advantage of optimum farming conditions. It was built around A.D. 1040 during an eighteen-year drought that began in A.D. 1030, in an isolated and exposed area high on the grassy plains above Chaco Canyon along the southern crest of the Escavada Valley. The location subjected its inhabitants to some of the driest and poorest terrain in this area, but if one wants command of the view and canyon traffic, this isolated and exposed land is prime real estate.

Much of what archaeologists know now is due to the way in which Pueblo Alto was excavated and analyzed. At one time, archaeologists excavated sites wholesale, producing more information than was manageable and making it difficult to separate artifacts into time periods. Pueblo Alto was chosen for study because of its relationship to the roads. A pair of attendant houses, New Alto and East Ruin, attached to Pueblo Alto by an east-west wall, and the huge mound to the southeast of that wall added to the interest. The project used sampling techniques and computer-assisted analysis. By design, researchers dug up only 10 percent of the Pueblo Alto rooms and trash mound. They discovered that a small number of people used an inordinate amount of pottery.

Archaeologists found more than 200,000 pieces including potsherds, flaked stones, and food remains; 70,000 of them were from a nearby trash mound that occupied 2,400 cubic meters of space and stood four meters tall. More than 150,000 pottery vessels alone were discarded in this one trash mound over a sixty-year period. If the estimate of permanent residents at Pueblo Alto is correct, that amounts to 2,500 vessels per year or twenty-five pots per person per year. Hardly likely.

What appears to have actually happened, ascertained by the new minimalist style of archaeology, was that an enormous amount of material was carried into Pueblo Alto and stored or purposefully broken. The fact that the cultural material was layered in the trash mound indicated that the population inflated seasonally. Therefore, it is believed that the heavy, seasonal traffic patterns were due to a ceremonial industry, formalized by the roads.

The main house at Pueblo Alto contained seventy-seven rooms, later expanded to 133, and three to five kivas. At least fifteen of the new rooms were dead space created by walling off earlier rooms to build the kivas. The 133 rooms and enclosed court plaza covered eight hectares. Including the two exterior plazas, the grounds measured 16.9 hectares total.

At Pueblo Alto, researchers found three different kinds of suites: household, big-room, and road-related. Together they made up three-fourths of Pueblo Alto's floor area. The number of household suites (a living room connected to a storage room) was low—only five of the eighty-five rooms originally constructed were domestic.

Two of the household suites contained stone- and adobe-lined hearths, storage pits, mealing bins for grinding corn, and special niches for food. The presence of pollen and burned seeds from plants showed that food had been prepared and eaten in these rooms. The floors had been replastered many times and were badly worn as the result of heavy use. These rooms had more evidence of activity than any other room at Pueblo Alto. By comparison, in modern pueblos, the Zuñi built large rooms into their homes to accommodate the high number of spectators and participants at the Shalako dances, perhaps as an ancient architectural practice left over from Anasazi times.

Once these household suites were identified, archaeologists looked in other great houses. Pueblo Bonito and Pueblo del Arroyo had only five household suites each, and Una Vida had no more than eleven. Whereas it was believed that as many as 5,000 people occupied a single great house, now it is generally accepted that only twenty-five to fifty people actually lived at Pueblo Alto. Because other great houses had similar features, some believe that no more than one hundred people resided in them. The populations of the great houses may have also swelled seasonally as multitudes of Anasazi arrived on the ceremonial highways to Center Place.

Big-room suites at Pueblo Alto and other great houses are another mark of a limited number of people living in residence there. Big-room suites, or large rooms of limited domestic use, adjoin a room-size closet and a small kiva. As much as one hundred square meters in area, they are twice the size of household suites. People probably slept in one corner of the big room suites, but they did not eat or cook there. No doors connect one big-room suite to another, a sign that the rooms were defined by political or social boundaries. Five big-room suites were built when Pueblo Alto was first constructed and three more were added on later.

Road-related suites were small, interconnected storage rooms that were built in rows along the exterior of the building and opened directly onto the adjacent roads. They were completely inaccessible from inside the house. If great houses were meant for habitation, then the storage rooms would have been accessible from inside the house. Since the rooms opened to the roads, they were built to serve the roads; it is questionable whether Alto residents had authority over the content of or activity in these rooms since they couldn't get into them from inside the great houses. From this, archaeologists have speculated that someone other than a Pueblo Alto resident controlled the rooms. On the other hand, pedestrians leaving items in the storage rooms would not be able to stray into the great house, either. Such road-related rooms were built into Pueblo Alto, Pueblo Bonito, and Chetro Ketl.

Pueblo Alto, like all the larger great houses, had a central plaza: a large open area within the building's walls. The plaza was periodically resurfaced with thick coats of clay, unlike other plazas that were compacted by foot. Obviously, the plaza was an important gathering place at certain times of the year. A second plaza was located outside the building at the juncture of several roads and may have related more to trade than ceremony.

The official modification of the Chaco-as-ecosystem theory came out in a July 1988 *Scientific American* article, "The Chaco Canyon Community," written by Stephen Lekson, Thomas Windes, John Stein, and James Judge. The archaeologists now say that Chaco Canyon was a ceremonial center, and the reasoning stems from the research done at Pueblo Alto.

According to the most commonly accepted Chaco-as-ceremonial-center theory, ceremonialism coalesced and became more formalized at the same time the roads were built, as indicated by an increase in religious structures (shrines, kivas, and great kivas) and artifacts associated with the classic period, as well as the geoastronomical placement of new or remodeled great house architecture. Because Chaco had few tangible resources to exchange for goods, ritual may have been the prime mechanism for drawing resources to Chaco. The Chacoans may have enjoyed such charisma that they had authority over ritualistic calendars as well as over rituals designed to control the weather. The Anasazi, for instance, employed the use of calendars based on when and where the sun rose or set along the horizon.

The Anasazi also used light-and-shadow calendars. The infamous example is on Fajada Butte, where the sun pierces a spiral petroglyph on the solstices through a set of three rectangular boulders. This shrine also marks the lunar standstills. The Chacoans might have used the line-of-sight visual communication network of pinnacle shrines to call the people to the center from across the Colorado Plateau for ceremony at appropriate times of the year. The people in the outliers perhaps responded in massive numbers, moving in procession along the roads bearing food, goods, and their willingness to join construction crews—all, perhaps, out of devotion to the Center Place. Apart from their symbolic significance, the roads at Pueblo Alto may have been part of a conservation program to protect Chaco's fragile ecosystem from the massive numbers of people pouring over the flaky sandstone into the canyon.

Researchers point to the exotic goods stored at Chaco Canyon as evidence that the canyon was the center of a regional system. Turquoise from the Santa Fe region 160 kilometers to the east, ornamental shells from the Pacific Coast, and copper bells and macaws from Mexico are more abundant at Chaco Canyon than any other contemporary Anasazi site. More remarkable is the number of utilitarian goods that were imported from outside the canyon. As much as a third of the chipped-stone debris found at Pueblo Alto came from distant quarries, such as Washington Pass in the Chuska Mountains eighty kilometers away. Up to half of the many thousands of pottery cooking vessels were made from a special clay that has also been identified as coming from the Chuska area.

Pueblo Alto provided some other interesting clues that led to other theories about Chaco Canyon: the roads were used not only to draw people in, but to mark their safe return. "Our work at Pueblo Alto, and a resurvey of small houses in Chaco, have brought into clearer focus the possibility that out-migration and general mobility were practiced options long before the eventual demise of the Chacoan system mid-1100s," writes Thomas Windes, in *Investigations at the Pueblo Alto Complex, Chaco Canyon, 1975–1979*, the document summing up the NPS/UNM Chaco Research Project at Pueblo Alto.

Windes, an archaeologist with NPS, believes that when temperatures soared and the skies dried up, the Anasazi routinely relocated to cooler, wetter climes, and returned when the *shiwannas,* the ancestors, brought the rains to Center Place. Chaco Canyon, in Windes's estimation, became important to people because it was a home they were often forced to vacate.

THE PUEBLO ALTO ROAD SYSTEM

The road system in the vicinity of Pueblo Alto, with its interconnecting gateways, stairways, and parallel segments, is quite extravagant. Few people actually lived at Alto, but many stopped by on a regular basis. Pueblo Alto had neither great kivas nor nearby small houses like other great houses. Only the roads. These facts led many to believe Pueblo Alto was built to manage the roads, a task which may have been embellished by or for ceremony, the storage of offerings, and symbolic spatial relationships.

Pueblo Alto's primary role, according to Windes, was to converge with areas outside Chaco Canyon via the prehistoric road and communications systems. Windes says this marked a shift to regional interaction, possibly in response to climatic changes and dwindling resources. The roads would have relieved some of the pressures of a growing population by allowing rapid transportation of goods into Chaco and rapid dispersion of people out of it.

Roads may not have been necessary to effect these changes, says Windes, but they did allow greater flexibility and may have expedited the events. The care that went into road construction suggests that they were not designed to be short-term features, but rather were a partial solution to problems presented by a rising population and an unpredictable environment. Windes views the roads as an adaptive result of the reorganization of a system that had been sustained for more than a century without major disruptions. Until more refined dating for events can be achieved, however, the determination of which came first, the stress caused by a rising population and resource depletion or that from a deteriorating environment, cannot be made satisfactorily.

Chaco Canyon was sometimes seen as an oasis, but archaeologists now know its suitability for sedentary farmers was marginal, particularly during dry periods, despite elaborate water control systems. Anasazi migrated from location to location, following the rain. They may have even built more than one residence and rotated between them depending on the weather. Seasonal mobility was practiced by the historical Pueblos, even in areas of permanent stream flow (for example, along the Rio Grande). Some Navajo today move between a winter hogan and a summer hogan.

This may explain the proliferation of Bonito outliers. A great house near Chaco Canyon, Bis sa'ani, apparently served as a part-time residence for the inhabitants of the associated small-house sites, where, not unlike Pueblo Alto, groups may have gathered. Contemporary Anasazi sites in the Chuska Valley and other areas outside Chaco Canyon may have been areas of retreat. Chuska Valley figured prominently in Chaco's classic period, particularly as a resource for the import of a certain style of ceramics. The Chuska Valley had wood for firing ceramics, but Chaco Canyon did not, making import necessary. During the dry 1000s in Chaco, the population fell, and when an above-normal precipitation period began in the early 1100s, the population greatly increased.

Windes found evidence of Anasazi mobility at Pueblo Alto. The Great North Road, which begins at Pueblo Alto, leads traffic to a canyon about a mile from Salmon Pueblo, the entranceway to the powerful San Juan community of Aztec further north. One would assume that the road was built to connect Chetro Ketl and Pueblo Bonito to important cultural or economic allies to the north and that Pueblo Alto was built as a checkpoint.

Pueblo Alto may have indeed been built as a checkpoint or some other type of facility designed to control traffic coming from the north, but not right away. Pueblo Alto was built around A.D. 1040, and it is significant that it was built before the communities in the north and, probably, so too was the road that apparently connects them. Anasazi materials on the interconnecting road date between A.D. 1050 and 1125, although some archaeologists would date the formalization of the road around A.D. 1080, when Salmon Pueblo was built. Aztec East and Aztec West were built after the turn of the century (A.D. 1100 and 1100–1120, respectively).

The dating sequence may not be as mysterious as it sounds, at least not as far as the road is concerned. The Anasazi in Chaco Canyon may have been traveling north over the same route for quite some time to draw from more abundant supplies of timber, food, and water. Windes's colleague, Frances Joan Mathien, who edited the Pueblo Alto report, says that the Anasazi were importing ceramics long before the roads were built. A formal road would have been an expensive method to ease the movement of timber. Nevertheless, the time-honored practice was formalized around A.D. 1050.

Windes says evidence shows that Pueblo Alto was abandoned around A.D. 1080, about the time Salmon Ruin was built; this conclusion was reached after excavation of only a tenth of the rooms at Pueblo Alto. "Pueblo Alto's involvement in a regional system may have been sharply reduced or altered in the late 1000s when the initial residences may have been abandoned, possibly during a major drought in the 1080s and 1090s," Windes says in his report. It is difficult to determine how long and how often the buildings stayed vacant, but by the turn of the century, the Pueblo Altoans returned, he says. But the returning Pueblo Altoans were different.

By the dawn of the 1100s, Pueblo Alto had changed. Windes wrote, "There are many things, however, that establish continuity of the Chacoan system into the new century—among them were the continued use of the roads and the establishment of new great houses north of the San Juan River." Yet in the 1100s, occupation was substantially different. There were changes in the use of space, trash deposition, plaza maintenance, road use, subsistence resources, ceramics, and other features which, according to Windes, mirror those characteristics of Chacoan sites later reoccupied by Mesa Verdeans in the 1200s.

The occupation at Pueblo Alto and other canyon sites in the early 1100s reflected a northern influence in the style of construction, the type of architecture and ceramics, if not an outright migration from the northern regions. At the same time, the road down into Chetro Ketl fell into disuse after A.D. 1100, implying that the ties were weakened or severed. Corresponding with these changes were the wettest years of the Bonito phase, indeed for the previous one hundred years. The newcomers may have been a different group of people or the same group with new tastes picked up in the north. Windes writes:

> Shifts in the direction (from the Chuska Mountains and black-on-white ceramics) of influences impacting the Chacoan Phenomenon are a hallmark of the Bonito phase, but the latest, in the early 1100s, is the most tantalizing because of its involvement with a people whom archaeologists have traditionally considered a distinct cultural entity—the Mesa Verdean. There is little doubt that the two groups, Chaco and Mesa Verde, are tightly interwoven in the final act of the Chaco Phenomenon if they were not previously.

Frances Joan Mathien disagrees on this point, as do many others, she says. The group of people who were once thought to be Mesa Verdeans may actually have been Chacoans with a new ceramic and architectural style. It isn't unreasonable to assume that the Anasazi would easily acquire new tastes the way a contemporary person might switch from Early American to Santa Fe-style. Tastes do not necessarily identify origin. Furthermore, she argues, the Chacoan may not have been a Chacoan at all, but a member of a pan-Anasazi culture that spread across the Colorado Plateau. This interpretation is discussed in the next chapter.

Walled-off rooms along the north wall of Pueblo Bonito may have been road-related. The Hyde Exploring Expedition cut the doorways into the north wall of Pueblo Bonito to get to the ceramics inside. (Photos by Robert Gabriel.)

It is possible that the Chacoans planned Pueblo Alto as the first stage of expansion into the region, Windes says. Similarly placed great houses above the canyon, such as Penasco Blanco to the west and Pueblo Pintado to the east, have roads extending from them and may have served the same purpose of formalized expansion beginning around A.D. 1050. Tsin Kletzin, built in the early 1100s on a higher mesa south of the canyon in a setting of wide visibility, may have eclipsed Pueblo Alto's duties.

Windes says the road-related storage suites built between A.D. 1040 and 1050, specifically at Pueblo Alto, Pueblo Bonito, and Chetro Ketl, represent mobility. Pueblo Pintado, Penasco Blanco, and other great houses on the periphery and those near good cultivating soils were probably also built or modified at this time to accommodate goods transferred into Chaco. These suites, along with the big-room suites, marked a departure in the use of space seen in previous Anasazi sites.

The three types of suites found at Pueblo Alto, which make up 74 percent of the initial total room space, reflected user mobility rather than permanence, according to Windes. The rooms accommodated only the number of people local resources could support.

It may seem contradictory that a reaction to drought was to build new houses. More than any other site, Pueblo Alto reflects the new cultural response, which is not so preposterous when you stop to consider the role of this house in the new scheme. Whether Pueblo Alto preceded the drought of A.D. 1030–1048 or followed it cannot be determined with certainty, but Windes suspects that by that time, Pueblo Alto was at least planned and the foundations were set in anticipation of future use. Construction of some great houses in Chaco Canyon that remained uncompleted may be testimony to the advance planning of great houses before their need and use was desired. Windes has said that any people who have lived in the same place for a millennium, and on the fringes of survivability at that, should be able to sense environmental changes such as the approach of a drought and plan accordingly.

The question remains: was the road formalized to the north in A.D. 1050, prior to the out-migration, or in A.D. 1080, after the San

Juan shift in ceramic and architectural styles? If there was a gap between the construction of Pueblo Alto and the northern out-liers, then considerable long-range planning for expansion must have existed, or else Pueblo Alto was built initially for purposes other than monitoring far-flung road activities.

Although fluctuations in the environment existed, they may not have been adequate enough to cause major changes. But a soar-ing population would have strained existing resources, if not ex-ceeded them, unless the Anasazi could establish a system of re-ciprocity with those outside the canyon. Leaving the canyon and then returning during better weather conditions was the only vi-able alternative. Windes writes:

> In addition to the calamity of overpopulation and increasing ex-ploitation of an always marginal resource base in Chaco, with in-creased numbers of small-land holders and landless laborers, the environmental variability must have cast a pall of uncertainty and stress on the inhabitants.
>
> The Chaco area was poor for agriculture at best, with the fewest frost-free days in the San Juan Basin. According to climatic recon-structions, climatic disaster, after more than a century of average or slightly above-average precipitation, loomed in A.D. 1030 and lasted eighteen years, would have prompted the Anasazi not to sit it out. A drought of this magnitude should have had a psychological effect upon the inhabitants of the San Juan Basin, with a growing aware-ness over the generations that the drier conditions were normal. This could have influenced future decision making. A second, major, drought in the 1080s and 1090s should have reinforced this attitude.

In the meantime, it is difficult to tell whether the other great houses, particularly Pueblo Bonito, were temporarily abandoned during the same droughts because of the layers of occupation. Pueblo Bonito was expanded during this period to its present form. Windes continued to bore wood samples in the canyon for further tree-ring dating well into 1990.

If the Anasazi were mobile, then Chaco Canyon was not the cen-tral authority, ceremonial or not, many believe it to be. At least not all the time. Windes's last word in his Pueblo Alto report stated, "It is a narrow view to see Chaco Canyon as the sole center for an en-terprise that incorporated the San Juan region and beyond."

The Anasazi Corridor

Most archaeologists believe that by A.D. 1100, many of the communities across the Colorado Plateau were not isolated, but integrated in a political, economical, or religious system centered at Chaco Canyon. This realization has been based on the presence of a regional ceramic style, a similar set of architectural elements and stylistic conventions used in the construction of such social structures as great kivas and Bonito-style buildings, and the presence of an apparent interlinking road system.

In the spring of 1990, David Doyel and Stephen Lekson presented a paper to the 55th Annual Meeting of the Society for American Archaeology in Las Vegas, Nevada. The paper, "Anasazi Regional Organization and the Chaco System," proposed expanding the model describing the system to include a 250- to 300-mile wide corridor that begins laterally in Utah and Colorado and butts up against the Hohokam and the Mimbres systems in Arizona and New Mexico, respectively.

The Chacoan region Doyel and Lekson propose is about eight times larger than was defined in the 1970s and early 1980s:

> The Chacoan region has expanded well beyond Chaco Canyon, beyond the San Juan Basin, and almost beyond the limits of the Anasazi. This new scale is simply too large for the economic and ecological underpinnings of existing Chaco models, which were developed for the San Juan Basin.

The Great House/Great Kiva System

The expanded region was determined by the Bonito-style great house/great kiva complexes of the eleventh and twelfth centuries. The pattern is so widespread, one has to ask if the motive to build such monuments was ethnic or sociopolitical. In the past, the assumption has been that extracanyon copies of the Chacoan originals implied social or political connections to a system centered at Chaco. But could a system of such proportions be managed by administrators living in the dry trenches of Chaco Canyon?

The alternative is that the community structure identified as Chacoan could instead have been a nonspecific, pan-Anasazi pattern. Such structures may have been necessary for survival during the centuries between A.D. 1000 and 1200. In this scenario, Chaco Canyon was the exception, a supernova in the constellation of great house/great kiva clusters, rather than the sun of a solar system.

Doyel and Lekson expressed concern that the expanded Anasazi region may have become so large as to be meaningless; but the roads challenge this bleak conclusion. They argue:

> Roads in the San Juan Basin are the skeleton of a regional system, centered on Chaco Canyon; indeed roads are the least ambiguous archaeological evidence of a regional system yet discovered in the Anasazi southwest.

If the roads connect the most distant outlying great houses to Chaco and if all the roads were built between the eleventh and twelfth centuries, then the expanded Chacoan system may be real. With several exceptions, however, including roads found near the new site of the Puerco-of-the-West group, the physical connection has not yet been made. According to Doyel and Lekson, "We do not know enough about roads, and indeed may never know enough about roads, to resolve this important problem."

While Doyel and Lekson's Chaco region now includes most of the known Anasazi groups, it excludes the Anasazi of the Kayenta and upper Rio Grande regions, because these groups did not build identifying great house/great kiva towns. One great kiva has been found in the Pojoaque Grant Site in the upper Rio Grande and a deviant Unit House Community has been found near the Cerrillos turquoise mines. These two exceptions may prove the rule. If the great house/great kiva community pattern is not completely pan-Anasazi, then the pattern may define the borders of the Chaco-centered territory.

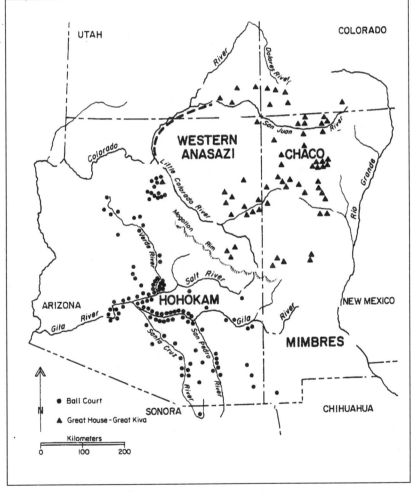

The great house/great kiva and the ball court systems as proposed by David Doyel and Stephen Lekson. (Diagram courtesy of Doyel and Lekson.)

The Anasazi region is characterized by great house/great kiva communities like Chetro Ketl in Chaco Canyon. (Photo by Michael Mouchette.)

The great house/great kiva system can be compared to the ball court system of the Hohokam to the south. The Hohokam regional system, which underwent its own period of elaboration and expansion, consists of 150 villages containing more than 200 Mesoamerican-style ball courts in a region larger than the San Juan Basin. Many of these villages, especially in the Phoenix Basin, share characteristics such as central plazas, platform mounds, specific architectural and ceramic styles, and the way they developed their neighborhoods. Although there is regional variation, settlements outside of the Phoenix Basin with built-in ball courts share many of the same attributes.

Hohokam villages have no roads or a recognized center such as Chaco Canyon, although Snake Town in the lower Salt River Val-

The Hohokam system is characterized by ball courts such as this one at Snaketown, Arizona, under excavation c. 1925. (Photo courtesy Museum of New Mexico, Negative 80123)

ley is a candidate. So far, scholars do not agree on the extent and form the Hohokam system took, not unlike Chacoan studies.

"Roads themselves are not a panacea for regional definition, but the relational criteria developed from the roads are a critical point-of-entry into the taxonomy of regional patterning," Doyel and Lekson say. The roads were multifunctional. They helped to define the great house/great kiva communities and some can be seen as elements of the architecture and local social expression. On the other hand, some of the roads may link to resources, such as timber, salt, stone, or ceramics, and were not meant to define a political territory.

Roadblocks in the Regional Highway

If the regional system theory depends solely on the fact that the prehistoric roads connect the outliers to Chaco Canyon, John Roney, an archaeologist with the Bureau of Land Management who is intimately familiar with the Chaco roads, expresses reservations about the validity of the theory.

Although two, maybe three major arteries emanate from Chaco

Canyon, most of the prehistoric road segments so far identified begin at local Chacoan outliers and have no obvious destination. Moreover, Roney, an Anasazi roads veteran, says that a series of arguments cast doubt on the notion that prehistoric road construction was undertaken in order to reduce transportation and communication costs:

> This notion is embedded in the very term "roads" which we have affixed to these prehistoric features. Under prevailing interpretations the roads were built in order to formalize a transportation network which linked participants into a regional economic, political or religious system coordinated or controlled by a centralized authority in Chaco Canyon. In fact, it is far from clear that the prehistoric Chacoan roads were built in order to make economic transport and region-wide communication more efficient.

If the roads were intended to address communication, transportation, or political needs, several expectations should be met, Roney argues. First, the Anasazi would have invested most of their labor in the road at the most difficult portions and greatest obstacles in the route. Labor invested in these areas would yield the highest return in terms of increased transportation efficiency. In negotiating their pack trails in the San Juan Basin, for instance, the Navajo spent much effort in improving routes up the canyon walls. There is often no evidence of deliberate construction once the trail veers up over mesa tops or along canyon bottoms. This is different from roads built by the Inca, for example, who built bridges and road cuts in areas of difficult terrain.

The many elaborate stairways and platforms which clearly aid in the movement of people in and out of Chaco Canyon do not aid in traversing rough terrain across the region. Instead, labor investments are greatest in the immediate vicinity of Chacoan buildings, great kivas, and formal shrine-like features called *herraduras*. Outside of these conditions, the roads stretch uninhibitedly across open, rolling countryside that poses no serious obstacles to pedestrian traffic. Here the roads are usually thirty centimeters or more in depth and nine meters in width. When major topographic obstacles were encountered, such as the Dutton Plateau, there was little, if any, investment in road construction.

Roney noted that it was relatively easy tracking a road from distant outliers (such as San Mateo, Haystack, Kin Ya'a, Muddy Water, and Aztec), but once the road entered particularly difficult topography, all traces of it would disappear. If the roads were built to aid in transportation, these exact areas would have had more elaborate construction.

The roads have a nonutilitarian nature to them. The excessive width, the disregard for ease of passage in selection of their route, the double, sometimes quadrupled parallel segments, the effort expended in pecking elaborate stairways and grooves into sandstone bedrock all show how the major labor investments did not serve to promote hauling cargo or traveling between distant towns.

Roney's second argument against prehistoric roads as a long-distance transportation system concerns the timing of their construction. If the Chacoan roads were built to support a regional system organized and centered at Chaco, these roads would have ended abruptly with the demise of the Chacoan system, characterized by the cessation of large-scale construction in the canyon. The period following the collapse is marked by a decline in population, evidence of strife and warfare, and regional disintegration reflected in the increased variety of ceramics. Under these unstable conditions, exhaustive road construction would slow or cease altogether.

In fact, more roads were built well into the thirteenth century. The best documented post-Bonito roads are those Roney found on Chacra Mesa, where there is no evidence of occupation until the 1200s. The Hikson Ranch site is another post-Chacoan site that is positioned near a number of road segments. Pueblo IV (A.D. 1300–1540) sites that have prehistoric roads include Calabash Ruin near Grants, New Mexico, and possibly Posipa-Akeri near Española, New Mexico.

It was once thought that lithic and ceramic scatters, burned rock, grinding stones, and other evidence of camping would be found along the transportation corridors. Many highly decorated jars have been found on the roads, and jars have been found near other camping sites, but no other evidence of camping has been found on the roads. Stone instruments, ground stone, and burned rock on the roads are rare. Ceramic scatters, expected to be found on one side of the road or the other, are instead found in long, linear swaths within the road itself.

If the roads were meant to aid in long-distance trade, then the ceramics found on the roads would be imports. The import business was indeed high in the eleventh and early twelfth centuries in Chaco Canyon. However, the ceramic scatters on the road are of local origin. Finally, if roads were built for the transportation of goods, the endpoints would bear some relationship to the goods being transported. The roads would lead from economic resources to areas of storage or consumption and the existence of such resources would warrant the construction of the roads.

Some of the roads are usually associated with resources. The South Road ends on Lobo Mesa, an area of large timber, and the Poco Road at Chaco Canyon passes through a major quarry area. It has been said that the North Road was used to connect to higher elevations in the Animas River and San Juan River areas, but this has been disputed. The Zuñi Salt Lake Road heads toward a major source of salt, a seventy-two-mile route, but only two miles of this road have been documented. Several roads in the Chaco Canyon area could be directed toward water sources.

Roney says that when the roads are considered as a whole, "there is no consistent theme which links the roads to resources." He noted that most roads are a kilometer or less in length, originating at a Bonito-style building with no known endpoint:

> The strongest rationale relating prehistoric roads to resource exploitation and transportation is the theoretically derived assumption that the labor investment should provide a direct economic return. I have argued that labor investments are not distributed in a way which achieves this end, and I believe that the lack of a consistent association between roads and a limited set of resources further undermines this interpretation.

Most endpoints (or starting points) for the roads are Chacoan buildings or great kivas. This suggests to Roney that the roads are intimately related to the function of these buildings.

Roney believes the validity of the published reconstructions of the Chacoan road system has not been verified. Roads that have been verified by gumshoe archaeology are the North and South Roads which do link distant outliers to the canyon. The destinations of the confirmed Ahshislepah Road and South Gap Road are unclear. The other postulated major road arteries, including the Southeast Road, the Kin Ya'a Cutoff, the Latrine Road, and the Mexican Springs Road have not been confirmed. (The Mexican Springs Road was pulled from the maps during the BLM survey.) The Chacra Face Road has been verified from the air, but not on the ground.

Outside of Chaco Canyon, recent investigations have discovered a number of additional prehistoric roads but to date none of these can be traced for any appreciable distance. An intracanyon road system was verified by Thomas Windes, but has no bearing on the proposed regional transportation system.

The evidence that the roads comprise a coherent, integrated system is far from clear. The only two major arteries emanating from Chaco Canyon are the North and South Roads. Two other long segments, the Coyote Canyon Road and, potentially, the Zuñi Salt Lake Road, are not obviously linked to the canyon. A six-kilometer-long road segment recently reported along the Comb Wash in southeastern Utah also fails to show up near the canyon. The majority of the Anasazi roads do not connect to the canyon; many roads don't even connect outliers to each other. Such outlying communities as Andrews, Casamero, Chambers, and Navajo Springs, have roads with no apparent destinations.

It may well be that many of the prehistoric roads are purely local phenomena, associated with local Bonito style buildings and are not part of a larger integrated road system. For a relatively brief period between 1050 and 1130, the great kivas were either supplemented or replaced by what Roney calls large, special function buildings—referred to as great houses by most archaeologists.

Roads, as architecture, may have been another aspect of the

Only the North Road to Pueblo Alto (pictured) and the South Road possibly linked Chaco Canyon to the outliers, according to John Roney. An intricate network of roads connect great houses in the canyon, such as to Pueblo Bonito and Chetro Ketl in the picture, but not to the region. (BLM Low Sun Angle, 1981, No. 1-003, courtesy Thomas R. Mann and Associates, Albuquerque.)

great house/great kiva/small house community pattern that prevailed over much of the Colorado Plateau. The special function buildings (usually only one per community) are characterized by massive multistory construction with a preplanned layout (as opposed to a hodgepodge of annexes and additions), large room size (often four times the size of rooms in residential sites), formal enclosed plazas in front of the building, blocked-in kivas, and earthworks. Many of the buildings are also embellished with stairways, ramps, and towers. The grand entryways were landscaped with berms or earthworks often encircled by ramparts and sets of two (or infrequently four) perfectly parallel roads. Herraduras, shallow horseshoe-shaped shrines of standing rock, are common features on most roads. The roads may be seen as one more ornamentation of the local communities, complementing earthworks, aureoles (roads that wrap around houses), great kivas, and the other trappings of these buildings.

In Chaco Canyon, the architectural development is on an order of magnitude greater than the communities outside the canyon. The long North and South Roads reflect that magnitude, according to Roney. The roads extending from other communities outside of Chaco Canyon served a function similar to the role of a kiva. Kivas were the focus of activities, such as ceremonies and meetings, which integrated members of villages and villages with other villages across a region. The roads, says Roney, might have been formalized preexisting routes of transportation and communication, but it is equally plausible that they were raceways, avenues for ceremonial processions, or even cosmographic expressions.

The pan-Anasazi communities, characterized now by the presence of a road, or more fittingly, a ceremonial entryway, implies a relationship to Chaco Canyon, but to what end is unknown. To Roney, they played a role in which the labor investment itself was the end goal in achieving social cohesion.

In the broader context of Southwestern prehistory, construction of the Bonito-style buildings and their associated features, including the prehistoric roads, represented an increasing intention to organize society on a local as well as on a regional level. Roney

The roads may have served as architectural embellishments to the great houses. The roads (E and F) around Pueblo Pintado (G) created the appearance of sitting in a dish—an effect archaeologists call an aureole. Letters A, B, C, and D point out areas where archaeologists dug trenches and counted rocks in the roads. (Photo courtesy NPS.)

sums up: "I suspect that the ethnological comparisons will eventually lead us to conclude that this regional system supported a network of mutual rights and reciprocal obligations which operated to the benefit of the local communities, at least during periods of low to moderate stress." In other words, the Anasazi region participated in a cultural ecosystem with no consistent political center.

Anasazi Roads in Utah: The Exception to the Rule?

The Anasazi roads recently discovered in Utah further challenge Chaco Canyon's role as the center of political power in the Anasazi system. While research is continuing, the preliminary reports suggest that the Anasazi roads in Utah were formalized around the late 800s, two and a half centuries prior to the dates used for the roads around Chaco.

In a telephone interview, Dale Davison, an archaeologist with the Bureau of Land Management in Monticello, Utah, said:

> We don't see Chaco Canyon as the center of a system. It was important over a period but not the only focus of Anasazi culture. Finding roads in Utah doesn't footnote what we know about Anasazi thinking. The roads show far more integration and sophistication than we ever would have thought.

If the formalized roads in Utah go back to the seventh and eighth centuries, long before Chaco fluoresced, then the roads may have been formalized versions of ancient trails. Pottery shards found in the Utah roadways suggest that the routes, unformalized, were used as early as Basketmaker III times, as is true for the routes in Chaco's southern periphery and those in Arizona. So far, roads have not been found linking the four great house/great kiva complexes in Utah to Chaco Canyon, but Davison is confident the missing links will be found. The discovery of roads between Utah and Chaco Canyon would not prove to the archaeologists in Utah that Chaco was the center, but that there was an interrelationship between the groups living in the two areas.

The fact that the roads in Utah may date to Basketmaker times creates yet another detour in the proposed superhighway system.

It means that if the roads in Chaco Canyon weren't built until A.D. 1050, then it was not always the center of a cultural network. Instead, Chacoan power may have become centralized around that time, or at least an attempt for power was made.

Winston Hurst, curator of the Edge of the Cedars Museum in Utah, said in an interview that the disparity in dates just means that the roads in the Chaco area can be proven to exist after A.D. 1040, and not before. "It depends on how much weight you give to what you know and what you don't know."

Basketmaker III and earlier sites are known to exist in the area of the South Road, southwest of Chaco Canyon. In the first BLM report in 1983, John Stein said he saw a road swale in association with a room block, ceramic scatters, and a herradura dated between A.D. 950 and 1000 near the South Road.

BLM's phase one survey revealed early occupation in the Kin Klizhin Valley along the South Road in sites scattered along sandy ridges flanking laterals to the Kin Klizhin Wash. Individual structures were small and pit houses were not visible from the surface. Anasazi occupation in this corridor apparently began in the eighth century A.D. at the locations of LA 34209, an extremely dense shard scatter near Casa Patricio, and LA 34223, a three-room slab structure. Seven locations, including several small-camp processing areas may have been built as early as A.D. 850. Most notably, the great kiva at Casa Patricio was constructed at this time.

By A.D. 950 most of these sites were abandoned. According to the report, seven new locations were occupied, including three room blocks, one visible segment of roadway with associated ceramic scatters, and La Mesita de la Junta. Sometime between A.D. 950 and 1000, the Upper Kin Klizhin tower kiva replaced Casa Patricio as a community focus. Use of Casa Patricio was probably discontinued although it later functioned as an aspect of the South Road. "Sites showing beginning dates of A.D. 1000 include a roomblock, a road swale and associated ceramic scatter, and an herradura," Stein writes.

Roney, when questioned on this point, said that although Basketmaker sites have been found in the area of the South Road, this does not mean that the Basketmakers built them. The roads are more abundantly connected with great houses in the eleventh century. On the other hand, Basketmaker sites may have been used later as shrines. (These assessments were made before the Utah material became available, and therefore comparison of the Basketmaker sites in both areas in relationship with the roads had not been possible.)

Nevertheless, the great houses in the southern periphery may have been built around A.D. 1000. Even the herraduras in the south—which are *always* road associated (except for the Rams Pasture Herradura on the unconfirmed Southeast Road) and often mark a change in the bearing—were built around A.D. 1000 or much earlier, with continued use well into the thirteenth century. The sites could have been built first, and then the routes between them could have been formalized later. And just because there are roads near the Basketmaker sites does not mean they were built that early. The roads may have been built later to include these sites, perhaps out of a sense that they served some sort of homage to ancestors, for instance. In at least one case, the road cuts right through a Basketmaker III village (see Road Cut Ruin) as if oblivious to it.

Thomas Windes also was able to comment in an interview on the dating problems. He said that at first, BLM archaeologists thought the roads in the southern periphery were built around the 900s based on dating the ceramic scatters found in the road. Then they settled on the 1000s because that's when it appears that the great houses were built. Windes is beginning to think BLM archaeologists were right the first time, but for the wrong reason. The ceramic scatters may have been a part of whole fields of potsherds that were later dissected by roads. His recent work in Chaco Canyon on sites that haven't been touched by the wholesale excavation of the 1920s and 1930s has showed him that great houses were built in the 900s across the region, but it is difficult to tell what the order of events were because of the constant remodeling and reoccupation of the houses.

Windes said that the problem is in our perception of what we

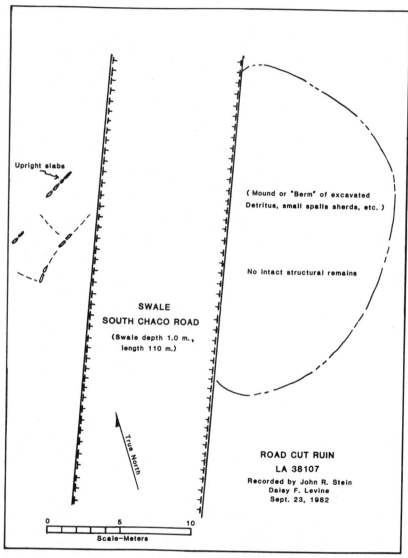

Upright slabs

(Mound or "Berm" of excavated
Detritus, small spalls sherds, etc.)

No intact structural remains

SWALE
SOUTH CHACO ROAD

(Swale depth 1.0 m.,
length 110 m.)

True North

ROAD CUT RUIN
LA 38107
Recorded by John R. Stein
Daisy F. Levine
Sept. 23, 1982

0   5   10

Scale—Meters

Sometimes roads passed near Basketmaker III sites randomly, and at least one time, the road cuts right through a ruin as if oblivious to it, in the case of the Road Cut Ruin. (Illustration courtesy BLM.)

call roads. "I'm not sure the whole road system was one massive superhighway connected to Chaco. What we call the Chaco Phenomenon (the classic period between A.D. 900 and 1150) was actually regional, a phenomenon that didn't blow in Chaco until the mid-1000s when they began their excessive building."

The fact that the southern periphery road paraphernalia predates northern periphery roads could be a further illustration of the "northward shift" to influences around the San Juan River and beyond to Mesa Verde. Windes said that there may have been more shifts than the record shows.

Davison says that he is a phenomenologist right now rather than an archaeologist because the research in Utah is so new. Perhaps a dozen or more road segments have been found, but no real archaeology has been performed to date. However, many archaeologists have visited the area to see it for themselves, and were inclined to believe that the roads were built as early as Basketmaker times.

Some roads connect sites to each other, some are local, and some are regional. Three of the great house/great kiva complexes (which are not Basketmaker III structures, but rather Chacoan contemporaries) in the area are related to the roads. The Utah roads are Chacoesque in nature with typical staircases, pecked bedrock grooves, and huge malls that lead into the great houses with cribwork for ramps. The roads lack berms of rock bordering them because the geography is different. They were cut into the terrain about a meter deep and are generally five to fifteen meters across. The biggest cut is near Cottonwood Falls, northwest of Blanding, Hurst said. About a half of the roads are not straight and crisscross major drainages.

Davison and Hurst say the roads in Utah are multi-functional. They were used for long distance routes of communication, had ceremonial implications, reinforced social cohesion, and were thoroughfares for trade. The travelways were constructed north and south among major drainages into San Juan River, Butler Wash, Comb Wash, and Cottonwood Creek. "I don't see the different explanations of the roads as being competitive," Hurst said.

"They are probably all right. Without question the roads were used for different things at different times." Each road has to be evaluated on its own terms, he said.

"Chaco is like an onion. As we peel off the layers, we may find the core that is germane to Chaco only, but some of the peels may be pan-Southwestern phenomena," Davison said.

New World
Archaeoastronomy

Aᴮᴼᵁᵀ ᵀᴴᴱ ᵀᴵᴹᴱ ᴹᴬᴶᴼᴿ ᴬᴿᴄᴴᴬᴱᴼᴸᴼᴳᴵᴄᴬᴸ ᴱˣᴾᴱᴰᴵᵀᴵᴼᴺˢ were being conducted on Pueblo Alto and the greater Chaco region, a volunteer artist began recording rock art for the field school in the canyon. In the summer of 1977, she was charged with surveying and sketching petroglyphs on the butte the Navajo call *Tsé Dighin*, or Holy Rock, at the south entrance of the canyon. Just before midday on June 29, she climbed the 423-foot Fajada Butte and serendipitously witnessed a dagger of light pierce a spiral petroglyph. The entire episode took about eighteen minutes. The artist, Anna Sofaer, has since dubbed the light-and-shadow phenomenon the "Sun Dagger."

The "rock clock," as it has been nicknamed, consists of two spiral petroglyphs pecked into the cliff face of the butte behind an unusual configuration of three stone slabs, each about two meters high. Every day, just before noon, icicles of light stream through the slabs, piercing the spirals in different places depending on the time of year. The vertical light and shadow patterns thus go through an annual cycle marking the solstices and equinoxes. (That is, until recently. Because of the amount of sightseeing and study, the Sun Dagger no longer accurately marks the solar cycle.)

Sofaer's discovery topped off a watershed decade for Chaco

Canyon. The use of new technology led to the discovery of the roads. Private organizations ordering exploration of the outlying communities led to the recognition of the scope of the Anasazi region. Innovative archaeological techniques applied at Pueblo Alto redefined the Chacoan system. It is paradoxical that with so much money, so many researchers, and such new technology, the refined explanation of the Chaco Phenomenon, by the 1980s, leaned toward the esoteric.

The prevalent thinking may be due to the birth of a new field of study in the 1970s: archaeoastronomy, the study of the practice of astronomy in the archaeological record. The knowledge that the ancient cultures practiced astronomy is nothing new, but archaeologists and astronomers interested in researching these practices, for the most part, either did not have a background in each other's field, or lacked a method for communicating with those who did. Their work was not considered mainstream. It wasn't until archaeologists met with astronomers for the first time in Mexico City in 1973 that the two fields married. The quickly growing field has had an impact on our understanding of Chaco Canyon.

The choice of Mexico City as the meeting spot for the first symposium of archaeoastronomers was no accident. First of all, it established that archaeoastronomy existed outside Stonehenge. Studies of ancient astronomy at Teotihuacán and among the Maya and the Aztec were proliferating. The Teotihuacán Mapping Project, for instance, was just discovering that the city was built on a grid oriented to a specific geometry determined by the stars (geoastronomy). I cannot help but think that the work in Mexico was also being applied to the Chaco Canyon culture by Chacoan researchers.

Teotihuacán and the Seventeen-Degree Family

One of the most prolific authors and researchers in the new field of archaeoastronomy is Anthony F. Aveni, who, in the 1970s, began making discoveries about the incorporation of astronomical and cardinal alignments in Mesoamerican architecture. Although scholars, even as early as 1928, recognized the planned nature of most Mesoamerican cities, ceremonial centers, and roadways, the idea that astronomical factors went into the planning slowly dawned on a few. Inspired by the work of K. Macgowan, Aveni was the first to conduct an organized study of the extent of astronomical orientations throughout ancient Mesoamerica.

In a note to *American Antiquity* in 1945, Macgowan was the first to notice that the plans of many Mesoamerican cities exhibited an east of north axiality. He noticed that the orientations fell into three groups, or families: true north, seven degrees east of north, and seventeen degrees east of north. Only a few oriented west of north. The seventeen degree family included a number of sites: Teotihuacán, Cholula, Tenayuca, Mexican period buildings at Chichén Itzá, Tula, and the pyramid adjacent to the Zócalo in Mexico City.

Aveni tested Macgowan's speculations and published his results in "Possible Astronomical Orientations in Ancient Mesoamerica," in *Archaeoastronomy in Pre-Columbian America*, in 1975. Fifty of the fifty-six sites Aveni examined were oriented along axes slightly east of north. Of these sites, Teotihuacán seems to have been the archetype for the orientations, although an historical time line for these orientations has not yet been established. One source speculated that the orientations may have come from the Olmecs, who lived between 1200 and 300 B.C., although the orientation of the Olmec site is two to three degrees west of North.

Teotihuacán, in the Valley of Mexico, emerged around 200 B.C., became the leading cultural, religious, and political force in all of Mesoamerica, and retained power for six centuries. Around the birth of Christ, some astute theologians at Teotihuacán conceived of a plan. They would not build just one temple aloft a pyramid, but groups of temple-pyramids neatly aligned with a central axis, an avenue oriented along a straight, north-south line roughly seventeen degrees east of magnetic north.

For the next 150 years, the population expanded from five thousand to thirty thousand people who were probably lured in to help build the pyramids. Labor was needed to mine stone, manufacture tools, dig and maintain canals, and construct great buildings that attracted more laborers. Teotihuacán was "like a vacuum that sucked up the population of the neighboring villages." News of the religious mecca must have spread as far away as Oaxaca, for there's evidence that groups of people moved to Teotihuacán from that area. By A.D. 150, Teotihuacán had achieved total domination over the Valley of Mexico and perhaps the entire highland area. The ceremonial center eventually accommodated 85,000 people. The aristocracy lived in special residences, and large apartment-type communal dwellings housed farmers, craftsmen, and specialists.

The Pyramid of the Sun was the linchpin for the city plan and the exact positioning of the building may have been determined by a four-chambered cave. Judging from the artifacts found in the cave, it may have represented the entrance to the underworld where a shrine was built perhaps to attract pilgrimages during the developmental stages of the city.

In the early 1970s, the Teotihuacán Mapping Project discovered that the buildings were oriented on a grid nearly nine square miles in area. A line passing from the summit of the Pyramid of the Sun to the Pyramid of the Moon ran parallel to the principal

Street of the Dead (right) at Teotihuacán, Mexico, underscored one of two important alignments in the city. View is from the Pyramid of the Moon. (Photo by V.L. Annis, courtesy Museum of New Mexico, Negative 70973.)

north-south axis and crossed the exact center of the citadel. Teotihuacán had two sets of alignments: north-south orientation 15° 28' east of north, as emphasized by the Street of the Dead (so named later by the Aztecs), toward the sacred mountain of Cerro Colorado; and an east-west axis 16° 30' south of true east, as emphasized by a major street and a canal, toward the sacred mountain of Cerro Gordo. The bisecting lines divided the city into four parts. Buildings in the citadel obeyed one orientation or the other. So important was the grid that it was retained in the barrios and the landscape was modified to fit it. Even the Rio San Juan and its tributaries were diverted to the mystical specifications.

A clue to the grid is the large, sun-like petroglyph of two concentric circles overlaying a cross pecked into the plaster floor of a building dead center of the citadel adjacent to the Pyramid of the Sun. Two more cross-within-circles markers were pecked into Cerro Colorado and Cerro Cordo; these crosses align with the first cross in Teotihuacán. The east-west axis of the grid may have been oriented toward Cerro Colorado because that is where the Pleiades star group set in A.D. 150. That year, the Pleiades underwent heliacal rising, or first rose after being hidden by the sun, on the first of two days a year (May 18) when the sun cast no shadows at noon, thus demarcating the changing of the seasons. Furthermore, the Pleiades crossed the zenith on this same day. Given the dramatic spectacle this star group must have presented to the ancient astronomer, the Pleiades understandably took a prominent position in Mesoamerican star lore.

The other dotted line between Cerro Gordo and the Pyramid of the Sun is 17° east of north, almost exactly perpendicular to the Street of the Dead. Dubhe, the brighter of the pointer stars of the Big Dipper, could have served as the stellar reference for this unusual geometry.

Other crosses have been found in Teotihuacán, and more than seventy have been found in the remotest limits of the empire. Some have even been found in Teotihuacán-influenced buildings in Maya temples. The pecked cross behaves as a surveyor's mark or bench mark. The circles underlying the crosses are outlined with specific numbers of holes, leading many to believe that the marker also served as a calendar.

Nearly all sites that lie within one hundred kilometers of Teotihuacán belong to the 17° east of north family. Even ceremonial centers like Tula, Chichén Itzá, Tenayuca, and the House of Tepozteco near Tepoztlán, built much later, revealed the alignments. Later it was discovered that these cities were oriented out of nostalgia for Teotihuacán, although the orientations were nonfunctional since the Pleiades no longer set on the east-west axis.

The civilization at Teotihuacán was followed by that of the Toltecs at Tula around A.D. 500 and yet the 17° orientation persisted. Even when Tula's influence spread among the Maya, the orientation came along as part and parcel of the cultural baggage. At Tula the earliest set of buildings align 10° to 12° east of north, the next 16° to 18° east of north, and finally 21° to 23° east of north. The meaning of the first set of orientations is not known. The second group falls into the Teotihuacán family of orientations, and the third aligns with the solstices at sunset. Tula's city plan was duplicated at Chichén Itzá, although the two are fifteen hundred kilometers apart. Copán, a classic Maya site in Honduras, also reoriented its grid three times to the same specifications.

A rare handful of sites possessing west-of-north orientations were part of early Mesoamerican development. La Venta, an Olmec site in the state of Tabasco on the Gulf Coast dating to a thousand years before Christ, was oriented six degrees west of north, and Huitzo, another Olmec site, was built two to three degrees west of north. The orientations are repeated at Poverty Point in Louisiana, suggesting to some an Olmec influence.

There were as many exceptions to as there were members of the 17° family. Monte Alban was built on a predominantly north-south grid with buildings erected on the diagonals to point at astronomical features. Uxmal (with a sacbe running to Kabáh), was one of the largest sites in the Yucatán. Most of the structures there are aligned nine degrees off the cardinal directions. The House of the Magician is oriented 9° 17' north of west. The astronomical base line at Copán is 9° 14' north of west. The Palace of the Governor deviates from the 9° axiality and is skewed 20° relative to the common axis, probably to face Nohpat, a ceremonial center six kilometers to the east. The alignment from the Governor's Palace to Nohpat points almost exactly to the azimuth of Venus when the planet attained its maximum southern declination around A.D. 700. Venus rising directly over Nohpat as seen through the doorway of the Governor's Palace must have been spectacular. Other astronomical alignments take place at Uxmal.

Not all deliberate alignments were astronomical ones. As Horst Hartung pointed out, there exist significant lines and dominant axes in the structure of Mesoamerican ceremonial centers which cannot be related to astronomical events. On the contrary, many followed certain orientations in the composition of the ceremonial center solely because of formalism or order. In designing an urban center, many Mesoamerican architects probably worked on the basis of relations between the surrounding space, the constructions, and the additional sculptural elements, all fixed visually. Take for example the special relationship between a temple, a ball court, and a sweat bath at Piedras Negras in Guatemala. These align on an east-west axis in an otherwise irregular urban plan. Generally, those buildings with astronomical orientations exhibit lines that tend to extend to the horizon, while those buildings with urbanistic relationships exhibit lines that remain inside the city or ceremonial center.

Mysterious Computers of Chaco Canyon

In 1974, the Denver Post's *Empire Magazine* published an article titled, "The Mysterious Computers of Chaco Canyon," by H.M. Kaplan, in which claims were made that the canyon had a solar/lunar observatory similar to Stonehenge in the Old World. The sensationalized article had come out on the heels of Erich von Daniken's *Chariots of the Gods* (1971), which argued that primitive cultures capable of marking with surprising precision a complex set of astronomical feats a thousand years ago must have possessed a technology more advanced than our own. This was the popular sentiment of the early 1970s.

In debate since the sixties, the only uncontested statement that can be made about Stonehenge in England is that its deliberate orientation is toward midsummer sunrise and midwinter sunset. The position of the fifty-six Aubrey holes, chalk-filled depressions evenly spaced around the monument, could be functions of a computer used to count intervals between the eclipses of the moon. Likewise, it has been argued, that the lower Caracol at Chichén Itzá, as well as many other Maya temples, was built to check on the timing and location of relevant astronomical events, particularly of Venus as the Evening Star, and of the Pleiades and solsticial settings. These events are crucial to the various Maya calendars.

Perhaps it is no accident that since then, dilettantes and scientists alike have been looking for a Stonehenge or a Caracol in Chaco Canyon. They may have found one.

Casa Rinconada, one of six great kivas in the Chaco Canyon, comes closest to the British and Maya analogs. In 1974, Ray Williamson, Howard Fisher, and Donnel O'Flynn took a tape measure to this great kiva and discovered that it does have solstice and equinox alignments. Built on a hill isolated from other structures on the south side of the canyon across from Pueblo Bonito and Chetro Ketl, it has two sets of unusually regular wall niches. One set is composed of twenty-eight niches evenly spaced and shaped at a constant height around the kiva. The other set contains six slightly larger niches; two of these niches were built in the east wall and four on the west wall. In addition, there is a window in the northeast wall and another in the southeast wall.

Depending on the time of the year, the sun will shine through the windows and illuminate certain wall niches. The kiva has a summer solstice sunrise line between the northeast wall opening and a lower niche along the northwest side of the interior wall. On the winter solstice, the sun enters the corner of the T-shaped south doorway and illuminates a wall niche, but this may accidentally occur due to the height of the wall when it was reconstructed. It isn't clear if the great kiva actually allowed observation of certain solar events or if it was built to symbolically mark them.

The kiva is roofless now, but when it was roofed, it would have blocked most of the sun niche choreography.

Archaeoastronomer Ray Williamson commented on whether the great kiva's orientations were intentional in his article, "Casa Rinconada, A Twelfth Century Anasazi Kiva," published in *Archaeoastronomy in the New World* in 1982. He observed that:

> The totality of the evidence indicates that Casa Rinconada, built and used during the flowering of Chaco Canyon culture, was meant to serve as an earthly image of the celestial realm; that it was not an observatory, but a ritual building whose structure reflects the central place astronomy had in ancient Pueblo religious practice.

Casa Rinconada was a carefully made circle. The four holes that served as post sockets for the logs that originally supported the massive roof nearly form a square, and the sides of this square are oriented to the cardinals. The square falls on the major and minor axes defined respectively as the center line between the north and south doorways and the line between small niches eight and twenty-two, counting clockwise from the north. The floor vaults on either side of the major axis of symmetry are oriented along north-south lines. The kiva as a whole was built due west of the edge of a mesa. At sunrise near the equinox, the sun appears momentarily to the north of the mesa edge and casts a shadow across the south half of the kiva before disappearing again behind the mesa due south.

Casa Rinconada was built in the 1100s and seems to represent everything the Chacoans had learned about geoastronomy in the century previous to the building. In the early 1970s, while Teotihuacán was being mapped, Williamson, Fisher, and O'Flynn reported other findings concerning the alignments of Chaco Canyon. Pueblo Bonito, for instance, exhibits several cardinal alignments and at least two solstice alignments. The axis of Great Kiva A at Pueblo Bonito is a north-south line. In addition, the wall to the west of the kiva, which divides the great house roughly in half, is aligned nearly north-south. Furthermore, the western side of the straight wall is oriented east-west. Cardinal alignments, Williamson said, are of solar significance: a north-south wall casts no shadow at midday, and an east-west wall aligns with the sunrises and sunsets on the equinoxes. However, the high mesa wall behind Pueblo Bonito block these solar manifestations at sunset and sunrise. Six corner doorways in Pueblo Bonito mark winter solstice sunrise, but they are entrances to inside rooms; they never would have seen the sun.

In 1978, Sofaer, the artist introduced at the beginning of this chapter, founded the Solstice Project, a nonprofit group, to study, document, and preserve the Sun Dagger. Since then, the group has expanded its efforts into other Chacoan phenomena and has conducted interdisciplinary investigations by enlisting the help of different scientists and agencies depending on the project. Throughout the 1980s, Sofaer and various teams of researchers began taking a closer look at the orientations in Chaco Canyon, expanding immensely on Williamson's report.

Sofaer's intuitions, perhaps inspired by Aveni and others, were well founded. Between 1984 and 1989, Sofaer conducted a series

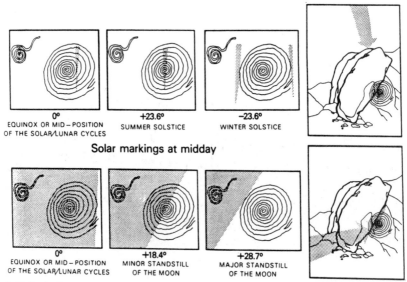

At Fajada Butte, the light shaft of the "Sun Dagger" pierces a spiral petroglyph (top) at midday on the solstices and equinoxes; another pattern may be created by the shadow cast by the rising moon (bottom). (Illustration courtesy of the Solstice Project.)

Around A.D. 1050, Chacoans began aligning their structures to the cardinals and certain astronomical events. Casa Rinconada lies a quarter degree off true north. The close-up of the great kiva's doorway shows its alignment with New Alto, the notch above the beam. New Alto, on top of the north mesa of the canyon, lies along Pueblo Alto's east-west axis as emphasized by a wall connecting the two Altos.

Pueblo Bonito's principal wall (projecting from camera) is 65 meters long and lies just a quarter degree off true north. The wall appears to be lavish, filling no practical architectural need. (Photo by Robert Gabriel.)

of surveys with the help of her partner, physicist Rolf Sinclair of the National Science Foundation, and astronomer Joey Donahue of Los Alamos Scientific Laboratory. The following results of the Solstice Project's survey of Chaco building orientations were presented to the *Proceedings of the Colloquio Internazionale Archeologia e Astronomia,* at the University of Venice in May 1989.

At about the time the roads around Chaco Canyon had become formalized (the latter 1000s), the Anasazi were making extensive alterations to their structures in the canyon and were building new ones to astronomical specifications, as if to modify the landscape to mirror their metaphysics. By that time, the north-south axis had become primary in the architecture in Chaco Canyon. Most of the great kivas were built on approximate north-south axes and generally had niches in the northern edge of the circular walls. Pueblo Bonito had been expanded and realigned to within a quarter degree east of north, just prior to the construction of the roads, as had Hungo Pavi, a great house in the canyon about halfway between Chetro Ketl and Fajada Butte. Pueblo Alto and its counterpart on the south mesa, Tsin Kletzin, which are within view of each other, were constructed on a bearing of a half degree east of north. Casa Rinconada, mentioned above, was also built (in the next century) within a quarter degree east of north.

New buildings were given their geoastronomical orientations and existing buildings were modified and expanded to meet these new standards during the most intensive construction period, which ran from the latter half of the eleventh century through A.D. 1115.

Sofaer and Rolf Sinclair found that the markings using shadow and light patterns on the petroglyphs on Fajada Butte, which mark the solstices, equinoxes, noon, and possibly the major and minor lunar standstills, also involved the north-south axis. The light patterns pierce the petroglyphs within a few minutes of meridian passage of the sun, when the sun is due south, thus further confirming the Chacoan's interest in and knowledge of the north-south axis. Furthermore, the evidence at Fajada Butte exemplifies the importance of the sun and the moon to the Anasazi.

Chaco architecture integrated the sun and the moon, and the midpoints and extremes of both cycles, and did so redundantly and comprehensively. The Chaco buildings were probably not used as observatories in the practical sense. Like the light markings on Fajada Butte, one purpose of their construction was probably to express symbolically a knowledge of the relationships among the earth, sun, and moon. These structures were not built to predict astronomical events, but to incorporate the events into their architecture.

At one time, it was thought that the Sun Dagger calendar on Fajada Butte was built to determine the solar cycles and thus control ceremony because of its hard-to-reach location. It was supposed that the proclaimed sun watcher would wait for the dagger of sunlight to pierce the spiral marking the solstice, and then he would put out an alarm to all corners of the region via the signaling network to beckon the people to Center Place. Astronomer Michael Zeilik pointed out that the key to historic Pueblo ceremony is anticipation. The winter solstice ceremony generally requires four days of ritualistic preparation and additional days for

Corner doorways in Pueblo Bonito marked the coming of the winter solstice. Anticipation of the event is important to the ritual. However, outer walls may have blocked the visibility of the doorways. Instead, the doorways may have represented, to the Anasazi, the importance of acknowledging the event.

planning and gathering. The markers on Fajada Butte do not give advance warning that the solstices are coming. Historic Pueblo sun watchers do not travel to out-of-the-way places to tell time. The sun watcher does that by watching the horizon from a certain (and always secret) place closer to home. The Hopi, in fact, watch a specific butte; the sun passes certain markers as it moves southward and northward along the butte, ticking off planting cycles. The markers like those on Fajada Butte are actually shrines. Many such shrines, in various stages of sophistication, were plentiful in Chaco Canyon, indeed the entire Anasazi region, and may have been accessible to the general public.

Incidentally, the question of who carved the spirals on Fajada Butte is an interesting one. Sofaer says they were probably carved between A.D. 950 and 1150. Archaeoastronomer John B. Carlson, however, says that there is no evidence for that dating. In fact, the only known archaeological remains found on Fajada Butte are two sites attributed to the late occupation of Chaco Canyon by Mesa Verdean people—or Chacoans with Mesa Verdean cultural traits— between approximately A.D. 1220 and 1300, well after the first large-scale abandonment of the canyon in the mid-1100s.

At any rate, architectural manifestations relating to solar and lunar cycles were not limited to Fajada Butte, Casa Rinconada, or Pueblo Bonito's winter solstice doorways. The Solstice Project surveyed fourteen of the largest buildings in the Chaco system in search of a pattern of geoastronomical orientations. Their suspicions were confirmed: the Anasazi intentionally brought the choreography of the sun and the moon inside their great houses.

Ten of the fourteen buildings studied were inside the canyon: Pueblo Bonito, Chetro Ketl, Pueblo del Arroyo, Penasco Blanco, Wijiji, Una Vida, Hungo Pavi, Kin Kletso, Pueblo Alto, and Tsin Kletzin. The four extracanyon houses studied were Pueblo Pintado (twenty-seven kilometers to the southeast), Kin Bineola (seventeen kilometers to the southwest), Salmon Ruin (seventy-one kilometers to the north), and Aztec (eighty-six kilometers to the north).

The Solstice Project found that all but Wijiji and Kin Bineola were intentionally aligned with either the cardinal directions or the full set of solar (both solstice and cardinal) and lunar (both minor and major standstill) azimuths. In addition, a number of the major Chaco rectangular buildings in this list shared a common internal geometry which also correlated with solar and lunar cycles.

Kin Kletso, Pueblo del Arroyo, Salmon Ruin, Chetro Ketl, and Pueblo Pintado were all oriented with the minor lunar standstill. Penasco Blanco and Una Vida were oriented toward the major lunar standstill, and Aztec to the solstice.

The orientations of each of the twelve buildings listed above, again excluding Kin Bineola and Wijiji, were near one of the four solar and lunar azimuths. (The orientations were sighted on the principal, or longest, walls of nine of the great houses and the perpendiculars to the longest walls in three buildings.) Pueblo Bonito, Pueblo Alto, Hungo Pavi, and Tsin Kletzin were oriented within 0.3 to 1.7° of the cardinal directions; Aztec was oriented within 2.1° of the solstice azimuth; Una Vida and Penasco Blanco were oriented within 0.5° of the lunar standstill; and Chetro Ketl, Pueblo Pintado, Salmon Ruin, Pueblo del Arroyo, and Kin Kletso were oriented within 1.4° to 3.1° of the minor standstill.

The above values were assigned as though the astronomical events were viewed on a flat horizon. The topography at each site showed that the horizons changed the astronomical azimuths viewed from each building by at most one degree, while there was no appreciable difference in the correspondence between the building orientations and the solstice and lunar azimuths.

To identify the position of a star in the heavens, Western astronomers do so by specifying its two coordinates: azimuth and altitude. The system turns the horizon into a flat 360° circle, which is domed by the sky. The zenith of the domed circle, or celestial sphere, is the uppermost point. Placing themselves at the center of this circle, astronomers identify the azimuth of a star by counting its position in degrees on the horizon clockwise from the north. The altitude of a star is measured by degrees upward from the horizon toward the zenith. Since stars and other bodies are constantly on the move, the coordinates are constant.

Solstice literally means "sun standstill" in Latin. During the solstices, the sun rises at the same position each day for a week. To most ancient cultures, it looked as though the sun traveled along the horizon and then came to a dead stop. Historical Pueblos (and most probably their predecessors) feel it is their duty to make sure the sun is "turned back" so that it won't get stuck in winter or summer. The moon also travels along the horizon as it rises, although it can rise farther to the north of sunrise on summer solstice. When the moon reaches its maximum northern or southern declination, it has a standstill similar to the solar solstice. Due to the gravitational pull of the sun, the moon's orbit about the earth is slow. A major standstill takes place every 18.61 years, while a minor standstill takes place every 9.3 years. There is much controversy regarding whether ancient cultures, such as those associated with Stonehenge or those of the pre-Columbian Southwest, or even the historical Pueblos, actually used horizon calendars or buildings to predict the lunar standstills.

The Solstice Project survey established references at the sites by using one of two methods: orienting to the sun, Venus, or Sirius, or to Polaris at night. From ten to thirty points were pinpointed along each wall (depending on the length and condition of the wall) with respect to the established references. The orientations of the walls were then found by averaging the points, usually by method of linear regression. The orientations were determined by the direction of the longest wall, termed the "principal wall," or by the perpendiculars to these walls.

The great houses aligned with the cardinal directions were Pueblo Bonito (north), Hungo Pavi (east), Pueblo Alto (east), and Tsin Kletzin (east). Their orientation set them apart as a distinct group, isolated from other orientations and they averaged .59° off the cardinal with the maximum deviation of 1.68°.

The Chacoans seem to have tolerated some error in the astronomical orientations of the exterior walls. The standard deviations and maximum differences in these angles are comparable to the standard deviation and maximum difference in the relationship between the orientation of the building and astronomy.

The probability of the Anasazi randomly choosing angles that happen to correlate so closely with the cardinals and the solstice and lunar azimuths is less than one percent.

The Chacoan buildings stand free of the cliffs and their specific orientations are not constrained by natural obstructions. The need to face the great houses toward the south to optimize solar heating may have influenced the general orientations of certain buildings, but it probably did not constrain these orientations to the specific azimuths. In fact, the buildings weren't necessarily built for residential households, but as public buildings. Thomas Windes says that the great houses weren't even built in the warmest areas. The small house residences were built in areas that are warmer than the great houses.

The Solstice Project could find no topographic or practical reason why the building orientations clustered near the points on the horizons at the extremes of the solar and lunar cycles, except to incorporate the visual effect of the cycles into the architecture. From many of the buildings, the sun and moon, rising or setting in the extreme points of their cycles, would be seen along the long back walls or across the plazas at angles perpendicular to the back walls. In the buildings oriented to the lunar standstill azimuths, the moon near its extremes must have been framed by the doorways and windows. In these formal, symmetric buildings, doorways and windows were regularly constructed perpendicular to the back walls.

Finally, the Solstice Project discovered what may be the first ancient recording of the Anasazi relationship between architecture and cosmology: a D-shape on Fajada Butte surmounted by a spiral. The shape, unusual in rock art, corresponds with the floor plan of Pueblo Bonito, also D-shaped, and to the building's solar cycles. Two lines on the petroglyph's diameter and perpendicular radius correspond with two principal walls at Pueblo Bonito that are accurately aligned to the north-south and east-west axes. A hole drilled into the petroglyph corresponds with the position of the primary kiva at Pueblo Bonito. The spiral over the D-shape may refer to the great house's cardinal and solar alignments. The

D-shape is similar to the bow-and-arrow design used by historic Pueblos in depicting the sun. In Pueblo tradition, a bow and arrow offered to the sun will ensure hunting prowess. If the reading is accurate, the petroglyph may be the first recording of the relationship between the Anasazi's great houses and their beliefs.

The story of Chaco Canyon is reminiscent of Teotihuacán, although to a much lesser degree. The propensity of Teotihuacán's builders to incorporate specific geoastronomical orientations in their designs spread across cultures and even centuries suggesting political influence, nostalgia for Teotihuacán, or a reverence for the Pleiades.

Similar to the priests of Teotihuacán, the Anasazi priests seem to have conceived of a plan for an earthly version of the cosmos in Chaco Canyon, and labor to build the houses and roads was drawn from the outliers. The fact that extracanyon great houses exhibit similar orientations to the great houses inside Chaco Canyon confirms a regional tendency that suggests centralized planning.

But orientations vary from house to house, leading me to believe that they were not dictated by an elite in Chaco Canyon. The fact that Aztec is among the outliers sharing these orientations challenges Chaco Canyon as the geoastronomical authority. Aztec is already suspected of influencing styles at Chaco Canyon and of being its political rival, if not its successor. If the Solstice Project's calculations are to be believed, it would appear that each community was able to align itself with the event most appropriate to local culture: the sun, the moon, the cardinal directions, or a combination of all three.

In describing the orientations of buildings in Chinese cities, such as the north-south line of Beijing's Hall of Supreme Harmony as defined by its central mall, Paul Wheatley said that those religions that equate the creation of the universe with the origin of mankind tend to reproduce on earth a miniature version of the cosmos as they see it. Those that relate divine revelation to the meaning of human existence do not find gods in the landscape, and their rituals bear little connection to the environment. Thus, where creation myths are heavily emphasized, religion is consulted in the planning of most construction projects. Theologian and historian Mircea Eliade said that a place could be considered divine through certain signs in the environment: a cardinal direction, the abundance or lack of certain plants and animals, or the cycles of a particular celestial body. Once revealed, the citizen worshiper feels compelled to emulate it in the architecture.

But orienting architecture to astronomical cycles is probably more a case of patient observation than geomancy. To the Anasazi, and other high civilizations of the New World not situated near the equator, celestial bodies rose and fell on paths nearly perpendicular to the horizon while journeying north and south along the horizons. Finding the north-south axis is not as easy. The celestial bodies appear to move east to west across the sky dome because the earth rotates on its axis in a counterclockwise direction. Polaris is historically used to determine north because it is one of the stars that stays close enough to the north pole to never sink below the horizon. But Polaris was probably not used in prehistoric navigation. The axis of the earth wobbles, making the North Star crawl across the sky over a period of 26,000 years. The bright star has not always shined over the north polar point. During Chaco Canyon's florescence between A.D. 900 and 1200, Polaris moved from 5° to 6.7° away from the pole. Still, the Chacoans exhibited remarkable accuracy in orienting some of the buildings in the canyon to within a quarter degree of the north-south axis.

Lunar standstills are probably the most esoteric of all proposed astronomical observations, according to Aveni in a 1987 argument, "Archaeoastronomy in the Southwestern United States: A Neighbor's Eye View." The Anasazi may have spotted a lunar standstill, but probably were not able to predict it. Nor were they capable of predicting eclipses. "There is no evidence that people living in the southwestern United States either desired to predict or were capable of predicting eclipses," Aveni said. The Mayans, on the other hand, did demonstrate an ability to predict eclipses using a relatively complex mathematical equation, which, coincidentally, was also used by the Babylonians.

Lunar standstills are probably not so difficult to align to. A sunset, for instance, casts dramatic shadows across the landscape. A sun watcher standing on a building or a hill would also cast a shadow that would point across the landscape opposite the rising or setting sun. Similarly, capturing the point at which the moon rises or sets would rely on the ability of the watcher to imagine that the moon is casting long shadows as does the sun. If the moon has not yet risen, the watcher need only make a mental note of the place on the familiar horizon that was marked by the sun and wait to see if the moon appears at that point.

Pueblos regularly watch the fixed marks for the sun along the horizons. The shifting sun is the landmark for the moon. Evidence indicating observation and recording of a major lunar standstill cycle, an 18.6-year cycle, has not yet appeared in the historic Pueblo record, although the Hopi and the Zuñi have ceremonies that rely on the position of the moon. The Shalako ceremony, which marks the end of the Zuñi calendar year, is particularly complicated because it must be conducted at winter solstice when the moon is full. Consequently, the date for this ceremony changes from year to year.

A final comment on shadowplay, for what it is worth. I was in Chaco Canyon around noon on the autumnal equinox. The shadow I cast was true north, according to my compass. Perhaps the Chacoan buildings orientated to north were built to recognize the sun at Center Place: noon on the equinox.

The role of Anasazi geoastronomy in their belief system is unknown. They left few clues. We can compare the archaeological record of Chaco Canyon to their descendants, the Pueblos (see Chapter Eight), and to another New World civilization, the Maya, who had a written language.

Maya Cosmological Engineering

The peculiar alignments within Chaco Canyon and Teotihuacán are not unique among the ancient megalithic cultures of the world, or even that mysterious. Nearly every major culture is thought to have observed the sun at the horizon on the solstices,

This Uaxactun temple, E-VII sub, marks the sun's journey as it ascends and descends the steps in one day. (Drawing by Ricketson and Ricketson, 1937.)

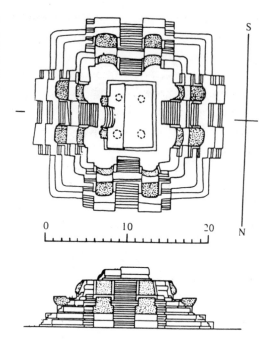

and most of them also observed the equinoxes. Sophistication of astronomical knowledge largely depended on geographical location, and not extraordinary intelligence.

In "Archaeoastronomy in the Southwestern United States," Aveni noted that among the cultures of the tropics, the observance of the zenith (the two days of the year when the sun passes directly overhead at noon) and the antizenith (the two days when the sun passes its lowest point at noon) supplements or replaces the solar solstice observation in the calendar. The observance is unique to tropical cultures because this is the only place in the world where the sun is directly overhead. The event is associated with the start of the planting and rain season.

The Maya, whose roots extend back to 2000 B.C., began settling villages around 900 B.C. and urbanizing around 300 B.C., when they developed long-range trade routes and a hieroglyphic writing system. The three hundred years between A.D. 600 and 900 saw the fruition of the Maya civilization. In sharp contrast to Teotihuacán-dominated central Mexico, no one center emerged as a political or religious nucleus in the lowlands. Lowland Classic Maya centers numbered in the hundreds and held varying degrees of power. Not unlike the Anasazi, the Maya centers were independent yet interrelated, and strong cultural themes persisted throughout.

Maya ceremonial centers also served as concrete calendars that marked astronomical events. The site of Uaxactún (300 B.C.), a five-hour walk on a sacbe from Tikal, is known as the archetypical Maya solar observatory. One building (known specifically as Structure E-VII Sub) literally marked the cycle of one day, or *k'in*. The stuccoed pyramidal platform had four sets of stairways leading to a temple on the top. Conceptually, the sun ascends steps or levels to the top or highest heaven, then descends down another set of stairs toward evening and mythologically traces a similar journey through the underworld to the foot of the stairs in the east. From this building one could view the sun as it rose over one of three temples east of it on the equinox or solstice. These

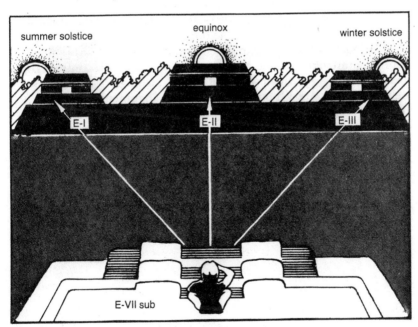

Sunrise alignments of Group E solar observatory at the Maya site of Uaxactun. This type of building arrangement was used at a number of Maya cities. (Diagram courtesy of Peter Dunham.)

temples were aligned on an eastern platform in a north-south line. The sun rises over the northern and southern temples at the summer and winter solstices and the central temple was set by the sunrise at the equinoxes. Collectively, these buildings were known as Group E buildings and this arrangement was duplicated throughout the region.

What we know of Lowland Maya geometry and astronomy comes down to us through the records of the Spanish conquistadores, the alignments of the ruins, and Maya hieroglyphic texts. The alignments of their sacred structures show obvious concern with the behavior of the sky deities, whose actions vitally influenced human affairs, but the hieroglyphics primarily recorded the activities and pedigrees of the rulers; astronomical events or any other historical information concerning the life and times of the people were only indicated indirectly.

Unlike Teotihuacán and Chaco Canyon, there is enough information known about the Maya to piece together an idea of their cosmology. Maya astronomers built models of the drama that daily occurred in the sky and sketched the relationship between sky gods and royalty, as if there was divine connection between the two. Of prime importance was the ability to predict the cycles of the celestial deities who influenced the fate of the earthbound mortals.

The Maya recorded their data, as it pertained to rulers, on large stone slabs called stelae, and planted them upright in the temple analogues of the heavens at different intervals. Some have argued that the temples, encoded by the stelae, were ancient computers of time. But the Maya were not as interested in computing time, as they were in predicting divine activities and linking them to their rulers.

The Maya developed three overlapping calendars, the names of which are courtesy of modern scholarly research. The Sacred Round was a ritual cycle of 260 days and followed a pan-Mesoamerican calendrical tradition. The "vague year" calendar had 365 days. Most historical dates were specified in both 260-day and 365-day calendars, in that order, and formed the 18,980-day cycle

Stelae were chiseled at katun-ending (20-year) intervals to document the lives of the Mayan elite. This stela at Copan, Honduras, was photographed in 1912. (Photo by Jesse L. Nusbaum, courtesy Museum of New Mexico, Negative 60211.)

called the Calendar round. A given date in this calendar would recur about every 52 years.

The Maya also used a cumulative calendar called the Long Count, which indicated a count of the days that have elapsed since the base date of the calendar in 3114 B.C. This count, like other Maya counting systems, was based on units of 20, and time was recorded in a place value system in units of single days (the *kin*), 20-day months (the *uinal*), 360-day years (the *tun*), 20 tuns (the *katun*), and 400 tuns (the *baktun*).

Basic calendar structure is reflected in the twenty-based counting system used throughout Mesoamerica (which is related to the number of fingers and toes of the human body). Subdivisions of cycles of twenty days is a common feature of all three Maya calendars. The system parallels the subdivision of lunar months into groups of ten days as is illustrated in the calendar sticks of the Zuñi, among other North American Indians.

The four surviving Maya bark-paper books (or codices) contain, among other things, planetary tables that indicate the timing of repetitive astronomical events. The Dresden Codex included a lunar eclipse table and five pages of Venus tables. Synodic periods of Mars, Jupiter, Mercury, and Saturn have been identified in other tables. Temple 22 at Copán, for instance, is a sculpted doorway adorned with symbols representing Venus as illustrated in the Dresden Codex. A window on the western side of the temple, the only window at Copán, marks the sunset on April 12 and September 1; these dates were also recorded on two markers, or stelae. The site seems to be aligned to a baseline formed by these stelae. One theory is that the window provided the priests with a sighting of sunset at the start of the agricultural year while ceremony was conducted at the base of one stela on a hill to the east. The shell, flame, and crossbands on Temple 22 may represent firemaking and could be associated with the annual ritual of the burning of cornfields.

Maya directions were oriented east and west following the path of the sun, according to Clemency Coggins. East was associated with the rising sun, birth, and the right hand, and was depicted as the right head of the two-headed Celestial Serpent. West meant setting sun, death, and the left hand, and was represented by the lower head of the Celestial Serpent.

In Maya cultures, north and south are not as clearly defined as east and west. North, when it was represented, was associated with portraits of rulers with their dead ancestors who resided in the uppermost heavens. Temples placed at the northern end of ceremonial centers usually represented the divine place where the ancestors of rulers resided. A picture of a ruler, for example, was chiseled into the center of the north side of a quadripartite platform at another stela at the twin pyramid group 4E-4 at Tikal.

South is sometimes identified with the underworld, which is divided into nine parts. On an Early Classic cache vessel depicting the underworld, a mortal holds the two-headed serpent in his arms, with the eastern head on his right and the western head on his left. Below is the long-nose skeleton head like those found beneath trees in tablets at Palenque.

Coggins says this view of Maya cosmology can be seen in modern Chamula beliefs. In their organization of space, east is the primary position, and north is up, or the position of the sun at the zenith. Together they form hot, light, right hand, and male. West and south represent the position of the sun in the underworld, or down, and together they represent cool, dark, left hand, and female.

Coggins believes that the Maya had no concept of north and south that approximates ours. The symbolism of the directions is based on the ecliptic, the band that describes the apparent annual path of the sun and includes the heavens. North and south, called *xaman* and *nohol*, are points in between and complete the quadripartition so necessary in building anything on the two-dimensional surface of the earth. The concept of quadripartition was probably introduced by the Toltecs in the fourth century.

This is only a thin slice of Maya cosmology as demonstrated in architecture and is not meant to be a definitive explanation. The great variety of sources available to researchers on the Maya culture are complex and sometimes contradictory. Clues are sifted from European records, from both the Conquest and Colonial eras; the archaeological record; the ever-increasing abundance of cultural material; hieroglyphic texts; ethnographic accounts by early native writers and colonial sources; and comparison to contemporary cultures and their descendants.

Sources of information for the Anasazi are considerably scarcer than those for the Maya culture. Nevertheless, the Anasazi no doubt revered the sky beings enough to commemorate them in their important architecture. But what role did the roads play in this scheme? When the dust settled on the BLM's survey of the roads, Anna Sofaer and the Solstice Project reevaluated the Great North Road on the suspicion that the true north bearing of the road was no accident and that the cosmological orientations of the Chacoan buildings had been incorporated into the roads as well. Their findings are discussed in the next chapter.

Road Cosmology

In the New World, with varying degrees of sophistication, temples and shrines were raised along elaborate and simple lines to mark the places where the sky gods appeared and vanished. Turning the landscape into calendars was a widespread phenomenon, and this practice takes many forms, from the medicine wheels of North America to the *ceque* lines of Peru. Such centers as Teotihuacán, Tikal, Cuzco, and Chaco Canyon served as calendars in the round, and ritualistic movements through them were incorporated into the daily life of those who believed time, space, life-forms—and economics—were inseparable.

Interconnecting these ceremonial centers are roadways. In Mesoamerica and South America, specifically the ancient cultures of Peru, roadways served a variety of purposes. The roadways around La Quemada (in Zacatecas, Mexico), for instance, were largely military. The Incan roads in Peru formed the backbone of a state, but also incorporated mystical elements. Streets in the Valley of Mexico helped define a cosmological grid that was replicated across the Teotihuacán empire. Numerous trade routes snaked along the entire length and breadth of the Maya World, separate from the short, but geometrically defined, sacbes. Even in our preliminary work at Chaco, it appears that at least one road, the Great North Road, combined geoastronomical and religious elements.

North Road to Sipapu

Following a long-held suspicion that the true north bearing of the North Road was no accident, artist Anna Sofaer organized the Solstice Project to resurvey the road in the mid-1980s. She and physicist Rolf Sinclair enlisted the help of archaeologist Michael Marshall, who had led the survey of Chaco Canyon's outlying area in 1979. The results were presented to the Second Oxford International Conference on Archaeoastronomy in January, 1986. They found quite a number of peculiar features that may together form another template of Anasazi cosmology.

The North Road is the westernmost of five roads radiating from the gate in the north wall of Pueblo Alto. Through Pueblo Alto, the road connects by way of a series of cliffside staircases to Pueblo Bonito and Chetro Ketl in the canyon below. The road holds a bearing of one half to two degrees east of true north for 50.5 kilometers to its end point at the isolated Kutz Canyon.

The North Road inefficiently cuts through vast stretches of badlands such as in the Pierre's Ruin area in the photograph. A more direct route to Salmon Ruin could have been laid down to the west of this area. (Photo by Robert Gabriel.)

The road cuts through rolling sage-covered plain broken by vast stretches of badland flanking the major drainages across sandy loam. John Stein, a leading road archaeologist, said that from a surveyor's standpoint, the sighting of the road must have been difficult. The landscape lacked features that would have been useful for triangulation and ground orientation. Excluding the far horizon, the only visible prominent features from the North Road are El Huerfano and Angel Peak to the north; Tse Nizhoni and Tse Ka'a to the west; and the junction of the Chaco and Escavada Washes, the rim of Chaco Canyon, and Pueblo Alto to the south.

The road leaves the Pueblo Alto gate with a bearing of 13° east of true north. At Escavada Wash, a point 3.1 kilometers from the gate, the road shifts to within a half degree of true north for sixteen kilometers. It then passes through the Pierre's Ruin area, an unusual set of buildings marked by towers on pinnacles. (Pierre's Ruin is the proper name. Pierre's Ruin complex refers to all the ruins in the vicinity.)

The North Road takes a turn after Pierre's Ruin, a deviation from the almost true north bearing. It then continues close to two degrees east of north for thirty-one kilometers. This angle change was designed to bring the road to the dramatic edge of Kutz Canyon and to connect the two most prominent symmetrical cones in the area: El Faro at Pierre's Ruin complex and Upper Twin Angels. For sixteen kilometers, however, the Chacoans kept the road on a straight bearing of one half degree east of north, thereby demonstrating the importance of that particular orientation. "The purpose of the deviation appears to have been a blending of astronomic north and symbolic use of topographic features in a cosmographic expression," according to the Solstice Project report.

A stairway discovered by the Solstice Project descends from the Upper Twin Angels Mound on the edge of the steepest slope of the Kutz Canyon escarpment to the canyon floor. Now largely collapsed, the stairway was built as a series of platforms that were supported by juniper posts and crossbeams packed with earth. This is presumably the end of the road.

It is commonly accepted that the North Road linked Chaco

Canyon to those important centers north of the San Juan and Animas Rivers. On most maps, the road extends to Twin Angels Pueblo and then a dashed line representing a projected road bears north by northwest for another twelve to eighteen miles to Salmon Ruin. Aztec is another ten miles farther north. The Solstice Project team found no evidence in aerial photographs or during a ground check that the road, in fact, goes to these pueblos. Twin Angels Pueblo is six kilometers from the actual end of the road. Travel to Salmon Ruin and Aztec would have been more efficient by a more direct and easier route farther to the west from Chaco Canyon. Rather than going west, the road goes north and descends a slope into Kutz Canyon that is almost too steep to climb.

Twin Angels Pueblo is a relatively small pueblo and has only seventeen rooms—less than a tenth the size of Salmon Ruin or Aztec. The Solstice Project report points out that although the road does not seem to continue to or near Twin Angels Pueblo, the site lies only one half degree east of north from the start of the road near Chaco Canyon. It therefore bears possible relationship to the roads.

The arrow points toward an avanzada, a simple masonry structure, on a mesa near Twin Angels Overlook near the end of the North Road. Avanzadas are thought to be related to the road by virtue of their elevated positions above the road, projected, in this case. (Photo by Denise Galley, courtesy BLM.)

This aerial photograph shows how the visible and projected road segments align with the major structural sites at Pierre's Ruin. Parallel segments (A) enter the complex from the south, the easternmost segment diverges slightly toward the ramp (B) ascending the large mesa known as the Acropolis (C). The roomblock (D) at the foot of the pinnacle, El Faro, served a mysterious purpose. The hearth (E) at the top of El Faro may have been a lighthouse. (BLM Low Sun Angle, 1981, No. 1-020, courtesy Thomas R. Mann and Associates.)

The North Road area was the most remote area in the region and it still is today. Most of the outlying Chacoan communities are to the south, west, and east of Chaco Canyon. With the possible exception of Pierre's Ruin, there are no residential communities on the North Road.

Much of the architecture along the North Road seems to be special-function architecture. A few shallow herraduras, the circular or horseshoe-shaped masonry structures mentioned earlier, were placed near the road where it can be watched in both directions for a good distance. Similarly, *avanzadas*, or shrine/lookouts, were built in high areas overlooking the road. Avanzadas cap three pinnacles in a row at the end of the North Road into Kutz Canyon. *Zambullidas*, such as Halfway House, are rectangular structures with rows of rooms, more sophisticated than a her-

This oblique aerial photograph shows a slightly different view of the three roomblock units (A, B, C) on the Acropolis; the ramp (D); the lower roomblock at El Faro (E); and the pinnacle structure crowning El Faro (F). (Photo by Tony Lutonsky, courtesy BLM.)

radura but less so than a great house. They were not inhabited, but served some other purpose related to the roads. Most of the structures contain three rooms, some as many as six.

The eeriest Anasazi roadside attraction is the cluster of structures around Pierre's Ruin, 18.9 miles north of Pueblo Alto. The ruin was named for its discoverer, Pierre Morenon, an archaeologist working on Salmon Ruin. He discovered the complex in the 1970s when he walked the roads south from Salmon Ruin. Pierre's Ruin is set amongst a complex of ruins on pinnacles and buttes. Pierre's Ruin is the main ruin and is known to archaeologists as the "Acropolis." Two Bonito-style room-block-with-kiva structures were built on the edge of a mesita on a massive earthwork, a deliberately formed dirt mound that dwarfs the great house it supports. A formal ramp enabled access to the summit of Acropolis, which is level with "El Faro," or lighthouse. At the base of the pinnacle is a housed kiva, and at the top of the spire is a hearth where many large fires had burned, which could have been seen in all directions. Not surprisingly, the spire marks the center of the projected alignment of the North Road. As many as twenty-seven shrines crown the pinnacles in the immediate vicinity.

While three of the structures in the Pierre's Ruin complex are the size of smaller Chacoan outliers, about a third of the structures are isolated rooms or nonhabitation sites. The site lacks a great kiva, which may indicate that not enough people lived there to warrant one, or that no one lived there at all. John Stein called the complex a "constellation of special-function architecture," which may have been determined by the placement of the road.

As John Roney has observed, an inventory of the road produced no evidence to support the idea that it served any intentional economic use. Only ten percent of the ceramics on the road were from the San Juan River communities; all of the rest of the ceramics were local in origin, further discounting the proposal that the road was used for trade. Moreover, if the road were built for trade, there would be signs of roadside camping, but there is a conspicuous absence of hearths and ground or chipped stone in the road inventory.

The ceramics that have been found in the road are peculiar. There are several concentrations of shards along the road. Unusually dense scatters were found along the segment several kilometers south of Pierre's Ruin. Another scatter was found along the Kutz Canyon stairway. The proportion of jars and nonutility ware shards was higher in these locations than is typical of a Chacoan site. The Solstice Project researchers believe that due to the lack of evidence for the practical use of the ceramic shards found in the roads, the ceramics may have been ceremoniously broken and scattered in the road.

Two closely spaced, parallel roads connect Pueblo Alto to Kutz Canyon for much of its length. For about a mile north of Pierre's Ruin, the two-lane road changes to four lanes. From a strictly practical standpoint, the road seems to be overbuilt and underused for all the effort that went into the construction of the parallel lanes, the stairways, ramps, earthworks, and road-related stations.

The North Road's excessive width and linearity, its lack of practicality and use, the long scatters of ceramics within the road itself, the redundancy of certain features such as the parallel routes, and its apparent terminus at an isolated canyon lead members of the Solstice Project to believe that the road was not meant to be functional. "The road apparently goes 'nowhere' and displays a level of effort far out of proportion to the meager tangible benefits that may have been realized with it," according to the Solstice Project report. The road, they proposed, was an expression of spiritual values.

The Solstice Project team looks to the historic Pueblos for these spiritual values. In that culture, First People emerged from the underworld through an entranceway called a *sipapu* and, simply speaking, migrated south. The Pueblos ritualistically return to the sipapu, or representatives thereof, to reenact the emergence. Kutz Canyon, with no apparent economic function, may have been a ceremonial sipapu and the North Road may have played a role in the reenactment of the emergence. The five isolated low-walled structures built on the pinnacles or ridge crests resemble shrines of the historic Pueblo culture, which are often built in high, out of

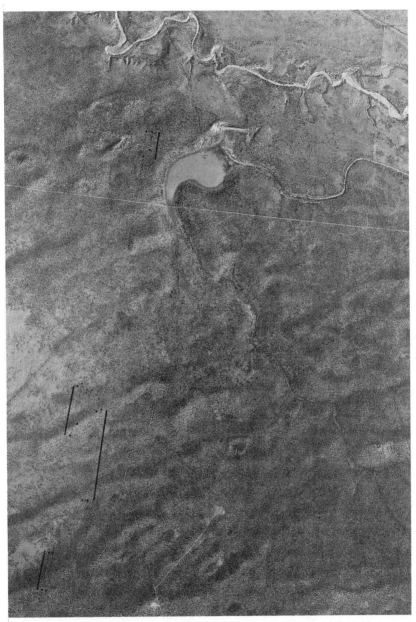

Multiple parallel segments, such as those north of Pierre's Ruin pictured between the dots and along the bold lines, served no obvious practical purpose. (BLM Low Sun Angle, 1981, No. 2-023, courtesy Thomas R. Mann and Associates.)

the way places. Chapter Eight will delve more deeply into Pueblo road and geoastronomical beliefs and ritual.

The North Road is not the only road that emerges as a ceremonial way. Although some roads do link outliers to each other or to resources, others represent formalized entrances to ceremonial locations such as great kivas; one such road leads to the Llave de la Mano, an elaborate platform tucked into an alcove in the side of a cliff on the South Road. Roads near public buildings are often wider and curbed with low masonry, and are frequently elaborated with large ceremonial earthworks such as ramps and circular mounds. The road often enters the buildings between platform mounds, which in other cultures do have religious functions. The pecked grooves and evidence of fire on ramps, burnt structures, elevated fire boxes, and fire pits may also indicate ceremonial significance. As many as twenty-eight herraduras have been documented, along with countless other peculiar structures, within the Chaco road system area.

The South Road, which is projected fifty-one kilometers from Chaco Canyon on the map (only a half kilometer longer than the North Road), is believed to be the major access into the canyon from the south. It may have passed into the canyon through South Gap or near Tsin Kletzin, but so far, that pass has not been verified from the ground. The road, which actually runs from south to southwest, first becomes obvious nine kilometers south of Tsin Kletzin, on the south mesa of Chaco Canyon near Upper Kin Klizhin. From that point it can be traced (with some gaps) for an additional thirty-nine kilometers, through Bee Burrow and Kin Ya'a and on to Dutton Plateau where it ends five kilometers short of the shrine-crowned Hosta Butte, one of the most prominent features in the San Juan Basin.

The South Road bears many of the same characteristics of the other roads, including related shrines, ceramic scatters, and a segment of parallel lanes. Three herraduras have been found in association with this road, as well as a six-room structure. The earthwork and great kiva at Kin Ya'a were pivotal elements of the South Road, which also bisected a structure of the Basketmaker III village of So'tsoh as if it may have been used by later groups as a shrine. Long linear grooves, similar to the one on the North Road near Pueblo Alto, were cut into the bedrock along certain segments of the South Road. All of these features suggest that more was on the minds of the Anasazi than the transportation of goods.

Some roads lead only to such places as pinnacles, springs, or lakes. The Ahshislepah Road, which extends from Penasco Blanco twelve kilometers to the northwest, connects with a group of cisterns, the site of a nonutilitarian structure, and then ends at Black Lake, now dry. A road near Zuñi may also lead to a lake. The list of road fragments is extensive and their related ruins countless. They are well documented in Chapter Twelve of this book, the Anasazi Atlas.

Archaeologist David Doyel said in an interview that the roads are clearly detailed in a ceremonial sense. But that doesn't preclude the fact that they connected Chaco to the outliers or that other roads may have been routed to resources, for practicality is often consecrated. The roads in general are more formal near the great houses, in much the same way that highways are more prominent near cities in our culture. Architectural embellishment may be a show of power and wealth as well as sacred aesthetics.

Doyel believes that the North Road does link Chaco to the San Juan Basin. By neatly terminating at Kutz Canyon, the road gets travelers down off the mesa not too far from Salmon Ruin and Aztec, which also have roads. Frances Joan Mathien said that a trade route between the two regions existed before it was formalized by a road, as demonstrated by San Juan imports that predate the North Road. The road may have celebrated the shift in power to the north or the return of those who migrated north until the rains returned, as Thomas Windes believes. A look at the use of overconstructed Maya sacbes and the Nazca lines in Peru may shed some light on Anasazi roads of Chaco Canyon.

The Maya Sacbe

In the mid-seventies, Edward B. Kurjack wrote one of the earliest descriptions of Maya urban development as it related to roads. He said that the Classic Maya settlements were organized into coalitions centered around core communities connected by intersite and regional causeways, and that the fragmentation of power was reflected in the groundplans of the communities. A hierarchy of settlements with at least four tiers must have existed within these communities, he thought. Primary and secondary sites held the first two ranks, while smaller communities along the causeways were the tertiary centers, and hamlets and scattered houses were the lowest order of settlement. The hierarchy was organized by strong, competitive kinship ties. Causeways provided access between clusters and underscored dominance of one cluster over another.

Some consider the sacbe to have been constructed for religious processions. Sacbes like the ones at Labná consisted of huge blocks of stone that were leveled with gravel and paved with plaster. Some sacbes link only to temple-pyramids or palaces, but at Cobá, in northern Quintana Roo, such causeways connect many scattered ruins. The sacbe between Cobá and Yaxuná (near Chichén Itzá) was sixty-two miles long.

In addition to aligning buildings to solar phenomena or any number of other complex astronomical events, the Maya may have employed numerology in their construction that was extended to their roads. In 1974, geographer Franz Tichy proposed that Mesoamerican angular measurements may have been divided into finite increments with certain azimuths occurring more frequently than others, according to the special times of the year when the sun rose and set in a particular direction. The azimuths that occurred most frequently were multiples of nine degrees.

The evolution of roads in the Maya world began as simply as most formalized roads. In the Yucatán, early settlements were determined by the availability of water. The climate there is arid and warm, surface streams and lakes are rare. The settlements usually sprung up around *cenotes*, caves with collapsed roofs that filled with water. The cave system in northern Yucatan is one of the largest in the world. When the Maya started to build in dressed stone and cement, paths were straightened and formalized. By this time, the Maya could build wells and reservoirs, as is evidenced by the fact that Uxmal and Tikal were not built near water. When cave mysticism was brought to the surface, cave symbolism was blended with imagery of the sky beings in the quadripartite world, and became memorialized in architecture.

Maya roads were laid out in what geographer Michael Romanov called a broken reed pattern, or a section at a time. Romanov, writing in 1973, thought that the roads may have been laid out from central sites at particular angles and pushed out until they intersected other roads. There is evidence of long survey roads, such as the one between Cocal and Katunil, which runs 120 kilometers across Quintana Roo and Yucatán. This road was routed through Chichén Itzá, Uxmal, Izamal, Cobá, Aké, and Dzibilchaltún.

The Maya didn't necessarily locate secondary sites around capitals for economically determined reasons, according to Romanov, but possibly for arbitrary geometric reasons. Romanov felt that the Maya may never have considered surveying the land in order to determine routes, but rather built the roads at pre-ordained angles in order to define the land itself in terms of the imposed system of roads. Romanov said:

> There is abundant evidence that the Maya mind did not think in terms of adapting his cultural achievements to the land itself, but rather thought (in very contemporary terms) of mastery of it. It seems consistent to suggest that the Maya first built his geometric space-covering network of roads, and then located his important places with references to the geometry wherever it coincided nicely with the natural features. The smaller parts were then much more easily dealt with.

Edward Kurjack said that causeways connecting spatially distinct groups of architecture must have been part of a complex of social practices designed to enhance community interaction. The amount of energy expended in their construction, he said, was far greater than that required for a convenient path between buildings, suggesting that "these costly artifacts were symbols of status intimately linked to key features of Maya social organization." The causeways may have symbolized alliances between high status families. Regional causeways between sites were probably constructed to create and maintain enlarged spheres of influence through extension of kinship ties.

Expanding on Kurjack's reasoning that sacbes symbolized alliances among the elite, they may have also symbolized alliances with the stars. The temple-pyramids at Uaxactun, for example, which recorded certain astronomical events, were linked to rulers on the stelae. Uaxactun was linked to the urban center of Tikal by a sacbe. Similar associations between temple stelae, sacbes, urban centers, and ruling families may be evident elsewhere. That the sacbes were constructed with specific angles to the centers only reinforces the geoastronomical alliance.

As discussed in Chapter Four, archaeologist John Roney said that the Anasazi roads served to integrate society. Kurjack makes the same point about the Maya roads. The integration in both cases may have been strengthened by ritual. In 1633, ten years after the Conquest, Bernardo de Lizana recorded the following observation in his *Historia de Yucatán*:

> . . . they offered great alms and made pilgrimages from all parts, for which reason there have been made four roads or highways, to the four cardinal points, which reached to all the ends of the land . . .

This theme was elaborated in Michael D. Coe's 1966 book, *The Maya*:

> These [festivals] took place in every community . . . and involved the construction of a special road (perhaps like the Classic causeways) to idols placed at a certain cardinal point just outside the town limits; a new direction was chosen each year in a four-year counterclockwise circuit.

One final note on semantics. Romanov noted that the word sacbe is often synonymous with both causeway and road, but not all roads are sacbes. There is some confusion in distinguishing between the scores that are just a few dozen meters long and the few that are twenty or more kilometers long, which is similar to confusing a mall with a highway. The former are local sidewalks and not communication routes. Some roads are curbed cause-ways, others are just dirt trails. The word *be* is Yucatec for "road" and is depicted hieroglyphically as a footprint on the center of a circle. *Sac* means "white"; the variant spelling *zac* means north, clay, built-up, cemented. All refer to the color white, which is the color of a paved road. *Sahscab* is white limestone which, when mixed with pebbles and water, provided a good pavement. Hence *sacbe* means "the white road."

Andean Ceque and Nazca Lines of Southern Peru

To most pre-Columbian cultures not near the equator, time flowed around the horizon like a wheel. A landscape calendar was built along lines of the ceque system surrounding the ancient city of Cuzco in Peru. Not unlike other geoastronomical systems, the ceque lines have religious and political implications.

Centered on the Temple of the Sun, the radial cosmo-political map integrated astronomy with ritual kinship and kingship in a system of hierarchical order. It also served as a calendar in which the huacas, or sacred places of worship, functioned like the cords and knots of a *quipu,* used to tally the days of an agricultural year.

Mijones, or pillars, were placed on the horizon in as many as forty-one directions around the temple, and solar events were marked at the center someplace in the city. Because the Spaniards later destroyed the configuration, it is difficult to determine how many lines or pillars there were or where they were placed. At its greatest width the ceque system is five kilometers across.

Linearity and radiality is present in another Peruvian phe-nomenon not fully appreciable from the ground. It wasn't until ge-ographer Paul Kosok took to the air in 1941 that the Nazca lines of Peru were announced to the world. Etched in the high desert bor-dering the valley of the Nazca River is a maze of geoglyphs of con-necting geometrical, animal, and human shapes one to ten kilome-ters long over an area of a thousand square kilometers.

The ray patterns of some of the lines are reminiscent of the ceque lines. Anthony Aveni measured and analyzed eight hundred straight lines on the Nazca pampa and described a pattern. With rare exceptions, the lines radiate from more than sixty well-defined positions surrounding the pampa. These focal points are situated on the surrounding hills that flank tributaries or that lie in the intersection of waterways with the principal drainage, the Nazca River. Many of these positions lie in the lowermost group of Andean foothills that protrude onto the pampa like a pointing finger. Thus Aveni discovered that the lines appeared to connect points in the landscape to the descent of water from the mountains to the pampa on its way to the sea. The huge trapezoids and triangles in particular are so oriented to catch the water run-off.

The creators of the Nazca lines may have intentionally associated their irrigation system with certain astronomical events, reflecting that these two phenomena were somehow entwined in their world view. Consider the conditions under which they lived.

The Peruvian Coast has one of the most arid climates in the world. The long, narrow desert has been created by a number of factors. The Humboldt Current, or Peru Coastal Current, creates an upwelling of cold water in the Pacific near the coast (creating one of the richest fishing zones in the world, particularly for anchovies). The cold water cools the air, reducing evaporation, and as the air moves overland, the higher temperatures hinder rather than encourage rainfall. Since the westward moving air from the Atlantic Ocean sheds its moisture over the eastern Andes, the annual rainfall in this ecological niche is less than one centimeter. The coast is transected by more than fifty dry riverbeds that cut westward from the Andes to the Pacific. Rainfall above 2,500 meters elevation, between October and March, fills these streams but less than ten carry water year round. These rivers are critical to coastal inhabitants since they support a high table for drinking water and irrigation systems.

In an introductory paragraph to *World Archaeoastronomy,* which he edited and published in 1990, Anthony Aveni argued that one of the astronomical hypotheses that can be drawn from the association of the lines with water is that there might be a significant correlation between line orientation and the position of sunrise on the day of the late October solar passage across the zenith, a date which can be correlated both astronomically and ethnohistorically in other segments of Andean culture with the time of appearance of spring rains that precede planting. Statistical data do not bear out the relationship between "water and zenith sun appearing," Aveni said, but they do offer more than a subtle hint that such an association was possible. Aveni writes:

> The water that comes to Nazca rarely comes from the sky. It appears in the rivers only after dark clouds form over the distant mountains at a certain time of the year, and once it arrives it is gone in a flash as it concludes its dramatic, precipitous descent from the high Andes to the Pacific.

Water often comes to Chaco Canyon in much the same way. Dark clouds form above the mountain peaks on the periphery of the San Juan Basin, and in a flash water floods the arroyos to places like Chaco Canyon at the bottom of the basin. The Chacoans built elaborate waterworks to catch the flow. Recall in Chapter One how archaeologists mistook stairways and roads for canals—and for good reason: they overflowed with water during one of these flash flood episodes. The Ahshislepah Road connects Penasco Blanco to an aqueduct. Perhaps there was some ritualistic connection between astronomical alignments and the flow of water in Chaco Canyon, as well.

At least thirty years before Aveni analyzed the Nazca lines, Paul Kosok discovered, quite by accident, that the lines might bear possible astronomical orientations. While cleaning and surveying the first of the rectangles he found, he noted that sunset occurred almost along the direction of the figure. That day was June 22, the winter solstice south of the equator. Further examination led to other discoveries. The long neck of a bird aligns with the winter solstice at sunrise. In 1969, Maria Reiche discovered that two other animals align with the summer solstice at sunrise and sunset. The largest rectangle aligns with the point where the Pleiades rose in about A.D. 600—a date which corresponds with potsherds on the site. Some lines point to lunar extremes and such bright stars as Castor and Antares.

The summer solstice line markers might also guard against the devastating effects of the phenomenon known as El Niño, which occurs upcoast from Nazca, and brings heavy rains to the north and central coast of Peru. El Niño is named for the Christ child because it occurs once or twice a century around Christmastime—or summer solstice south of the equator. The mechanism that triggers El Niño is under extensive study as far away as New Mexico. Basically, a change in the temperature of the ocean currents, the atmospheric conditions, and the trade winds combine to produce the rainfall which lasts several weeks and often destroys villages, burying people in the mud. It upsets the marine ecosystem, producing an absence of fish along the coast and causes the death of birds and other animals dependent on marine life for survival. Surely the effects of El Niño reached the Nazca culture just to the south, who created effigies of bird and marine life in ceramic water vessels.

Maria Reiche, a mathematician, proposed in 1969 that the people traced the continuous lines in a religious procession. She also suggested that the crossings of triangles and trapezoids represented kinship patterns. Aveni found, after careful examination of the surfaces of the Nazca lines, that they were indeed intended to be walked upon. Perhaps, he said, the act of walking helped to keep order in the cosmos. Aveni noted that study of post-Conquest documents suggested that the assignment of water rights among the coastal people, at least at the time of conquest, was based on complex principles of kinship. Thus people would have had good reason to walk across the pampa from one valley to another in accordance with prescribed social rules.

In summary, Aveni said that at least one category of straight lines and line centers constituted a system that almost surely was associated with water, and that some of the lines may have been associated with a calendar and astronomy. Finally, people walked on these lines. Aveni argued that all of these characteristics must be brought together through the pan-Andean concept of radial hierarchical structure derived from the ceque lines analog at Cuzco.

Evidence that the Maya sacbe and the Nazca lines reflected cultural cosmology is speculative, but strong. The fact that Chaco

Canyon's North Road exhibited the same kind of deliberate construction oriented to geoastronomical specifications suggests that it, among the other Chacoan roads, also reflected an alliance between great houses and their sacred places. Researchers have shown that the Maya sacbes and Nazca lines were intended for ritualistic movement—an interpretation that might also be applied to the Great North Road at Chaco Canyon.

Poor preservation might explain gaps in the North Road of up to twelve and a half kilometers. On the other hand, the gaps in the road might never have been closed. In terms of moving great numbers of people from the San Juan River area to Chaco, the road segments might have been very much like the sections of moving sidewalks in an airport, but rather than moving the people through congested traffic, they moved people across rugged terrain. If these disjointed segments were nonutilitarian, then movement along them would have been deliberate and ceremonial, perhaps like the Roman Catholic ritual of systematically praying in front of the Stations of the Cross. To date, no Chaco Canyon scholar has imagined, at least for publication, that the North Road may have been a form of a horizon calendar, that ritualistic movement along the road may have correlated with certain astronomical events marked by the unusual structures spaced at odd intervals along the way.

The similarities between the use of architecture as it related to the sky among New World cultures so distant from one another is striking. Consistently, that cosmology reflected associations between sun and water, so desperately needed in Chaco Canyon, the Maya Lowlands, and the pampa of Peru. The next chapter will explore the various explanations behind the similarities.

The Pochteca Trail

In 1849, First Lieutenant James H. Simpson—yet another civil servant on reconnaissance in the Chaco area, this time with the Army Topographical Engineers—remarked in his report to Congress that he could not "with certainty fix an Aztec origin on the ruins of the Chaco, but they go to show that, as far as is known, there is nothing to invalidate the hypothesis." Mesoamerican stimulation has been proposed as an alternate explanation for the precocious society in Chaco Canyon since it was first discovered.

No book on Chaco Canyon is complete without a discussion about Mesoamerica as the catalyst for Chaco's meteoric growth. Although this subject has been thoroughly explored and challenged, it is reintroduced here because of the conceivable bearing Mesoamerica may have had on the development of the Chacoan roads.

The Mesoamerican Connection

A 1955 paper entitled "Trail Survey of Mexican Southwestern," by Edwin N. Ferdon, Jr., introduced the concept that long-distance traders, the *pochteca*, linked Mesoamerica to such outposts as Chaco Canyon and played a prominent role in the transmission of ideas, objects, and people. The term pochteca refers to a class of professionally trained merchants, or families of merchants, who conducted trade over long distances outside their own political domain. Although the pochteca system was a feature of four-teenth century Aztec culture, well after the fall of the Anasazi, it is presumed that earlier cultures had similar merchant classes. Hold-ing a unique station in life, the self-effacing Aztec pochteca were equal to craftsmen in status, were granted private ownership of land, yet wore plain clothes, and therefore could slip in and out of territory unnoticed. As a result, the pochteca were often used as spies and were privy to civic secrets.

Ellen A. Kelley and J. Charles Kelley, in their 1975 paper, "An Alternative Hypothesis for the Explanation of Anasazi Cul-ture History," embraced the claim that the pochteca inspired the grand architecture at Chaco Canyon. The paper stated that such traders came north from Mexico specifically in search of turquoise.

Some of the most explicit statements regarding both direct and indirect Mesoamerican influence on Southwestern peoples have been those of Charles C. DiPeso. He said that "the presence of a mercantile system in certain New World cultures created an eco-nomic motivation that often fostered islands of exploitable cul-tures in various seas of indigenous traditions." DiPeso identified the Chaco area, and Pueblo Bonito in particular, as one of the northernmost outposts of what he called the *Gran Chichimecan pochteca*. The Chichimecs were the ancestors of the Aztec, who had moved into the Valley of Mexico from the north by the eleventh and twelfth centuries.

Who exploited, manipulated, or instigated the Chaco culture? This question is not easily answered. There is widespread dis-agreement and confusion concerning the dates when some of the major cultures thrived, making it difficult to pin down the contem-poraries of Chaco culture. In an area where the number of groups was high, it is difficult to completely determine which culture pre-ceded which and who influenced whom. Scholars have charted complex distinctions in an effort to define groups culturally and geographically.

In 1943, Ralph L. Beals came up with the phrase "Greater Southwest" to define an area that extended from the Anasazi re-

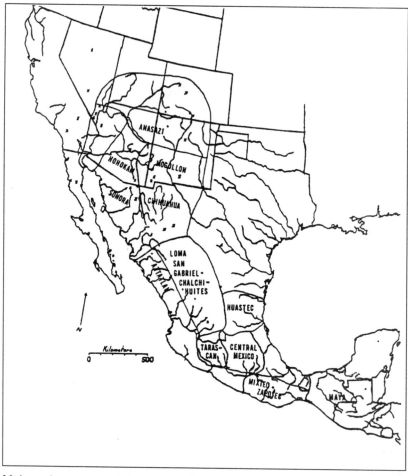

Major culture areas of the Greater Southwest and Mesoamerica. (Courtesy
Frances Joan Mathien.)

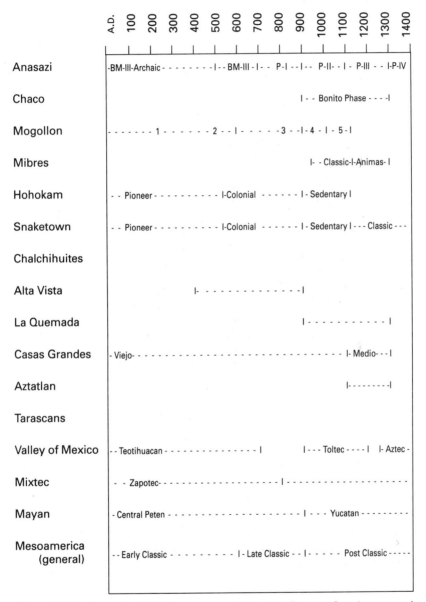

	A.D.	100	200	300	400	500	600	700	800	900	1000	1100	1200	1300	1400

Anasazi   -BM-III-Archaic - - - - - - - -I - - BM-III - I - - P-I - -I - - P-II- - I - P-III - - I-P-IV

Chaco   I - - Bonito Phase - - - -I

Mogollon   - - - - - - - 1 - - - - - - 2 - - I - - - - -3 - -I - 4 - I - 5 -I

Mibres   I- - Classic-I-Animas- I

Hohokam   - - Pioneer - - - - - - - - - I-Colonial - - - - - - I - Sedentary I

Snaketown   - - Pioneer - - - - - - - - - I-Colonial - - - - - - I - Sedentary I - - - Classic - - -

Chalchihuites

Alta Vista   I- - - - - - - - - - - - - I

La Quemada   I - - - - - - - - - - - I

Casas Grandes   - Viejo- I- Medio- - - I

Aztatlan   I- - - - - - - -I

Tarascans

Valley of Mexico   - - Teotihuacan - - - - - - - - - - - - - - I   I - - - Toltec - - - - I   I- Aztec -

Mixtec   - - Zapotec- I -

Mayan   - Central Peten - - - - - - - - - - - - - - - - - - - I - - - Yucatan - - - - - - - - -

Mesoamerica (general)   - - Early Classic - - - - - - - - - I - Late Classic - - I - - - - - Post Classic - - - - -

Chronologies for selected culture areas within the Greater Southwest and Mesoamerica. (Courtesy Frances Joan Mathien.)

gion in Colorado and Utah to the southern limits of the Maya culture in Honduras. The Greater Southwest is not to be confused with the "Southwest" which consists of the sedentary populations of Anasazi, Mogollon, Hohokam, and other cultures that lived in the modern states of New Mexico, Colorado, Utah, and Arizona.

The term "Mesoamerican" was invented by Paul Kirchhoff in 1952 to describe the prehistoric inhabitants who had developed elaborate cultures and who were superior agriculturalists. The high cultures of Teotihuacán and the Toltec and Maya areas are popularly thought to be the instigators of the Chaco culture. The Mesoamerican cradle and the Greater Southwest overlap in northern and western Mexico.

DiPeso's "Gran Chichimeca" is the area above the Tropic of Cancer as far north as the thirty-eighth parallel, which dissects the following Mexican states from west to east: Sinaloa, Durango, Zacatecas, San Luis, Nuevo León, and Tamaulipas. DiPeso disliked the term "northern Mesoamerica" because it presumed an unproven cultural affiliation with Central Mexico.

In 1943, Donald D. Brand subdivided the region differently. One area encompassed the northeastern plateau of the Southwest where the Anasazi culture lived. The Gila/Sonora area formed a second subdivision, comprised of the Trincheras, Hohokam, Sonora, Mogollon, and Chihuahua cultures. Brand called a third area Nueva Vizcaya; it consisted of the coastal cultures of Sinaloa, Durango, parts of Nayarit, and Zacatecas. A fourth area included the Lerma-Chimalhuacan area or drainage basins of the Balsas and Lerma rivers. It was through this last area that he felt many cultural traits provided "the basis for the archaic in the Valley of Mexico and for the various sedentary agricultures in north and western Mexico."

The term "Chalchihuites" was first coined by J. Alden Mason in 1935. It refers to a more or less homogeneous culture living in a broad area between western Zacatecas and northern Durango and included the Alta Vista and La Quemada cultural groups, both of which were road builders. In their 1975 paper, Kelley and Kelley earmarked the Loma San Gabriel culture as the best example of the Chalchihuites tradition. The Loma San Gabriel traded with the Mogollon in southern New Mexico. Artifacts from the Loma San Gabriel culture showed a closer relationship with the Mogollon than with Mesoamerica. Thus it is through this Chalchihuites/Loma San Gabriel/Mogollon cultural district that the first Mesoamerican traits reached the Anasazi. Kelley and Kelley noted: "Essentially, Loma San Gabriel and the Mogollon represent parts of a continuum of related sub-Mesoamerican cultures along the Sierra Madre, with a high degree of cultural similarity."

By A.D. 1000, La Quemada in southern Zacatecas may have had a long-distance trading group or pochteca tied to Casas Grandes, according to Kelley and Kelley. DiPeso, on the other hand, said that Casas Grandes, a two-hour drive south of the New Mexico/Mexico border, was a Toltec outpost and a stepping stone to Chaco Canyon. Kelley and Kelley proposed the following scenarios for Chaco Canyon. The putative takeover of the Chaco Canyon sites between A.D. 1030 and 1040 could have been accomplished through Casas Grandes in Northern Mexico, or directly from Guasave on the west coast. This network supposedly disintegrated because of the abandonment of the Four Corners area a century later. On the other hand, they said that the Chacoan system may have collapsed between A.D. 1250 and 1300 because of the withdrawal or rebellion of the pochteca, the deteriorating environment, and the aggression of nomadic tribes, in that order.

MESOAMERICAN IMPORTS

Mesoamerican archaeologists point to the exotic imports and styles found in Chaco Canyon as evidence that there was influence from the south. Certain artifacts found in Chaco, such as copper bells, marine shells, and macaws, must have been carried from their areas of origin in the south to Anasazi sites, particularly Pueblo Bonito. The question is whether these traded goods verify extensive Mesoamerican influence on the Anasazi. The list of acknowledged similarities includes the areas of architecture, ceramics, wooden objects, water diversion, watch/signal tower systems, geoastronomy—and the roads.

If every scholar who made a comparison between Anasazi and Mesoamerican architecture were correct, then the great houses of Chaco Canyon would be a hodgepodge of mismatched parts. Come to think of it, this describes most American cities today. Speculative Mesoamerican origin for specific great house embellishments have been broad: cored masonry from Maya or Teotihuacán influence; square columns (at Chetro Ketl and BC-51 small house site) similar to those at Teotihuacán; round columns are found in Oaxaca, Tula, and La Quemada; mounds and platforms are pan-Mesoamerican; circular buildings are from Malinalco, Chichén Itzá, and Mayapan. This is only a brief list from a variety of scholars.

Kelley and Kelley actually went to the trouble of charting Mesoamerican influence on Chaco and categorizing specific imports into specific time periods of influence. The first contact the Mesoamericans made with the Anasazi, they said, was from A.D. 400 to 600. From A.D. 800 to 925, there was a hiatus in Mesoamerican contact because of the fall of Teotihuacán and the florescence of the Toltecs.

The period between A.D. 1020 and 1300 represented maximum exploitation by the Mesoamericans, according to Kelley and Kelley. This period not only covers the rise of the Toltecs, but their move from Tula and their subsequent displacement by the Aztecs, who by 1300 began to establish their reign in the Valley of Mexico. According to legend, the Aztecs arrived in the valley from the mythical Aztlan, Place of the Heron, which lies someplace in the north, after wandering the countryside for a hundred years.

The list of archaeological finds supporting Kelley and Kelley's chronology of Mesoamerican contact is extensive. Between A.D. 450 and 600, the Mogollon transferred ceramics, pithouse design, some cultigens, the bow and arrow, stone mortars, bowls, and grooved mauls from the Chalchihuites in the Loma-San Gabriel area to Chaco Canyon. From A.D. 600 through the Basketmaker III/Pueblo I transition, around the 700s, the Anasazi borrowed the sipapu, ceramic designs of Lino black-on-grey (A.D. 500–700), new types of cotton, lima beans, moschata, squash, and corn from the Chalchihuites culture, through the Mogollon. The great kiva apparently came from Rio Bolanos (Totoate) and was used as headquarters by the Mesoamerican traders, but the use of wood supports in the kiva came from Teotihuacán by way of the Chalchihuites, Kelley and Kelley report.

There is no evidence of Mesoamerican contact between A.D. 800–925, and no great kivas were built in the American Southwest during this period, according to Kelley and Kelley. By A.D. 1030, the Anasazi had in their possession the following Mesoamerican imports: crafts, copper bells, macaws and parrots, shell trumpets, pottery stamps, cloisonné-decorated sandstone, painted wooden birds, ceremonial sticks, effigy vessels, and exotic forms. From the pochteca, the Anasazi may have learned how to design and build columns, circular towers, platform mounds with forecourt, stairways, and balustrades, and how to use core masonry and cut rock stairways. They also learned about water control, human sacrifice, and, most notably, roadway systems.

MESOAMERICAN INFLUENCE IN THE Mississippi VALLEY

Traces of Mesoamerican influence showed up in the archaeological record in the Louisiana Valley 3500 years ago. The culture at Poverty Point may have been the first to align their buildings cardinally and to build a formal road in North America. This advanced development in the lower Mississippi Valley emerged 1500 B.C. and peaked circa 1200 to 800 B.C. and may have had an Olmec influence. The culture had not yet engaged in agriculture, yet it built earthworks along the banks of the Bayou Macou. Nor had the inhabitants invented cooking pots, yet they made ingenious use of clay cooking balls in their pit-flamed pots.

Of the 150 Poverty Point sites, five have been identified as regional centers with exports to distant sites. At one site, four sets of concentric ridges intersected by aisles are laid out in a horseshoe shape between the Bayou Macou and two mounds. The two central aisles point to the sun at the solstices. A road angles across the site. Centered behind the horseshoe of ridges is a mound which

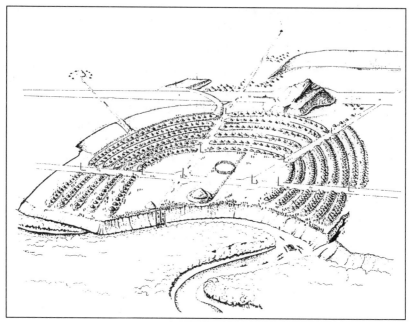

Reconstruction of the Poverty Point site reveals the six man-made concentric ridges and four aisles that radiate outward like roads. The main road dissecting the site from left to right is nearly aligned true north. (Courtesy the Department of Culture, Recreation and Tourism, Louisiana Archaeological Survey and Antiquities Commission.)

may have been a bird effigy. The mound is seventy feet high and 680 feet on the north/south line (to form the wings), and 690 feet on the east/west line. The eastern side of the ramp falls away to a low earthen platform or ramp, suggesting the tail feathers.

The Olmecs, who lived a thousand miles south (1200 to 300 B.C.) also built earthworks and it is believed by some that the Olmecs influenced the people of Poverty Point, who were making crude replicas of the artistic Olmec pregnant women figurines.

"It is hard to imagine that there wasn't some kind of connectedness between the Mississippi Valley and the shores of Mesoamerica," David Doyel said in an interview. The Mesoamericans could have traded across the Gulf Coast by boat.

Shaping the earth into mounds and the forms of animals, such as the snake effigy in Ohio, continued through the Adena culture in the Ohio Valley (500 B.C.–A.D. 200), the Hopewell in the heart-land and later across the eastern half of the United States (100 B.C.–A.D. 350), and the Mississippian culture in basically the same area (A.D. 800–1500).

Malls and roads tended to connect the mounds of these cultures. Geoastronomy was practiced among the Mississippian culture, a contemporary of Chaco culture. The third and fourth terraces of Monk's Mound at Cahokia Site (A.D. 900–1250), on the banks of the Mississippi, were aligned six degrees east of north in later stages of construction, according to a survey published in *American Antiquity* in 1968. The mounds and ruins were built on north-south and east-west axes in relationship to Monk's Mound. Cahokia may have participated in what ethnologists are calling the sun/water cult.

THE SUN/WATER CULT OF THE NEW WORLD

"We cannot imagine seed and techniques for growing corn having been transmitted [to the Anasazi] without added instructions as to gods and rituals believed necessary for success," said Florence Hawley Ellis, who brought tree-ring dating to Chaco Canyon in the late 1920s. Ellis says that the striking parallels in world view between Mesoamerican beliefs and historic Pueblo beliefs cannot be ignored. Something as simple as maize could have been the bearer of a mythology. First cultivated in Central Mexico, it later became a staple of the Anasazi diet and evolved into a symbol of power for historic Pueblo religious leaders. The mechanism by which corn was brought to the Anasazi region is not known.

Pueblo and Navajo legends describe traders, gamblers, and wise men who either came from Mexico or went there after leaving the Anasazi area. Most of them taught life skills and ritual practices. In a Zia origin legend, one hero, Poishaiyanne, a gambler and cultural hero from a community at Pecos, New Mexico, helped the Zia set up their medicine and weather controlling societies before he headed south to Chihuahua, Mexico, where he married the daughter of the chief of the Pueblo there. Noqoilpi, the gambler that the Navajo place at Chaco Canyon, destroyed the

Anasazi culture in one version, but in another version, he became Nakaii Cigíni, or the God of the Mexicans.

In that version, as described in the *Journal of American Folklore* in 1889, Washington Matthews said that the Chacoans shot No-qoilpi into the air until he came to the home of Bekotcice, the god who carries the moon. Bekotcice, taking pity on him, gave him a new people (the Mexicans) to exploit, as well as farm animals, including the horse, and bright colored clothing. The people multiplied and moved north near Santa Fe, building villages along

The sun/water cult, underlying most New World cultures, is the basis of the all-pervasive directional scheme. (Photo is of a western window at Pueblo Bonito.)

the Rio Grande on the way. Noqoilpi returned to Mexico where he still lives as the God of the Mexicans.

Alexander Stephen documented a similar legend about Masau, a cultural hero who was not from Mexico but had Mesoamerican counterparts. The legend was told to him by the Powamu Chief at Walpi, a Hopi village, in 1883:

> When my people learned to build houses and men had grown accustomed to life in the kivas, Masau [the spirit who helped the Hopi emerge from the underworld and who greets them when they return after death] came and taught them many things concerning growth and trees and instructed them about planting beans when the moon should be at a certain angle and after the sun had come a certain distance on his way back to the north. Many days this has been the custom and we have no right to forsake the ways of our fathers.

Masau also gave the Hopi four sacred tablets. One tablet, inscribed with cryptic markings, had a piece broken off from one corner. Pahana, the lost white brother, was supposed to arrive from across the salt water with the missing piece and save the Hopi from disaster. According to Frank Waters, the Hopi did not forget the prophecy and still wait for Pahana at designated places. Likewise the Aztecs waited for the return of Quetzalcoatl, and the Mayas waited for Kukulcan.

However it was brought to the Anasazi, corn became ingrained in the culture of their descendants. But corn, planted in the earth, requires sun and water to grow. Hence sun and water became intimately connected in the cultural traditions of agricultural civilizations, and as they developed, they built monolithic temple-calendars to mark the sun's path and the rainy season.

The sun/water cult, underlying most New World cultures, is the basis of the all-pervasive directional scheme with accompanying color symbolism and emphasis on ritual and numerology. "The vast network of symbolic associations generated by these two principles is derived not only from the apparent motion of the sun, but also from the belief in its interconnection with rain and water," said ethnologist M. Jane Young in a 1989 article comparing the ideology of Mesoamerica to that of the Western Pueblos.

The Zuñi, a Western Pueblo, shape space and time into the semi-cardinal directions, for instance, which refer not only to the solstices at sunrise and sunset but to the four oceans and the places where the rain priests dwell. Aztec deities also related to both sun and water. The relationship between sun and water is seen as the basis for human and agricultural fertility.

Polly Schaafsma said that rain cult iconography took hold in the Southwest by A.D. 1050, about the time the roads were built around Chaco Canyon. She says the goggle-eyed monster found in southwestern petroglyphs is Tlaloc, the rain god of Mesoamerica who is derived from the Olmec dwarf or infant, the symbol of maize. Another Mesoamerican deity is Quetzalcoatl, associated with the Morning Star and portrayed as the feathered serpent. Serpents are ubiquitous in Pueblo ritual and Anasazi petroglyphs. The zigzag lines symbolize lightning bolts or rain.

The deities connected with sun and water may be intrinsic components of an agriculturally based society and not necessarily borrowed from another culture. Nevertheless, sun and rain were important needs of the Anasazi. But did the Chaco Canyon culture belong to an intercontinental sun/water cult? That would be difficult to prove scientifically. There is an abundance of sun shrines and alignments to the solstices, and there was a lack of water, which would cause any primitive culture to look toward the supernatural for help. The infamous sun calendar on Fajada Butte marks the solstices with a sun dagger stabbing a spiral—a symbol for water. Serpentine zigzag lines also interplay with the sun markings on the butte. Furthermore, many of the sun shrines are in high places, which are closer to the sun but also symbolic of mountain ranges, the origin of rain.

Ellis said that early ideology north and south of the Mexican border was based on caves. The Pyramid of the Sun at Teotihuacán was built directly on top of a cave. Early Maya shrines were built near cenotes, collapsed-roof caves filled with water. Pueblo mythology centers around the sipapu, the entrance to the underworld, which includes caves, crevices, natural hot springs, or any opening in the surface. Ellis says the sipapu was borrowed from the Mogollon, the intermediary culture between the Anasazi and Mesoamerica. Cave ideology was elaborated with the addition of geoastronomy throughout the New World, but the connection between sun and water, and even earth, did not change.

Ellis noted that Feather Cave, discovered more than forty years ago in the Mogollon region of southern New Mexico, which dates to Chaco contemporary times, linked the Southwest to Mexico. An inner chamber served both as a sun shrine and an earth shrine. It was discovered in the late 1960s by graduate students and is chock-full of petroglyphs, prayer sticks, arrows, and other offerings. Ellis said iconography from Mexican and Anasazi cultures was found in the cave.

Some southwestern investigators make the claim that the kachina cult of the Pueblo culture is an outgrowth of Mexican deities working their way into New Mexico in the fourteenth century. This claim is made on the basis of a change in the rock art, and the date is much later than Ellis's estimate. Sometime after A.D. 1300, a new rock art style pervaded the Rio Grande Valley and extended as far west as the Hopi in Arizona—a style that includes masked figures similar to kachina dancers. Astronomer Michael Zeilik says that the motifs were derived from Jornada Mogollon of southern New Mexico and included the Mexican de-

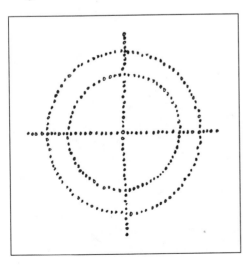

Crosses within concentric circles in various misshapes and sizes were pecked into the floors of pyramids or cliff walls and used, many of them, as survey markers for Teotihuacán geoastronomy.

ity Quetzalcoatl incorporated with Venus as the morning or evening star.

The Teotihuacán pecked cross, seen in more than seventy sites throughout Mexico, is prevalent in the Mogollon region as well, but is much less common in the Anasazi area. These crosses may have come from the Chalchihuites, who were thought to have influenced the Chacoans through the Mogollon. Two were found hundreds of kilometers north of the Teotihuacán Valley at the Chalchihuites Alta Vista site in the Mexican state of Zacatecas, which, in the early stages, showed strong architectural influence from Teotihuacán.

The disparity in dates probably does more to show repeated contact with Mesoamerica, than it does to indicate one overwhelming period of contact. One date does not necessarily discount the other.

Young says Pueblo deities were created from Mesoamerican prototypes and reflect the belief in the reciprocity between human beings and gods. Many similarities between the deities of the

Numerous cross and circle configurations were pecked into a virtual gallery of petroglyphs at Three Rivers in the Mogollon area north of Tularosa, New Mexico. The crosses all align with prominent peaks along the horizon. The symbol may have come to the Mogollon through the Chalchihuites at Alta Vista in Mexico, who also used the Teotihuacán bench mark.

Hopi, the Zuñi, and the Aztecs existed in function, attribute, and appearance. The Aztec sun, Tonatiuh, for instance, is represented by a disk and is known, among other names, as the eagle that soars. The hands are tipped with eagle claws clutching human hearts. The Hopi sun, Tawa, is sometimes portrayed as an eagle and wears a plaited circle of eagle and parrot feathers around his head like the rays of a sun. Tawa is gentle and kind, but legends do hint at human sacrifice: "Sun had to be helped to move across the sky by killing a child."

Other similarities between kachinas and Mesoamerican deities exist in great number, but most of them probably postdate the Anasazi. Besides parallels in deities, the two geographical regions held common perceptions of astronomical phenomena as well.

The Aztecs and their predecessors, as well as the Zuñi, believed in a dual creative principle. The Aztec Ometecuhtli/Omecihuatl generative pair can be compared to the Zuñi Awonawilona, who characterizes both the Sun Father and Moon Mother, translating in the plural as "The Ones Who Hold the Roads." Awonawilona, both male and female, also stands for the entire class of supernaturals. The Hopi tradition also traces descent from a male-female creator pair.

Both the Pueblo and the Mesoamericans believe that the sun travels between east and west houses. The Mesoamericans believe the houses are paradise where one goes after death. The Aztecs, Mayas, and Pueblos perceive the universe as layered. The Mayas had nine underworlds and thirteen heavens. The Zuñi have four underworlds, each associated with a tree and a direction; four upperworlds, each associated with a bird, and a middle world, or the familiar world. Together, the worlds total nine.

Both Aztec and Zuñi traditions include belief in an afterlife. Zuñi priests join their deified counterparts. Others, after four reincarnations that involve working one's way through one underworld per reincarnation, can return to the living as an animal, depending on knowledge acquired during life. Eastern Pueblos and Hopi journey the north road to the sipapu where they can return to their ancestors in the underworld.

Aztec souls, in contrast, were assigned to certain realms of the cosmology depending on one's occupation and manner of death. Those assigned to the north had to work their way back up through the nine underworlds. Those who died in combat or were sacrificed went to the sun's house or paradise on the eastern horizon, and returned in four years as hummingbirds or other exotic birds. Fray Diego Duran noted in the late 1500s how the hummingbird, *huitzitzlin* in Nahuatl, plants its beak into the bark of leafy trees for nourishment during winter, seemingly dead for six months, after which time it is reincarnated, or so the natives believed. The Aztec god, Huitzilopochtli, "Hummingbird from the Left," is portrayed in a gruesome springtime ceremony which includes the flaying of captives. Waters said that the flaying of the skin symbolizes the shedding of man's earthly clothing, and the freeing of his spirit. A *huitziton* is a macaw and hummingbird feather bunch, symbolizing newborn corn, that sits atop a long pole, or *coatl*, the serpent staff of the Quetzalcoatl in the corn dance at Santo Domingo Pueblo. Venus as the Morning Star is reincarnated as the Evening Star, an event incorporated into the mythological death and rebirth of Quetzalcoatl.

Ritual life of both Zuñi and Aztec cultures includes a period of fasting and abstinence of four days before some ceremonies and a period of idleness following the ceremonial calendar.

The Mayas, Hopi, Aztecs, and Zuñi all have six points of orientation, although the Western Pueblos assign different colors to the directions than do the Mesoamericans and refer to the semi-cardinal directions or solstitial directions, rather than the cardinals. For all, the ritual direction of time is generally counterclockwise and includes the zenith, nadir, and center in the scheme. All groups believe that there were four worlds before this one.

As the Zuñi were instructed to leave their home in search of the center, so were the Aztecs by their god Huitzilopochtli. All groups extend their directions to symbolically include birds, mountains, trees, and animals. The Aztec assign certain gods to specific directions, as well as human beings, depending on the birth date. The Zuñi assign rain priests or *uwanammi*, and the

Hopi the Cloudyouths to the six directions. These cloud spirits are associated with specific mountaintops, as were the Aztec rain gods, or Tlalocs. The Keresan Pueblos also appeal to the six directions for rain.

Responding to the cross-cultural comparisons made by Ellis, Young, and others, Zeilik said that the Southwest lacked important Mesoamerican features such as written calendars, a numerical system with long counts, 260-day ritual years, close attention to conjunctions of Venus, a system of year bearers, and zenith passages of the sun. (The Pueblos do have a simple calendric system which will be described in the next chapter.) Zeilik agrees, however, that the use of solstitial points and cardinal points, rather than the European notion of north, south, east, and west at right angles, show cultural borrowing. Zeilik calls for more investigation of Venus sightings and references among the Pueblos. He said that the Isleta practice of pulling down the sun through a small hole in the roof with a crystal may be an analogy to Mesoamerican zenith tubes, although the sun does not transit the zenith at southwestern latitudes.

Mesoamerican Highways

The mechanism for bringing corn, macaw feathers, and architectural design to the Anasazi is not understood. A surprising number of archaeologists I talked to said that they wouldn't doubt that roads existed between the two zones, while just as many rejected the idea. The fact that roads have been discovered as far south as the Zuñi area in southern New Mexico and as far north as Casas Grandes, Mexico, leads many to believe that a trading route between them existed and that the route may have been formalized by a means long faded. In fact, DiPeso found that ancient trailways not only connected population centers within the Casas Grandes sovereignty, but were also traceable as shell trails to the Gulf of California.

So far, no evidence of panregional routes from Mexico to Chaco have been found, and the dates of such road-encompassed centers as La Quemada and Casas Grandes do not exactly coincide with those of Chaco Canyon. Although the panregional route would not have to be as formal as those around the urban centers, there would be some telltale signs of routes, such as way stations paced a day's travel apart, not unlike modern highways. None of these signs have presented themselves. However, I have already suggested that the Anasazi roads were for architectural embellishment and ritualistic use. In this context, a constructed panregional highway seems unlikely. A marked trail would have been more appropriate.

Cultural material from the cradle of Mesoamerica doesn't show up at Casas Grandes until around A.D. 1060, according to DiPeso. By that time, most of the great houses at Chaco Canyon were already built, using the techniques attributed to Mesoamerica. Furthermore, it was not until A.D. 1205 that Casas Grandes reached its most complex stage, with high-rise apartments.

However, the disparity between the time Casas Grandes cultivated a taste for Mesoamerican culture (A.D. 1060) and the time when Chaco Canyon peaked (A.D. 1040) is only twenty years. That's when the Chacoans began reorienting their major buildings on a north-south axis and formalizing their roads. Just because no formal route between the distant centers of Chaco Canyon and Mesoamerica has been found does not mean that the very idea of building roads was not introduced to the Anasazi from a traveling corn peddler.

Casas Grandes had a road system comparable to Chaco Canyon. "This transportation system apparently helped to weld the Casas Grandes province into a functioning whole, although it was not as sophisticated or elaborate as those produced by other New World groups," DiPeso said. The roads were banked and engineered. Sometimes the trails were protected with stones and walls on the outside and steps were cut into steep inclines of rock.

The roads were banked by single room way-houses and signal towers (*atalayas*). When fire signals were not conveyable during the day or on stormy nights, the military may have resorted to conveying messages along the network of connecting pathways. Runners could have been strategically stationed in various towns for this purpose, says DiPeso. Adolf Bandelier, who studied the area in 1884, said the structures served a dual purpose as a line-of-sight communication route and as religious structures used in worshipping the wind god, Ehecatl (the Nahuatl name of the Aztec god). Not unlike the La Quemada system, the system around Casas Grandes had hillside fortresses.

Formal routes did exist in the Chalchihuites area in the modern Mexican states of Zacatecas, Nayarit, Jalisco, Guanajuato, and Durango. Remember that the Anasazi kivas, sipapu, irrigation system, and much of its other cultural hardware reportedly came from the Chalchihuites culture.

The examples of roadways in the Chalchihuites region are numerous. Five sites with causeways have been identified in the Rio Lajas drainage (a northern tributary of the Lerma River) and in the Bajio of Guanajuato dating to the Classic period. Among these are two roads at Cañada de Alfaro dating to Early Classic times. Later Classic period sites with causeways include: Graceros; Rancho Viejo, with a causeway extending from a series of plazas for four hundred meters; Cañada de la Vergen on a six-hundred-meter road ten meters wide extending from a pyramid/

Roads were probably used by the military to gain access to the Citadel at La Quemada. (Aerial view of the south face of La Quemada, Zacatecas, courtesy Charles Trombold.)

plaza compound; and the Cerro de la Mona-Morales group, which sits on a super-causeway reaching halfway across the Rio Lajas Valley to a series of ceremonial structures. San Bartolo Aguacaliente in central Guanajuato is connected to a spring via a causeway more than two hundred twenty-five meters in length and eight meters in width.

Charles Trombold, in *Ancient Road Networks and Settlement Hierarchies in the New World,* said that these and related sites at this early date are especially significant because of their architectural similarities (such as round and square columns, sunken plazas, and stepped pyramids) to those of the La Quemada region and the Chalchihuites tradition in general. The influence is from the Chalchihuites tradition from the Bajio, Rio Lajas, and middle Lerma, which predates the cultures of the Basin of Mexico.

The Caxcans of Zacatecas were also cultural descendants of the Chalchihuites tradition. Aerial photos have revealed roadways in the vicinity of Las Ventanas, a large Caxcan stronghold and ceremonial center in southern Zacatecas, 140 kilometers south of La Quemada. Although it was still occupied at the time of the Spanish conquest, it dated to the Classic period. Formal routes may also be tied to the large fortified Caxcan center of Teul de Gonzales Ortega in southwestern Zacatecas.

Formal routes were also found on the northern edge of the Chalchihuites culture at the Schroeder site in north-central Durango. Although carbon 14 dates have not yet been firmly established, the major occupation of the Schroeder site dates around A.D. 900-1100. In terms of the Chalchihuites, this is somewhat late. Trombold said, "Almost certainly the practice of road building was well known beforehand in this region . . . ."

La Quemada, in Zacatecas, featured formal causeways that helped troops gain access to their fortifications on the hills. The La Quemada causeways have been compared to Chacoan roads relative to their straightness, width, connections to outlying sites, construction of stairways to overcome topographic obstacles, and perhaps roadbed preparation.

At first glance, Trombold said, this might suggest direct contact between Chaco Canyon and La Quemada. The two cultures, however, are separated by two hundred years and more than eighteen hundred linear kilometers. Trombold says that the roads functioned differently in the two cultures. They were also structurally different—unlike the Chacoan roads, those at La Quemada were rarely depressed or bermed. Trombold noted:

> Although direct contact between them thus appears very doubtful, a general Mesoamerican presence seems evident at Chaco based on (among other things) the comparatively widespread occurrence of earlier road networks in north central Mexico. The macro-morphological similarities found in association with traditional Chaco architecture may indicate that the practice of road building was "grafted on" an already established cultural tradition.

Trombold says that the mechanism for this is not clear, but he suspects "especially strong cultural waves were sweeping northward from somewhere in north central Mexico between A.D. 600 and 800." The wave might have been the result of the political upheaval further south, realignment of exchange patterns, marriage alignments, religious ferment, conquest, or a combination of these factors. "Whatever it was," he said, "it manifested itself suddenly and decisively—and primarily in certain aspects of architecture and intra-site layout." It may be more than just coincidence, then, that formal routes were constructed at La Quemada between A.D. 600 and 800, at Schroeder between A.D. 900 and 1100, and at Chaco between A.D. 1050 and 1140, according to Trombold.

DOWN-THE-LINE TRADING

Frances Joan Mathien, who challenged the so-called Mesoamerican connection and provided most of the historical detail of the thinking in this area, doubts that the pochteca would come all the way from Tula just for turquoise, even if there was a road to follow.

Besides turquoise, the Anasazi could have conceivably offered the pochteca such worthwhile commodities as peyote, salt, selenite, copper, skins, herbs, and themselves as slaves, but the Mesoamericans could have obtained all these closer to home. Although Cerrillos turquoise has been found at Chalchihuites sites,

Mathien has not been able to prove that the Chacoans themselves used the mine, situated south of Santa Fe, New Mexico;
there are turquoise mines closer to Mexico. Furthermore, she
says, the evidence in Chaco Canyon of imports from other cultures is just too sparse to suggest that a major Chaco-Mesoameri-
can network existed.

Mathien says that apart from the fact that the amount of foreign
material found in the canyon is too small to indicate major trading, there are more differences between Chaco and Mesoamerican
cultures than similarities. For instance, Mathien points to the C, D,
and E shapes of the great houses, which are not found in Mexico.
Contrasting with the Mesoamerican pattern are the pre-planned
layouts of the great houses. The Mesoamericans' use and style of
core-veneer masonry also differs. Mathien would prefer to think
that the culture in Chaco Canyon evolved on its own.

In any event, Chaco Canyon is a long walk from Tula. According to an equation devised by DiPeso, if the trader could walk
twenty-five kilometers a day or a thousand kilometers in forty
days, it would still take fifty-six days to reach Chaco Canyon from
Tula. The Spanish missionaries of the mid-1600s, with travel-effi-
cient beasts of burden and wheeled carts, took a year and a half
to journey to New Mexico and back to Mexico, including a six-
month layover at their destination.

Casas Grandes would have been more accessible. Although it
was probably part of the trade network as an intermediary center, it may not have been interesting enough to the pochteca to
warrant a trip until long after Chaco Canyon culture was well
established.

The claims of Mesoamerican influence on Chaco Canyon are
not widely accepted. No real proof exists to credit, or blame, a
real pochteca trader for the meteoric rise of the Chaco civilization,
not even a skeleton, unless one counts the extravagant burial beneath Room 33 of Pueblo Bonito. Twelve bodies had been buried
in this cramped six-foot area labeled Room 33. Beneath this room
were two more skeletons; one adorned by ten turquoise pendants
and nearly six thousand beads, and the other, nearly seven hun-

dred pendants and more than nine thousand beads. Compare this tomb to Room 320, where eight women and two girls were buried. This grave was relatively unadorned, containing only a few pots and baskets and the mats and robes on which they were lain. The burial in Room 33 is the most lavish of the few grave sites found in Chaco Canyon. Some have speculated that Room 33 was the final resting place of a pochteca.

Mathien proposes an alternative to direct trade with Mesoamerica. The items and ideas transmitted from Mexico to Chaco did not require a single bearer, but could have been traded up and down the line by more localized trade systems. Mathien said the Anasazi themselves may have traveled when farm work allowed, but could only go as far as they could carry their cargo and as far as they could afford, a radius of about seven hundred to nine hundred miles.

As early as 1945, archaeologists began thinking that ties which linked the Anasazi to Mexican cultures were more general in nature and were probably transmitted through the Hohokam and that direct Mexican connections were not necessary. Mathien says that the Hohokam lived too far west to be part of the direct chain from the Chalchihuites.

David Doyel prefers the Hohokam explanation. On a map, the Chacoan great house/great kiva system is on the hem of the Hohokam ball court system, which is so close to Mesoamerica that the exchange of goods and ideas is very likely. There are even ball courts in sites that are not Hohokam, which indicates how a culture, tied perhaps economically into a network, can be influenced. Hohokam ceremonial features, plazas, irrigation systems, and big mounds indicate information sharing across thirty to fifty thousand square miles, according to Doyel. The ball court itself may be a link to Mesoamerican cultures.

The Hohokam ball court, built on elliptical mounds, is one of the most distinctive features of public architecture. More than two hundred courts have been recorded at more than one hundred sixty sites and were built in the early Colonial period. They were widely distributed within a radius of one hundred kilometers or more in the four cardinal directions from Snaketown in the Phoenix Basin, where the largest ball court is found. David Wilcox, in "Evolution of Hohokam Ceremonial Systems," noted that the most striking attribute of the ball court system is the closeness of adjacent sites in the Phoenix Basin, where more than forty percent of the ball court sites were recorded. Most are only five or six kilometers apart, although some are as far as fifteen to twenty kilometers apart. "This closeness of spacing probably indicates a continuous social integration throughout the ball court network," Wilcox said. "Most of the flow of intercommunity exchange was probably structured by these linear networks . . ."

Mesoamerican ball courts, built in dressed stone and cement and much more elaborate than what is left of the Hohokam ball courts, often align with important buildings within urban centers. The ballgame battles were violent and deadly according to interpreters who examined the layout of the architecture, Conquest descriptions of the game, mythological accounts recorded in the *Popul Vuh*, illustrations of the game on pottery and murals, and the equipment and protective clothing found in the archaelogical record. Each team may have represented a religious faction or elite family and scenes of human sacrifice often accompany depictions of the game.

Doyel said some trade may have existed between the two cultures as evidenced by the presence of turquoise from the Cerrillos mines (which many believe to be a resource for the Chacoan turquoise industry) in Hohokam sites, as well as the presence of a Hohokam pyrite mirror found at Pueblo Bonito. The copper bells, marine shells, cotton, macaws, and the Mesoamerican ideas of architecture and organization could have reached the Anasazi through the Hohokam.

It is just as likely that the building patterns of the Anasazi filtered southward. The adobe village of Casas Grandes in Mexico looks more like a great house settlement than a Maya or Teotihuacán pyramid.

There is some overlap between the two systems at Wupatki Pueblo north of Flagstaff, which contained both a great kiva and a ball court. Other evidence of intercultural mixing includes the material culture of the Salado peoples, who moved in among the Hohokam and built great adobe structures such as Casa Grande in Arizona.

"Archaeologists are becoming too specialized," Doyel said. "They are not thinking about the big picture from Mexico City and Cortez, Colorado, between the time of Christ and 1100 A.D."

J. Charles Kelley thought about the big picture. In 1974, in "Speculations on the Culture History of Northwestern Mesoamerica," he proposed the idea of cultural drift, which may account for similarities between cultures. Certain lineage groups—small numbers of farmers, for instance—"budded off," taking a portion of their basic heritage with them. These basic traits, and the cultural baggage carried by organized trade endeavors, combined with the traits of a new area in such a way that the next generation of colonization carried with it mixed variations of the basic pattern.

Thomas Windes and Frances Joan Mathien believe that the Anasazi were mobile and possibly lived in more than one great house because of climatic changes that occurred not only in the Southwest but the Greater Southwest. And like modern folks, they changed their tastes as they sampled the wares of others, adding new pottery styles to their cupboard and carrying with them such grand ideas as building roads.

ONE LANGUAGE, ONE COSMOLOGY, ONE PEOPLE

A Zuñi man told me a story about two groups who, after the emergence from the Grand Canyon, were sent to find the center of the world. A priest held a parrot egg in one hand and a raven egg in the other and ordered the religious leaders of each group to choose an egg to determine which direction each group took. One group chose the exquisite parrot's egg, while the other chose the plain black raven's egg. The holders of the more ornate egg were sent south into Mexico, while the holders of the simple egg were sent eastward. That group migrated through many prehistoric sites, including Chaco Canyon, and historic Rio Grande Pueblos to the Village of the Great Kivas near Zuñi.

Humans probably migrated into the New World at least eleven thousand years ago (and perhaps as many as twenty thousand years ago, depending on one's sources), when mountain glaciers still covered much of New Mexico and large lakes filled basins like that of the San Juan. Paleo-Indians hunted the large mammals driven south by the ice ages as early as 8500 B.C. Suppose, for example, that Clovis hunters were the first hominids to enter the New World. Suppose they brought with them a single language, a single cosmology, and a single culture from which nearly all other aboriginal cultures of the New World evolved.

Archaeologist David Wilcox made that supposition. "Similarities among the Southwestern cultures and between Southwestern cultures and those in Mesoamerica may derive from an original unity of New World culture and parallel evolution thereafter," he said, remarking on the striking similarities in ceremonial systems in the New World.

Wilcox said that the Hohokam and the Chacoan Anasazi, who both developed a calendrical system around A.D. 1000, may have diverged from other cultures in western North America and maintained a closer similarity to the evolving cultures of Mesoamerica. "This implies participation in the evolution of Mesoamerican civilization." The mechanics of this interaction remain highly controversial, Wilcox warned. They do indeed.

Frances Joan Mathien's elaborate studies of the Mesoamerican trade and exploitation systems amounted to disproving them and led her to propose an alternate system—one that is holistic. The idea is reminiscent of Wilcox's single linguistic group.

According to a linguistics map drawn after the Spanish conquest in the sixteenth century, a string of Uto-Aztecan language groups extended from the Great Basin in Nevada throughout the western half of Mexico as far as Zacatecas. Mathien added to the map the Nahuatl speakers in the Valley of Mexico who were the descendants of the Chichimec of the north and who moved into the central plateau of Mexico by the eleventh and twelfth centuries.

Mathien says the sheer range of Uto-Aztecan language groups shows long-term occupation by a single people who had migrated to the New World in early antiquity. Many of the Uto-Aztecan languages in this family had splintered into dialects by the sixteenth century. Language and cultural variations would naturally develop over the centuries.

However, little variation existed in the dialects among the widespread Pima-Tepehuan group—a branch of the Uto-Aztecan mother group—which survived the sixteenth century map. This group spanned a vast region, from the Middle Gila River in Arizona south nearly to Guadalajara. Furthermore, the Pima and the Tepehuans themselves were separated geographically by other Uto-Aztecan groups. Despite the obstacles, the Pima-Tepehuan groups shared many similarities, suggesting that they somehow maintained contact for the exchange of both information and goods, a tradition solidified by close cultural ties.

A parallel situation existed in the Old World, where a basic set of cultural ideas united Western Europe during the Roman Empire and still underlies much of Western civilization. If a comparable range of cultural ideas were in existence in antiquity, then it would not be unusual for west Mexican groups to decorate their ceramics with similar patterns and designs or worship the same gods or build on grander scales as they evolved, adapting these cultural elements to the tools and building materials at hand.

The Hohokam culture shows greater similarities with Mesoamerican cultures than do the Anasazi or Mogollon. The latter two do not have ball courts, for instance. While neighbors do communicate and interact, the Mogollon and Anasazi may not have had the same underlying linguistic and cultural bases and therefore may have adopted west Mexican ideas or items to a lesser degree according to their needs. The non-Uto-Aztecan speaking Anasazi were linked to Mesoamerican culture through the Uto-Aztecan speaking Hopi and Paiute.

Based on this argument, Mathien says that many of the cultural traits originated in Mesoamerica and spread north without major movement of people from the core area. If the groups in west Mexico, particularly in the areas of Lerma-Chimalhuacan, seeded the Archaic and Formative cultures of the Valley of Mexico, then later groups, particularly the Toltec and Aztec, brought new ideas and information to the Mesoamerican core from their Chichimecan relatives.

If information and goods could pass through a down-the-line network with ease, then many similarities in cultural traits on either end of the line would develop. Each group would evolve its own variation on a common theme as reflected in the differences in styles. When ideas were transferred across the Uto-Aztecan language/cultural barrier into the territory of the Anasazi (who were the ancestors of the Keresan-, Tanoan-, and Zuñi-speaking peoples in the San Juan Basin) new styles would grow.

Linguist Joseph Greenberg, author of *Language of the Americas*, takes Mathien's theory to the extreme. He unites most American Indian tongues—from southern Canada to southernmost South America—into one family, which he calls Amerind. For the Amerind family to exist, American Indians would have had to migrate from Asia to the New World at least twelve thousand years ago.

Greenberg's opponents say that there are roughly two hundred language groups in the New World. Separating language families older than seven thousand years is futile because of the rapid changes, the experts say. Greenberg agrees with theories established decades ago that group the Eskimo-Aleut language in northern Canada and Alaska with the Na-Dene family in northwestern Canada, southeastern Alaska, and a small pocket in the American Southwest. The rest, says Greenberg, belong to the Amerind family.

To arrive at his highly controversial conclusions, Greenberg used a technique called multilateral comparison, which involves comparing many languages at once and identifying underlying grammatical and vocabulary patterns among them. In the past, a small number of languages were matched for common themes using the method of sound correspondence.

In a *Dallas Morning News* article, published in December of 1990, writer Adam Friend reported on studies in other disciplines that support Greenberg's claims. One archaeologist, Christy

Turner of Arizona State University, studied dental anatomy and, in 1977, determined that three groups of people, which closely relate to Greenberg's language families, migrated from northeast Asia. The first group would have migrated twelve to fifteen thousand years ago.

Anthropological geneticist Stephen Zegura, at the University of Arizona, examined published material for patterns among American Indian genes in cell nuclei. In 1987, he discovered three individual families relating to the same language groups. Luigi Cavalli-Sforza, a Stanford Medical Center geneticist, examined 110 genes in cell nuclei studied during the past sixty years, and in 1988, in the *Proceedings of the National Academy of Sciences*, he published results that concurred with Greenberg's theory. Finally, biochemist Douglas Wallace, of Emory University, examined genes in mitochondria, the power source of the cell, among three separate tribes in North, Central, and South America and found that they all had a similar origin. He released his findings in the *American Journal of Human Genetics*, in March 1990.

We know now that similarities between Mesoamericans and historic Pueblos exist. We also know the Anasazi built miniatures of their cosmos with materials and skills at hand, as did many New World cultures, with greater and lesser degrees of sophistication. It is still not clear if the Anasazi culture was a mosaic of shards pieced together from other cultures, or if their sandstone masterpieces were intrinsically designed, a stage in their development. Another avenue of inquiry is to examine more closely the metaphysics of the historic Pueblos for clues to their past.

Traveling The Straight Road

WE, THE ANCIENT ONES, ASCENDED FROM THE MIDDLE of the world below, through the door of the entrance to the lower world. . . . We entreat you to send your thoughts to us that we may sing your songs straight, so that they will pass over the straight road to the cloud priests that they may cover the earth with water, so that she may bear all that is good for us.

The above is an excerpt from "A Rain Song of the *Sko'yo Chaian* (Giant Society)," loosely translated by Matilda Coxe Stevenson, in *The Sia, Eleventh Annual Report for the Bureau of Ethnology, Smithsonian Institute*. (Sia Pueblo, more popularly known as Zia, is an East Keresan village just northwest of Albuquerque, New Mexico.) Stevenson collected a volume of Zia weather control, hunting, healing, and fertility songs, all of which maintain the same theme of the emergence and appeal to the various guardians of the cardinal points. The songs were the property of various Zia societies, or highly secretive and exclusive cults, which were charged with the duties of weather control, hunting, agricultural and ceremonial timekeeping, and the like.

The song can't be compared to Maya stelae or hieroglyphic texts, but it can still offer some clues to Pueblo cosmology and, idealistically, the Anasazi culture. But be warned: Pueblo songs and myths tend to be ahistorical. There is no tribal memory of historical origins—the story of the emergence from the underworld is *the* important account for Pueblos.

Pueblo Cosmology

The cosmos and one's relationship to it can be likened to the Zia sun sign: four sets of four lines protruding in each direction from a circle. At the center of this quadripartite world is the Pueblo. Around the individual member revolves the Pueblo village, the clan, the societies, and the duties—all of which must be kept in balance. The four sets of lines represent a direction, and each direction is associated with a color, a spirit, a mountaintop, and, therefore, a society chief. The ultimate duty is to walk the straight road, and the ultimate blessing is to finish one's own road, or to attain an equilibrium in old age, and to return to the underworld through the sipapu. The parallel lines represent the divergent roads one can take throughout life.

The Pueblo four-part world is divided into three strata: the sky, the earth, and the underworld—the latter sometimes with four subdivisions. Of these, the underworld, from which human life pushes through the crust of the earth in stages like a corn plant, is of prime significance.

Mountains, holes in the ground, canyons, lakes, rocks, trees, and fissures in the cliffs are all points of reference in the sacred Pueblo landscape connecting the upper and lower worlds. Shrines at these places provide a means of communication with the supernaturals.

Two ceremonial structures—the sipapu and the sun shrine—artificially replicate geographical orifices and projections and permeate the Pueblo culture today. The sipapu is a hole in the ground that represents the place of emergence. The sun shrine, such as the one at the modern pueblo of Laguna called the *Osach Kamuh* (Place the Sun Comes From), is a low-walled cairn on a plateau or high mesa sometimes adorned with a sun petrogylph. Offerings to the sipapu bring about fecundity. Offerings to the sun shrine bring luck in hunting and warring.

Kiva, Zia Pueblo, circa 1920. (Courtesy Museum of New Mexico, Negative 43107.)

As Pueblo architecture evolved, the formalized shrines became grander. The ceremonial kiva is an enlarged version of the sipapu. Climbing the ladder out of the kiva represents the emergence. The kiva can be thought of as a home, for it was home to the first people for a long time. In his 1942 report in the Bureau of American Ethnology Bulletin, Matthew W. Stirling described the mythical first kiva at Acoma. He explained the origin of the kiva and its orientation to the cosmological world:

> When they built the kiva, they first put up beams of four different trees. These were the trees that were planted in the underworld for the people to climb up on. In the north, under the foundation they placed yellow turquoise; in the west, blue turquoise, in the south, red, and in the east, white turquoise. Prayer sticks are placed at each place so the foundation will be strong and will never give way. The walls represent the sky; the beams of the roof (made of wood of the first four trees) represent the Milky Way. The sky looks like a circle, hence the round shape of the kiva. . . .
>
> On the north is a hollow dugout place that represents the door of North Mountain, East Mountain, West Mountain, South Mountain, Sun and Moon.

The pueblo apartment complex is an elaborate shrine to the sun. It is generally accepted that the pueblo complex evolved from the Anasazi great houses. Pueblo villages were also built to reflect their metaphysics, as is the case with other earlier New

Pueblo apartment complexes, different architecturally from the megalithic great houses of Chaco Canyon, nevertheless still orient their construction to the cardinal or solstitial directions. Pictured is the "Dancing the Ka-k'okshi, or Good Dance," Zuni Pueblo, June 19, 1897. (Photo by Ben Wittick, courtesy of New Mexico, Negative 56120.)

World cultures, and cosmological order is manifested in village planning. Pueblos are usually no more than five stories high; this may reflect a desire to avoid exceeding the number of worlds, gone by plus the Fifth World in which we live. Fires in hearths in the eastern portion of the kivas are kept stoked. Symbolic elements are integrated in the buildings, and openings are positioned in the walls to measure the sun and constellations. Streets and houses are almost always aligned to the cardinal directions. All but Sandia, Zia, Zuñi, and the Hopi villages other than Mishognovi are oriented to the cardinal points. Even the stucco homes of the Zuñi not living in the original pueblos still radiate from the center along solstitial lines. Leaders who laid out the villages buried a shrine offering in the plaza and from there estimated directional shrines on each periphery. Sun and sipapu shrines dot the horizons.

In contrast to the organization of space, time is less important, according to Alfonso Ortiz in *New Perspectives on the Pueblos*. There is little speculation on origins beyond the emergence; and beyond the yearly cycles based on solar and lunar movements, there is little concern for the passage of time. The sun father and the earth mother continuously interact, with the solstices and equinoxes providing the winter and summer divisions that are variously symbolized and represented throughout the Pueblo world.

Pueblo Timekeeping

In "A Thousand Years of the Pueblo Sun-Moon-Star Calendar," Florence Hawley Ellis argued that the sun calendar, with its moon and star counterweights, is a thousand years old. The controversial sun-moon-hand petroglyph at Penasco Blanco in Chaco Canyon is said by many to be a recording of the explosion of the Crab Nebula in A.D. 1054 (about the time the roads around Chaco Canyon were formalized). Ellis believes the petroglyph site was a sun watcher's station and shrine because it consists of a handprint (which she interprets as a signature), an upside down crescent moon, the Great or Morning Star, and, nearby, the sun symbol (two concentric circles with a center dot).

Ellis says that Pueblo ethnology has not yet turned up other recordings of such events as a supernova. She believes the Pueblo calendar is a thousand years old because of the striking similarity between two sun watching stations, one Anasazi and the other at Zuñi.

Shabik'eshchee Village, a Basketmaker III site (A.D. 500), sits on top of the south mesa of Chaco Canyon. Pecked into a boulder below the village is one of the simplest solar petroglyphs at Chaco: two concentric circles with a dot at the center. Based on Pueblo translation, the outer circle represents the rays around the sun and the inner circle the sun's body. The dot at the center is the umbilicus through which flows sustenance to the earth.

The stone marks sunrise on the fall equinox. The sun rises over a landform projection on the east horizon, and the first rays hit the stone. On a line between the stone and the projection at 94° azimuth, at a point two-thirds of a mile from the stone on a small point below the cliff, is a collapsed cairn believed to have been a sun shrine.

In an 1893 article in *Century Magazine*, Frank Hamilton Cushing described an event he observed while living among the Zuñi that may demonstrate the way the Anasazi used their sun watching stations. Cushing watched the *pekwin* (Sun Priest) walk three miles up to Matsakaya (a previous Zuñi site abandoned during the 1680 Pueblo Revolt) at dawn in late February and early March. The Bow Priest, the representative of the Elder War God (Morning Star), followed the pekwin every morning and sat a distance from the small tower he entered. The pekwin sat before a pillar marked with sun symbols also found at Chaco Canyon, and waited for sunrise. The pekwin returned to the site every morning until, as Cushing wrote, the "shadows on the solar monolith, the monument of Thunder Mountain and the pillar of the gardens of Zuñi lay in a single line." The pekwin thanked the sun, and the Bow Priest cut a notch in his "pine wood" calendar and both hurried back to announce the time to begin farm work, which meant moving from the village to the field houses near the plots.

Cushing's comment on the drama included the following note:

> Nor may the sun priest err in his watch of Time's flight; for many are the houses of Zuñi with scores on their walls or ancient plates embedded therein, while opposite a convenient window or small porthole lets in the light of the rising sun which shines but two mornings in 365 in the same place. Wonderfully religious and ingenious are the rude systems of orientation by which the religion and even the pastimes are related.

Astronomer Michael Zeilik observed that most of the existing Pueblos have been documented as having astronomical practices. Each pueblo had a religious officer, usually a sun priest invested with sunwatching responsibility. The priest observes the sunrise, and less often the sunset, from within or close to the pueblo. The watching place is rarely marked. Horizon markers are most commonly used to establish the sun's seasonal position. Marking the sun through windows and doors is not frequently done. Solstices are the most important event of the ritual calendar, especially the winter solstice. The sun priest also keeps track of the basic planting calendar from April to June and announces the solstice ahead of time. Anticipatory observations begin two weeks before the solstice when the sun is still moving a noticeable amount every day.

Ellis said that when the summer solstice approaches at San Juan, the sun watcher scatters cornmeal (to form a spiritual "road") and walks a short distance north of the pueblo to a stone slab on which he stands while waiting for the sun to reach its "summer house" as it rises over a narrow peak known as the heart. At sunset on June 24, close enough to June 21 to count as the summer solstice, the head war captain and war priest go to the solar monolith on the western edge of the pueblo. This white outcrop stands two feet high and is marked with an equal-armed

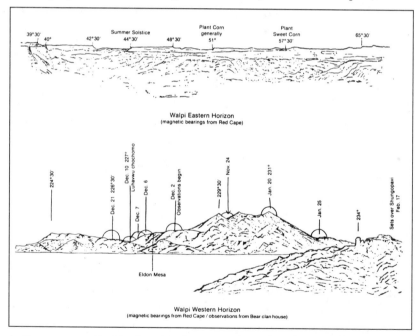

In the summer, the Hopi watch the sun as it moves along the eastern horizon at sunrise marking the agricultural cycles. In the winter, the western horizon is watched at sunset for ceremonial periods. (Both illustrations of the Walpi horizon calendar were published by Stephen in 1936.)

cross on the east side. If the shadow of the mountain range completely covers the stone, a long summer is ahead. If not, there will be an early frost.

Alexander M. Stephen, who lived among the Hopi on and off beginning in 1881, kept a journal, which has come to be called his "Hopi notebooks" and consists of letters to J. Walter Fewkes of the Bureau of American Ethnology. Stephen noted that at the edge of the mesas some ten kilometers across the valley to the southeast from each Hopi village are small sun shrines called *Tawaki,* or Sun's House, marking the solstices. *Tawa-mongwi,* Sun Chief, watches the rising sun as it travels along the horizon, notes its arrival at specific natural landmarks, and announces the various chores of farming. Planting season takes advantage of the optimum number of frost-free days between May 21 and autumn.

In 1925, Crow Wing, a Hopi Indian, wrote in *A Pueblo Indian Journal,* "Sometimes if the Snake Chief does not watch the sun right, they dance early, then it freezes early, too. That is the reason why they must try and watch the sun closely." Such are the responsibilities of the sun watcher.

When the sun leaves the summer house, the Hopi turn to ceremonial aspects of the calendar. The sun is now watched as it moves south along the western horizon. The watcher is the *Powuma* society chief from the *Kachina* clan, who checks the sun for the homecoming of the *Kachina* or *Niman* in July. The Singer's society chief from the Tobacco clan watches the sunset for the Tribal Interaction of *Wuwuchim* in November, and the Sun Chief watches the sun for the winter solstice. *Soyal,* the winter solstice ceremony, turns the sun back toward summer.

The new moon is watched for weather patterns as well as planting cycles that divide the year into monthlike periods. In the spring, during the vernal equinox new moon of *Kel-muya,* the crescent always appears on its back, a sign that spring would be dry and dusty, which it always is. At the fall equinox new moon of kel-muya, the crescent stands upright, a sign of rain, as is usually the case. Seasonal rain usually comes in late summer and early fall. Year after year, the omen predicts the same outcome.

The Zuñi year is from solstice, or *tepikiwaiipa*, to solstice, while some might argue it might just as well be from *itiwonna* to *itiwonna*, or from "corn-ripe to corn-ripe." The Keresan calendars divide the year into periods that reflect planting times and generally ignore the moon titles. The Hopi calendars divide the year into moons, disregarding the fact that there are thirteen moons in a year. The Hopi year is lopsided: five months for the growing period. The *Wuwuchim* ceremony in "initiate moon," or November, carries the second half of the year through May, or "too cold to plant corn moon." Nevertheless, all Pueblos view the world as being divided between winter and summer.

The Pueblos unify. time with space. Zuñi, called *Itiwanna*, or Center or Middle Place, is not only the geographical center, but also the center of time. The winter solstice is thought to be the center of the year, which pivots at the center place—all created, of course, by *Awonawilona*, "The One Who Holds the Roads," the way of life, the way to the center.

So important is the sun that the Pueblos align their towns according to its path. The eastern Pueblos—Acoma, Cochiti, Isleta, Jemez, Laguna, Nambe, Picuris, Pojoaque, Sandia, San Felipe, San Ildefonso, San Juan, Santa Ana, Santa Clara, Santo Domingo, Taos, Tesuque, and Zia—are said to orient their villages to the cardinals, but this is a misperception. The eastern Pueblos are concerned with where the sun rises and sets on the equinoxes, and the annual shift between winter (north) and summer (south). That the eastern Pueblos orient on the cardinals may be an imposition of several centuries of European contact.

The western Pueblos—Hopi and Zuñi—on the other hand, divide the world along the solstitials. The Hopi, the only Pueblo group in Arizona, remained relatively isolated from Euro-American contact during the Spanish period and were not Christianized like the Rio Grande Pueblos. Therefore, their directions stayed intact.

Imagine the elation Stephen must have felt when he finally realized that the Hopi world was slightly askew of the western world:

> Doesn't that please you? . . . As soon as it flashed upon me, I hastened in to apply the key to some of the old fellows' knowledge

boxes. And then they one and all declared how glad they were that I now understood and how sorry they had been that I could not understand this simple fact before.

Interestingly, the map Stephen drew in 1891 of the directions of the altar in Goat Kiva shows a north (which stands for the above and the color black) and a south (which is the below and all colors). Could it be an error on Stephen's part to mark the zenith

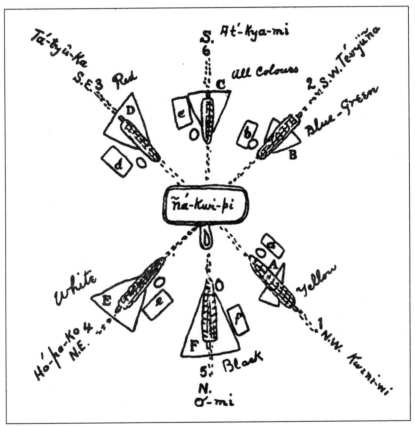

Alexander M. Stephen recorded the Hopi's Directions Altar from Goat Kiva in 1891 and published it in 1936. The specifications are the following as he recorded: 1. NW, yellow corn ear, A. oriole skin, a. unidentified bird skin; 2. SW, blue-green corn ear, B. jay skin, b. bluebird skin; 3. SE, red corn ear, D. red-shafted woodpecker skin, d. house finch skin; 4. NE, white corn ear, E. whippoorwill skin, e. magpie feathers; 5. above, black corn ear, F. blackbird skin, f. robin skin; 6. below, sweet corn ear, C. unidentified bird skin, c. warbler skin.

and nadir directions with an *N* and an *S*? Or, as with the Mayas, were north and south equal to up and down? Furthermore, perhaps this directional scheme is a holdover from more ancient times, preserved before there was pressure from the Euro-Americans to reorient to the cardinals. Pueblo Bonito features a mixture of both cardinal and solstitial point references, for reasons that may have been lost.

The Pueblos had no way of recording their geoastronomical and calendrical practices. The information exists in the mental indices of the priests who pass it down to initiates orally. In the 1890s, Reverend H.R. Voth recorded a ritual at Oraibi (Hopi) following the *Powamu* chief's sighting of the first crescent of the *Powa-*moon. He called the elders of the *Powamu* society to the kiva for "smoke talk." One of the songs had twenty variations of this verse:

> The sun he is bringing
> The sun he is watching
> When at Apoonivi the sun is setting
> The plants are being clothed.

Voth said that the first ten verses named the points where the sun set on the western horizon during the ceremonial season, and the next ten verses named the points where the sun rose during planting season. The ritual is an example of how, through repetitive recitation, key measurements were passed on.

Pueblo stories also contain geoastronomical information such as the one Matilda Coxe Stevenson recorded in *The Sia* in 1889. Notice the numerology as you read:

> Kochinako, a virgin, the yellow woman of the north, when journeying to the center of the earth, lay down to rest. She was embraced by the sun, and from this embrace, she became pregnant. In four days, she gave evident signs of her condition, and in eight days it was still more perceptible, and in twelve days she gave birth to male twins. During her condition of gestation her mother, the spider woman, was very angry . . . as soon as the daughter complained of approaching labor the mother left, but her heart softened from the birth and she soon returned. In four days from the birth of the boys they were able to walk.

Stories of the sun impregnating a maiden may contain clues to astronomy. Archaeoastronomer Ray Williamson says stories that particularly show the sun entering a porthole or crack in the wall of a room may demonstrate evidence of purposeful astronomical alignment in Pueblo structures. The numerology would represent the days of anticipation and preparation.

If Pueblo geoastronomical information is oral, then it is likely that the Anasazi calendar was also. It is intriguing to wonder how much of the Chacoan oral tradition has been salvaged over the last millennium.

Ted Jojola, a University of New Mexico professor of architecture from Isleta, said that storytelling helps to balance the supernatural with human reality. The keepers of astronomical knowledge are the intermediaries between the two dimensions. The passing of the solstices, the phases of the moon, and the seasonal positioning of constellations are personified in the stories. Storytelling reveals the behavior of the celestial personae and reinforces their role in human life. The stories also reinforce the listener's responsibility to maintain natural order by assuming a productive role in the village.

Road Mythology: A Morality Play

Road metaphors, as translated into English, are used heavily in Pueblo storytelling. Alfonso Ortiz, an anthropologist from San Juan Pueblo, said the Isleta express their cosmological and philosophical system as a Wa?e, meaning "life-road" or "life-way." "This life-way—the ceremonies and the rituals—embodies Pueblo attitudes toward the ultimate conditions of man's existence and serves to focus the meaning of social institutions as well."

In 1929, Mary Roberts Coolidge recorded the following generalized translation of a Yuma Indian song in *The Rain-Makers* which conveys the meaning of the road of life:

> The Mocking-Bird sings only when it is happy . . . It sings that the world is fair, the clouds are in the sky, and it is glad at heart. Then I, too, am glad at heart and go on my up-hill road, the road of goodness and happiness.

In Tewa, the word "road" translates as "channel for the life's breath." Elsie Clews Parsons explained in *A Pueblo Indian Journal* that, "Life is a road; important spirits are . . . keepers of the roads, the life roads. All spirits or sacrosanct persons have a road of cornmeal or pollen sprinkled for them where their presence is requested."

A few lines from a Zuñi tale, taken from Ortiz's book, *New Perspectives on the Pueblos*, demonstrates how the road metaphor expresses a method of seeking knowledge:

> . . . she
> took out her corn meal
> and
> spoke the way her great grandfather had told her:
> she asked that this would bring her daylight
> that the day would not be wasted, that
> she would enter upon the roads of the raw people, that they would
>   enter her house
> with their waters, forever bringing in their roads as they lived.

The above excerpt describes a prayer for a personal emergence into daylight and enlightenment. The raw people are the innocent and naive ones who first came up from the underworld.

Notice the use of the road metaphor and the cosmological detail in Matilda Coxe Stevenson's version of the Zuñi creation myth, published in 1904 in *The Zuni Indians, Twenty-third Annual Report, Bureau of American Ethnology:*

> The place for coming into this world is called *Ji'mi(t)kianapkiatea*, a word full of occult meaning, having reference to an opening in the earth filled with water which mysteriously disappeared, leaving a clear passage for the A'shiwi [Zuñi] to ascend to the outer world. . . . The outer world . . . was reached just as the Evening Star, who is second warrior to the Sun Father and follows after him, rose above the horizon.
>
> In the lower world the A'shiwi had rain priests (*A'shiwanni*) of whom were assigned to the six regions. . . . The *Kia'kwemosi*, *Shi'wanni* of the North, sat next to the road, on the south side, the road being the dividing line; the *Shi'wanni* of the West and *Shi'wano'kia* sat on his right. The *Shi'wanni* of the South sat next, the Shi'wanni of the East being on his right. The *A'shiwanni* sat on

the other side of the road with *Wats'usi* north of them. *Ya'nowwu-luha*, a man of great heart and wisdom, sat before the meal painting to the north of the line, and the *A'shiwi* gather around on the north, west, and south . . .

The myth, in meticulous specifics, continues as the Sun Father sent the Divine Ones to the underworld to bring the *A'shiwi* into the light. The trek was arduous. The Divine Ones lead the *A'shiwi* on a sacred meal road to the north where they planted a Ponderosa pine, which they shinnied to get to the next world. A new direction and a new tree is taken in each subsequent world to get to the next, until they emerge into the light through a lake. From there, the *A'shiwi* were sent to search for the middle place, which took many years, and many villages were built and abandoned along the way. The Zuñi pantheon of deities was collected during the journey. The middle place was determined by stretching the legs of a water strider to the four oceans.

The Zia version of the creation and emergence story is also replete with geoastronomical references. The one Stevenson recorded is only "the nucleus of their belief from which spring stories in infinite numbers, in which every phenomenon of nature known to these people is accounted for." The following is paraphrased from her report on the Zia:

> In the beginning there was but one being in the lower world, Sus'sistinnako, a spider. . . . Sus'sistinnako drew a line of meal from north to south and crossed it midway from east to west; and he placed two little parcels north of the cross line, one on either side of the line running north and south. . . . Sus'sistinnako sat down on the west side of the line running north and south, and south of the cross line, and began to sing, and in a little while . . . two women appeared, evolved from each parcel. In a short time people began walking about. . . . The two women first created were mothers of all; the one created on the east side of the line of meal Sus'sistinnako named Ut'set, and she was the mother of all Indians; he called the other Now'utset, she being the mother of other nations.

Utset and Nowutset are both heavily involved in the creation of the directions, the sun and its path, the moon, and the stars. In one version of the story, they fall into competition and fight on a mountain. Utset kills Nowutset and cuts out her heart with a knife, slices it into little pieces and scatters them. The heart pieces transform into rats, and Utset explains that those who fight are similar to rats. Finding a cactus in her heart, Utset proclaims that the rats will live forever among cactus. In another version of the story, Utset scatters the heart and it begins to rain. The stories not only contain a morality lesson, but probably interpret geoastronomical information.

The stories parallel an Aztec story which also brings geoastronomy into play by way of the Templo Mayor, the main Aztec pyramid in Tenochtitlan. In this story, Huitzilopochtli, god of war, fights with his sister, Coyolxauhqui, at Coatepec or "serpent hill." The battle may have been an actual event. A Nahuatl story tells how Coyolxauhqui led Huitzilopochtli's many brothers, the Huitznahua, against him. Huitzilopochtli took up his shield and weapons and prevailed. Because his sister, who "spoke to all the centipedes and spiders and transformed herself into a sorceress . . . was a very evil woman," he beheaded and dismembered her. At the main Aztec pyramid at the center of what is now Mexico City, the myth is preserved in a round stone which lies at the bottom of the hill-like pyramid marked with serpent imagery where human sacrifices were made, reenacting the mythical battle. A statue of Huitzilopochtli stood at the top of the pyramid.

After the battle, Utset, sometimes known as Iyatiku, or Corn Mother, led the Zia into this world through the sipapu in the north. Stevenson, in her report on the Zia, continues the story:

> Utset selected for the people the tiamoni, religious leader, who was to take her place with the people and lead them to the center of the earth, a man of the corn clan, saying to him, "I, Utset, will soon leave you; I will return to the home whence I came. You will be to my people as myself; you will pass with them over the straight road. I will remain in my house below and will hear all that you say to me. I will give to you all my wisdom, my thoughts, my heart, and all. I fill your head with my mind."

Stevenson said Utset then gave the tiamoni instructions to make the *Iarriko* or *yaya* (mother), a perfect ear of corn attached to

Corn dance at Zia Pueblo, circa 1915. (Photo courtesy Museum of New Mexico, Negative 27902.)

eagle and prayer feathers. Utset then says, "This is as myself," and all the people clasped the staff and drew a breath from it. "Be sure to follow the straight road for all years and for all time to come."

By breathing in the symbol that represents Utset, the people have communion with divine intelligence. That divine intelligence is embodied in the underworld, and because north is the direction one must travel to get to the gateway to the underworld, it is a very sacred direction. After death, the Pueblo travel the north road to the sipapu, which is "crowded with spirits returning to the lower world, and with spirits of unborn infants coming from the lower world," according to Stevenson. When a person dies, a road of cornmeal is scattered to the door of his or her house so that the spirit can find its way to the sipapu. The souls come back to the pueblos of their living relatives to eat the food placed for them on the road to the north. In some beliefs, the dead turn into the cloud spirits, or kachinas, who bring rain to the living.

North to Sipapu

The Great North Road of Chaco Canyon, studded with its peculiar pinnacle shrines, great kivas, parallel lanes, rock-cut grooves, and stairways, was most likely used for ceremonial purposes, as noted in Chapter Six. Those purposes may still be carried out in Pueblo ritual today.

In her article, "The Inner Sanctum of Feather Cave," Florence Hawley Ellis said that Pueblo society members often make spiritual treks, some as long as five hundred kilometers round trip, to reenact their emergence. They would stop along the way at specific caves, cliff crevices, and small lakes representing the sipapu.

One such shrine is *Temapo* (Keresan Holes), a cave a few miles north of Ojo Caliente (fifty-five miles northwest of Santa Fe). A Tewa informant told an anthropologist that Keresan men from Santo Domingo used to pass by him on their way to their cave shrine and an ancestral village site.

Another shrine is at Soda Dam, in the Jemez Mountains north of Jemez Pueblo. This is sacred to the Underworld Chief's society members who foretell the future from what they see and hear there.

The people of the pueblo at Pecos annually returned to a cave there after the Pueblo moved to Jemez in 1838. The pilgrims would drop prayer sticks into a hole in the floor. If the sticks stayed down, despite the draft of air deflecting them, their heart was good. The floor was covered with prayer sticks.

Photograph is simply titled, "Stone Markers, Zuñi pueblo, circa 1890," but the shrine commemorates a battle between the Spanish and the Zuñi. Upright stones sometimes represent the ancestors. (Photo by Frederich Maude, courtesy Museum of New Mexico, Negative 103194.)

Some distance north of their pueblo, Cochiti ceremonialists used a cave where the entrance was said to be partially closed by lightning. A person going into the cave had to bring along someone to guard the entrance. "If even a bee or a fly entered the cave while he was in there, he could never leave," Ellis said. If he was fortunate, he could collect water near the opening; otherwise, he would have to go in deeper.

Cochiti members also use sipapu substitutes. Circular stone enclosures with large central upright stones represent inconveniently distant shrines. The elongated stones represent the "old stone people of the underworld."

At Acoma, at least until 1902, the men traveled twice a year to a sipapu shrine in southwestern Colorado with their solar offerings packed on burros. They would leave offerings at the sun symbol petroglyph at the village of Shabik'eshchee. They also stopped at Jackson's Butte, the chimney rock near Highway 666, and then finally at a small spring near Cortez, Colorado.

In older caves, artifact offerings found have included old bows, prehistoric sticks, and fending sticks used for digging, as well as darts and atlatls. These artifacts would have been offered to the sun. Feather bunches, prayer sticks, food images, or small food pieces would have been offered to the Earth or Corn Mother. Other objects in the cave included images of plants and animals they wished to increase, and zigzag wooden objects that represent lightning. Pueblos also leave miniature or full-size kickballs for the Cloud People in hopes that they will bring rain as they kick the ball across the sky in play. At one time, the sipapu and sun shrines were one and the same.

Some pilgrimages are conducted on what are referred to as roads. In 1925, Parsons, in *The Pueblo of Jemez*, said that the Jemez religious leader, upon emergence from the sipapu, chooses the direction toward the south and then makes four roads by clearing away brush for the people to travel on in search of the place of settlement. K.B. Kelley, writing in 1984 in *Historic Cultural Resources in the San Augustine Coal Area,* reported an important pilgrimage to Zuñi Salt Lake on roads that have been described as very straight and with shrine-like sites similar to those on the Chaco roads. Parsons reported many references to running in Pueblo ceremony and myth, sometimes on north-south roads and parallel courses symbolic of the emergence, and in certain instances on ritually swept east-west roads to aid the journey of the sun.

Without too much stretch of the imagination, it is conceivable that the roads around Chaco Canyon could have been used for the same ritualistic processions described above. The North Road in particular was engineered due north, wide and straight, and passes near elevated mounds, platforms, and shrines and terminates down a staircase into a steep canyon. Along the way, scores of ceramic vessels are scattered in the road. The North Road would not only be a route to the place of the emergence for the living, but also for the dead. In death rites, some Keresan and Tanoan Pueblos take offerings that represent the person's soul, such as ceramic vessels, and deposit them in a canyon or mesa crack. Sometimes a vessel containing food is put on the road to the north, or broken at the rim and then thrown out to the north.

White Village of the North

Chaco Canyon is not recognized in Pueblo origin myth. When asked where his or her people originated, a Pueblo member will say somewhere up north. But Chaco Canyon may have become the mythical Keresan village of Kush Karet. Returning to Stevenson's rendition of the Zia creation myth where we left off, Utset had just given the leader the *Iarriko*, the corn ear fetish meant to represent her:

> The Sia alone followed the command of Utset and took the straight road, while all other pueblos advanced by various routes to the center of the earth. After Utset's departure, the Sia traveled some distance and built a village [Kush Karet] of beautiful white stone, where they lived for four years (four referring to time periods).

In his book *Pueblo Gods and Myths*, Hamilton A. Tyler said that life was not easy for the people when they first emerged. Their experience at Kush Karet, or White House, which the Keres believe to be somewhere in the north, was something of an initiation. "The people took stock of themselves and their rites were amplified. With this gathered strength they again set out to locate the center." He noted:

> The migrations were certainly historical events leading up to present success, or at least to present equilibrium, but all of the migration stories have proved to be a confusion, rather than an illumination of actual history. They represent a kind of progress of the soul, or more simply a search for the basic securities of water, food, and safety from enemies.

According to Navajo legend, the decline of the Eastern Anasazi system in the mid-twelfth century A.D. marks the end of the fourth world. If this were the case, then the mythical Keresan northern house made of white stone, Kush Karet, where the people took stock of themselves, might have been Pueblo Bonito in Chaco Canyon.

Indeed, the residents of Chaco Canyon entered a new phase, a new world, once they left the canyon and other great houses in the area. Anasazi culture as we know it vanished. Certainly, Pueblo villages are still built according to a macrocosmic blueprint. Sipapus and sun shrines still figure heavily in the Pueblo cosmology, but with much more subtlety. Never again was so much invested in making such grandiose overtures to symmetry.

Since it is assumed that most of the San Juan Anasazi migrated south in search of the center place in multiple stages to the present locations of the Rio Grande pueblos and Zuñi pueblo on the Arizona/New Mexico border, as their own legends bear up, then the ceremonial processions northward may be a symbolic reenactment of the migration itself, an emergence from the depth of Chaco Canyon and an old way of life.

Furthermore, archaeologists talk about a political, if not stylistic, shift to the north (San Juan district) toward the last century of Chacoan occupation. Recall that Thomas Windes suggested that there was as much migration from the canyon as there was migration to the canyon as a response to cycles of dry years and wet years. On the other hand, the society may have been ordered like that of the nineteenth century Zuñi, who moved near their fields during planting season upon the sanctified announcement of the pekwin sun priest. In either case, if the Chacoans moved to secondary, or even primary, homes in any number of wetter areas ringing the canyon, then the roads may have been used to *return* to Chaco Canyon—the place of emergence—in the south. North, as a sacred direction, takes on a whole new meaning.

North indeed has other meanings to the Pueblo. North is synonymous with winter and south is synonymous with summer. The following Acoma tale is set at Kush Karet—where the Keres first met the kachinas and learned the ways they should follow in order to survive. At Kush Karet—midway between the North and South Mountains—the directions and the seasons merge. The tale tells how the villagers gain some control over their environment and establish an equilibrium.

Shakak, the spirit of Winter and ruler of North Mountain, discovers that Miochin, the spirit of Summer and ruler of South Mountain, has seduced Shakak's wife, Yellow Woman, and was now living in his home at White House. Shakak could not go home, for fear of melting.

Yellow Woman, the chief's daughter and leader of the Corn Maidens, had strayed far from home where she met Miochin dressed in a yellow shirt woven from corn silk, moss leggings, and corn tassel hat. Against her principles, for she was a married woman, she brought him home. Her parents and her people cheered the affair. Their corn plants usually shriveled in the cold climate and as long as Yellow Woman remained married to Shakak, they would be forced to continue their days on a diet of cactus.

Rising to Shakak's challenge, Miochin's phalanx of summer animals and birds advanced from the south. Bat shielded his face from the icy winds with his wings as Miochin lobbed hot volcanic rock and summer lightning on the winter marchers, turning them white. Although Shakak had Magpie to fan him, his icicle shirt melted, exposing the cattails beneath the frost.

Defeated, Shakak called a cease-fire. Miochin would keep Yellow Woman, but each ruler would alternate his reign every so many moons. To hold them to the pact, the people learned the ritual and dance step necessary to switch the power from one spirit to the other when appropriate.

During certain ceremonials, the Keresan literally transfer the *iyani* (also spelled *ianyi*), the power, from one season to the next. They "call back the sun" at the solar standstills. Keresan corn dance choreography looks as though the dancers are trying to synchronize with energy, something like rewinding a clock. Songs and dance steps, sometimes borrowed from the Plains Indians, are performed on the plaza by two groups, or moieties, alternately representing winter and summer. When not performing, each moiety waits in either the winter kiva to the north of the center of the village or the summer kiva to the south. When their turn comes, the dance groups, queued in double rows of alternating males and females, and dressed in costumes of the corn maiden or the animals present at the emergence, wind around the plaza in circles of various shape and size, spinning like connecting cogs. When they abruptly change direction, there is the sense that the motive is to alter the energy.

As Alfonso Ortiz noted in *New Perspectives on the Pueblos*, "Just as an almost impenetrable moral, conceptual, and spatial organization is attributed to the cosmos, so also do the undulating rhythms of nature govern their whole existence, from the timing and order of ritual dramas to the planning of economic activities." Tyler said that curing ties in with weather control, which deals with seasons and directions. During the battle between winter and summer, the summer spirit fights with lightning bolts, which are depicted petroglyphically as zigzag snake icons. Summer brings crops as well as snakebite and lightning shock, which must be cured by the North Priests. The North Priest's kit, called a snake-jar, is used to cure snakebite, treat tuberculosis, and petition for warmer weather during a severe winter.

The Zenith and Nadir at Chaco Canyon

Looking for Pueblo analogs in Chaco Canyon is a challenge. The Chacoans and Pueblos were both interested in aligning their buildings to certain azimuths. The sipapu and the sun shrine may have had their prototypes in Chaco Canyon as early as A.D. 500, or Basketmaker III. In the pit house at Shabik'eshchee Village, there is a hole dug into the dirt floor between the fire pit and the north wall. The nearby sun watching station has already been described in this chapter. Of course, Fajada Butte is the classic solar/lunar shrine, but it isn't an isolated feature. Thousands of rock art sites are scattered across southwestern cliffs, boulders, and cave walls, even as far away as California. The meaning and function of many of these are lost.

The group archaeologists call Basketmaker III (A.D. 500) lived in pit houses, a form of a sipapu. According to accepted scientific lore, this group began building square rooms around the pit houses for storage and then began annexing and layering the square rooms. One theory states that around A.D. 700, some of the younger, more adventurous members of the group moved into the storage rooms (emerging into the light of a new world, in effect). The older ones, or more traditional ones, stayed in the round, underground rooms. The pit became a ritualistic symbol of the return to the old ones or to tradition.

Around A.D. 900 (Pueblo III) the sipapu, square room, and sun shrine took on grand proportions. Although the Anasazi still built modest square room/round room complexes, they began building multistoried square rooms around large round rooms. The square room complexes were usually four stories high and seemingly reached for the sky beings. The pit houses were still in use at this time.

By A.D. 1050, the great houses and great kivas, as they are now called, were synchronized to certain astronomical events, and great ceremonial ways were laid out to join sacred places. Certain other structures, perhaps shrines in exaggerated forms, were built along the ceremonial ways.

These road-related structures—the herraduras, zambullidas, and avanzadas described in Chapter Nine—are an offshoot from the evolutionary progression of architecture from Basketmaker pit houses and ramadas to great houses and kivas to Pueblo apartment-plus-kiva dwellings. Pueblo shrines are simple—perhaps a few standing stones in a line or a circle, or prayer sticks around a spring hardly noticeable to passersby. Pueblos don't have formal roads and thus lack the road-related structures used by the Anasazi. These structures are more like Inca *huacas* or other way stations. Yet the Anasazi way stations were not used for overnight camping, but may have been more closely related to road control and ceremony.

For more than a decade, many archaeologists have argued that great houses were not domiciles, but public houses used for storage, administration, and ceremony. Ceremony, it was believed, took place underground in the round rooms of the great house complexes. John Roney argued that, at least between A.D. 1050 and 1130, the great kivas were replaced or substituted by the multistoried great houses as special function architecture.

Stephen Lekson believes that during the period between A.D. 900 and 1300, the round rooms, called kivas, were in the last stages of pit houses. They had not yet become kivas.

The Great Kiva Caper

Pueblos speak variations of six languages: Hopi, Zuñi, Tiwa, Towa, Tewa, and Keresan. Few Pueblos can speak any other language than their own, while most can speak English, which replaced Spanish as the dominant second language. Each Pueblo is stylistically and organizationally different. Hopi and Zuñi structure their society by clans. The other Pueblos have divided themselves into moieties, or two groups which alternate leadership and ceremonial responsibilities. The matrixes of social organization in either case are complex and vary from pueblo to pueblo.

Although historic Pueblos suffered severe acculturation pressures from the Spanish and Anglo cultures, and earlier from the Navajo, they remain culturally intact. Some Pueblos to this day enforce tighter rules with their members than others. Yet all are dynamic and borrow heavily from neighboring groups. Navajo and Plains Indian songs are integral to their ceremonial dances.

However tempting, it is risky to use modern Pueblo thinking as

This small kiva, some-
times called a blocked
or housed kiva, at Pueblo
Bonito, may have been
the living room of a do-
mestic suite of rooms,
a carryover from the pit
house era several cen-
turies earlier, rather than
a ceremonial kiva.

a baseline for interpreting the behavior of a people who lived a thousand years ago. So much has changed in the Pueblo culture. The urge to build on a grand scale—great houses, great kivas, and great roads—is gone. Even the pueblos are dwindling in number: only twenty of the more than eighty pueblos that existed when the Spanish arrived in the New World are still functioning.

And yet, retaining the ancestral ways is crucial to Pueblo life. The archaeological record is full of many coincidences between the Anasazi and the Pueblos. Intuition confirms this—as if Utset herself is whispering in your ear.

But just when you thought it was safe to call a round room a kiva, someone like Lekson comes along and quietly suggests that you may be wrong. Such is the nature of archaeology, especially at Chaco Canyon. Lekson argued that the underground round rooms in the great houses were trumpeted as kivas as part of a public re-lations plan designed by nineteenth century intellectuals to save whatever was left of the Indian population in the Southwest.

The great kivas, such as this one at Pueblo Bonito, were probably the proto-types of the ceremonial chambers of historic kivas, but did not develop until around AD 1300.

Misdefining the kiva began in the late 1800s, according to Lek-son, when intellectuals sought to end Native American genocide as the United States encroached on the frontier. Up to that point, the population had survived because Spanish colonial tradition in-corporated indigenous people for their souls and their free labor. The United States, on the other hand, employed a hearty Jackso-nian policy of removal. In 1869, the Navajo were rounded up and taken to Fort Sumner.

To those whose professions concerned antiquity, the Pueblos offered an opportunity for study and humanitarianism. The New Mexico Territory, for instance, was seeking to become a state. One way to become a state was to show enough sophistication to have a university. Hence, the University of New Mexico, created in 1889, sought to build its reputation by using New Mexico as a laboratory in anthropology from the beginning.

By this time, the Pueblos had lived through three centuries of Spanish colonization and Mexican government. The Spanish gov-ernment had given the Pueblos grants to prime land, which the

United States promised to honor in the Treaty of Guadalupe-Hidalgo. When the Supreme Court ruled that the grants were real estate and not reservations, some of the land was grabbed through squatting, purchase, and fraud amounting to more than three thousand non-Pueblo claims.

The pueblos looked like some Mediterranean buildings and were quite formidable compared to the buildings of the major American cities of the time. They weren't like the Indian huts and tents the government had removed from the Southwest—these were settled farming communities. In 1925, Chaco archaeologist Neil Judd said, "No other apartment house of comparable size was known in America or in the Old World until the Spanish Flats were erected in 1882 at 59th Street and Seventh Avenue, New York City." How could civilized Americans despoil a people whose architectural prowess rivaled their own?

Well, the United States expansionists argued that the Pueblos moved into the area and copied the exquisite great houses of Chaco Canyon and Mesa Verde, built and abandoned by the Aztecs or some other Lost Race. The Aztecs were in vogue at the time due to the publication of Prescott's *History of the Conquest of Mexico* in 1856, and, after all, the Aztecs said they came from the north. The Pueblo villages were cheap imitations of the real thing, according to this justification, and therefore not a major hindrance to manifest destiny.

But the first anthropologists—Frank Hamilton Cushing, Adolph F. Bandelier, and later, Jesse Walter Fewkes—set out to establish that the ruins of Chaco and Mesa Verde were built by Pueblo ancestors. Lekson said that Cushing "greatly muddied the waters by initially pronouncing Southwestern ruins to be Toltec, and the Zuñis to be descendants of that central Mexican group," and at the same time seeking to demonstrate continuity between the Zuñi and prehistoric ruins. The archaeological evidence used to trace the Pueblos into prehistory was primarily architectural. Lekson noted that in doing so, the early archaeologists helped to prevent the imminent loss of Pueblo lands, but also created a major historical error. That error lies within the kiva.

After decades of court and congressional battles, Pueblo lands were granted reservation status and the non-Pueblo claims were disallowed by establishing continuity between the grand prehistoric architects and the historical Pueblos. The kiva was the piece of evidence that tied the Pueblos to the Anasazi. Lekson defined the kiva as "a remarkable subterranean structure seen at almost all Pueblos, housing male ceremonial societies that cross-cut kin and clan, and kept the loose Pueblo social fabric from unraveling. Kivas are the architectural expression of a particularly strong social glue that integrates inherently disparate village structures." The kiva was not the result of superficial copying, the argument went, but was a primary element of Pueblo life. The kiva represents antiquity, and dozens of them existed at Mesa Verde and Chaco Canyon. In fighting for the lives of the Pueblos, their advocates turned pit houses into kivas before their time. Lekson argues that the hundreds of small "kivas" seen at Chaco through A.D. 1300 were actually the last stages of the formalization of pit houses.

Lekson says that there is no scientific proof that the pit houses were ceremonial chambers beyond projecting backwards the use of these structures by modern pueblos. Kiva chasers, he says, searched for a continuum between the Anasazi and the Pueblos, and some even to Toltecs. Archaeologists debated the term kiva at the first Pecos Conference in 1927. They agreed not to agree on the definition of a ceremonial chamber, as reported by Alfred Kidder:

> It was agreed that ceremonial rooms varied so greatly in form and in interior arrangements, and the types shaded into each other so imperceptibly that no valid distinctions as to essential function could be drawn between, for instance, round and square, or between aboveground and subterranean examples. The following very broad definition was therefore adopted: A kiva is a chamber specially constructed for ceremonial purposes.

It was Edgar Hewett, founder of the American School of Research and the Museum of New Mexico and the first chair of the University of New Mexico's anthropology department, who solidified the Pueblo III "kiva" as a kiva, and that was final.

Lekson says that archaeologists have no idea what a pit house actually looked like. Although dug into the ground, most of the structure was above ground and lost to the record.

Through time, the pit house became another room in the basic domestic unit, like a parlor in a Victorian home. Excavation around pit houses reveals many hearths, work areas, plaza surfaces, and post-holes that represent the remains of ramadas or porches where most of the chores were done. Instead of a radical shift from sunken living rooms to penthouses, Lekson says both pit houses and above-ground buildings developed slowly, beginning with fairly crude structures, to become the great houses which included six or seven stacked rooms and a fairly elaborate pit house. The largest prehistoric sites, such as the Mesa Verde cliff dwellings, are grander versions of the smaller units, with fifteen to twenty seven-room-and-a-pit-house complexes stuffed into the sandstone alcove. Lekson says that about seventy-five pit houses were in use in the central Chaco Canyon great houses, which could accommodate to about 1,900 to 2,025 people.

Most have assumed that kivas underwent a transition around Pueblo I or II, but the archaeological record suggests that the pit house became a kiva after Pueblo IV or about A.D. 1300, when great kivas went out of style. The record shows that the number of pit house/kivas doubled during Pueblo III, during Chaco's peak, and then dropped off dramatically. During Pueblo III, the pit houses were probably still incorporated into domestic architecture, and when their number declined, they became ceremonial and helped to integrate society.

Small kivas may have been the equivalent of our living rooms, while the great kivas may have been the precursor to the modern kiva, Lekson says, where the Anasazi would rendezvous for ceremony, meetings, and smoke talk. There is no indication, however, that the great kivas were used to attract large numbers of people to the canyon. Given the low population count, the central Chaco Canyon settlement might not have quite reached the stage of political prowess which would give the Chacoans the power to control the vast Anasazi system. But they were making a good start.

There is even continuing research on the intermediary kiva called the "proto-kiva." The kachina cult began to take hold around the fourteenth century when the Pueblos began constructing kivas similar to those used today almost exclusively by men.

As a sidebar to the kiva saga, Lekson sees another architectural element among Chacoan cities not seen in historical Pueblos. He feels that Pueblo Bonito and Chetro Ketl, less than three-tenths of a mile apart, were joined by an enclosed plaza-like area. He said that the Pueblo Bonito–Chetro Ketl complex included Pueblo Alto, Pueblo del Arroyo just to the south of Pueblo Bonito, and smaller structures such as Hillside Ruin, Talus Unit, Kin Kletso, New Alto, and a number of great kivas and mounds. The pueblos were enclosed by a surrounding two-mile-wide rectangle of low masonry walls and a system of intracanyon roads. In addition, more than one hundred smaller houses were clustered on the south side of the canyon and between the larger structures. A second area of concentration, although not as heavily used, centers around Una Vida.

Remnants of the megalithic architecture were clearly retained in the historic pueblos, and perhaps some of their deities and ritual as well. Pueblo resistance to change, coupled with their opposite willingness to assimilate new ideas, has kept the culture from becoming extinct, though they are an endangered species. They built their culture as meticulously as they built their houses, which, remarkably, have not been eroded away by the Cloud Spirits of time.

The Road Engineers:
Knowledge and Power

THE ANASAZI'S PENCHANT FOR CONSTRUCTING MONUMENTAL ARCHITECTURE, for straight lines, and astronomical orientation would have necessitated a certain amount of planning, skill, and leadership. Just exactly how these skills were acquired, who was making decisions, and how far the power of the decision makers was taken is anyone's guess. Whatever their level of sophistication, it isn't known, and may never be known, what the Anasazi intentions were.

The Anasazi were good engineers; this much is known. Peak period buildings in the canyon were preplanned rather than annexed, and the roads were laid out in straight lines according to a prescribed course disregarding the landscape. One wonders what the Anasazi would have accomplished with earth movers and a little dynamite.

In most cases, road construction consisted of removing and compacting a broad trench and piling the remains along the downhill side of the road. Remote sensing studies indicated that the Anasazi scooped out countless cubic yards of topsoil to form the roadways. The roadbed was then surfaced with sandstone, which had to be carried in. The Anasazi took the time to build curbs and berms along the roads and to add ramps to keep the bearing of the road true. Hills, mesas, and canyons were overcome with steps, ramps, or roadcuts; there are forty-five stone-cut staircases in the Chaco Canyon area alone.

In comparing a section of the North Road to the modern Chaco Canyon–Blanco Trading Post road, the North Road, although going straight over the obstacles, is the more efficient of the two. Both have the same general north-south trend, and both are perpendicular to the topographic grain, yet the North Road has less total elevation change and a shorter distance between endpoints.

The roads were actually built in a series of straight segments that together *appear* straight. Much like the Maya sacbes, which Romanov described as broken reeds, the Chacoan segments sometimes deviated slightly from the trend. The broken lines may have represented adjustments to the desired course, accomplished through subtle angle changes at ridge tops or drainage bottoms. But rather than veer the road to a particular site, the Anasazi engineers built in an abrupt dog leg angle.

The simple techniques of road construction described above were expensive in terms of labor, but were not difficult to execute. The surveying may have been no mystery either. Archaeologists James Ebert and Robert Hitchcock argued that the Anasazi may

This portion of the Penasco Blanco to Ahshislepah Road is marked on the west edge by stones (C). The view is southeast toward a stairway complex just below the canyon edge (visible in next photo). A: Chaco Wash, B: Escavada Wash. (Photo by John Roney, courtesy BLM.)

This stairway complex on the Penasco Blanco to Ahshislepah Road, near the ruin, aided access to the Chaco Wash. (Photo by Gwinn Vivian, courtesy BLM.)

The Chaco intracanyon road system is embellished with 45 stone cut staircases. These masonry stairs, excavated by Vivian and Buettner in 1970-1971, are at the base of the slickrock near Chetro Ketl in Chaco Canyon. (Photo by Gwinn Vivian, courtesy BLM.)

Note the straightness of the prehistoric road segments (C, E) compared to the sinuosity of the historic road (G). Also shown is a gravel pit (A), pre-historic wall near Pueblo Alto trending EW (B), and another trending NS (D), and the Chaco Culture Historical Park boundary fence (F). (BLM Low Sun Angle, 1981, No. 1-004, courtesy Thomas R. Mann and Associates.)

have simply sighted on some distant or intermediate landmark and walked straight toward that feature, thus forming the "navigational route." Fred Nials, commenting on the physical characteristics of Chacoan roads in the 1983 BLM report, said that fence builders will testify that walking an absolutely straight line with only a single distant landmark as a point of reference is a virtual impossibility. The surveying probably consisted of a combination of three land-marks or people, or a calculated system of aligned markers used as multiple points of reference. This would have enabled minor course changes at ridge tops, where realignment on the distant landmark or backsighting could have taken place.

Colleen Beck surveyed an Inca road that was similarly constructed. The Incas outlined the trajectory of a road for a considerable distance by constructing lines of stones to mark each side of the road. Then the roadbed was leveled and ramps and cuts were constructed in extremely uneven terrain before the road was opened to traffic. The Spanish ethnographers of the sixteenth century noted that the Inca king would send experts to lay out the route of a road, and then the local Indians would construct it. Pedro de Cieza de Leon, a sixteenth-century ethnographer, said that part or all of the road could be built within a very short period of time.

Beck found a road construction project which had been abandoned after only a few meters had been laid out. If the section was aborted, the labor crew responsible for building that section may have made an error—they were either not lined up correctly with the rest of the crews constructing the road, or they were building from the middle out, and miscalculated.

Straightness in Chacoan roads, however, is modern folklore, Winston Hurst, an archaeologist with the Edge of the Cedars Museum in Utah, said in an interview. The roads he has seen in Utah *meander* along major drainage areas. He said that the course of the road largely depends on the geography. The terrain in Utah is complicated by an abundance of canyons and mesas. Although the terrain in the San Juan Basin makes walking long distances difficult, the basin provides wide open spaces which would allow the luxury of long, rolling thoroughfares. The situation is similar to the Moche Valley, a vast desert in Peru, which would have allowed for the type of construction Beck described. Most of the other road characteristics seen in the San Juan Basin apply to the roads in Utah.

The BLM survey report on the Chacoan roads also revealed a few curves. Aerial photographs show broad sweeping curves in the southern third of the Penasco Blanco to Ahshislepah Road, and in the road extending from Hungo Pavi to the small mesa in the northern Chaco area. The South Road makes a "sweeping curve over the foothills of South Mesa and assumes a bearing to Upper Kin Klizhin," says the BLM report. These curves do not necessarily conform to the topography. Some roads meander up particularly steep canyon walls and rims.

Curved or straight, the roads were a major effort. But who did the roads serve, and how powerful were the road engineers? The answers to these questions depend on whether Chaco Canyon was the center of an empire, a cultural network, or just a shining example of what all the great houses were doing.

When the actual extent of the Anasazi roads across the San Juan Basin were discovered in the 1970s, archaeologists interpreted them as a regional superhighway system with Chaco Canyon as the depot. It is important to remember that the roads weren't all built at the same time, and relatively few were planned by administrators living in downtown Chaco Canyon. In Chapter Four I stated that archaeologists believe the roads in Utah, at least according to preliminary reports, were built as early as Basketmaker III times, or around the late A.D. 800s. I also mentioned that some archaeologists are reconsidering the dates of the roads immediately south of Chaco Canyon, which predate the official estimate of A.D. 1050 by a century or so. If roads were built throughout Chaco's florescence (from A.D. 900 to 1150), then they do not prove or disprove that Chaco was the center of political power, but rather suggest that they served many different purposes—as trade routes, ritual procession ways, architectural embellishments, *and* avenues of political aggression. But, as Utah archaeologist Dale Davison said, "The vision of Anasazi armies marching on roads of a vast empire has no luck with me."

Versatile Roads of Mesoamerica and Peru

Soldiers marching in a phalanx six abreast and eighteen strong on the causeways around La Quemada, in Zacatecas, Mexico, are exactly what archaeologist Charles Trombold imagines. The avenues linked fortress-like buildings such as the Citadel at La Quemada and helped soldiers gain access to upper levels of these fortresses. The roads would have allowed for rapid deployment of troops from one trouble spot to another.

Trombold says that the hilltop structures could have been ceremonial, because they do present an axial symmetry typical of Mesoamerica, but he believes they were also fortifications, because no cultural material was found in them. There are numerous isolated strategic outposts or lookout points, major hilltop fortifications, and defensively situated habitation sites in the area. They were often the termini of the roads. Roads didn't connect to the habitations, nor were the habitations necessarily connected to each other.

The labor costs, engineering, and the extent of the La Quemada road network indicate to Trombold that centralized planning and an extensive power base were necessary to carry out the projects. The cost of the monuments reflected an acute sense of importance, as well. The roads and causeways around La Quemada symbolized the authority of those in charge.

A chapter in a book Trombold edited, entitled *Ancient Road Networks and Settlement Hierarchies in the New World,* explains the huge labor expenses and ceremonial aspect of the La Quemada road systems:

> If that polity was benign to its resident population, the causeways could have represented security and stability. If the polity was antagonistic, however, they may have been a constant reminder that retribution would be swift in the event of civil disorder. Almost certainly they were associated with ritual activities as seen by the location of small altars found occasionally near prominent architectural complexes. Likewise . . . [they] also seem never to have missed an opportunity to impress others of their importance. This is amply seen in the embellishment of various entrances to the citadel and the axial symmetry created by the placement of stairs, altars, and major structures.

The La Quemada causeways have been mentioned here not to say that Chaco Canyon administrators used the roads to deploy armies necessarily, but that such wide, paved avenues were a show of power drenched in local religion. The Maya sacbe was similar in that it may have tied the ruler of an urban center to a corresponding ceremonial center, and the ceremonial center connected the ruler with geoastronomical events, as described in Chapter Six. The constructed alliance between the ruler and divinity via the sacbe and temple is much like an organizational flow chart in dressed stone.

Andean roads are also a show of power. The superhighways of the Inca empire joined the Andean highlands, the tropical rain forest, and the desert coastal strip. The royal road along the spine of the Andes ran 3,450 miles from the Columbia/Ecuador border to Central Chile, and it was linked by lateral roads to the 2,500-mile-long coastal highway. The Inca, however, were not the first to build roads in that vast region. Although most of the ethnological record of the Andean roads concerns the Inca, the Inca roads made up only a small percentage of roads in the area Beck surveyed in the Moche Valley along the coast of modern Peru.

The earliest roads in this valley may have been built a thousand years before Christ, although humans may have occupied the area ten thousand years before that. Archaeologists have found it difficult to follow the ebb and flow of the different cultures, but generally the power volleyed between Chavín de Huantar (850-200 B.C.), the Moche or proto-Chimú (100 B.C. to A.D. 750), the Chimú at Chan-Chan (A.D. 1000 to 1470), and the Inca (c. 1438-1532). The Inca were a south sierra people with a different prehistory, culture, and language than the people in the Moche Valley, but both cultures built roads. The Inca occupied the valley for only eighty years and had moved into the existing city of Chan-Chan. Their presence is well documented on the roads, Beck said. The complexity of road systems constructed and abandoned through time in the area Beck studied made it difficult to distinguish between culture and use. This is true with Anasazi roads as well.

Early roads were cleared, sometimes graded, and lined with stones or high walls. The engineering techniques declined during the intermediary period and picked up again during the time of the Inca. Although some of the roads have been interpreted as ceremonial ways or astronomical markers, Beck found only a few roads in the Moche Valley that could be interpreted ceremonially, but she assumes there are more that cannot be reconstructed archaeologically. She found that the roads predominantly either aided or controlled the movement of people within a site, between sites, or over long distances within or between valleys. The roads controlled whether direct access into a site would or would not be permitted.

Beck says that the Roman's strategic use of the road to move armies and define boundaries of power applies to the Incas and "there is no reason to think that roads were not used in the same manner in earlier times when a region was conquered."

"It must also be kept in mind that the purpose of a road can change through time," she added. A road built to define territory may eventually have become a trade route as two territories bordering the road developed commerce with each other. The Great North Road at Chaco Canyon may have similarly served different purposes linked with travel, commerce, or ceremony through time.

Tambos, or way stations, used for shelters or storehouses, were positioned near entrances into the Moche Valley and at a day's journey apart not only to aid travelers but to control traffic. The earliest dated tambo was built in the Early Horizon (about 1000 B.C.). That's how long ago the rulers began to control the roads.

In the Chaco area there seems to be much duplication of roads in the area north and east of Pueblo Alto. Similarly, Beck found a great amount of duplication in the Moche Valley which may have some implications for the Chacoan Roads. Sketches of the roads in small sections of the Moche Valley look like the lines in the palm of one's hand—the sheer number alone is impressive, but that they crisscross and superimpose each other is confusing. New roads were built in the area as new groups took over, as a new purpose warranted, and as they were destroyed by nature. Roads were either reconstructed or rerouted if they were destroyed by natural forces such as the storms of El Niño, earthquakes, or moving sand dunes.

Humans, in their constant need to expand and improve, would have instigated the construction of new roads. When the Incas moved into the Moche Valley, they used preexisting roads, but also wanted to build their own. A tradition of the dominant authority reinforcing its power by constructing its own roads could account for some of the roads built in the same area.

A striking similarity between the Peruvian roads and the Chacoan roads is the parallel routes. The parallel routes in the Chaco area are seen as ceremonial, but they could also be an indication of power. Cieza de Leon, in the sixteenth century, counted three or four parallel roads outside of Vilcas, Peru. The townspeople explained that each succeeding Inca ruler wanted new roads built, longer and wider than his predecessor's. "Such an endeavor was not the most advantageous choice economically but does reflect the desire of specific rulers to establish their authority, power, and prestige by building roads," Beck said. Such ostentatious use of labor may have resulted in the earlier parallel, and very wide, roads at Chaco Canyon.

The parallel roads could have also applied to a formalized stratification of people. As new groups moved into the Moche Valley, they built on top of what already existed and as a result, adopted some of the local social mores. Apparently, the Inca system of segregation between lords, bureaucrats, and artisans came from the Chimú, who had derived some of their cultural habits from the Moche people. Beck pointed out that there was a separate road for message runners, who were called *chasquis* (meaning "to exchange"), and another for fishermen. There were separate entrances to a *huaca* (shrine) for coastal people, sierra people, and women.

The *chasquis* system was developed into the 1400s by Pachacuti Inca Yupanqui, the Ninth Inca (ruler), according to Indian running expert Peter Nabokov. Ritual running may have preceded this institutionalized group of message carriers drawn from elite families. By the reign of the Eleventh Inca, Huayna Capac (1493-1528), oven-shaped way stations, called *c'oklya*, were built into the system; runners waited at these stations to relay messages on down the line. A message could be delivered from Cuzco to destinations five hundred to six hundred leagues away within two or three hours, or 150 miles in a day. The runners wore white feather bonnets and carried their messages in bags. They were paid for their fifteen-day shifts from local taxes.

Specialized knowledge was required to engineer the roads and align the buildings in Chaco Canyon much as it was in the other high cultures of the New World, but does the evidence of precise engineering or astronomical observation imply a specialized class of engineers or astronomers and a supervised class of laborers? If so, what was the power structure?

The Chacoan Road Engineers

Given that the Anasazi indeed had the skills to build well-laid-out roads and cosmically orientated buildings, there must have been a group of planners who made the decisions to do so. The roads connecting Chaco to alleged outliers and the abundance of small houses in Chaco Canyon suggests to many scholars a political hierarchy that centered in the canyon, perhaps at Pueblo Bonito. But just as many scholars believe the Anasazi great houses were autonomous and egalitarian like those of their Pueblo successors.

Quite a number of archaeologists have suggested that sociopolitical organizaiton at Chaco Canyon was more complex than at historical Pueblos, as noted by Stephen Lekson. Gordon Vivian (1964) suggested a pluralistic society with a budding theocracy (1959). His son, Gwinn Vivian (1970), saw two societies, with micro-environmental differences living side-by-side. Paul Grebinger (1978) proposed a pristine, ranked society based on differential access to production (irrigable farmlands). Jeffery Altschul (1978) saw the presence of a managerial elite in Chaco, with the canyon as a focus for a large regional interaction sphere. Charles DiPeso (1968 and 1974), Edwin Ferdon (1955), J. Charles Kelley (1986, and with Ellen Abbot Kelley in 1975), and Albert Schroeder (1966) have suggested a colonial hierarchy with an imposed Mexican elite. James Judge (1979) proposed an elite based on the administration of an internally developed redistributive system and later a (1983) ceremonial center for the large Chacoan region.

Archaeologist Lynne Sebastian (1988) said that it is much easier to redistribute people than it is to redistribute food. Rejecting the model that the complex society was organized to redistribute food, Sebastian created a model based on comparisons of productivity to climatic change. She concluded that a stratified society was developed in which those who had high-yield landholdings assumed leadership and were able to obligate poorer landholders. When drought hit the richer landholders, they called in their chips. The obligated ones, believing their debtors to be favored by the supernatural, donated labor to build the great houses and the roads in order to attract more people into the canyon, or to reach further into the region. Sebastian said that the existence of multiple great houses suggested competitive powers.

Lekson, in his 1988 dissertation, "Sociocomplexity at Chaco Canyon, New Mexico," read the record very differently. "The basic premise that all great houses were part of a regional system may be questioned." The great houses (and particularly the small extracanyon great houses) may have been an aspect of broader Anasazi settlement architecture, rather than a colony or imposition from the central Chaco core. Lekson counted the number of hearths in the kivas he called pit houses located in the central Chaco Canyon and determined that less than 2,500 people lived there, which was not enough people to achieve "social complexity" or to hold sway over a vast region. He says, however, that the Chacoans were right on the cusp of social complexity.

Many believe that the Eastern Anasazi system was egalitarian but that planning occurred at Chaco Canyon, probably Pueblo Bonito. The system was fueled by Chaco's religious charisma, and labor was, possibly, volunteered. But caution must be observed in labeling the functions of all great houses as ceremonial. Just as geography may have influenced the straightness of a road, purpose may have defined Anasazi architecture more than anything else—including culture and power.

"Size may not be determined primarily by power and status, but may relate to other more important factors, such as function," Thomas Windes said. It is true that Pueblo Bonito stands alone in yielding an exceptional amount of high-quality cultural material, but the inventory of this material differs only in quantity and not in quality from the other great houses and from the small houses. Cultural material alone is not enough to prove status. Perhaps the perception of the Chacoan system has been obscured by assuming that all great houses served similar functions. The similarities between great houses is biased by their impressive architecture.

The great houses may have been divided into several different functions which may not be perceptible, and these functions may have changed over time. Pueblo Alto, for instance, was built for the purpose of the roads, but the fact that it straddles several different roads doesn't necessarily mean its residents were among the elite. Windes said that the road system at Alto reflects less emphasis on hierarchical power and control of the system, and more on equality among various units. Pueblo Alto is not the only great house built, or retrofitted, for the roads.

Someone made the decision, or to put it in bureaucratic terms, a decision-making policy existed, to make those modifications. Windes said that decision-making crisscrossed individual sites but was not beholden to all of them, another example of widespread interaction.

Clearly Pueblo Alto was no Pueblo Bonito; it may have been subordinate to Pueblo Bonito as well as to Chetro Ketl. Pueblo Bonito is the older and larger of the three houses and those who ran it must have achieved some measure of influence and prestige by the time Pueblo Alto was built. If Pueblo Bonito and Chetro Ketl were major centers within a hierarchically organized system for the redistribution of goods, then Pueblo Alto would not have been built astride the multitude of northern roads without influence and direction from the residences who ran those two great houses nearby, to which the roads ultimately connected. Pueblo Bonito and Chetro Ketl would not have allowd Pueblo Alto to have been built if it threatened direct or indirect economic competition.

It's the hundreds of small houses in the canyon that throw off the equations. Not as glamorous as the great houses, they are nevertheless present and cry out for an explanation which most would choose to ignore, unless, of course, one wanted evidence for a feudalistic society in Chaco Canyon. The problem is the attention the great houses seem to command from us. They are the first to have been excavated, but the last to have been built. The people in the small houses may have built the great houses for their purposes, but the small houses did not necessarily exist at the pleasure of the great houses.

It was Michael Marshall who, in 1979, found the satisfying argument on the egalitarian side. He said that a socially complex, but basically nonstratified, populace lived in the small structures and used the larger structures, which he called public architecture, for storage, and for periodic sessions of special tasks related to public obligations and decision-making. These tasks included periodic ceremony, meetings, market, accommodations for visiting relations, and storage.

Windes and Frances Joan Mathien agreed with him. Only a few caretakers or upper-echelon ceremonial types may have lived in the great house, they said in an interview. The small house people controlled or at least participated in the great houses, perhaps by owning storage or participating in ceremonial activity.

Windes, who surveyed the small house communities in Chaco Canyon in 1972, revisited his work in the late 1980s. Four discrete communities were found in Chaco Canyon that have "continuity through time." These communities include the Fajada Gap Community, South Gap/Pueblo Bonito Community, Padilla Well/Penasco Blanco Community, and the East Chaco Community seven miles east of the park. The small house communities began in the early 900s, about the time when the Chaco civilization began to flower. Over time, the neighborhood around Pueblo Bonito became the most densely populated and complex.

During his survey, Windes discovered a cottage industry of turquoise manufacturing in about 94 percent of the small houses. Fajada Gap, the small house site near Fajada Butte where the sun calendar rests, contained a staggering number of artifacts: seventy thousand pieces as opposed to the normal two or three thousand, plus "multitudes" of turquoise—not whole pieces, but small flecks and unfinished beads. These flecks were accompanied by small drills and polishing stones.

Few whole beads were found in the small houses. However, exquisite small black beads made from shale were found with the small house burials. By contrast, Room 33 in Pueblo Bonito had a great deal of turquoise associated with its burials.

Windes suggests that the turquoise could have been used by small house residents as an economic hedge, that even if they were farmers by day, they were jewelry manufacturers by night. As evidenced by its use in great house burials, the turquoise was ceremonially connected, but it could have been traded by manufacturers for food or other goods.

"My assumption is the great houses and small houses go together as a unit contrary to what others believe," Windes said. He is testing the idea that great house/great kiva complexes were born out of small house communities when a certain population was reached.

Incidentally, turquoise has been found in large quantities in the great houses and kivas in the canyon, but not systematically in the outlying communities. This does not mean that turquoise is not there, but that it is hard to see, unless an archaeologist is looking for it specifically.

A large turquoise cache was found at Aztec, north of Chaco, and represents the second greatest find after Pueblo Bonito. The number of pieces found there may represent the shift in leadership from Chaco to Aztec in the later 1000s to early 1100s, and may have been one destination for Chacoans after the major depopulation of the 1150s.

Windes does not believe that the great house people were in control, although they had some status as evidenced by their turquoise-laced burials. The small house people may have chosen their habitats based on comfort. The small houses are built on high protected ground as opposed to the canyon floor where it is colder. "Clearly, the south-facing great houses reflected knowledge in solar engineering," he says. "But the small house communities were built to take advantage of sunrises and to avoid cold air drainages." Most of the small houses were constantly being refurbished through time, which suggests that the units were temporary because the Anasazi were constantly on the go. The exception to this rule, so far, is Marcia's Rincon in the canyon, which seems to have been occupied continuously for three hundred years.

Archaeologist Marcia Truell, for whom the rincon is named, has a slightly different idea of who the small house people were. She says the small house rooms became larger at the same time the great houses became larger. "It would be handy if the number of small sites also rose instead of showing a moderate decrease," Truell says, because then she could say that the small house people were drawn in as labor for the large house construction boom. Instead, the increased floor plans show temporary occupation, or a shift in style. "It seems reasonable to suggest that people involved in the transportation of goods into Chaco would have established settlements of either a temporary or permanent nature within the canyon," she said.

Truell found diversity among small house architectural styles and suggested that the small house people themselves were a cultural mix. Gwinn Vivian, on the other hand, said the small house, or Hosta Butte, people were a culturally different group than the people living in the great houses. He suggested that "this variability is a manifestation of two essentially egalitarian sociopolitical bodies whose cultural traditions had evolved along diverging trajectories. However, these linkages did not involve political control of small house populations by a great elite."

Pueblo Egalitarianism

Individual historical pueblos did not belong to a regional political system. No one pueblo had power over another, although they have been competitive and periodically have gone to war with each other. Hence, the Pueblos are said to have an egalitarian society, but that doesn't mean the individual pueblos did not have their own ranking practices.

An egalitarian society is one in which the members all have equal political, social, and economic rights. An egalitarian society has many opportunities for reciprocity and many stations of prestige. An examination of the religious order of the Pueblos shows that the system is not egalitarian.

Jonathan Reyman, in "Priests, Power, and Politics: Some Implications of Socioceremonial Control," said that a nonegalitarian society is one in which "positions of valued status are limited so that not all those of sufficient talent to occupy such statuses actually achieve them. Such a society may or may not be stratified."

Most modern Pueblos have two systems of leadership in place. One is the religious leader, called the *cacique* by the Spanish, or the *tiamoni* by the Keresan, and numerous other names by other pueblos. The second is a governor. The first is inherited; the second is an annually elected official, an authority imposed on the Pueblos by the American government when the pueblos became reservations. At one time, Pueblos were lead by a town chief, also called the cacique, and a war chief who took care of external affairs. Both offices were steeped in religious authority as well, because civil and ecclesiastic duties were not seen as separate. It is often said that Utset and Nowutset, introduced in Chapter Eight, were the prototypes for these offices.

Generally, Pueblo people are classified according to their religious function, which is largely inherited and decorated with privilege. The Hopi have three classes, for example. The people are governed by the chiefs (*Mongwi*), village criers (*Chakmongwi*), and priests (*Momwit*). The people are classed as common, middle, and upper class, and the members of each class are identified as follows: The *Mong-cinum* are the leaders of the kivas, priests, and high priests; the *Pavun-cinum* hold no office but belong to societies and participate in ceremonies; and the *Sukavung-cinum* do not participate in the religious functions.

Another class distinction is the order in which one's clan arrived in the Hopi area according to the creation myth. Clans are not the basic unit for hereditary transfer of office, but specific lineages within the clans control these offices.

The line of succession for office is similarly observed at Zuñi and Acoma. At Zuñi, the Dogwood Clan controls two major offices: the *Shiwanni*, or Chief Priest of the North, and the *Pekwin* (now extinct), the Sun Priest. A son or brother of the *shiwanni* fills the vacancy. At Acoma, a specific line within the Antelope Clan controls the office of the *ha'actitcani*, "a person who symbolizes the whole pueblo."

The Hopi, Zuñi, and Acoma believe that the people who do not have ceremonial property or connection are poor and not valuable to the pueblo, according to Reyman.

The Keres have a religious class structure, as well. At Santo Domingo, a *sishti* is someone who does not do ceremonial or governmental work. The Cochiti refer to nonsociety people as *sir'shti*, or "raw people," and are members of the general public, as opposed to the *Ku-sha'li* and *Kwe'-rana*, who are "cooked people," or the village's elite. The raw and cooked people references refer to how people were created as described in their creation myths.

At Zia, the cacique comes from one of five specific clans. The Cochiti, on the other hand, cannot select a successor from one's own clan. At Jemez, the cacique and two assistants are from the Young Corn or Sun Clans, but not from societies.

The Tewa have two caciques, one for the summer moiety and one for the winter moiety and alternate control. Apparently, inheritance is strictly not involved in the selection of their caciques. But the Tewa do distinguish between the Dry Food (or common) People and the six native officials, the *Towa'e*, chosen to serve both the Dry Food People and the Made People (society chiefs). The Dry Food People are also called *Whe Towa* (the Weed or Trash People) or *Nayi wha Towa* (people who sweep before the dances). The Made People are hierarchically stratified into eight groups. The Made People are a large group but not the majority. To be a member of the Made People is to have prestige. The Dry Food People, the Towa'e, and the Made People are the three levels of existence which correspond with three ways of being in the Tewa spirit world.

After the religious leaders, the society priests or chiefs are next in line. Some systems include assistants and a war priest or bow priest. These priests, chiefs, and acolytes assume positions in similar hereditary manner.

The ranking system is more clearly defined among western pueblos than eastern pueblos. To take a high-ranked office, one must be able to demonstrate considerable knowledge, but unless one is of a particular lineage, one may never be able to acquire that knowledge, since it is passed down the line as property. Access to the knowledge is restricted through institutionalized secrecy.

Ritual knowledge and performance alone does not carry power. Power would also come through control, perhaps ritualistic, of valued resources. The person who keeps the calendar would have control, sometimes more than the town chief, although many residents have their own way of detecting seasonal cycles. But the Sun Chief is the one who has the authority to decide when planting is done or, in the past, when to move near planting fields. Chiefs who watch the ceremonial calendar also have authority to call the ceremony. When the announcement is made, it is an order. The pace of activity on all levels in the village quickens and the economy benefits.

When Jonathan Reyman first introduced this argument to a symposium on "Astronomy and Ceremony in the Pre-historic Southwest," in 1983, he met with much controversy and criticism, especially from the Zuñi and Hopi attending the conference. They said that priests are responsible to the pueblo as a whole, and their behavior must be for the good of the village, not for personal gain. Above all, priests must have good hearts. Secondly, priests do not have the power to command.

Nevertheless, generally speaking, membership has its privileges. The high-ranked priests who work for the good of the village are relieved of their other duties. Their fields are planted for them. Food, water, and firewood are provided for them through communal labor and hunts. Their homes are maintained. The town chief has access to seed surplus and seed reserves. Most pueblos keep one to two years supply of seeds in reserve in the event a bad year produces little seed. The chief is able to allocate seed and can give the best seed to his own lineage. He has control over the assignment of land and water rights. The Hopi *Kikmongwi* can award his own land allotment to anyone who has acted in good service.

Reyman said that the chief's own lineage will eventually control a good portion of surplus wealth and will eventually gain economic dominance. His lineage will unite with other privileged lineages through clanship, resulting in village-wide systems of stratified lineages and clans. Reyman says that this is what happened at Hopi, and to a lesser extent, at Zuñi and elsewhere. Priests can maintain authority through such means as gossip, public ridicule through clown antics at ceremonial dances, and by fining heavily.

A system of checks and balances keeps the leaders from getting too far out of hand. The priest is limited by rules of morality and proper conduct. If there is a trend of bad weather, the priest is not doing his job. Historically, priests have been known to be impeached and, in the worst of cases, executed.

One fact remains that shows the priestly power was not absolute. Unlike the case of the Maya, priests are not associated with divine power. When a Pueblo chief dies, he dies a human being and is buried in the same manner as the other members of the pueblo. With the exception of perhaps a few ornaments to show office, and one or two elaborate burials, the Pueblos do not practice status burials.

The Anasazi did have status burials. Fifteen people were buried at Pueblo Bonito, in rooms 32 and 33, and two men were buried in the subfloor, with thousands of artifacts. The small house people at Chaco Canyon, on the other hand, did not have elaborate burials.

The fact that the Pueblos do not have status burials precludes the use of their ethnography in deciphering the power structure at Chaco, according to Reyman. Pueblos cannot be used to support the argument that the Anasazi were an egalitarian society.

Returned to Sender

The story is told that long ago there were many anaasázi living in pueblos throughout what is now Navajo country, traditionally defined by the four sacred mountains of the cardinal directions. Something happened which caused the anaasázi to begin fighting each other. Nobody is sure what caused the struggle, but soon a general civil war ensued. Finally, the anaasázi completely destroyed each other and many of their pueblos. That is why only ruins are left, though one can occasionally find a room in one that looks as if the people simply went to their fields and never returned. Someday, the story goes on to predict, the same thing will happen again and years afterward people living on the land will again be asked about ruins by strangers.

A Navajo living near Two Grey Hills, New Mexico, told this story to Dennis Franstead, who recorded it in an unpublished manuscript, "An Introduction to the Navajo Oral History of the Anasazi Sites in the San Juan Basin Area," in 1979.

Anasazi ruins figure prominently in Navajo legends, but not in Pueblo legends. In one version of the Navajo Gambler legend, recorded by LuLu Wade Wetherill and Byron Cummings in 1922, Noqoilpi demanded the Chacoans build him a great village, a race track, and an arena. He managed to destroy whatever was left of the people's enthusiasm for ceremonial duty by amassing power through addiction to blue gum. The Chacoans finally killed the

Gambler, but they were compelled to leave Chaco Canyon and settle near Zuñi.

It is interesting to compare myth to the archaeological record. It is equally interesting, but not practiced widely by many Chacoan archaeologists, to extrapolate from the record at hand. Frankly, that's not their job. Their job is to sift for clues and test hypotheses. The focus is on the smallest bits of evidence, rather than the big picture. Each new generation of archaeologists brings fresh perspectives and questions to the field. The puzzle may never be solved and that's the challenge.

What follows is my extrapolation of the record.

By A.D. 900 the population of most of the communities in the San Juan Basin had expanded enough to build public houses and great kivas, and a distinct panregional culture had developed. This is not unlike the explosive development of urban centers in medieval Europe, where population centers in Normandy, France, England, and Spain grew up around a multitude of cathedrals. Although those people spoke different languages, they borrowed architectural styles from each other. The Anasazi towns were competitive but autonomous—and the population at Chaco Canyon functioned in much the same way. No one great house could amass too much power, because climatic conditions caused the residents to move frequently.

An elaborate and stratified religious order was established at the different great houses across the Anasazi region. The highest ranking priests watched the sun's movements and called for ceremony, planting, or moving to other great houses when climatic conditions changed. As channels for life's breath, the roads facilitated kinship alliances between the towns, formalized geoastronomical alignments, and established routes to resources and shrines. These alliances were reinforced by ceremony. I suspect that the roads were not built all at once in A.D. 1050, but were built in stages beginning perhaps as much as a century or two earlier. Long before A.D. 1050, the inhabitants of the so-called outliers in the greater San Juan Basin built roads for their own local purposes. Routes existed north and east of Chaco Canyon to serve the purposes of the great houses, but may not have been formalized at that time. Meanwhile, ancient trade routes snaked throughout the region.

But after A.D. 1050, something happened. Pueblo Bonito and Chetro Ketl mounted an unprecedented campaign to expand influence beyond the canyon walls with the aid of the road turnpikes at Pueblo Alto, Penasco Blanco, and Tsin Kletzin. The North Road, South Road, and Coyote Canyon Road in particular stretched into the outer region like tentacles to beckon people to the charismatic but water-starved Chaco Canyon. The residents of the great houses in the canyon, perhaps in response to a single calling, had begun reorienting their houses to specific cosmic alignments. Scores of volunteers were needed to assist in the building, and they came bearing offerings, perhaps out of belief in divine reciprocity.

The heavy construction in the canyon during this time was obviously masterminded. Whoever was in power, priest or ruling class, ordered the obsessive building well beyond what was necessary for productive living. This effort was briefly thwarted by a drought at the end of the eleventh century and then remounted by the beginning of the next century, but with a different emphasis. At about this time, Aztec Ruin to the north was built, and architectural and ceramic styles, if not power, in Chaco Canyon shifted to the styles of the Aztec region. Perhaps Aztec became the seat of the new archbishop. Cosmic geomancy was still important—Casa Rinconada, with its cardinal and solar alignments, was built during this time.

When this population left the canyon again around A.D. 1150, as was the custom during dry periods, it used the great roads for ritualistic return to the place of emergence. The roads still symbolized the channel of life, the route to the past. When Chaco Canyon was abandoned, because of drought or political deterioration, many people may have moved to Aztec.

By the time the population returned again in the 1200s, something happened that caused the Chacoans to no longer favor grandeur. Building styles began to change. Eventually, the roads were lined with combustible plant and other material and ceremonially burned, and the people left again, this time never to return.

After the abandonment of Chaco Canyon, the population in the outliers carried out their respective life spans, moving when necessary to greener mesas, adopting new beliefs and kachinas along the way. They refined their architectural taste and left the more elaborate elements behind for the Navajo.

Perhaps Chaco Canyon was indeed Kush Karet, the mythical Keresan village of the north, the place where the people learned many lessons and took stock of themselves. I suspect that the Pueblos, in all their various forms, retained and refined remnants of Anasazi practice over the past thousand years. They continually borrowed the best elements from other cultures while preserving the ancient ways in adobe and song.

The pueblo, a blend of the small house/great house prototypes, bespeaks of a cohesive community in harmony with the cosmos rather than a grand reflection of the awesome sky. The priests, though treated with respect and well paid for their duty, no longer occupy majestic palaces but live in rooms of proper proportions. It is as if the Pueblo have integrated the cosmological elements into community life; before, their ancestors stood in wonder and fear of it. Clearly, the sky gods, whatever their names, were much larger than they are today.

The great roads, though no longer visible in Pueblo architecture, are still present among them. Just as the emergence became a metaphor for migration and leaving one's ancestral home, taking the straight road became a metaphor for a centering process. One follows the straight road without deviation throughout a life of service to one's pueblo. Migration is symbolized by a coiled snake, the sign for water—like the one marking the winter solstice on Fajada Butte. Ultimately, the straight road takes one back to the place of emergence. Thus the straight road becomes a circle, a snake swallowing its tail for all eternity.

Marcia Truell said, "It's a pity that we don't know what we don't know. . . . It seems that how this information is construed depends largely on how rash you are willing to be."

Discovering the Roads

In 1872, Mark Twain, in *Roughing It*, wrote about the chilly thrill of losing track of a road. He noted that "Having a cake of ice slipped down one's back is placid comfort compared to it," and described a situation in which:

> . . . in any direction that you proceeded (the same as in a well-laid-out orchard) you would find yourself moving down a distinctly defined avenue, with a row of these snow mounds on either side of it—an avenue the customary width of a road, nice and level in its breadth, and rising at the sides in the most natural way, by reason of the mounds. But we had not thought of this. . . . it finally occurred to us, far in the night, that since the last faint trace of the wheel tracks had long ago been buried from sight, we might now be wandering down a mere sagebrush avenue, miles away from the road and diverging further and further from it all the time. . . . There was an instant halting and dismounting, a bending low and an anxious scanning of the roadbed. Useless, of course; for if a faint depression could not be discerned from an altitude of four or five feet above it, it certainly could not with one's nose nearly against it.

John Stein, one of the leading Anasazi road experts, and Chris Kincaid, who edited the first BLM report on the roads, said Mark Twain was describing a syndrome known in the business of archaeological survey as the Rorschach Approach. They described it this way: "The ground observer, intent on verifying a road on a segment by segment basis is placed in the extremely frustrating position of 'knowing something is there' as demonstrated by the photographed image, but not being able to see the tangible reality in front of him. It is at this point that the observer might begin to imagine he sees a swale. . . ." A swale is a low place in a tract of land, often subtle and difficult to perceive in flat light.

Using the Rorschach Approach

Trying to trace by foot a road that appeared as a faint, but long, hairline in an aerial photograph is frustrating work. Since the eight-hundred-year-old roads could not usually be "seen," the survey archaeologists, by the soles of their boots, developed sighting methods that would coax the roads to the surface. But the challenge was more difficult than that. The archaeologists not only had to document the photo-visible or ground-visible alignment by following a physical swale or depression, but search for cultural material as well, in order to determine affiliation, age, and function. In this case, these surveyors were required to do exactly what Twain advised against: bend low and put their noses nearly against the ground.

The tedious process of forming routines for surveying the roads spanned more than a decade. The methodology culminated with the BLM project in the 1980s, in which surveying was conducted in two phases. The first phase concentrated on an area within ten miles of Chaco Canyon. The second phase concentrated mainly on the portion south of Chaco Canyon. The project pulled in the expertise and data gathered prior to 1980 and compiled the most comprehensive report to date. Methods for surveying the roads were refined during this period.

By the Way

The first step in locating a road is to know where to look. Surveyors of the prehistoric roads began with field notes. Some early researchers mentioned road sightings in their reports as an afterthought, such as that noted by Paul Martin near Lowry Ruin in 1936:

I should, however, like to call attention to the shallow, dry foss or ha-ha about one foot in depth and from fifteen to twenty feet wide. This ditch lies between the great kiva and the Pueblo extending for a half mile or more north and south beyond the ruin. I was unable to determine whether or not this shallow depression was of a natural or an artificial origin or to determine its purpose.

Most who had investigated road segments mentally filed away their findings for that someday when they would write it up. Edgar Hewett, director of the American School of Research in the 1920s and later head of the University of New Mexico field school in the canyon in the 1930s, knew about the roads but left them out of his reports entirely, according to Gwinn Vivian in the BLM report. Neil Judd, director of the National Geographic Expedition in the canyon, was not only versed on the roads, he planned to publish a separate volume on them, but never did. His data on the roads was given in short references in his two volumes on Pueblo Bonito of 1954 and 1964, some forty years after his initial work in the canyon began. However, he apparently supplied road information to the anonymous author of "Prehistoric Chaco Canyon 'Roads' Puzzle Scientists," a brief article in the *New Mexico Highway Journal* in 1928. He is credited in the article with suggesting that the roads were used for transporting logs.

Judd questioned the Navajo for information on the roads:

> When asked about the so-called 'roads' on both the north and south cliffs, Hosteen Beyal remarked that they were not really roads, although they looked like them. He says they were built by the Chaco people. One road lead from Pueblo Pintado to Pueblo Bonito and on to Penasco Blanco. Another led from Pueblo Bonito to Kin-yai; a third, from Kinbiniyol to, or through, Coyote Canyon and on to a point near Fort Defiance. On each of these 'roads' one could see, until recently, cuts where the road passed through small hills.

Chris Kincaid, in the 1983 BLM report, commented on the occasional opportunity to talk to Navajos whose families had lived in the area close to the roads for many generations. At one such time, a Navajo met the crew as they stood within a segment of the South Road which was difficult to see from the ground. After greetings were exchanged and the crew's presence explained, the individual was not in the least perplexed but rather confirmed that the crew had accurately located the road. He said that the road could be followed into Chaco Canyon and that during early morning and late evening light it could be seen continuing to Kin Ya'a. He implied that the knowledge of the roads was restricted to a few individuals and that there were others who knew much more than himself. He was not allowed to play as a child in or near the South Road.

Research on road and trail systems is hampered by a dearth of information for two reasons, said Benjamin P. Robertson in the 1983 BLM report, which compared prehistoric roads to ancient trails. The first of these is a failure on the part of the ethnographers, historians, and archaeologists to recognize the importance of the roads. It reflects a series of conscious or unconscious assumptions on the part of both informants and ethnographers. James T. Davis explained it this way:

> It would not be unreasonable to suppose that if one San Franciscan informed another that he was going to Oakland, both parties would probably assume that the route followed would be over the San Francisco–Oakland Bay Bridge. Similarly, an Achomawi informant, for example, might offer the information that 'we go to Glass Mountain to get obsidian,' and unless further information is elicited by the interrogator as to the route traversed in getting there, such intelligence probably would not be volunteered because the Indian, possibly unconsciously, assumes that anyone knows how to get to Glass Mountain. . . .

The second difficulty in researching a road is that even if writers described the routes taken by prehistoric trails or roads, they often did not indicate the actual characteristics of the roads. "One gains the impression from the literature that the only important features of a trail are its point of origin and destination, since everyone obviously knows what a trail looks like," said Robertson.

By Air

Knowing where to look and the possible bearing of a road relieves an otherwise monumental task in interpreting aerial photographs of possible roads, according to Margaret Senter Obenauf in the 1983 BLM survey. During the first phase of the BLM survey, five different sets of photographs were used in searching for roads: Soil Conservation Service black-and-white, BLM in-house photography in both black-and-white and color, and low sun angle photography of two different scales. Most of the known Chacoan outliers and the distance between neighboring outliers were covered in the photographs.

The first step in the process of interpreting the photos was to identify the area of interest using either the mapped location of a previously known road, or a defined area to be examined for the presence of a road. Aerial photographs were then examined stereoscopically for lineations. When a lineation was found it would be directly marked on the photo with a grease pencil by placing a dot at each end with a line alongside it. The interpreter would then follow the line for more segments, mark it, and continue.

Many short linear features show up in aerial photography of the San Juan Basin that are not roads. By following the line outward from the outliers, this problem was reduced to manageable size since roads are more distinctive near the outliers.

When examining photos between outliers, the interpreters were more successful if a "highly probable" road segment was visible at one of the endpoints, but in a few cases "highly probable" segments were discovered between the outliers or near road-related features even when none were found near the outliers themselves. Field crews were then sent to verify the "highly probable" road segments and extend them to outliers.

Not all projected roads were verified. In fact, very few roads were contiguous lines from outliers to Chaco Canyon. Nevertheless, they appear on maps as contiguous lines.

Photointerpretation for the first phase of the project was performed using a Topcon mirror stereoscope mounted on a scanning track. Lenses were available to provide 3-power magnification. Three-power magnification of imagery at scales of around 1:30,000 proved to be the most productive.

Possible roads marked on the photographs were transferred to

USGS topographic maps using a Bausch and Lomb Stereo Zoom Transferscope in the monocular mode. Scale adjustment, especially in areas with few landmarks, was often difficult. Accuracy of the transfer using the Transferscope was approximately equal to the accuracy gained using a Mapograph.

A variety of aerial photography techniques at several different scales was used for the exploration of Phase II of the BLM Chaco Roads Project, which concentrated on the roads south of the canyon. In addition to photointerpretation, Phase II elected to use aerial reconnaissance and ground examination. Although most Chacoan roads were located through photointerpretation, this is a limited and sometimes misleading means of locating roads. The experience of the interpreter and the wide range of characteristics exhibited by both prehistoric and historic roads in photographs can limit interpretations.

Aerial reconnaissance proved to be one of the most useful means of locating and evaluating previously unrecognized road and photointerpreted road segments. Fixed-wing aircraft, more economical than the helicopter, although not as well suited to the task, were flown shortly after sunrise when the low sun angle usually enhanced the visibility of the roads.

The Pueblo Pintado to Chaco Canyon Road was enhanced by the growth of sagebrush between road margins as indicated by the brackets. (Photo courtesy BLM.)

Reconnaissance of this type offered several advantages over using aerial photography in locating roads. The roads are easier to spot in person due to the oblique perspective and the ability to search for signs. From the air, an archaeologist can more quickly place the roads in context with the landscape.

This method led to the discovery of several unknown road segments. For example, the Penasco Blanco to Ahshislepah Road was extended beyond the Ahshislepah Wash by aerial reconnaissance after intensive conventional photointerpretation and concentrated ground survey failed to show one trace of these segments. In some cases prehistoric roads were much more apparent in 35mm oblique photographs taken during aerial reconnaissance than in either conventional or low-sun-angle aerial photography.

By Foot

Topographic relief is probably the single most significant factor effecting the visibility of a prehistoric road, according to Fred Nials in the 1983 BLM report. Primary relief is the term archaeologists use when referring to the marks in the landscape caused by prehistoric construction, maintenance, or natural erosion during use of the road. Secondary relief is the topographic expression developed since the abandonment of the road. It is not always possible to distinguish the two unless the original road was embedded in rock, or archaeologists have excavated a trench in the road for a better view of the way the dirt was layered or eroded through time.

Most road segments have been partially filled by the natural processes of wind and sheetwash deposition of the road's surface since abandonment. Border walls and road edges collapse in the road. In other cases, the road has been deepened or widened by wind erosion or run-off water. Water can be seen standing in these roads today after a rain, which is part of the reason they were mistaken for canals earlier in this century.

These water-deepened road segments become fertile ground to such plants as sagebrush and other native plants. However, a decrease in vegetation can also characterize a road segment. Archaeologist Fred Nials noted in the 1983 BLM report that vegetation is most commonly noticed outside historic roads, but inside prehistoric roads.

The sediment within the road is often darker than surrounding sediments. This is due to a variety of factors: increased organic content, increased density of small annual plants, or increased moisture content.

Cultural interaction can affect the visibility of the prehistoric road. Overgrazing, for example, reduces vegetation cover so that run-off in the road is likely to be more rapid and damaging.

Don't expect to see a road in a valley bottom, near an arroyo, or on a slope where the run-off can do the most damage. Some road elements, however, can be found on cliff faces and steep bedrock from the ground, not from the air, if they included rock-cut steps, grooves, and toeholds and handholds. Identification of a road is best on a flat or nearly flat terrain, especially if the roads were well constructed. Flat surfaces are generally well suited for the preservation of prehistoric roads because erosion is kept to a minimum, although the extent to which the road was constructed won't be visible.

The road will most likely be visible if it is parallel to the local prevailing winds that scatter the dirt across the road, often exaggerating its features. However, in these areas, especially where the wind builds up a sand dune to one side, the original character of the road is lost.

Roads on sandy substrates, that portion of the earth lying within a few meters of the surface, whether unconsolidated sediments or bedrock, are often highly visible from the air and the ground. Only a trace of the road is visible here, however, rather than the actual surface.

Theoretically, roads should become less visible with age as a consequence of natural geographic deterioration. In the Chaco area, however, many highly visible prehistoric roads still exist, while historic roads are barely visible at best.

Another expectation is that the roads that were used the most would be the ones most visible today. Almost the opposite is true.

Roads in the most remote regions tend to be most visible. Visibility seems to have less to do with use and more to do with geographical processes. Roads closest to great houses are of course the most visible. That may seem like a contradiction except that the roads were more elaborately constructed the closer they were to architectural features.

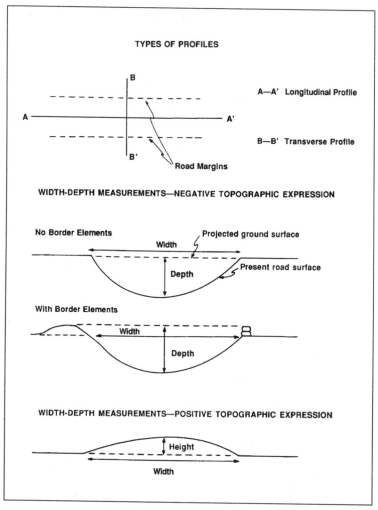

Schematic diagrams showing the types of road profiles, and methods of measurement of width, depth, and height of prehistoric roads. (Illustration courtesy BLM.)

Prehistoric roads can normally be differentiated on the basis of width, depth, border elements, and nearby structures. But to distinguish them from historic roads and geographic depressions, the roads have to be verified archaeologically. During Phase I of the BLM project, archaeologists discovered that they could follow a linear distribution of artifacts along the roads. These cigar-shaped shard scatters were used to date the road. As with the physical characteristics, there are relatively few instances where artifact density alone is sufficient to verify a road, nor should dating rely solely on the artifacts.

Several archaeological structures are almost always found near a road segment and help in determining the general presence of a road. These include a variety of Bonito-style structures, such as great houses, great kivas, herraduras, avanzadas, and zambullidas. Bonito-style great houses are usually considered to be a part of the road design and construction. Lesser features such as ramps or landings, toeholds and handholds, formal pecked or constructed stairways, and long grooves pecked into slickrock are also road signs for surveyors.

Ramps, landings, and stairways are road signs for surveyors. An example is a set of rock-cut steps (B4) and an eroded ramp (B5). (Photo by Gwinn Vivian.)

One of the more common means of exploring Anasazi roads has been to first locate the great houses and then trace the roads outward. There are instances in which a great house has no apparent road nearby, but this could be due to general erosion. Unfortunately, accurately projecting a road is limited by the great distances that separate the houses.

Road-Related Architecture

Great houses are the highest level of architectural sophistication on the roads and are often the nexus of several roads. This architectural form first took hold in the San Juan Basin around A.D. 900. By A.D. 1050, classic great houses were engineered and constructed in association with the formalization of the road system.

A peculiar characteristic of the outlying great houses is that they seem to be encircled by road-like swales. At Manuelito Ruin, for instance, a massive berm encircles the great house on the east and south sides and where artificial fill on the west side of the great house maintains a level surface around the ruin. At Kin Ya'a a broad, shallow swale, which seems to have been scooped out by hand, encircles the great house and is particularly visible along the northwest edge. At Haystack Ruin the side of a very low hill was removed, resulting in a broad swale around the northern and western margins of the great house. Similar features are present though more subtle at Kin Nizhoni, Standing Rock, and Lake Valley.

The Anasazi also modified the landscape at the community of Muddy Water. Although some of these excavations appear to have been quarries, most of the excavated rock would not have been suitable for building. "The purpose of these excavations remains obscure," according to the BLM report.

Great kivas, which became formal in the eleventh century and grew to twelve to twenty-five feet in diameter, are another road-associated feature. The relationship between the kiva and the great house varies. Most often the kiva is contained within a plaza or otherwise joined to the great house. At Padilla Well, Kin Ya'a, and Muddy Water, the kiva is set apart from the great house a

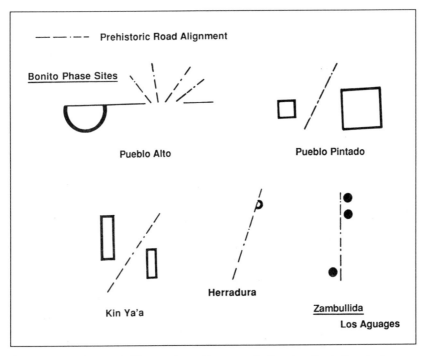

Plan view schematic illustration of types of direct articulation between road alignment and structural sites. (Illustration courtesy BLM.)

short distance and is connected to the house by a road. Roads run adjacent to the great kiva at Haystack, at Penasco Blanco on the West Road, Pueblo Pintado on the East Road, and at Kin Ya'a on the west fork of the South Road.

Another structure tied uniformly to the roads is the small, horseshoe or circular shaped herradura. Ranging from 3.5 meters to 12 meters in diameter, they were built at major breaks in the topography in areas where visibility in both directions along the road is clear. Fifteen of the twenty-five herraduras documented by Phase II of the BLM project were oriented in an easterly direction, although sometimes they open onto the road. Preference for the eastern orientation overrode opening onto the road, but to have done both was ideal.

Because of the location in topographic breaks, herraduras often mark the location of a roadway bearing change that is so subtle it

Herraduras often mark subtle angle changes in the bearing of the road, but the herradura (A) marks the convergence of the west fork (B) of the road leading from Casa del Rio to the Lake Valley ruin and a northwest fork (C) of the road leading to an unknown destination. Part of the road (D) was used in historical times. (Photo courtesy National Park Service.)

is only detectable with a compass. The Casa del Rio Herradura sits on the intersection of two roads, but this is rare.

The road surface near herraduras was often scooped out, resulting in a deep, bermed depression. An example of this is the Gasco Herradura where the road surface is deeply excavated into the bedrock and the spoils from the excavation were used in building the roads and the herradura itself. (Confirmation of an actual road at Gasco is inconclusive.) There is a tendency for the roadway near a herradura and otherwise deeply excavated segments to narrow, sometimes to six meters in width. (The standard width of the Chacoan roads is nine meters.)

Herraduras (literally "horseshoe") are the most predominant characteristic of the roads and were built in the late eleventh and early twelfth centuries (although those along the South Road may have been built in the tenth century), judging by the small amount of ceramics scattered nearby. These are C, D, or horse-

shoe-shaped enclosures with simple to compound coursed masonry walls up to one meter in height and up to seven meters in
diameter.

Herraduras are the most useful in locating a road, because they
behave like survey markers. Survey crews relied upon them heavily for extending known roads and verifying potential alignments
because they were always built in high areas near the roads, often

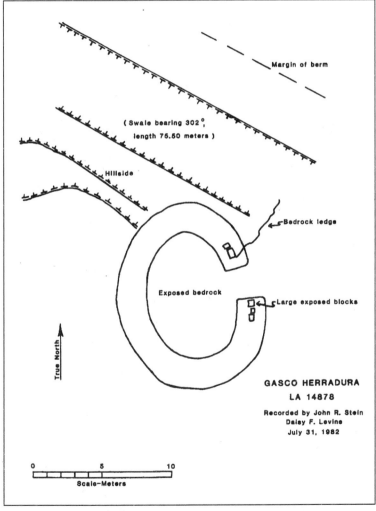

Gasco Herradura. (Illustration courtesy BLM.)

at the crests of major drainage divides, and because the surface of roads as they approached herraduras were always excavated and bermed. Confidence was developed as a result of both locating herraduras by following imaged ground-visible roadways and locating roads that are not easily ground visible by first finding the herradura. The Kin Klizhin to Kin Bineola Road is not conspicu-

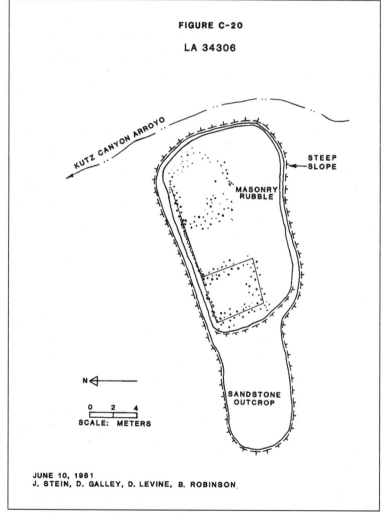

FIGURE C-20

LA 34306

KUTZ CANYON ARROYO

STEEP
SLOPE

MASONRY
RUBBLE

SANDSTONE
OUTCROP

N

0   2   4
SCALE: METERS

JUNE 10, 1981
J. STEIN, D. GALLEY, D. LEVINE, B. ROBINSON

Lower Kutz Canyon Overlook, an avanzada at the end of the North Road. (Illustration courtesy BLM.)

ous on the ground, for instance, but the Yellow Point Herradura was documented on a projected alignment, and the road was presumed real on that basis. Subsequent low-sun-angle aerial reconnaissance showed a clearly visible roadbed depression near the structure. Knowing this, the possibility of confusing herraduras with other Anasazi or Navajo structures was lessened.

The avanzada ("outpost"), a shrine-like structure found in high places near the road, may have been a variation of the herradura. Avanzadas, are squared or rectangular buildings that include one to four rooms made of simple coursed masonry or jacal, and are built on low buttes or badland pinnacles above the road. Avanzadas are not to be confused with one-room field houses found near farmland or with the residential three- to ten-room small houses, which are *U* or *L* shaped, and usually associated with a subterranean kiva. All but one of the seven discovered were on the North Road.

The zambullida is more sophisticated than a herradura, but less so than a great house. Described as "fancy herraduras," these circular or horseshoe-shaped structures were built on lofty overlooks and were connected to the roads. On the other hand, rectangular-shaped structures such as Kimbeto Point, Los Aguages, and Halfway House lacked the housed surface kiva that characterizes a great house and are therefore categorized as zambullidas. These structures may have been roofed and contained rows of rectangular rooms. Because of the lack of a kiva, the zambullida may have differed from the great house in function. Only one zambullida was found during the BLM Phase II survey project.

Archaeologists looked for the so-called constructed road by excavating down to the layer of compact earth on segments of the North Road, the Penasco Blanco to Ahshislepah Road, and the northern portion of the South Road. Berms often line these depressions in the relatively flat areas that resist erosion. In most cases the berms were mixed with rubble and earth. The Kin Ya'a West Fork Cut is an example of massive removal of earth. The segment near the Gasco Herradura had a rubble berm.

Roads were more extensively prepared near great kivas, great houses, and herraduras. In many areas, the roads were flanked by long mounds of dirt, called earthworks, such as at Holsinger's Great Kiva west of Kin Ya'a, Muddy Water, Haystack, Penasco Blanco, Lake Valley, and Standing Rock. Earthworks often contain trash and have been referred to as trash mounds or middens, but may have actually been deliberately built. Earthworks are usually much larger than trash mounds and lack the usual substances found in trash mounds with the exception of ceramics and a mixture of ground or pecked stone.

Until now, the earthworks have been unnoticed although their unnaturalness was commented on as early as the 1930s, especially in the case of one east of Casa Rinconada. Two parallel mounds actually retained by a wall run parallel to the front of Pueblo Bonito. Mounds like these are elements of Hohokam architecture between A.D. 500 and 1100, and of the Mississippian Culture at Cahokia between A.D. 900 and 1100.

The purpose of the earthworks is not known, nor are archaeologists certain of the source of material that went into constructing them. Earthworks have been a highly overlooked area of archaeology. Since Anasazi peers, such as the Hohokam and the Mound Builders, built great mounds near their architecture, the mounds around Bonito-phase great houses may need to be looked at more closely. It appears as though the earthworks are the tailings of the road or kiva construction, but that doesn't explain the ceramics on their surfaces. The earthworks may have been developed all at once or slowly over the years.

The Anasazi also built earth and rubble platforms, which incorporated landings, stairways, and ramps. Platforms and ramps helped the Anasazi enter the canyon. Llave de la Mano on the South Chaco Road, 5.4 kilometers north of Kin Ya'a, is a spectacular example of a platform that uses masonry steps and a landing to reach a herradura near the road. A less elaborate platform was built on the scarp below an unusual Bonito-style structure at Casa Papalote, but there is no road nearby.

Some causeways existed in the Chacoan road system, but they are not comparable to Maya causeways. Two of the few legitimate causeways were found near Penasco Blanco, where a low fill was placed to raise the roadbed in two low areas. One of these, an arroyo crossing, had masonry borders two feet high, twelve feet long, and six feet wide. They were filled with rock and soil and were probably no higher than several feet. Raised roadbeds were found on the roads to Kin Bineola and Pueblo Alto.

Road-related ramps were found at eleven sites. Usually at the foot of a stairway, they were built up with dirt, rock, or rubble fill and were held in place by a masonry wall and a natural cliff face. They were commonly built upon the rubble or talus slope, thus decreasing the amount of fill required.

Walls, curbs, berms, and mounds often bordered the roads near major sites and in topographically impeded areas such as cliff faces. Excellent examples of berms were found along the road to Pueblo Pintado for several hundred meters. Isolated piles of rocks of various sizes were built up along the road. They seem to have been used as survey markers or as a system of keeping the course straight. Cairns were also found along the roads. However, the cairns were probably built by the Navajo and indicate their possible later use of the roads.

The Anasazi Atlas that follows will describe the various road segments and tour the communities along the roads.

The Anasazi Atlas

Most researchers agree that the prehistoric Anasazi roads were at one time contiguous to Chaco Canyon and probably extend as far north as the San Juan Range in the Rocky Mountains and as far south as the Mogollon Mountains. Although less certain of the roads outside the Chacoan corridor, scientists believe the roads may have extended as far east as the turquoise mines in Santa Fe and as far west as the Little Colorado River valley, and maybe even as far as the San Francisco Peaks near Flagstaff.

The roadways are not accessible and are often difficult to see. The Four Corners region is a checkerboard of private, federal, or reservation lands and most of the roads are behind fences. The Kin Nizhoni road system, for instance, is in the heart of uranium mill tailings and ranch land among a myriad of indistinguishable mesas. El Rito and San Mateo are in a beautiful valley at the base of Mount Taylor on private and BLM land. A Sunday afternoon drive into most of these areas will not turn up a road or an Anasazi site without a guide. But there are some exceptions.

Roads and stairways are visible in the immediate Chaco Canyon area. One of the best and most accessible examples of a stairway/roadway configuration is on the north mesa above Kin Kletso on the way to Pueblo Alto. A well-marked path takes the hiker up a climbway via a tunnel between the canyon wall and a massive sandstone boulder. At the top, follow a marked path toward the Pueblo Bonito overlook and then turn left at the sign to Pueblo Alto. A cleared area on the east side of Pueblo Alto is part of a road. Steps cut into rock are part of the system as are curbed walls in the area. If you continue around the brim of the canyon beyond the Chetro Ketl overlook, you'll see the Jackson Stairs and cracks in the wall for other potential climbways. You'll need a back country hiking permit from the visitor's center in Chaco Canyon.

On Highway 57 heading into Chaco Canyon from the north you can see three clearly visible roads. Just after you enter the Chaco Canyon park and before you drive into the cliffs of the canyon itself, you will pass a park service gate on the left. In the distance you can see the ruins of New Alto on the horizon. In the space between, you can see a wide swath heading directly for the road right next to a curve in the park service road. It dips into Escavada Wash and is most likely the Great North Road. Two other roads crisscross in front of New Alto to the left. Parking on the road and walking into the area is not allowed. The service road is locked to the public.

Some roadside attractions are also visible from the modern road, if you know where to look. When a road isn't visible, it is sometimes gratifying to find the road-associated architecture by itself. On the side of the roads in the Chaco Canyon area, I have seen cairns that may be of Navajo rather than Anasazi origin. They may have been used as scarecrows to frighten coyotes, or as travel shrines for passersby who wanted to pray for luck, or perhaps as sites of rituals or "one night sings." There are two cairns together on a small hill south of Highway 57 (south of the canyon) near where the projected Southeast Road crosses over the highway a few miles west of the Seven Lakes Trading Post.

Another cairn sits on a hill on the south side of the road connecting 57 (north of the canyon) to 371 (the highway to Farmington). We got out of the car about a mile west of the cairn where you can look down on a series of buttes that make up the Pierre's Ruin complex on the North Road. A good pair of binoculars enabled us to see ruins on one of the buttes. Call the Bureau of

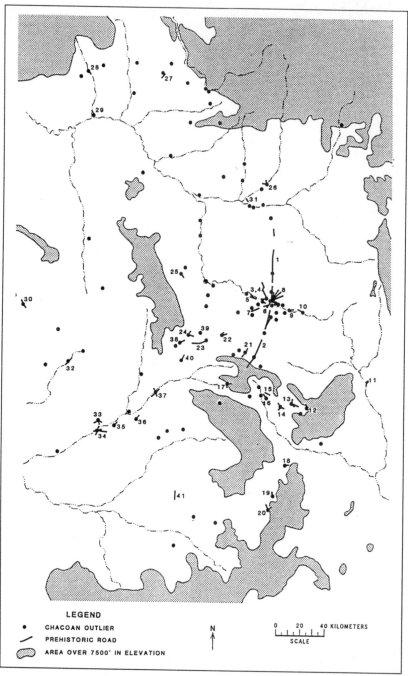

The Anasazi Atlas explores prehistoric segments and related ruins of the Greater San Juan Basin numbered in the map and the table at right. (Based on photo by John Roney, courtesy BLM.)

Lengths and Bearings of Chacoan Roads
(Ordered by Length)

Name	Length	Bearing*	Number
North Road	50.5	N 0 E to N 11 E	1
South Road	51.0	N 184 E to N 220 E	2
Coyote Canyon Road	11.5	N 266 E to N 251 E	23
Ahshislepah Road	9.5	N 324 E to N 390 E	3a
Poco	5.0	N 35 E to N 62 E	8a
Navajo Springs	5.0	N 73 E	34a
Muddy Water	4.5	N 199 E to N 228 E	21a
Pueblo Pintado	4.1	N 294 E	10
South Gap	4.0	N 225 E to N 245 E	6a
Greasy Hill	3.8	N 45 E	8a
Pueblo Alto	3.2	N 27 E	8c
Pueblo Alto	3.2	N 13 E	8d
Kin Nizhoni	3.0	N 104 E	13a
Muddy Water	2.5	N 20 E to N 35 E	21b
Red Willow	2.5	N 104 E	24a
Aztec	2.5	N 280 E	26a
Lake Valley	2.1	N 277 E to N 280 E	5a
Andrews	2.0	N 317 E	16
Kin Hocho'i	2.0	N 40 E to N 56 E	37a
Farmington	1.9	N 317 E	31
Aztec	1.3	N 334 E	26b
Haystack	1.2	N 330 E	14a
Guadalupe	1.0	N 346 E	11
Kin Nizhoni	1.0	N 342 E	13b
Chambers	1.0	N 220 E	33a
Navajo Springs	1.0	N 16 E	34b
Yellow Point	.8	N 70 E	7
San Mateo	.8	N 340 E	12
Coolidge	.8	N 96 E	17a
Red Willow	.7	N 73 E	24b
Haystack	.6	N 108 E	14b
West Road	.5	N 269 E	3b
South Gap	.5	N 235 E	6b
Kin Nizhoni	.5	N 145 E	13c
Gasco Herradura	.5	N 279 E	15
Standing Rock	.5	N 38 E	22a
Standing Rock	.5	N 72 E	22b
Chambers	.5	N 90 E	33b
Dittert	.4	N 310 E	20a
Haystack	.3	N 208 E	14c
Las Ventanas	.3	N 90 E	18
Dittert	.3	N 20 E	20b
Lowry	.3	N 214 E ±	27
Chambers	.3	N 163 E	33c
Kin Hocho'i	.3	N 246 E	37c
Lake Valley	.2	N 310 E	5b
Coolidge	.2	N 0 E	17b
Red Willow	.2	N 336 E	24c
Bluff	.2	N 344 E ±	29
Navajo Springs	.2	N 47 E	34c
Sanders	.2	N 50 E	35
Allentown	.2	N 40 E ±	36
Kin Hocho'i	.2	N 346 E	37d
Figueredo	.2	N 53 E	38
Padilla Well	.1	N 112 E	4
Chaco East	.1	N 80 E	9
Cottonwood Falls	.1	N 180 E ±	28
Skunk Springs	.1	N 121 E	25
Sunshine Springs	.1	N 72 E ±	32a
Sunshne Springs	.1	N 72 E ±	32b
Kin Hocho'i	.1	N 150 E	37b
Toh La Kai	.1	N 46 E	40
Cebolla Canyon	t	--	19
Dzil Nda Kai	t	--	39
Tse Chezi	?	--	30a
Tse Chezi	?	--	30b

*Most bearings were measured indirectly from 1:24000 scale topographic maps and are subject to some error. When an endpoint of a road, such as Bonito-style building, is apparent, the bearing away from the origin is given. When no such endpoint can be posited, the northerly bearing of the road segment is given.

Land Management in Farmington for directions to Pierre's. Since it is on BLM land, you can walk into it but you will be swallowed up by the monumental badland formations. BLM warns of rattlesnakes in the area.

Just south of Crown Point is Kin Ya'a, on National Park Service Land, which is visible to the east from Highway 371, the Vietnam Veteran's Memorial Highway. You'd better be watching carefully. The chimney, maybe about five miles away, disappears quickly behind the buttes closer to the road as you drive by.

Barring accessibility and visibility, we'll have to rely on descriptions provided by the surveyors and illustrators to make the roads come alive. Sometimes the details are sketchy and all that is known is that a road segment was documented at a certain site.

Although archaeologists project as many as seven major roads in the greater Chaco area, not all of them have been verified as contiguous roads. Keep in mind the various interpretations of the roads as ceremonial ways, trade routes, intersite expressways, or logging and quarrying roads. The North and South Roads are the

A rock escalator behind Kin Kletso in Chaco Canyon enabled traffic to scale the sheer cliff to the upper mesa. Follow trail markers to Pueblo Bonito for more road sites.

most studied and have the most features and so have been described here more thoroughly than the other road vestiges.

The numbers of each description in the atlas correspond with numbers on the map and the table. The map, the table, and the backbone of the descriptions were provided by John Roney of the Bureau of Land Management. The atlas is supplemented with descriptions of roadside architecture from the BLM reports, a report by the Public Service Company of New Mexico, entitled *Anasazi Communities of the San Juan Basin*, Volume 1 of the *National Park Service's Investigations at the Pueblo Alto Complex*, and interviews with other archaeologists.

Navajo legends, when available, are also included in the road site descriptions. Although the Navajo are not descendants of the Anasazi, they ultimately inherited their homeland. The Navajo Reservation, or *Dinetah* (among the Navajos), spans from the San Juan Basin west to the Grand Canyon. The Navajo say the ruins, or *kits'iil*, are what is left of the *Anaasázi Bighan*, or Home of the Ancient Enemy of the Fourth World. As such, the roads and ruins are part of the Fifth World landscape and should be preserved in the interest of maintaining beauty and harmony.

Interestingly, these sacred places are *bááhádzid*, literally meaning "for it there is fear and reverence," and are considered dangerous because of the supernatural powers still lingering in them. Traditional practitioners who specialize in one or another chantway dispose of ceremonial items in these places, which are otherwise taboo to those who do not know how to approach them.

Many of the Navajo place names and anecdotes for the Anasazi ruins used here were collected by Dennis Franstead for the National Park Service in 1979 and Frederick York for the Bureau of Land Management in 1982. York walked along a section of the North Road with a peyote "road man," or ceremonial practitioner, who lived in the vicinity. The man told him that a number of the roads were used by the Anasazi (translated as ancient aliens in this case) and the first Navajos. He said that the roads looked like trenches and that the Navajo moved along them carefully watching for Big Monster or *Ye'iitsoh*. He called the roads *atiin* and said they were used by the Navajo for long distance travel. The *kits'iil* and the *atiin* figure prominently in the origin legends of the Navajo and are preserved in their ceremonial songs, or chant-ways. York mentions that the statement contrasts to one made by another Navajo informant to Neil Judd: "They were not really roads, although they looked like them."

York included no translation for the word "*atiin*," but a passage from *Diné bahane': The Navajo Creation Story*, by Paul G. Zol-brod, about twin boys who had left their clan to divert the attention of *Ye'iitsoh*, and his band of Alien Monsters (*Naayéé*) suggests that *atiin* is a trail of special significance:

> When their mothers awoke, they saw that the twins had taken flight. They went outside to look for them and examined the ground for fresh tracks. But they found only four footprints for the two boys, and these pointed toward *Dzil ná'oodilii* the Travelers Circle Mountain. It seemed that they had taken *Atiin diyinii* the Holy Trail so that they could not be followed. But by taking such a path could easily arouse the anger of *Haashch'ééh dine'é* the Holy People.

The story, by the way, parallels portions of the Keresan Pueblo creation myth. *Dzil ná'oodili*, also translated as "Sacred Mountain of the Center," is presumed by York to be Chaco Canyon, but others say the reference may be to El Huerfano, north of Chaco Canyon.

Not all Navajos believe that ancient sites are shrines. Anasazi potsherds are used by some Navajo to temper their pottery. Stone metates and manos are carried away for grinding corn in the traditional way, and projectile points are kept as charms and curiosities.

1. The Great North Road

The Great North Road, so nicknamed after the Roman road, was described in Chapter Five in terms of the significance of its true north bearing and the lack of evidence proving its use as a trade route with the communities north of the San Juan Basin. The masonry circles and rectangular buildings look like hilltop shrines and roadside chapels, or perhaps military check points and turrets. From a strictly utilitarian perspective, the roads and the structures were overbuilt and underused.

The North Road was the focus of most early projects. The initial reconnaissance by BLM of the North Road, as John Stein pointed out in the 1983 BLM report, began on the southern margin of Kutz Canyon at the Angel Peak Overlook, where restrooms had been constructed roughly on the centerline of the road. "This irony was offset by convenience, for the structures provided a means of sighting the road alignment from the canyon bottom."

The North Road leaves Pueblo Alto on a bearing of 15° east of north, but within four kilometers it assumes a bearing that varies little from true north. The North Road can be traced for more than fifty kilometers, past Kin Indian Ruin, the Pierre's Ruin community, and Halfway House to the traces of an earth and juniper stairway that descends into Kutz Canyon. In some areas there is no trace of a road for as many as twelve and a half kilometers. In other areas, the North Road exhibits double, or even quadruple parallel road segments. The ultimate destination of the road is unknown although the prevailing thinking is that the road continued down Kutz Canyon to Salmon Ruin. Some believe it went on to Aztec Ruin, which postdates the road, while others believe that if the road continued beyond Kutz Canyon, it would have stuck to the bearing of true north.

Interesting archaeological features along the road, listed here in kilometers from Pueblo Alto, include: Kin Indian Ruin, great house, 5.1; Pierre's Ruin, 18.9; Burned Jacal Herradura, 30.1; Halfway House (zambullida), 35.3; Gallegos Crossing Avanzada, 37.9; Angel Peak Overlook Group (avanzada), 46.4.

A spur from the North Road ends in a formal ramp to the summit of the Acropolis, the flat-topped mesita which supports much of Pierre's complex, between a gate formed by Units A and C. Unit C opens to the west on the southwest corner of the structure. The structure deviates from a true square to form a doorway or gate two meters in width. Unit A, or Kin Bi Dagha Chii, is oriented to the north, which is unusual for a structure of this kind. The third housed kiva on Unit A is presumed from a pile of rubble;

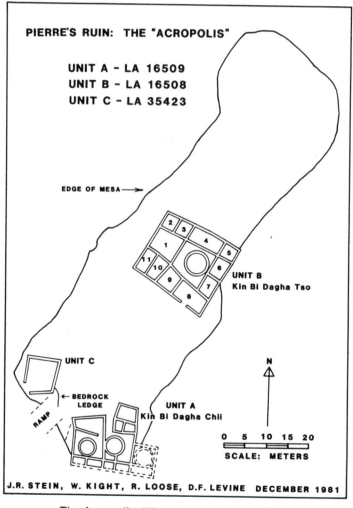

PIERRE'S RUIN: THE "ACROPOLIS"

UNIT A - LA 16509
UNIT B - LA 16508
UNIT C - LA 35423

EDGE OF MESA →

UNIT B
Kin Bi Dagha Tso

UNIT C

← BEDROCK LEDGE
RAMP
UNIT A
Kin Bi Dagha Chii

N

0   5   10   15   20
SCALE: METERS

J.R. STEIN, W. KIGHT, R. LOOSE, D.F. LEVINE   DECEMBER 1981

The Acropolis. (Illustration courtesy BLM.)

that the structure collapsed is understandable considering it was built on a downhill slope. Units C, A, and all but Room 1 at Unit B, Kin Bi Dagha Tso, were single story, but had high ceilings.

The Acropolis may have also been accessible from the northern end of the mesita, as well as via a possible route which ran diagonally from near El Faro and intersects the ramp approximately midway up the slope to a small structure. El Faro is a room-block at the bottom of a pinnacle supporting a hearth and

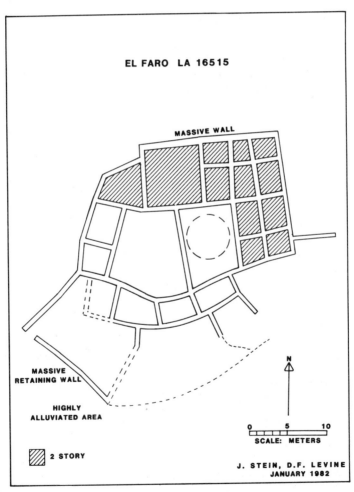

El Faro. (Illustration courtesy BLM.)

a now-collapsed kiva or platform. The alignment of swales and material scatters outline a possible mall entering or abutting El Faro from the south. Whether the road swings to the east or west (or both) of the El Faro pinnacle is not now known. The road may have followed a fingerlike ridge radiating to the west of El Faro, but for the North Road to have taken this route would have meant deviation from the true north bearing. It is more likely that the road passed or entered El Faro and continued up the narrow valley to the east of the pinnacle.

The Pierre's Ruin complex, 18.9 kilometers from Pueblo Alto, is the only structure along the North Road that may have been occupied. The complex at Pierre's Ruin does not conform to the way in which the Eastern Anasazi lived. Although units within the ruin group may have been residential, this has not been confirmed. The lack of a great kiva suggests that the population was too small to warrant one, or that no one lived there at all.

Pierre's Ruin was built about A.D. 1080 or later—at least fifty years after the road was formalized. This date marks the period when Chacoans may have shifted their interests to the north, or even moved north during that time, as evidenced by their inclination to stylize their pottery by the standards of the Anasazi living beyond the San Juan River. At this time, Salmon Ruin was built and another drought cycle had just begun.

Incidentally, Salmon Ruin is known to the Navajo as *Kin Dootl'izh*, or Blue House, and appears in Enemy Way, Blessing Way, Water Way, and Beauty Way ceremonies. The same name applies to the site of Wijiji in Chaco Canyon, among others.

The site for Pierre's Ruin was probably selected for the view. It is situated on the southern margin of the break from the elevated Chaco Slope to the south and the mesa and badland headlands of the Danain and Ahshislepah Washes to the north. A panoramic view of the basin north of Chaco can be seen from the Pierre's Ruin area, including the south rim of Chaco Canyon and the Lobo Mesa skyline to the south and Gallegos-Chaco divide to the north.

Fires on top of the Acropolis and El Faro could no doubt have been seen from the crest of the divide. From the south, Pierre's

Ruin could have easily been seen from Windes's Shrine above Marcia's Rincon on the south rim of Chaco Canyon and Pueblo Alto on the north. Every pinnacle, mesa top, and steep ridge slope within one kilometer of the Acropolis supported at least one small structure, twenty-seven in all.

The Navajo call Pierre's Ruin *Kl'eesh Shichíí,* or Flint Striking Stones. The Navajo say that their ancestors used the complex as a hideout when their people were being rounded up and taken to Fort Sumner in the 1860s. One old man remembered being told

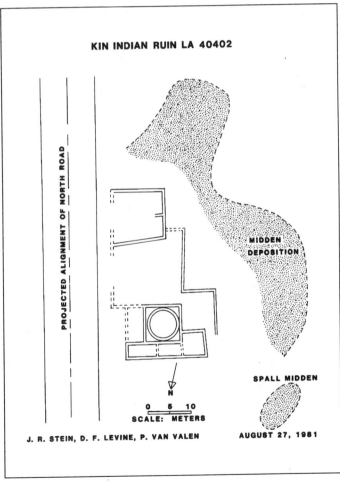

Kin Indian Ruin. (Illustration courtesy BLM.)

that a child was born there during the crisis. The sacred significance of the site, if any, has not been verified, but the name implies it is a place where *ts'iindii*, or ghosts, gather. Flint points are used to frighten them away.

Other interesting features along the North Road include Kin Indian Ruin, Burned Jacal, Halfway House, and the overlooks near Twin Angel Peak.

Kin Indian Ruin, 5.1 kilometers from Pueblo Alto, is the first archaeological feature encountered on the road as it leaves Pueblo

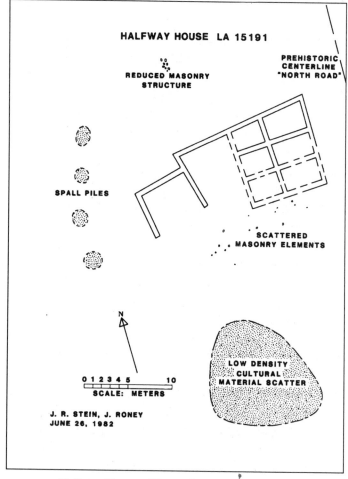

Halfway House. (Illustration courtesy BLM.)

Alto. It was built around A.D. 1000 on a crest of the ridge forming the northern margin of the Escavada Valley, just as Pueblo Alto was built on the southern margin. Smaller than Pierre's Ruin, its location may have been strategic as an outpost. The construction consisted of a Bonito-style room-block of four to six single story terraced rooms, flanking an elevated housed kiva and two plazitas. The road, quite elaborate at this point, passed to the east. The contemporary road from Nageezi to Chaco Canyon passes one hundred meters east of the ruin, which forms a conspicuous landmark for the informed passerby.

Archaeologist Anne Morris found a slab there in 1947 engraved with the name Col. H. F. Yumer and a pair of crossed sabers with a *C* above and an *L* below. Archaeologists considered naming the ruin after Yumer, but found no Yumer on the U.S. Army rosters.

Burned Jacal was built on an elevated landform known as Gallegos Divide on the lip of the North Road, within view of Angel Peak to the north and Pierre's Ruin to the south. The site consists of two concentrations of burned adobe representing remains of jacal structures destroyed by fire. A large amount of ceramics was found near the site. The use of the jacal—upright sticks covered and chinked with mud and clay—is noteworthy since this mode of construction occurred at few of the sites known to be of the late Chaco sequence.

Halfway House, a zambullida, is situated on the southern margin of a prominent ridge west of and overlooking an unnamed lateral to Gallegos Wash. The structure, which may have been burned, is elevated in a landscape characterized by rolling sage plano and exposed badland formations. Huerfano Mountain, the La Plata Mountains, and Angel Peak are visible to the north. Halfway House was built in the Bonito style of architecture but lacks an enclosed kiva. Six contiguous masonry rooms and two small enclosures on a single story are contained within a building measuring only 10 by 22 meters. The structure was oriented to the south, and the North Road parallels the building's east wall. It was probably not a great house, and because of its proximity and its elevation, it probably served the roads in some function.

The Navajo who live around Halfway House remember the road near it as being much deeper than it is now. A Navajo woman who owned the land said her grandparents told her that the road went to a rock quarry between the site and *Dzil Ná'ood-ili*, Sacred Mountain of the Center, still used by the Navajo. (Franstead believed Dzil Na'oodili was Chaco Canyon.) She said that the material for the ruin may have come from the quarry. The old people said that there was a road north of the ruin, but none to the south, curiously.

On three separate summits alongside the North Road leading in succession into Kutz Canyon are archaeological overlooks in an area called *Tsélgiizh*, or White Rock Gap. This area is the starting point for the origin legend of the Wind Way. From north to south, these overlooks are the Lower Kutz Canyon Overlook, the Upper Twin Angels Overlook, and a third overlook.

If traveling from the south, one would encounter the first over-look, as yet unnamed. The structural remains are situated atop a low dune, elevated somewhat above the surrounding sage flats. The site is approximately one hundred meters from the rim of Kutz Canyon and consists of reduced remains of scattered sand-stone masonry.

Slightly to the north and west of this overlook is the Upper Twin Angels Overlook at the top of a steep-walled badland pinna-cle standing several hundred feet above the floor of Kutz Canyon. The pinnacle stands near the canyon rim and flanks the North Road to the east where it drops into the canyon below. The spec-tacular nature of the setting is illustrated by the presence of Kutz Canyon Overlook at this location. Access to the top of the pinna-cle is precarious. Erosion prevented archaeologists from defining the exact dimensions of the avanzada, but there are the remains of a low masonry wall which conforms to the natural contour of the pinnacle. There is also the possibility that a 5 x 6 meter plat-form was built here. The structure hovers 150 meters from where the North Road drops into Kutz Canyon wash, a dramatic descent.

Below the Upper Twin Angels Overlook, and further north is the Lower Kutz Canyon Overlook on top of another isolated butte twenty-five meters above the Kutz Canyon floor. The upper over-look is visible from here and this is presumably where the North Road enters the canyon. Visibility is otherwise restricted. The re-mains of two noncontiguous masonry rooms connected by a low wall were found here. The easternmost area of the rooms may have been circular although, again, erosion makes it difficult to tell. The road angles down the canyon toward Kutz Canyon Ruin.

2. The South Road

South and west of Chaco Canyon, the landscape changes markedly from the high sage-covered plano and the expanses of badland of the Chaco Slope to a seemingly endless panorama of hills, slopes, and buttes rimming broad shallow valleys. Grass, rather than sage, predominates, increasing the chances of seeing a road from the ground. This southern area was occupied in late Basketmaker times in limited spots along the margins of drainages. The dark Menefee sandstone slabs used in the fine ma-sonry of Bonito-style construction are abundant. John Stein writes in the 1983 BLM report:

> The broken character of the southern terrain provides for a surreal and spectacular setting for the roads. Here the Anasazi monuments are literally swallowed up by the Basin floor, their presence masked by countless outcrops, pinnacles, rincons, and shadows which mimic the dark mass ruins. So effective is this natural camouflage that a structure of massive proportions only a few meters distant might easily go unnoticed.

The South Road passes near four great houses and seems to terminate near Hosta Butte, the most prominent feature in the area. As the North Road ends at the sipapu of Kutz Canyon, the South Road ends at the base of the shrine-crowned Hosta Butte. Several hearths were found along the South Road, unlike the North Road, but dating the fire pits is nearly impossible.

The South Road was surveyed by both phases of the BLM Pro-ject. It is believed by most archaeologists that South Road was the major formalized access to Chaco Canyon from the southern part of the San Juan Basin. "Ultimately, the South Road system links

Chaco Canyon with the Lobo Mesa–Dutton Plateau province, the western Red Mesa Valley, Zuñi, and possibly locations even further south," Stein wrote. "The outer limits of the South Road are poorly defined now but are expected to exceed 160 kilometers from Pueblo Bonito." The BLM report also states that many of the archaeological features near the road were built prior to A.D. 1000 See Chapter Four for information and implications of early dates in the southern periphery.

The South Road has not been legitimately connected to Chaco Canyon. In fact, trying to reconstruct the roads and fit them into the idea of an expressway from a few road scraps is frustrating. The South Road forks at Casa Patricio. The main alignment projects into South Gap and the spur projects to Tsin Kletzin on the south mesa of Chaco Canyon, which is the counterpart of Pueblo Alto on the north mesa.

John Roney investigated the northernmost lengths of South Road

The South Road does not legitimately connect to Chaco Canyon. Instead a spur is first noticeable ten kilometers to the south in the Upper Kin Klizhin area. Another fork projects into the South Gap area of Chaco Canyon. The South Gap (A) and the Upper Kin Klizhin (B) forks join near Casa Patricio (D). The main alignment of the South Road (C) continues south toward Bee Burrow. Historic corral is at E. The view is toward the north in this photograph. (Courtesy BLM.)

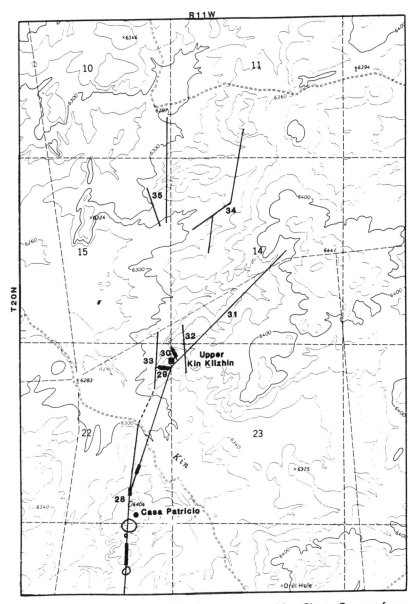

Map of the closest verified road segments approaching Chaco Canyon from the south. Thin lines are photoimaged alignments, and heavy lines are ground visible roads. Scale: 1.5 inches equals about 20 miles. (Courtesy BLM.)

and found it may not have been formally constructed, although its route is marked by linear shard scatters.

The spur does not become visible until it passes within two hundred meters west of the tower kiva at Upper Kin Klizhin, nine kilometers to the south of Tsin Kletzin. The South Road itself becomes visible as it jumps a mesa to the south near a large structural site and great kiva known as Casa Patricio, entering the area through a narrow break in the caprock now blocked by an historic corral. The road is again visible three hundred meters further south, and is characterized by alternating swales and shard scatters.

At La Mesita de la Junta, a lofty shrine on a prominent sandstone pinnacle, the bearing of the road changes to align with Kin Ya'a and Satan Pass. It was thought that Rincon Road, which passed through Marcia's Rincon in Fajada Gap, intersected with the South Road at Upper Kin Klizhin and again at Casa Patricio. The road, also known at the Latrine Road because it passed near the old Civilian Conservation Corps latrine camp, was checked by a remote sensing survey in 1973, and later by aircraft, but the results were inconclusive.

The road can then be traced with some gaps for an additional thirty-nine kilometers through Bee Burrow and Kin Ya'a and onto the Dutton Plateau where it ends about five kilometers short of Hosta Butte, a major topographic feature. Bearings along its documented portions vary from four degrees east of north to forty degrees east of north.

Upper Kin Klizhin (A.D. 1000-1050) is situated to view the Kin Klizhin Valley. The great house is a matrix of rectangular rooms constructed to terrace up to and support a tower kiva. In all, the structure had twelve single-story rooms and eight possible double-story rooms, plus a courtyard kiva, a plaza area, and a tower kiva. Bee Burrows (A.D. 1050 to 1200) is different from other great houses because the South Road, although it passes nearby, was not elaborately constructed as it approached the great house. Perhaps, in this case, the building was added onto an existing road. Bee Burrow may have been two stories high with at least eleven ground-floor rooms and two blocked-in kivas. A settlement existed

Looking south-southwest, the South Road (B) has just entered the area from the Casa Patricio area and passes La Mesita (A), the only avanzada not associated with the North Road. It changes directions at the topo- graphical break (C). The new bearing (D) shifts again slightly at Credibility Gap Herradura (E) on a ridge crest. Erosion is noted at F. (Courtesy BLM.)

some one and a half to three miles east by northeast of the Bee
Burrow. It was built by Pueblo II (A.D. 950 to 1050) at the latest.

Casa Patricio, a great kiva probably used between A.D. 850 and
950, fell into disuse before the road was built. The great kiva still
maintained some importance, however, for the road seems to
serve it. Three distinct swales exist in the Casa Patricio area,
which contains the great kiva and attendant rooms and middens.
One swale cuts thirty meters west of the kiva and the other two
shallow paths or roads pass directly beneath the kiva to the east.

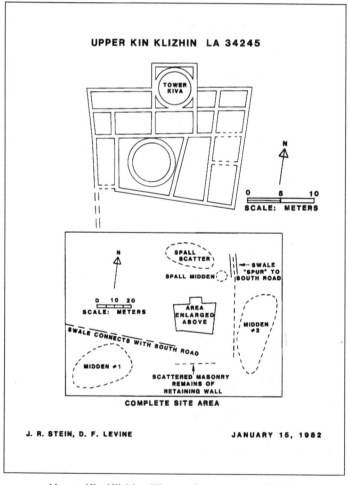

Upper Kin Klizhin. (Illustration courtesy BLM.)

Turn of the century corrals exist in the area as well as a hogan, pens, and shelters. At Provenience #2 in the illustration is a badly eroded petroglyph carved in a handwriting now barely legible: ". . . dad Fboriera (?) El Rito, NM . . . 1901." The kiva (A.D. 850-1000) is partially underground with three key-shaped alcoves. One is backed by a towering mound or platform, and a retaining wall forms an enclosure open to the south. Upright slabs within the enclosure remain of a slab-based jacal curtain wall and several slab-lined hearth boxes where food may have been prepared.

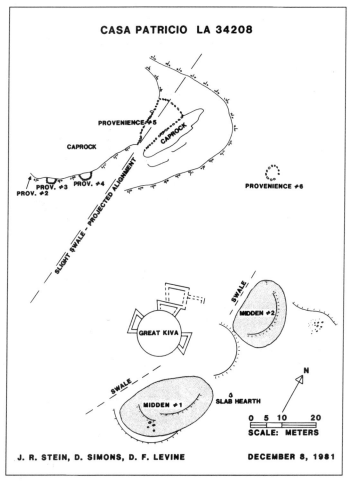

Casa Patricio. (Illustration courtesy BLM.)

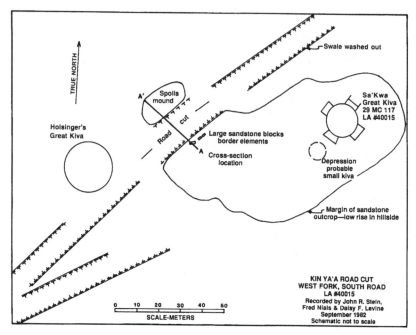

Kin Ya'a Road Cut. (Illustration courtesy BLM.)

The South Road forks at the Kin Ya'a complex built in open terrain. The West Fork, or Kin Ya'a Bypass, swings away from the South Road and connects with two isolated great kivas on a hillside 350 meters from the Kin Ya'a great house. A low sandstone outcrop was removed in order to join the road with the southern margin of Holsinger's Great Kiva. The other great kiva, Sa'Kwa, is forty meters to the south of the alignment on an elevated natural feature. The road at Holsinger's Kiva is 1.5 meters deep and 15 meters wide. The spoils from the excavation, including large blocks of sandstone used as a border, were piled in a mound north of the road.

Kin Ya'a itself contained twenty-six ground-floor rooms, three subsurface kivas, nine second-story rooms, a third story, and a tower kiva four stories high, perhaps to represent the four underworlds, as suggested by anthropologist J. Walter Fewkes in 1917. The terraced great house was oriented toward the winter sun. The inventory shows 104 sites within four square miles of Kin Ya'a.

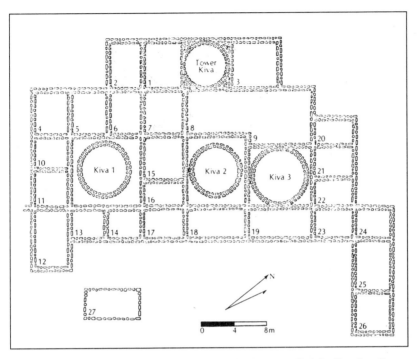

Kin Ya'a Ruin. (From Marshall, et al., 1979, courtesy Public Service Company of New Mexico.)

These range from shard scatters and hearths to large fifty-room pueblos with multiple kivas. The density is highest around Kin Ya'a on the western slopes. Most of the sites span between A.D. 950 and 1100 with traces of earlier periods. Michael Marshall said that it is possible the great kiva served a religious function prior to the construction of Kin Ya'a itself.

Kii (or *Kin*) *Ya'á* is translated as Standing House or Towering House. *Kin Yaaa'á* is the house of Rainboy's parents in the Hail Way origin legend. Tall House is noted in the Excess Way legend. The place is considered the home of the *Kiiya'ánii*, one of the four original clans in most versions of the Navajo origin legend, particularly the Blessing Way, the most central of chantways.

The road between Upper Kin Klizhin and Kin Ya'a is littered with shrines, herraduras, and small house structures as well as Basketmaker III villages. The first BLM survey of the South Road found twenty-nine prehistoric components alone. After La Mesita de la Junta comes Credibility Gap Herradura (A.D. 1000 to 1050), Nose Rock Herradura (A.D. 870 to 1175), and Seven Lakes Herradura (A.D. 800 to 1250). Ko'Pavi Herradura (A.D. 850 to 1130) and Crownpoint Herradura (A.D. 850 to 1250) lie between Hosta Butte and Kin Ya'a, both on formalized road segments. South Road from Crownpoint to Kin Ya'a turns into a formal stairway, a set of possible toeholds and handholds, and a badly eroded

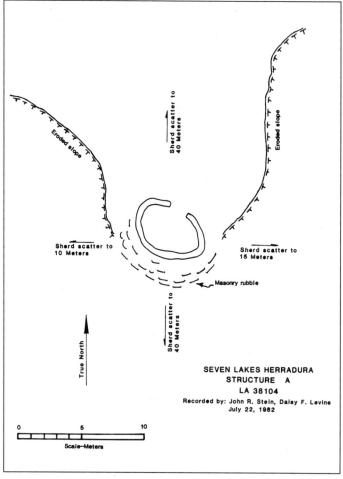

Note the shard scatters to the four directions in the sketch of Seven Lakes Herradura. (Courtesy BLM.)

groove in sandstone slickrock. The stairway provides access from a drainage to the slickrock.

Probably the most splendid roadside attraction found to date is the Llave de la Mano Platform tied to the ceremonial aspects of Kin Ya'a, but situated near So'tosh, a Basketmaker III/Pueblo I settlement which may have been built in A.D. 450, "300 to 400 years prior to the construction of the South Road," states the BLM report. The road is only verifiable in the vicinity of Llave de la Mano, and was elaborately constructed in this area.

The Llave de La Mano Platform is a massive earth and rubble construction measuring thirteen meters north-south by thirty meters east-west and standing four meters high. The structure was built against a sheer cliff face and functioned as a ramp to allow access to a natural shelf formed in the cliff face four meters above the ramp, and twenty by thirty meters wide. Steep cliff walls surround the embayment on three sides. A stairway cuts the man-

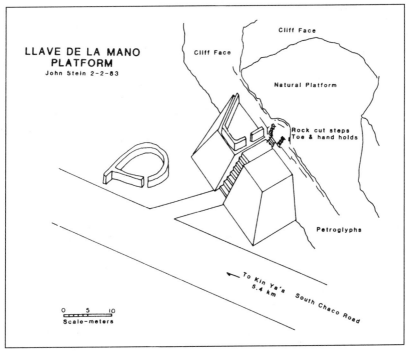

LLAVE DE LA MANO PLATFORM
John Stein 2-2-83

Cliff Face

Cliff Face

Natural Platform

Rock cut steps
Toe & hand holds

Petroglyphs

To Kin Ya'a
5.4 km
South Chaco Road

0   5   10
Scale-meters

Llave de la Mano Platform Reconstruction. (Illustration courtesy BLM.)

made platform while two toe-and-hand-hold staircases were cut into the shelf. Flanking the masonry steps of the ramp are two lesser platforms about eight by eight meters in size. An herradura was constructed on one of these platforms and another herradura flanks the South Road alignment ten meters to the south. ·

The alignment of the ramp and platform makes it look as though they were meant to accommodate the road, but the road does not proceed along the mesa top. Instead the road is a "cere-

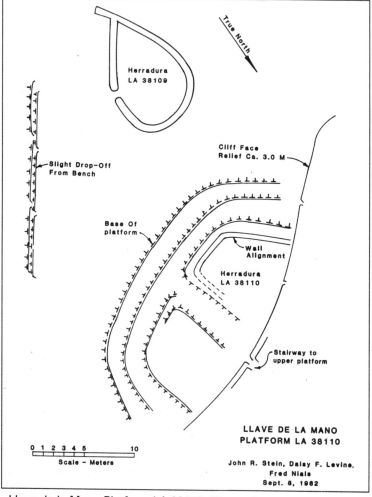

Llave de la Mano Platform LA 38110. (Illustration courtesy BLM.)

monial avenue" culminating at the top of the platform which commands a striking view of Satan Pass and Kin Ya'a.

3. Penasco Blanco Roads

Penasco Blanco, a major great house built at the west end of the Chaco Canyon, was associated with two roads: the Ahshislepah Road and the West Road. The Ahshislepah Road projects from the base of the wall of the Chaco Canyon 347 degrees from Penasco Blanco. Here the road makes a vertical ascent of 240 feet over sheer cliffs and narrow talus-strewn benches. As the road approaches the lip of the mesa, a series of seven rock-cut and masonry stairways eases traffic to the mesa top. From the margin of the mesa the roadway cuts a gentle arc through the relatively flat mesa top at a general bearing of 330 degrees. The road then drops into Arroyo de los Aguages, a minor lateral of the Ahshislepah Wash, at a distance of 5.2 kilometers from the mesa edge.

As the road drops off the mesa cap, the remains of a Bonito-

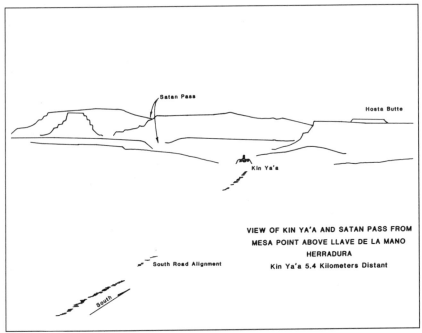

VIEW OF KIN YA'A AND SATAN PASS FROM
MESA POINT ABOVE LLAVE DE LA MANO
HERRADURA
Kin Ya'a 5.4 Kilometers Distant

The end of the South Road. (Illustration courtesy BLM.)

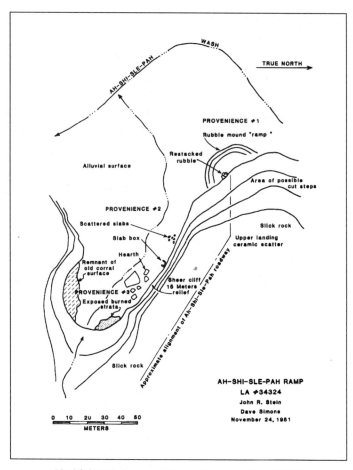

Ahshislepah Ramp. (Illustration courtesy BLM.)

style zambullida called Los Aguages becomes immediately visible. Los Aguages (A.D. 1000 to 1125) gleans its name from the bedrock water tanks in the bottom of the wash. The main ruins are located near the largest of these tanks, called El Cenote, which was found to contain water even following considerable dry periods. A reservoir could have been created downstream from the well and the holding capacity of the upper tanks was large. A substantial amount of surface water is available in the tanks at almost any time of the year and must have provided a steady supply of domestic water within easy reach of Penasco Blanco.

This road contained some ancient artifacts. A plano-convex scraper, characteristic of the Jay Phase of the Archaic period (dating as early as B.P. 8000) was found in the sandy bottom of the Ahshislepah Wash. Two projectile points, one a serrated point of white chert and the other made out of basalt, from the En Medio Phase (B.P. 3000 to 1600) of the Archaic Period, were also discovered. The tools that made these items were not found. In fact, no formal tools were found and little evidence of camping, tool manufacturing, or processing was found.

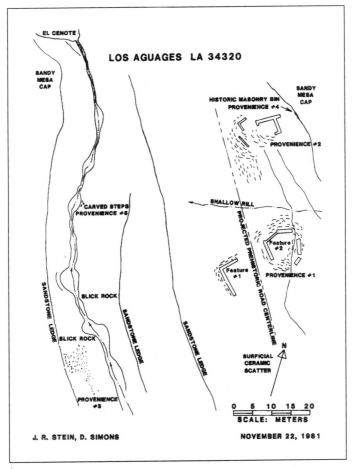

Los Aguages. The features and bins are remnants of a prehistoric reservoir. (Illustration courtesy BLM.)

A glyph from early Basketmaker times of "broad shouldered men" were discovered on the rear wall of a rock shelter. A trace of ceramics dating from A.D. 930 to 1098 was found near the Los Aguages tanks, but the greater mass of the ceramics found in this corridor dates to the early twelfth century.

From Los Aguages the road continues along the bearing of approximately two hundred degrees following the slickrock bench for nearly one kilometer, then again crosses the sandy mesa cap for another kilometer to a point on the eastern margin of Ahshislepah Canyon. Here the road turns sharply to the west, following the natural contour of the slickrock, and drops sixty feet down a series of cut-rock steps onto a masonry mound, which was probably a ramp of fire-reddened sandstone. Here the road ends, 6.3 kilometers from Penasco Blanco.

The Solstice Project believes that at the northern end of this road is a shrine-like site on the margin of Black Lake. If projected beyond Black Lake, this road would enter a vast area in which intensive surveying has found no likely destinations. Its last documented bearing is N 324 E.

West Road is a five hundred-meter-long segment which lies just to the south of Penasco Blanco and which must have accommodated one of the great kivas at this site. To the east a road segment continues into Chaco Canyon, where it becomes part of an elaborate intracanyon system. Its bearing as it enters Chaco Canyon is approximately N 89 E.

4. Padilla Valley Road

A road segment is visible immediately south of the Padilla Well Great Kiva for 150 meters. It links the kiva to its associated Bonito-style building along an axis bearing N 112 E. Beyond the great kiva, the projected road enters rougher terrain and no trace of a road has been found even in aerial photographs.

5. Lake Valley Road

Three road segments have been found on mesa tops in an area of dissected badlands, pinnacles, and buttes just west of Chaco

Canyon. The longest of these segments is five hundred meters and bears N 100 E. A second segment, two hundred meters long, generally parallels the first, 1.4 kilometers farther west. These road segments could conceivably link the Lake Valley outlier to Chaco Canyon. A third segment, about five hundred meters long, intersects with the first two on a bearing of N 130 E, but appears to go nowhere. An herradura was built at this intersection.

The Lake Valley outlier comprises several single-story, kivaless houses and middens. Although the number of rooms is small, the masonry is massive and the rooms are large. Marshall said the

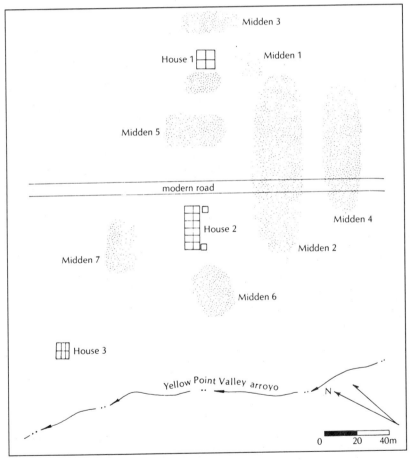

Lake Valley (From Marshall, et al., 1979, courtesy PNM.)

archaeological record is contradicted by the Navajo name for the site: *Kin Laní*, or Many Houses. On the other hand, Franstead said that the sites are numerous, sometimes no more than fire pits and potsherds. These sites are considered by the locals as the place associated with Kin Bineola and where the Anasazi made their pottery.

This road in the past has been referred to as the Casa del Rio to Lake Valley Road. Margaret Senter Obenauf noted that, in aerial photographs, this road is first visible a few hundred feet west of Casa del Rio and is distinct for about a mile, after which visibility diminishes for about a mile and the road becomes a series of discontinuous segments. Two branches or forks are evident near Casa del Rio, and perhaps this road was once part of a system linking the Skunk Springs/Newcomb area with Chaco Canyon.

Casa del Rio is an extremely large, *L*-shaped kivaless house with three large middens and an earthen bank reservoir. The West Road passes near the village on a steep mesa. Although Casa del Rio has no Navajo name that we know of, it was built near where Kin Klihzin Wash meets Chaco Wash, an area referred to as *T'iis eejin ch'inílíní*, or cottonwoods growing in a line flowing out.

6. South Gap Road

South Gap Road is a four-kilometer segment that leaves Chaco Canyon at South Gap, along the flanks of the West Mesa, and is eventually lost just beyond the southern tip of West Mesa. If projected seven to ten kilometers, this alignment could lead to either Kin Klizhin or the Yellow Point Road (see Road Description Seven). South Gap Road leaves the canyon on a bearing of N 25 E and its last known orientation is N 65 E. Another half-kilometer segment joins the main road at a bearing of N 55 E. No plausible destination for this road segment has been suggested, according to Roney.

Obenauf says that the complex of roads heading west from South Gap toward Kin Bineola and Kin Klizhin were visible in photographs of the vicinity of the gap but are generally less visible near the two great houses.

7. Yellow Point Road

Most have assumed that this 850-meter-long road segment connects Kin Klizhin and Kin Bineola on the west side of Chaco Canyon. The projected alignment of this road actually passes one and a half kilometers south of Kin Klizhin and three-quarters of a kilometer south of Kin Bineola. According to Roney the road segment has no destination at either end, but is associated with the Yellow Point Herradura.

In 1901, S.J. Holsinger described Kin Klizhin thusly, "Its characteristics are unity of design, uniform masonry, and large rooms with high ceilings. Though not large, this ruin was built on generous principles, with no niggard economy of space. . . ."

Kin Klizhin is a terraced house built in such a manner that the rooms provide a stepped buttress for the height of the tower kiva. The structure contained eight ground-floor rooms, six second-story rooms, two housed surface kivas, and a three-story tower kiva. An irrigation system consisting of an earth and masonry dam and irrigation canal was built two hundred meters northwest of Kin Klizhin. It was built during Pueblo III times, and the Navajo renovated the dam and were using it to irrigate a nearby field as late as 1979.

The Navajo call this house *Kin Lizhin*, meaning Black House, but it has also been referred to in the plural as *Kin Daalizhini* which shows up in the legend of Hail Way. This is an alternate name for Chetro Ketl and is the name of at least two other places.

"Striking in its singleness of design," as Holsinger said of the structure, Kin Bineola is a massive E-shaped house with 105 ground-floor rooms, fifty-eight second-floor rooms, thirty-four third-floor rooms, three hallway areas, eight single-story enclosed kivas, and two tower kivas surrounded by small houses, shrines, irrigation works, and roadways. Marshall documented several depressions, swales, and other linearities which could either be canals and dams or roadways and malls. Avenida Kin Bineola in particular was first described as a canal, but it may have actually been an elaborate ceremonial way for processions in connection with associated shrines or other features of sacred geography, as

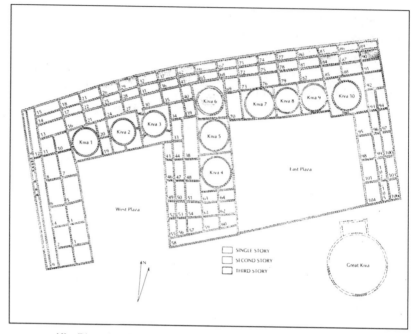

Kin Bineola. (From Marshall, et al., 1979, courtesy PNM.)

was suggested by Thomas Lyons (et al.) in 1972. David Bardé called the associated crescent-shaped mound, "The Great Wall of Chaco Canyon." The PNM team, led by Marshall, said the "canals" may be roadway segments, but this has not been verified.

Local Navajo call this house *Kin Bií Naayolí*, or House in which the Wind Whirls. A variation of this is *Kin Bil Dahnáyolí*, or House with Fabric in the Wind. This place is mentioned in the Excess Way legend. Another name for the house is *Kin Jo'leehí*, or Roping House, which is the name of an unidentified cliff dwelling near Navajo Dam. A rope was required to reach that ruin which implies that Kin Bineola may have also had some fairly inaccessible sections.

8. Pueblo Alto Vicinity

Pueblo Alto is the terminus for a complex of roads linking to the central canyon area and others heading in northeasterly direction.

In the central canyon area, road segments (designated RS)

merge with at least two (RS 33 and RS 40 on the NPS Pueblo Alto road system map; see page 47) or more major routes. Two roads extend north-south past the East and West Wings of the site. The western road (RS 33) runs 270 meters north past the Rabbit Ruin, and across the Escavada Wash to link with the Great North Road (see Road Description One at beginning of atlas). To the south, RS 33 crosses a number of benches and ledges, and then diverges to three ramps and stairs that drop into the canyon just west of Pueblo Bonito. Its exact route from there is assumed to pass south by Pueblo del Arroyo and links with South Gap Road.

At Pueblo Alto this route passes another road (RS 11) presumed to border the 210-meter-long masonry wall that extends due west of Alto past the north side of New Alto. The ultimate route of this road is unknown but it probably links several cut stairways descending the cliff southward to a gardening terrace (RS 34) and a cliff-ledge, rock art site (29SJ 2402) possibly related to astronomical sightings. The terrace was destroyed by the Civilian Conservation Corps road construction in the 1930s. Near the west end of RS 11, a cut in the crest may be another road that crosses RS 11 at right angles. The cut is about nine and a half meters wide and runs north past the only small house in the vicinity and may head south toward the Bonito Staircases.

Prescott College cleared a road (RS 40) in 1972 on the east side of Pueblo Alto that passes north through a meter-wide opening or gate in Major Wall 1. This road then splits into five or more routes and is considered the beginning of the North Road. Several routes angle to the northeast from the Pueblo Alto gate in the direction of a small house community along the Escavada Wash. Another section (RS 43) goes northwest from the gate across RS 33 past the Rabbit Ruin and on to nearby Cly's Canyon and further to Penasco Blanco. Yet another road (RS 37) runs due east from Pueblo Alto's east plaza past the East Ruin and on for another 430 meters, bordered by a masonry wall or curbing, to terminate close to RS 36, another curbed road. Road segment 35 runs southwest-northeast from the mesa edge and a series of stairs, just east of Chetro Ketl, past the Poco site, and on to sites along the Escavada Wash.

An extension (RS 40) of the North Road runs south through the gate across Plaza 2 at Pueblo Alto, past the Trash Mound, bordered by a major wall, and down the first set of ledges to the bench below where it runs parallel to a long groove hammered into the bedrock. Laguna and Zuñi stick-racers run in grooves like this one for their ceremonial races. The groove disappears at the point where the North Road as RS 40 forks into two segments (RS 40E and 40W) that lead to ramps and stairways behind Chetro Ketl. One can walk along the Pueblo Alto–Talus Unit Road (RS 40W) via a series of stairs, ramps, and wall segments to Talus Unit.

The other fork (RS 40E) continues around the bench top just east of Chetro Ketl and becomes RS 32, and then descends into the canyon via a series of closely-spaced stairways and possible ramps which may each link to specific roads merging here. Across the canyon from here is a spectacular cut-rock stairway, 29SJ 761, which connects to a road running to Tsin Kletzin on top of South Mesa (not shown on the map), presumed by the alignment of the two sets of stairways on either side of the canyon. Both sites are uniquely marked by stone animal figures. The Navajo call the road the Zuñi Trail because the Zuñi may have used it to deliver prayer offerings at Chaco Canyon, considered by the Zuñi to be an ancestral site.

Road Segment 43, which breaks out of Pueblo Alto and heads for Penasco Blanco, may have had multiple terminal points. The clearest of these lies directly west of Rabbit Ruin and is marked by a small causeway, several series of cut steps, and stone ramps. It descends Cly's Canyon near four active seeps that contain water. In 1901, Holsinger noted that the Navajo used a couple of the seeps. The Navajo named the seep "Great Gambler's Spring," and it is mentioned in one of the chantways. Jar fragments were found near this seep. A spur route between Pueblo Alto and Pueblo Bonito leads to the seeps, indicating that residents of Pueblo del Arroyo and Pueblo Bonito may have also used it.

Other road segments (RS 28, 30, 31, and 34) may actually be terraces or garden plots. These segments were once thought to be roads, but because of their position beneath a cliff and their orientation toward the sunlight, they may have been used as seeping fields, which were favored by the historical Hopi.

One of the longest Pueblo Alto roads, the Poco Road, actually originated at Chetro Ketl. This five-kilometer-long road extends northwest past the Poco Site, through a quarry toward a group of ruins known as the Escavada Complex. Another road extends nearly four kilometers northwest from Pueblo Alto to Greasy Hill

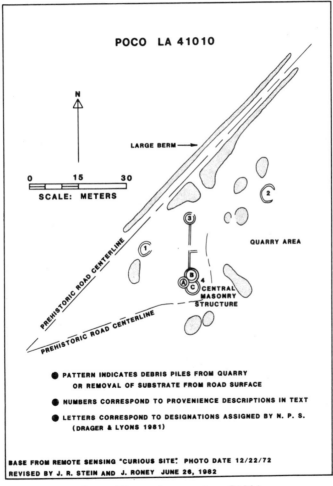

Poco. (Illustration courtesy BLM.)

Pueblo, in the same complex. Two other roads a little more than three kilometers long flank the North Road on the east and west, fanning from Pueblo Alto N 27 E and N 13 E. Several shorter segments branch from and interconnect these longer courses.

The Poco Site is an elaborate grouping of six herraduras six to eight meters in diameter. The "Central Masonry" herradura was three-ringed. A circular slab-lined firebox, hearths, and scattered burned areas in the herradura leads archaeologists to believe this site also served as a signaling station. The large area east of the Central Masonry was quarried as was the road. The presence of the Poco Site was dictated by the road.

Greasy Hill, a small six-room, two-kiva (one above, one below) structure, and a walled plaza house might have been the terminus of the road projected from Pueblo Alto.

Although not mentioned by Roney, or verified as a legitimate road, Kimbeto Point, a large, rectangular room, sits on the top of a small knoll on a projected road bearing twenty-six degrees from Pueblo Alto. The ruin may be the terminus for this road. Kimbeto Point is called *Giní Bit'ohí*, or Sparrowhawk's Nest, by the locals and is referred to in the Gambler legend from the Bead Chant which tells how the Navajo acquired sheep.

Windes said that the three or more stairways leading to RS 35 and RS 32 near Chetro Ketl suggest considerable influence and traffic. Of course, a number of roads also connect Pueblo Alto to the Escavada community, and others are suspected between the latter and Hungo Pavi and Penasco Blanco. Road ties between the canyon great house and the Escavada community may have facilitated much exchange of people and goods. Anyone traveling north from Pueblo Bonito, Pueblo del Arroyo, Chetro Ketl, or Talus Unit 1 would have borne inspection by the inhabitants of Pueblo Alto.

9. Chaco East

A constructed road segment east of the Chaco East site is visible for about a hundred meters and heads in the general direction of Pueblo Pintado and then becomes lost in the alluvium on the

Chaco Canyon floor. Another less distinct fragment may lead northwestward from the site, back onto the canyon floor where it too is lost. The road vestiges may have served a shrine near Pueblo Pintado.

10. Pueblo Pintado

Pueblo Pintado was reoccupied in the thirteenth century by a people who favored the Mesa Verdean style of ceramics and building. (See aerial of Pueblo Pintado, Chapter Four.) A trading

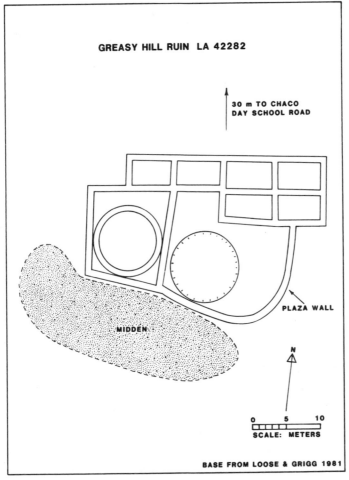

Greasy Hill. (Illustration courtesy BLM.)

post may have operated in the east wing of Pueblo Pintado intermittently since the beginning of the twentieth century. An historic house was built near the site, as well as a corral on the plaza. In 1889, Thomas Hye may have constructed a store at a site that fits the description of Pueblo Pintado, but was referred to as Pueblo del Alto. Silver jewelry, horses, and saddles were taken in trade. Indian agents said he sold whiskey to Navajos for a sheep a bottle. In the early 1900s, Mariana's Store was set up near the ruin.

Pueblo Pintado is a massive cathedral-like structure built just above the Chaco Wash floodplain on the lower north slope of Chacra Mesa ten miles from Chaco Canyon proper. It is the easternmost outlier excluding Guadalupe. The structure formed a massive right angle with terraced three-story arms. Twenty single-story rooms connect the ends of the arms to form a plaza. Pueblo Pintado has four kivas within the house (three of which are blocked in), fourteen to sixteen kivas on the plaza, and a single great kiva thirty meters to the southeast. True to cathedral towns, Pueblo Pintado is surrounded by a village of fourteen small houses, a total of 116 rooms, and nineteen pit houses or kivas.

A very clear road can be traced a little over four kilometers westward (N 294 E) from Pueblo Pintado in the general direction of Chaco Wash. The road wraps around the great house in the aerial photographs. Archaeologists have come to call this type of road an aureole. Dirt is piled up on one side of this aureole making the great house look like it is sitting in a dish.

The road disappears in the sand on the canyon bottom, but may well have continued down Chaco Wash to Chaco East. Two other faint traces are sometimes visible at Pueblo Pintado, one heading generally southward and the other northward from this site. Both are faint and unconfirmed.

Pueblo Pintado to the Navajo is *Kin Teel,* or Wide House, which is also the name of the Aztec great house. The name appears in the origin legend of Excess Way twice, as well as the Water Way, the Bead Way, and the Shooting Way. Pueblo Pintado is the starting point of the Bead Way, which is important in clan origin legends. The Shooting Way involves an old woman who makes men thin and is usually associated with *Tsé Dighin* or Holy Rock, which is probably Fajada Butte in Chaco Canyon. Kin Teel may have been associated with the Pueblo War incidents in many of the chantway legends, especially Enemy Way, Beauty Way, and Mountaintop Way. Chantway is a clumsy term which has become accepted based on questionable translations of Navajo phrases used to describe their ceremonials.

Holsinger, in 1901, said that the Navajo called the ruin *Kin Kale*, meaning great or grand house. Lt. Simpson, in 1849, said that the Pueblos called the ruin Pueblo de Montezuma and the Mexicans, *Pueblo Colorado.* "Hosta calls it *Pueblo Ratones*, Sandoval, the friendly Navajo chief with us, calls it *Pueblo Grande,* and Carrava-hal, our Mexican guide, who probably knows more about it than anyone else, Pueblo Pintado," Simpson wrote.

11. Guadalupe

A possible road heading south from Guadalupe shows up in aerial photography. It is last visible about a kilometer south of the site, and its destination is unknown. The road has not been veri-fied on the ground. Guadalupe Ruin, a relatively small one-story outlier, sits on a high, defensible ridge overlooking the Rio Puerco of the East. Built in the mid to late 900s, this E-shaped, twenty-five-room, three-kiva structure was remodeled several times in the Bonito style during the classic A.D. 1050 to 1125 period. Fifty-four miles southeast of Chaco Canyon and forty-five miles northwest of Albuquerque, this isolated outpost had no small house community.

12. San Mateo

Near Mount Taylor west of Albuquerque, San Mateo is the largest Chacoan Ruin in the Red Mesa Valley area. The house is a large, block-type building built around a fully enclosed rectangu-lar plaza area with up to 112 rooms and five kivas. A brief survey of the immediate San Mateo area revealed a number of small houses with substantial trash middens.

A clear four hundred-meter-long road cuts through a small ridge about four hundred meters north of San Mateo, near an area full of Anasazi rock art and shrines. A concerted attempt to trace this road northward into the Desliz Escarpment was unsuccessful. No one has any clues as to the road's destination. A faint swale to the south of San Mateo has not been evaluated, although it may head for El Rito, which has no corresponding road segment.

The San Mateo/El Rito/Kin Nizhoni triangle is known to the Navajo people living in the Haystack area, but they have little to say about the sites. The Navajos say that the region has been dominated by Mexican people who have had ranches there for as long as anyone can remember. Dennis Franstead, in his ethnography on the Navajo in the area, says that some fairly well-known New Mexican families of Spanish origin were early settlers in this region, which is now decimated by uranium mining.

13. Kin Nizhoni

Kin Nizhoni, built as early as A.D. 950, is a community of two multistoried public houses (Upper and Lower Kin Nizhoni) containing up to fourteen rooms and blocked-in kivas surrounded in a three-square-mile area by eighty-six residential houses. Two, possibly four, roads serve the two public houses. The longest road, three kilometers long, heads toward El Rito but does not connect to that site. A second segment connects Upper and Lower

Prehistoric roads from the direction of San Mateo and El Rito converge at Kin Nizhoni (A). 1930s. (Illustration courtesy BLM.)

Kin Nizhoni, five hundred meters apart. A third probable road trends northward from the Kin Nizhoni complex for about a kilometer; its destination is unknown. A fourth possible, but unconfirmed, swale heads for Haystack.

14. Haystack

Known to the Navajo as *Kits' Iil Ya'á*, or Standing Up Ruin, Haystack probably represents successive centers of development, from A.D. 850 to 1100. It includes a great kiva with associated surface rooms, a great kiva with a small associated Bonito-phase structure, and a large Bonito great house/great kiva structure with enclosed patio.

The Navajo may have renovated the prehistoric reservoir in 1960. Franstead said that the dam that formed Red Lake, *Be'ek'alchii'*, was believed by the Navajo to be Anasazi, and was reused by them as an antelope trap. Antelope hunting was conducted in association with a number of ceremonies called the Game Way or Corral Way. Corral Way uses a large corral made of cedar or piñon piled up to twelve feet high. Wings or chutes through which the hunted antelope entered the corral are several hundred yards to a mile long. It took a group of hunters five days to build the trap in preparation for the communal hunt participated in by both men and women. The practice decreased as the Navajo became dependent on animal husbandry as a source of meat.

Three likely roads have been found in the Haystack area. The best defined is a double swale which leaves the site in a north-northwesterly direction and can be traced for 1.2 kilometers, although its destination is unknown. A second swale projects from the site in a southwesterly direction, also toward an unknown destination. In aerial photographs it can be traced for three hundred meters. The third road at Haystack heads in an easterly direction, is six hundred meters long and is flanked by a huge earthwork near the main ruin. This road may lead to Kin Nizhoni, assuming the route swung around the southern tip of Mesa Montanosa. Concerted efforts have failed to establish such a connection.

15. Gasco Herradura

Gasco Herradura sits on a five hundred-meter-long road segment. Although it is in an area where a number of Bonito buildings are known to exist, no endpoints or logical destinations have
been found despite concerted efforts to trace the road.

16. Andrews

First established by A.D. 800, the Andrews complex grew to a
public structure containing five kivas, with twenty-one small houses
(106 rooms total) and three isolated great kivas within two square
kilometers from the great house. Two of the great kivas were built
as early as A.D. 800, and the great house was built between A.D. 950
and 1000, about the time the Casamero community was built nearly
five kilometers to the northwest. (Casamero is said to have been a
staging area for raids in the days of the Navajo warfare.) The presence and incredible size of the two early great kivas suggest that a
sizeable population was available to build these structures.

The BLM survey failed to verify a road segment near Andrews
known as Segment 192, but Roney says that aerial reconnaissance
since the 1987 report came out provided strong evidence that the
segment was indeed a prehistoric road. The road does not head
for Casamero as previously thought but instead heads for a pass
north of Casamero toward Coyotes Sing Here. No roads have
been found, however, at Coyotes Sing Here and no obvious connection turned up in aerial photographs.

17. Coolidge

The Coolidge community included two great kivas and two
Bonito-phase house mounds, all associated with trash mounds,
and a reservoir catchment area. In Marshall's estimation, the great
kivas were the center of community involvement. Great Kiva 1
was built during Pueblo I, and Great Kiva 2 replaced Great Kiva 1
during late Pueblo II–early Pueblo III. A road connects the second
kiva to the areas between east and west communities 165 meters
to the south. A second road heads almost directly east for eight
hundred meters (perhaps toward Coyotes Sing Here) ending with

a set of toeholds and handholds at the base of a massive sand-stone cliff. These roads are not well documented.

18. Las Ventanas

Now reduced to a mound, Las Ventanas was once an eighty-nine-room frontier great house surrounded by a substantial Anasazi constellation of communities. At the center of the house stood a two-story tower kiva, at least two stories high, contained within a room block. An isolated great kiva stood 250 meters away. Multistory architecture, great kivas, a roadway, and ceramics suggested an affiliation with Chaco Canyon, but in many respects, the site is atypical of most Chacoan outposts, and so must have been on the outer limits of the Chacoan frontier. Marshall said that a well-defined prehistoric road entered the site from the northwest. Las Ventanas is on the edge of the malpais just northwest of modern Acoma Pueblo south of I-40.

Roney, on the other hand, said that contrary to published description, the road falls on a near east-west axis. It is visible 150 meters east of the Las Ventanas Bonito building and can be traced no more than 130 meters to the tip of a nearby mesa. The destination is unknown.

19. Cebolla Canyon

Roney and Stein noted a Bonito-style structure in Cebolla Canyon, just under forty kilometers southeast of Las Ventanas. A short but definite road segment, defined by an ambitious cut-and-fill construction, projects northward into rugged country. The destination of this road is unknown.

20. Dittert

Roney and Stein noted a heavily constructed road segment heading N 310 E of Dittert, about twelve kilometers southwest of the Cebolla Canyon site. The road can be traced for four hundred meters toward an unknown destination. A second probable road trends N 20 E from the site toward broken country at the base of a mesa for 250 meters.

21. Muddy Water

Three Bonito great houses with housed kivas and a single great kiva form an impressive Anasazi cluster known as Muddy Water, or *Hashtl'ísh Bivi Kits'iil* (Ruin in the Mud), on the Northern margin of the Dutton Plateau west of Crownpoint. The largest great house, with the one great kiva, served the area throughout the Pueblo II era, while the other two were built in early Pueblo III. Within a square mile, forty-six Anasazi room blocks (255 rooms total) and six kivas were found. Six of these sites were built in early Basketmaker III times.

A major road passes through the Muddy Water community center. Two kilometers north of the sites is a short segment visible for only one hundred meters. Its northward destination is unknown. Two kilometers of well-constructed roadway are visible in the central portion of the Muddy Water complex. On the same alignment two kilometers farther south is a one and a half kilometer-long road segment which enters the canyon at the base of Dutton Plateau. A ceramic scatter can be followed onto the plateau, but no other evidence of the road could be traced on the mesa. The destination of this road is not known.

22. Standing Rock

The Standing Rock complex is comprised of a U-shaped house and great kiva and as many as fifty small to large village-type pueblos. It was built in the late Pueblo II/early Pueblo III times northeast of a geographical feature called Standing Rock. The Navajo call the area *Tse Ya'a* after the same feature, and it is recalled in the Hail Way Legend. Two roads leave this site, both heading in a northeasterly direction and both are visible for about five hundred meters. These roads are flanked by massive earthworks as they approach Standing Rock ruin. Neither road has an obvious destination. A new moon sliver of an herradura, named for the site, was discovered two miles away. It sits two hundred meters above a supposed ancient road, which was later found to have been an historic road. Early on, it was believed that Standing Rock may have aligned with the Coyote Canyon Road as it entered Chaco Canyon, but the road only connects Peach Springs to Grey Ridge.

23. Coyote Canyon Road

Archaeologist Harold Gladwin was the founder of the Gila Pueblo research institute in Arizona, and developed the "Gladwin Classification" for dating Pueblo Indians through time. In 1928, he wrote in his field notes:

> The Navajo say that a clay road [the Coyote Canyon Road] was once built from this ruin to Pueblo Bonito, a distance of thirty-five miles, on which pine logs were carried from the Chuskas to build the great pueblos at Chaco. Sections of the road are said to be still in use by the Navajo.

Coyote Canyon Road is the longest and best preserved road segment not directly connected to Chaco Canyon. With only a few gaps, it is visible for more than eight kilometers. Although the broad, shallow swale can first be seen three and a half kilometers west of the Peach Springs outlier, the ruin was probably the eastern terminus of the road. The western terminus was probably the Grey Ridge Community, near a post-Chacoan site.

The Grey Ridge Compound (A.D. 1000 to 1300) postdates the road by about a century, but is situated right on the road. This site consists of a masonry compound forming a rough square sixty meters on each side. Walls are made of rubble core and more than a half meter thick. Entry is through a wide gate in the east wall right off the road. A large circular depression was scooped out within the compound. The overall architecture resembles contemporary fortified sites in the Zuñi area or the great kiva at Yucca House National Monument in southwestern Colorado. The compound may have been built on the road accidentally, or the road may have been modified for reuse. Continued importance of the road system after the demise of the regional Chacoan system should not be overlooked.

Before surveying this road, BLM targeted two areas as the most likely sites for herraduras—sites that would offer the best view in both directions along the road. To their elation, they were right. These were named Little Ear and Coyote Canyon Herraduras. The

Anasazi road engineers cut through low ridges or sandstone, leveled slopes, formed berm borders, carved a groove (the Coyote Canyon Groove) into bedrock, built a stairway, kept a constant width of ten meters and constant straight course, scattered shards near herraduras, and sculpted three cairns. This was a serious roadway segment.

24. Red Willow

A road leaves the Red Willow site on a bearing of N 73 E, and can be traced seven hundred meters before it fades into a sandy surface. A second road passes to the east. It can be traced on aerial photography by a swath of vegetation toward Los Rayos Great Kiva two and a half kilometers away. A third possible road heads northwest from the Bonito-style building for about two hundred meters, but this has not been verified.

25. Skunk Springs

Skunk Springs, or Kin Lizhin (Black House) was first built in A.D. 850-950 (the West House Area), and later annexed in A.D. 1050-1250. The site is a great kiva complex, backed by a multi-story fifty-six-room great house. The great house contains three great kivas, two enclosed in a plaza. To the west of the great house, more than one hundred smaller houses line the upper edge and lower slopes of Grey Mesa and are scattered irregularly from the mesa to the valley floor in a two-square-mile area. The site was saturated and may have been one of the major Anasazi towns in the prehistoric southwest.

A prehistoric road appears in an eroded area on the mesa face immediately below Skunk Springs heading southeast from the site. It passes an herradura built immediately adjacent to the Bonito-style building. The road is only visible for 150 meters and requires further evaluation. A scar in the landscape between Skunk Springs and Newcomb Site appeared in a Soil Conservation Service aerial photograph taken in the 1930s, and ended up as a projected road between the two sites. The road may have been an abandoned historic road, and not a prehistoric road.

Local Navajo say that the irrigation system in the area is Anasazi. The main ditch ran for a considerable distance to the east or northeast. Older residents of the area can remember using the old irrigation system and cleaning it with digging sticks.

One man recalls spending his youth digging in "Kin Lizhin," despite the warnings and objections of others. In three small rooms on the outer edge of the ruin, he found pots containing corn and squash, which he said he planted, various projectile points, shell beads, and stone and antler tools including an ax still attached to the handle. He sold some of the material to a trader who promised to put it on display, but later disappeared. The same Navajo claimed to have found a burial in one room. He said the individual was quite tall—perhaps six foot six inches—and was buried with small, polished, marble-like pebbles around the skull and in the eye sockets. The bones were later taken by a medicine man who died within ten years.

26. Aztec

Aztec is said to have magnetized a shift in style and maybe politics in Chaco Canyon by the twelfth century. It is the third largest of all Bonito-style buildings next to Pueblo Bonito and Chetro Ketl. It is situated fifteen miles northeast of Farmington and almost exactly halfway between the cliff dwellings of Mesa Verde and Chaco Canyon, coincidentally or not. The main 405-room building was built fifty years after the North Road was built between A.D. 1100 and 1120. This building is the largest of the three built together and is surrounded by some ninety small houses in a mile and a half radius.

Aztec has two major prehistoric roads. One has a bearing of N 334 E and can be traced for 1.3 kilometers. Its destination is unknown. Another road segment leaves the Aztec Ruin complex on a bearing of approximately N 280 E. It can be traced for nearly two and a half kilometers in a 1930s aerial photo. The destination may have been a sandstone quarry, but this is disputed.

Much of the following information was gathered from research other than that of BLM and the National Park Service, and some of it was provided by archaeologists who have taken a busman's holiday to check the fields on the weekend and during vacation. Therefore, the information about these sites is not as complete as that for the sites listed above.

27. Lowry/Pigg

Roads at the Lowry/Pigg Complex have not been formally documented but Roney followed a clear prehistoric road for several hundred meters southwest from the Pigg site. The full extent and ultimate destination of the feature is not known.

28. Cottonwood Falls

Cottonwood Falls, an Anasazi site in Utah, is still under investigation. Roney has observed a one hundred-meter-long road segment leaving the great house toward the south and passing down Cottonwood Canyon; its destination is unknown. The roads in Utah exhibit many of the same characteristics as the roads closer to Chaco Canyon. Where roads in New Mexico tend to be straight, the roads in Utah tend to meander along drainages. Otherwise, the roads in Utah even have herraduras. See Chapters Four and Nine for more information about Anasazi roads in Utah.

29. Bluff

Like those at Cottonwood Falls, the prehistoric roads near Bluff, Utah, are still under investigation by archaeologists. John Roney says that the site has a definite aureole, and faint traces which may represent a prehistoric road are found about 150 meters north of the site. Others have found a probable road segment near Monticello, Utah.

30. Tse Chezi

Tse Chezi in Arizona has two road segments. No further information is available at this time.

31. Farmington

A probable road segment, nearly two kilometers long, near Farmington, New Mexico, was first noted in Soil Conservation Service photography in the 1930s. By the time it was field checked in the mid 1980s, most of the segment visible in the photo had been destroyed by construction. The origin of the remaining traces was ambiguous, yet they resembled the characteristics of roads and even included two parallel segments. The road headed south toward Sterling Ruin, about two kilometers beyond the end of the road trace. No specific destination presents itself to the north.

32. Sunshine Springs

Aerial reconnaissance shows a prehistoric road passing northeast-southwest through a complex at Sunshine Springs, Arizona, for about one hundred meters in each direction. The road has not been verified, nor is its destination known.

33. Chambers

The Chambers community center in Arizona has three roads. One leads southwest about 150 meters to a small building occupied in late Pueblo II times. A second can be traced eastward for about a kilometer, although it is not leading toward the nearby Sanders outlier. The third road leads southwestward from the site and can be traced for nearly a kilometer to a spring. A later Pueblo III building was built astride this road, but the intended destination of the road is not known. Interestingly, no road seems to lead from this site toward the nearby Navajo Springs center.

34. Navajo Springs

Navajo Springs, in Arizona, has a pronounced aureole which is broken in a number of places, indicating road entries. Three visible swales indicating constructed roads protrude from the Bonito-style great house/great kiva complex. Two other more ambiguous swales cut through this area and may also represent roads. One of the definite roads trends northeast and ends at residential complex 150 meters away. A second trends east-northeast and has been traced on the ground for nearly five kilometers. This road does not head toward any of the other known community centers in the area and its destination is presently unknown. A third relatively convincing kilometer-long swale progresses in gaps toward Chambers Ruin north-northeast of the site. A less distinct fourth swale, two hundred meters long, bears south-southwest toward the water source at Navajo Springs (not the ruin) six kilometers away. The fifth possible, but unconfirmed, road is a faint swale heading west-southwestward from the community center down the Rio Puerco drainage.

35. Sanders

A well-constructed road leaves Sanders, in Arizona, heading northeastward, up the Rio Puerco drainage. A faint swale leads southwest from the site, but the prehistoric origin of this feature has not been established. Neither road has an obvious destination.

36. Allentown

A massively constructed road runs northeasterly from Allentown, in Arizona, directly up the Rio Puerco. The road can be traced for about two hundred meters before it drops into a sandy bottom valley and is lost. Hocho'i is the next community center up the Rio Puerco, and a road does head toward Allentown from the Hocho'i end, but the twain do not meet. Further investigation might produce the missing link.

A second possible road leaves Allentown in a westwardly direction. This massive swale was traced for several hundred meters, but could be the result of natural shifting and not prehistoric construction. Further study is required.

37. Kin Hocho'i

Kin Hocho'i, in New Mexico, has four distinct prehistoric roads. The longest extends northeast up the Rio Puerco and can be traced in aerial photography for more than three kilometers. This roadway passes a great kiva 120 meters from the Bonito-style building. A poorly preserved swale on the southeast side of Kin

Hocho'i is probably the remnant of a road which extended up Manuelito Canyon, but it can only be traced for about one hundred meters. A third clear roadway can be traced southwest toward Allentown for three hundred meters to the edge of the Kin Hocho'i mesa. The fourth road leaving Kin Hocho'i is a shallow swale traceable for only 250 meters before it becomes lost in the alluvial canyon bottom. This road heads toward the mouth of Black Canyon and could lead to the Hunter's Point outlier, but Hunter's Point has no corresponding road.

38. Figueredo

When flying low over Figueredo, New Mexico, one can see a prehistoric road leaving this site heading northeast for two hundred meters along the projected alignment of the Mexican Springs Road leading to Chaco Canyon; this alignment, however, has long been discounted. A second faint and eroded swale leaves the site in a southwesterly direction. Neither has been ground checked.

39. Dzil Nda Kai

The Solstice Project discovered a large sixteen-meter-long earthen embankment on the southwest side of the ruin of Dzil Nda Kai which may well represent a road. Later flight over the ruin revealed a roadway heading south-southeast from the site for some distance. The road could not be detected in aerial photography and requires further study.

40. Toh La Kai

Toh La Kai, called *Bahast'aah* (Against the Cliff Wall) by the Navajo, is a multistory L-shaped Bonito-style house with a potential of thirty-one rooms and a couple of housed kivas. The great kiva at this site seems to dwarf the house. A Basketmaker III village is nearby.

A clear swale heading northeast from Toh La Kai toward Grey Ridge Community was seen from the air; the swale would seem to connect to the Coyote Canyon Road. The feature is visible for about two hundred meters, but has not been ground checked.

41. Zuñi Salt Lake Road

Fray Marcos de Niza documented what might have been the
Zuñi Salt Lake Road during the Coronado expedition in 1540. He
wrote that "on the first day we traveled over a wide and much
used road." A road seventy kilometers long connecting Zuñi
Pueblo to Zuñi Salt Lake is clearly visible on USGS topographical
maps. However, only two kilometers of this road have been inspected and confirmed as a prehistoric feature. These two kilometers contain clear evidence of construction and ceramics of both
Late Pueblo II and Early Pueblo III times.

Footnote on Anasazi Roads

Conspicuously absent from John Roney's list are Southeast
Road, Kin Ya'a to Ruby Wells Road, Chacra Face Road, and Mexican Springs Road as outlined on most maps of the Chacoan
roads. Roney excluded these from the list because they were not
confirmed.

The Southeast Road, previously seen in aerial photographs, was
not ground checked prior to Phase II of the BLM survey. The road
was believed to pass from Upper Greenlee Ruin to a road junction
near Ruby Wells Ranch and then southeastward to San Mateo ruin.
Long gaps in the projected road did exist in the photography but
could not be seen in aerial reconnaissance. Exhaustive hiking
along the imaged route for the usual roadside paraphernalia turned
up the short segment near San Mateo, the Rams Pasture Herradura,
seven kilometers south of Upper Greenlee, and little else.

BLM listed four possible explanations for its failure to find a
road along that route: The road never existed; the road has been
totally obliterated (highly unlikely); the road was not formalized
and therefore not well preserved; the wrong places were examined (the end points of the roads may have been presumptuous).
These explanations could apply as well to other roads seen in
aerial photographs and later ruled out by ground check.

Likewise, other lineations in aerial photography showed up between the Ruby Wells Ranch area and Kin Ya'a. Ground examination revealed a broad, deep depression similar to many prehistoric

roads three kilometers north of Kin Ya'a. The depression contained ruts (as if from wagon wheels), many historic artifacts from the Navajo site upslope from the road, and a single, shattered Anasazi vessel. Several obvious historic roads paralleled the imaged alignment. Despite superficial resemblance in places to a prehistoric road, the almost total absence of Anasazi artifacts and road-related sites, as well as the ruts and parallel historic road segments, have led archaeologists to believe this was an historic road.

The Chacra Face Road proved to be another disappointment, but deserves another chance. This road presumably paralleled the southern edge of Chacra Mesa starting at Fajada Gap and extended southeast, projecting to the Pueblo Pintado area and as far as Guadalupe. Aerial reconnaissance revealed an especially deep road cut near Fajada Gap and other visible segments which might extend as far southeast as Mesa Cortada, although the segments near Mesa Cortada were not verified. Segments were seen from the ground near Tse Lichii and Tse La Vie. However, after looking more closely, these roads were found to be narrower and more crooked than most prehistoric roads, and historic artifacts were found in the swale. But the prehistoric line seen in the photography lies upslope from this swale and was not examined. More work is needed on this road before it is thrown out completely.

The Mexican Springs Road, which was originally projected toward the Arizona border from Kin Bineola, was omitted from the BLM survey because what appeared to be swales in the aerial photographs were actually dunes and other natural erosion and drifting features.

Other roads not mapped by the BLM include lesser roads such as the Kin Bineola to Bee Burrow Road and the Kin Ya'a to Kin Bineola Road. The first road shows up in aerial photography near Kin Bineola and Bee Burrow respectively, but none of the features could be found on the ground. The second road was suspected because of an unrecorded great house along the Kim-me-ne-oli Wash between Kin Ya'a and Kin Bineola and a Navajo confirmation of a road. Prehistoric canals were found in aerial photos, but no road presented itself, although it could have been eroded.

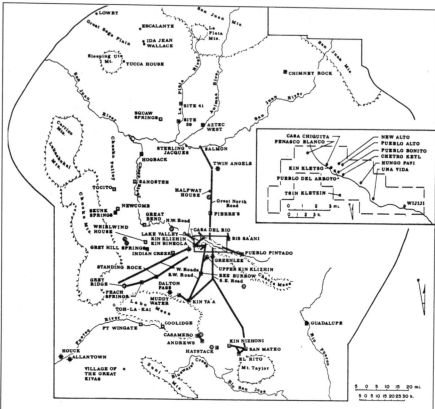

● Outlying Chacoan structure or major Chaco Canyon structure (treated in this study)

○ Outlying Chacoan structure (not treated in this study)

◉ Outlying Chacoan structure and associated community (inner circle or dot keys treatment of non-treatment)

⌖ Outlying Chacoan structure and probable associated community (inner circle or dot keys treatment or non-treatment)

◍ Other reconnaissance area

— Schematic interpretation of probable prehistoric road. With the exception of the Great North Road and the Southwest Road, road identifications are tentative, subject to future confirmation through ground survey.

Intensive survey areas include the Bis Sa'ani, Peach Springs, and Pierre's communities. Reconnaissance areas include the Twin Angels, Halfway House, Hogback, Great Bend, Grey Hill Springs, Standing Rock, Dalton Pass, Muddy Water, and Casamero outlying structures or communities.

An early version of the Chacoan road system (A.D. 1050–1175).

Bibliography

Altschul, Jeffery H. "The Development of the Chacoan Interaction Sphere." *Journal of Anthropological Research*. 34(1):20-37, 1978.

Aveni, Anthony F. "Possible Astronomical Orientations in Ancient Mesoamerica." In *Archaeoastronomy in Pre-Columbian America*. Anthony F. Aveni, editor. Austin: University of Texas Press, 1975.

Aveni, Anthony F. *Skywatchers of Ancient Mexico*. Austin: University of Texas Press, 1980.

Aveni, Anthony F. "Archaeoastronomy in the Southwestern United States: A Neighbor's Eye View." In *Astronomy and Ceremony in the Prehistoric Southwest*, John B. Carlson and W. James Judge, editors. Papers of the Maxwell Museum of Anthropology, No. 2, 1987.

Aveni, Anthony F. "Whither Archaeoastronomy?" In *World Archaeoastronomy: Selected Papers from the 2nd Oxford International Conference of Archaeoastronomy*. Anthony F. Aveni, editor. Cambridge: Cambridge University Press, 1989.

Bandelier, Adolph F. "Final Report of Investigations among the Indians of the Southwestern United States, carried on mainly in the years from 1800 to 1885 (Part II)." *Papers of the Archeological Institute of America, American Series 4*, 1892.

Bardé, David. Chaco Site data forms 29SJ-1578, 1579, and 1580 (Kin Bineola). On file at Chaco Center (National Park Service/University of New Mexico), Albuquerque, 1972.

Beals, Ralph Leon. *Acta Americana*. 1-6(4), January/March, 1943-July/December, 1948. Mexico, D.F. [etc.] The Inter-American Society of Anthropology and Geography, 1943-48.

Beck, Colleen Marguerite. "Ancient Roads on the North Coast of Peru." Dissertation, University of California, Berkeley, 1979. Manuscript on file, Albuquerque District Office, Bureau of Land Management, Albuquerque.

Byers, William N. "Ancient Trails." *The American Antiquarian*. 1(1):16-17, 1878.

Carlson, John B. "Romancing the Stone, or Moonshine on the Sun Dagger." In *Astronomy and Ceremony in the Prehistoric Southwest*, John B. Carlson and W. James Judge, editors. Papers of the Maxwell Museum of Anthropology, No. 2, 1987.

Cieza de Leon, Pedro de. *La Crónica del Perú* [1550]. Biblioteca de Autores Española, tomo 26. Historiadores Primitivos de Indias, tomo 2, Don Enrique, editor. Madrid: Edición Altas, 1947, pp. 344-358.

Cieza de Leon, Pedro de. *El Señorio de los Incas* (Segunda parte de *La Crónica de Perú*) [1553]. Lima: Instituto de Estudios Peruanos, 1967.

Coe, Michael D. *The Maya*. New York: Frederick Praeger, Inc., 1966.

Coggins, Clemency. "The Shape of Time: Some Political Implications of a Four-Part Figure," *American Antiquity*, 45(4), 1980.

Coolidge, Mary Roberts. *The Rain Makers*. Cambridge: The Riverside Press, 1929.

Crow Wing. *A Pueblo Indian Journal*. Elsie Clews Parsons, editor. Memoirs of the American Anthropological Association, No. 32, Menasha, Wisconsin, 1925.

Cushing, Frank Hamilton. "Outlines of Zuñi Creation Myths." In *Thirteenth Annual Report of the Bureau of American Ethnology for the Years 1891-1892*. Washington, D.C.: Government Printing Office, 1896, pp. 321-447.

Cushing, Frank Hamilton. "My Adventures in Zuñi." *The Century Magazine*, 25 and 26, 1892-1893. Palmer Lake, Colorado: Filter Press, 1967 reprint. Also appears in *Zuni: The Selected Writings of Frank Hamilton Cushing*. J. Green, editor. Lincoln: University of Nebraska Press, 1979.

Davis, James T. "Trade Routes and Economic Exchange among the Indians of California." *Reports of the University of California Survey*, 54, 1961.

von Daniken, Erich. *Chariots of the Gods*. New York: Bantam Books, 1971.

DiPeso, Charles C. "Casas Grandes: A Fallen Trading Center of the Gran Chichimeca," Vol. 2, The Amerind Foundation, Inc. Flagstaff, Arizona: Dragoon-Northland Press, 1974.

DiPeso, Charles C. "Casas Grandes: A Fallen Trading Center of the Gran Chichimeca." *Masterkey*, 42(1):20-37.

Douglas, William Boone. "The Land of the Small House People." *El Palacio*, 4(2):2-23, 1917.

Doyel, David E., and Stephen Lekson. "Anasazi Regional Organization and the Chaco System." Paper prepared for the symposium, "Anasazi Regional Organization and the Chaco System," 55th Annual Meeting, Society for American Archaeology, Las Vegas, Nevada, 1990, to be published by the Maxwell Museum.

Duran, Fray Diego. *Book of the Gods and Rites and the Ancient Calendar*. Norman: University of Oklahoma Press, 1971.

Ebert, James I., and Robert K. Hitchcock. "Locational Modeling in the Analysis of the Prehistoric Roadway System at and around Chaco Canyon, New Mexico." In *Cultural Resources Remote Sensing*, Thomas R. Lyons and Frances Joan Mathien, editors. National Park Service, 1980.

Eliade, Mircea. *Patterns of Comparative Religion*. New York: Sheed and Ward, 1958.

Ellis, Florence Hawley. "Distinctive Parallels between Mesoamerican and Puebloan Iconography and Deities." Paper delivered at Guanajuanto, Mexico, August, 1977.

Ellis, Florence Hawley. "A Thousand Years of the Pueblo Sun-Moon-Star Calendar." In *Archaeoastronomy in Pre-Columbian America*. Anthony F. Aveni, editor. Austin: University of Texas Press, 1975.

Ellis, Florence Hawley, and Laurens Hammack. "The Inner Sanctum of Feather Cave: A Mogollon Sun and Earth Shrine Linking Mexico and the Southwest." *American Antiquity,* 33(1): 25-44, 1968.

Ferdon, Edwin N., Jr. *A Trial Survey of Mexican-Southwestern Architectural Parallels*. Monographs of the School of American Research, No. 21. School of American Research and the Museum of New Mexico, Santa Fe, New Mexico, 1955.

Franstead, Dennis. "An Introduction to the Navajo Oral History of the Anasazi Sites in the San Juan Basin Area," 1979. Manuscript on file, Chaco Center, Southwest Cultural Resources Center, National Park Service, Albuquerque.

Frazier, Kendrick. *People of Chaco.* New York: W.W. Norton, 1986.

Friend, Adam. "Theory Stirs Up Linguistic Experts." *Dallas Morning News,* seen in *Albuquerque Journal,* December 9, 1990.

Gann, Thomas W.F. *Mystery Cities*. London: Duckworth, 1925.

Gladwin, Harold. Field notes—Wingate 8:4 site data form, Gila Pueblo, Globe, 1928. Published in "The Chaco Branch, Excavations at White Mound and in the Red Mesa Valley." *Medallion Paper,* 32, Gila Pueblo, Globe, Arizona, 1945.

Gregory, J.W. *The Story of the Road*. London: Adam & Charles Black, 1938.

Harrington, John P. "The Ethnology of the Tewa Indians." In *Twenty-ninth Annual Report of the Bureau of American Ethnology for the Years 1908-1909*. Washington D.C.: Government Printing Office, 1916, pp. 29-619.

Hartung, Horst. "A Scheme of Probable Astronomical Projections in Mesoamerican Architecture." *Archaeoastronomy in Pre-Columbian America*. Anthony F. Aveni, editor. Austin: University of Texas Press, 1975.

Hayes, Alden C. "A Survey of Chaco Canyon Archeology." In *Archeological Surveys of Chaco Canyon New Mexico*. Alden C. Hayes, David Brugge, and W. James Judge. *National Park Service Publications in Archeology* 18A:1-68, 1981.

Hirth, Kenneth G. "Interregional Trade and the Formation of Prehistoric Gateway Communities." *American Antiquity,* 43(1), 1978.

Hendley, Geoffrey. *History of the Roads*. London: Peter Davies, 1971.

Hewett, Edgar L. "The Excavations at Tyuonyi, New Mexico, in 1908," *American Anthropologist,* 2(3):434-438, 1909.

Hoffman, W.J. "Miscellaneous Ethnographic Observations on Indian Inhabitants of Nevada, California and Arizona." In *Annual Report of the U.S. Geologic and Geographic Survey of the Territories Embracing Colorado and Parts of Adjacent Territories, Being a Report of Progress of the Exploration for the Year 1876*, by F.V. Hayden. Washington, D.C.: Government Printing Office, 1878, pp. 459-478.

Holsinger, S.J. Report on Pre-historic Ruins of Chaco Canyon, NM. Called for by G.L.O. letter P, J.S.P. Dec. 8, 1900. Ms. on file, National Archives, Washington, D.C., 1901.

Jojola, Theodore S. "The Sun Personified: Some Preliminary Observations Regarding Celestial Cosmology and the Ordering of Pueblo Indian Society," In *Astronomy and Ceremony in the Prehistoric Southwest*. John B. Carlson and W. James Judge, editors. Papers of the Maxwell Museum of Anthropology, No. 2, 1987.

Judd, Neil M. "The Material Culture of Pueblo Bonito." *Smithsonian Miscellaneous Collections, 124*, 1954.

Judd, Neil M. "The Architecture of Pueblo Bonito." *Smithsonian Miscellaneous Collections, 147*, 1964.

Judge, W. James. "The Development of a Complex Cultural Ecosystem in the Chaco Basin, New Mexico." In Proceedings of the First Conference on Scientific Research in the National Parks (Vol. II). Robert M. Linn, editor. *National Park Service Transactions and Proceedings Series*, 5:901-905, 1979.

Judge, W. James. "Chaco Canyon-San Juan Basin." Paper presented at the seminar on Dynamics of Southwestern Prehistory. School of American Research, Santa Fe, New Mexico, 1983.

Judge, W. James, H. Wolcott Toll, William B. Gillespie, and Stephen H. Lekson. "Tenth Century Developments in Chaco Canyon." In *Collected Papers in Honor of Erik Kellerman Reed*. Albert H. Schroeder, editor. Papers of the Archaeological Society of New Mexico, 6:65-98, 1981.

Justeson, John S. "Ancient Maya Ethnoastronomy: An Overview of Hieroglyphic Sources." In *World Archaeoastronomy: Selected Papers from the 2nd Oxford International Conference of Archaeoastronomy*. Anthony F. Aveni, editor. Cambridge: Cambridge University Press, 1989.

Kaplan, H.M. "The Mysterious Computers of Chaco Canyon." *Empire Magazine, Denver Post*, March 24, 1974.

Kelley, J. Charles. "Speculations on the Culture History of Northwestern Mesoamerica." In *The Archaeology of West Mexico*. B. Bell, editor. Sociedad de Estudios Avanzados del Occidente de México, Ajijic, Jalisco, 1974, pp. 19-39.

Kelley, J. Charles. "The Mobile Merchants of Molino." In *Ripples in the Chichimec Sea*, Frances Joan Mathien and Randall H. McGuire, editors. Carbondale: Southern Illinois University Press, 1975, pp. 81-401.

Kelley, J. Charles, and Ellen Abbot Kelley. "An Alternative Hypothesis for the Explanation of Anasazi Culture History." In *Collected Papers in Honor of Florence Hawley Ellis*. Theodore R. Frisbie, editor. Papers of the Archaeological Society of New Mexico 2, Santa Fe, New Mexico, 1975, pp. 178-223.

Kelley, K.B. *Historic Cultural Resources in the San Augustine Coal Area*. On file at the Bureau of Land Management, Socorro District, New Mexico, June 1984.

Kidder, Alfred Vincent. "Southwestern Archeological Conference." *Science*, 66:489-491, 1927.

Kincaid, Chris. *Chaco Roads Project Phase I: A Reappraisal of Prehistoric Roads in the San Juan Basin*, Bureau of Land Management, Albuquerque District Office, 1983. (Including Chapter 2, "Other New Worlds and Trails," by Benjamin

P. Robertson; Chapter 3, "Identifying and Interpreting Chacoan Roads: An Historical Perspective," by R. Gwinn Vivian; Chapter 4, "Evaluation of Aerial Photography," by Margaret Senter Obenauf; Chapter 5, "Factors Affecting the Visibility of Roads," by Fred L. Nials; Chapter 6, "Physical Characteristics of Chacoan Roads," by Fred L. Nials; Chapter 7, "Archaeological Inventory Methodology," by John Stein and Chris Kincaid; Chapter 8, "Road Corridor Descriptions," by John R. Stein; Chapter 9, "Road Verification Summary," by Chris Kincaid, John Stein, and Daisy F. Levine; and Chapter 10, "Roads Management Plan," by Chris Kincaid.

Kincaid, Chris, John Stein, and Daisy F. Levine. "Road Verification Summary," *Chaco Roads Project Phase I: A Reappraisal of Prehistoric Roads in the San Juan Basin*. Chris Kincaid, editor. Bureau of Land Management, Albuquerque District Office, 1983.

Kincaid, Chris. "Roads Management Plan," *Chaco Roads Project Phase I: A Reappraisal of Prehistoric Roads in the San Juan Basin*. Chris Kincaid, editor. Bureau of Land Management, Albuquerque District Office, 1983.

Kirchhoff, Paul. "Mesoamerica." *Acta americana,* 1943.

Kurjack, Edward B., and Silvia Garza T. "Pre-Columbian Form and Distribution in the Northern Maya Area." Manuscript on file with the Bureau of Land Management, Albuquerque District Office.

Lekson, Stephen H., Thomas C. Windes, John R. Stein, and W. James Judge. "The Chaco Canyon Community." *Scientific American,* 259(1): 100-109, July 1988.

Lekson, Stephen H. "The Idea of the Kiva in Anasazi Archaeology." *The Kiva,* 53(3), 1988.

Lekson, Stephen H. "Sociocomplexity at Chaco Canyon, New Mexico." Dissertation, University of New Mexico, 1988.

Lister, Robert H., and Florence C. Lister. *Chaco Canyon: Archaeology and Archaeologists*. Albuquerque: University of New Mexico Press, 1981.

Lizana, Bernardo de. *Historia de Yucatán*. Valladolid, 1633.

Loew, Oscar. Report on the ruins in New Mexico. Appendix LL to *Annual Report of the Chief Engineers for 1875, Geographical Surveys West of the 100th Meridian,* pp. 174-178.

Lyons, Thomas R., David Bardé, et al. Notes concerning test excavations of the linear features adjacent to Tear Drop Mesa, Kin Bineola, 1972. Manuscript on file, Chaco Center (National Park Service/University of New Mexico), Albuquerque, New Mexico.

Lyons, Thomas R., and Robert K. Hitchcock. "Remote Sensing Interpretation of an Anasazi Land Route System." In Aerial Remote Sensing Techniques in Archaeology, Thomas R. Lyons and Robert K. Hitchcock, editors. *Reports of the Chaco Center,* 2: 111-134, 1977.

Macgowan, K. "The Orientation of Middle American Sites." *American Antiquity,* 1945.

Malville, J. McKim, and Claudia Putnam. *Prehistoric Astronomy in the Southwest.* Boulder: Johnson Books, 1989.

Marcus, Joyce. "Territorial Organization of the Lowland Classic Maya." *Science,* 180(4089), June 1973.

Marshall, Michael P., John R. Stein, Richard W. Loose, and Judith E. Novotny. *Anasazi Communities of the San Juan Basin,* for the Public Service Company of New Mexico and the Historic Preservation Bureau, Planning Division, Department of Finance and Administration of the State of New Mexico, 1979.

Martin, Paul S. "Lowry Ruin in Southwestern Colorado." *Field Museum of Natural History Anthropological Series,* 23(1), 1936.

Mason, J.A. *Late Archaeological Sites in Durango, Mexico, from Chalchihuites to Zape.* Philadelphia: Publications of the Philadelphia Anthropological Society, Twenty-Fifth Anniversary Studies, Vol. 1, 1937.

Mathien, Frances Joan. "Economic Exchange Systems in the San Juan Basin." Dissertation, University of New Mexico, 1981.

Matthew, Washington. "Noqolpi, the Gambler: A Navajo Myth." *The Journal of American Folklore,* 2(5), April-June 1889.

McClusky, S.C. "Historical Archaeoastronomy: The Hopi Example." In *Archaeoastronomy in the New World.* Anthony F. Aveni, editor. New York: Cambridge University Press, 1982.

Miera y Pacheco, Bernardo de. Quotation is from Herbert E. Bolton, "Pageant in the Wilderness." *Utah Historical Quarterly,* 18:45, 1950.

Morrison, C.C. Executive and descriptive report by Lieutenant C.C. Morrison, Sixth Calvary, on the operations of Party No. 2, Colorado Section, field season of 1875. Appendix JJ to *Annual Report of the Chief of Engineers for 1876, Geographical Surveys West of the 100th Meridian,* pp. 356-367.

Myer, William E. "Indian Trails of the Southeast." In *Forty-second Annual Report of the Bureau of American Ethnology to the Smithsonian Institution 1924-1925.* Washington, D.C.: Government Printing Office, 1928, pp. 717-857.

Nabokov, Peter. *Indian Running: Native American History and Tradition.* Santa Fe: Ancient City Press, 1981.

Nials, Fred, John Stein, and John Roney. *Chacoan Roads in the Southern Periphery: Results of Phase II of the BLM Chaco Roads Project,* Cultural Resources Series, No. 1, 1987.

Nials, Fred L. "Factors Affecting the Visibility of Roads." In *Chaco Roads Project Phase I: A Reappraisal of Prehistoric Roads in the San Juan Basin.* Chris Kincaid, editor. Bureau of Land Management, Albuquerque District Office, 1983.

Nials, Fred L. "Physical Characteristics of Chacoan Roads." In *Chaco Roads Project Phase I: A Reappraisal of Prehistoric Roads in the San Juan Basin.* Chris Kincaid, editor. Bureau of Land Management, Albuquerque District Office, 1983.

Obenauf, Margaret Senter. "Evaluation of Aerial Photography." In *Chaco Roads Project Phase I: A Reappraisal of Prehistoric Roads in the San Juan Basin,*

Chris Kincaid, editor. Bureau of Land Management, Albuquerque District Office, 1983.

Obenauf, Margaret Senter. "The Chacoan Roadway System." Master's thesis, University of New Mexico, 1980.

Ortiz, Alfonso. *New Perspectives on the Pueblos*. A School of American Research Book. Albuquerque: University of New Mexico Press, 1972.

Parsons, Elsie Clews. *The Pueblo of Jemez*. Papers of the Phillips Academy Southwestern Expedition, 3. New Haven: Yale University Press, 1925.

Parsons, Elsie Clews. *A Pueblo Indian Journal, 1920-1921*. Memoirs of the American Anthropological Association, No. 32.

Parsons, Elsie Clews. *Pueblo Indian Religion*. Chicago: University of Chicago Press, 1939.

Reiche, Maria. *Mystery on the Desert*. Lima: private publication, 1969.

Reyman, Jonathan E. "Priests, Power, and Politics: Some Implications of Socioceremonial Control." In *Astronomy and Ceremony in the Prehistoric Southwest*. John B. Carlson and W. James Judge, editors. Papers of the Maxwell Museum of Anthropology, No. 2, 1987.

Robertson, Benjamin P. "Other New Worlds and Trails." In *Chaco Roads Project Phase I: A Reappraisal of Prehistoric Roads in the San Juan Basin*. Chris Kincaid, editor. Bureau of Land Management, Albuquerque District Office, 1983.

Romanov, Michael Alexander. "Yucatec Roads and the Orientation of the Maya World." Dissertation, University of Oregon, 1973.

Roney, John R. "Prehistoric Roads and Regional Integration in the Chacoan System." Paper prepared for the Symposium, "Anasazi Regional Organization and the Chaco System," 55th Annual Meeting, Society for American Archaeology, 1990. To be published by the Maxwell Museum.

Sabloff, Jeremy A. *The Cities of Ancient Mexico: Reconstructing a Lost World*. New York: Thames and Hudson, 1989.

Schaafsma, Polly. "Rock Art and Ideology of the Mimbres and Jornada Mogollon," *The Artifact*, 13:2-14, 1975.

Schaafsma, Polly, and C. Schaafsma. "Evidence for the Origins of the Pueblo Kachina Cult as Suggested by Southwestern Rock Art." *American Antiquity*, 39:353-545.

Schroeder, Albert H. "Pattern Diffusion from Mexico into the Southwest after A.D. 600." *American Antiquity*, 31(5):683-704, 1966.

Sebastian, Lynne. "Leadership, Power, and Productive Potential: A Political Model of the Chaco System." Dissertation, University of New Mexico, 1988.

Simpson, First Lt. James H. "Journal of a Military Reconnaissance from Santa Fe, New Mexico to the Navajo Country, Made with the Troops under Command of Lt. Col. John M. Washington in 1849," *Senate Executive Document No. 64, 31st. Congress, 1st Session,* 1852. The report was edited and annotated by Frank McNitt and reissued as *Navajo Expedition, Journal of a Military Recon-*

naissance from Santa Fe, New Mexico to the Navajo Country Made in 1849. Norman: University of Oklahoma Press, 1964.

Sofaer, Anna, Rolf M. Sinclair, and Joey B. Donahue. "Solar and Lunar Orientations of the Major Architecture of the Chaco Culture of New Mexico." Paper to be published in the *Proceedings of the Colloquio Internazionale Archeologia e Astronomia,* held at the University of Venice, May 1989.

Sofaer, Anna, Michael P. Marshall, and Rolf M. Sinclair. "The Great North Road: A Cosmographic Expression of the Chaco Culture of New Mexico." In *World Archaeoastronomy: Selected Papers from the 2nd Oxford International Conference of Archaeoastronomy.* Anthony F. Aveni, editor. Cambridge: Cambridge University Press, 1989.

Stein, John R. "Road Corridor Descriptions." In *Chaco Roads Project Phase I: A Reappraisal of Prehistoric Roads in the San Juan Basin.* Chris Kincaid, editor. Bureau of Land Management, Albuquerque District Office, 1983.

Stein, John R. "The Chaco Roads—Clues to an Ancient Riddle?" *El Palacio,* 94(3), Spring 1989.

Stephen, Alexander M. *Hopi notebooks,* Vol. 1, "Legends" (Letters to J. Walter Fewkes of the Bureau of American Ethnology between 1883 and 1936, Washington SI/NAA, File 4408-4), Columbia University Library, Elsie Clews Parsons Collection; Hopi Journal, edited by Elsie Clews Parsons, Columbia University Contributions to Anthropology, 23, 1936.

Stevenson, Matilda Coxe. *The Sia.* Eleventh Annual Report of the Bureau of American Ethnology. Washington, D.C.: Smithsonian Institution, 1889.

Stevenson, Matilda Coxe. *The Zuni Indians.* Twenty-third Annual Report, Bureau of American Ethnology. Washington, D.C.: Smithsonian Institution, 1904.

Stirling, Matthew W. "Origin Myth of Acoma." *Bureau of American Ethnology Bulletin,* 135:1-123. Washington, D.C.: Smithsonian Institution, 1942.

Thompson, G. "Notes on the Pueblos and Their Inhabitants." In *Report upon United States Geographical Surveys West of the One Hundredth Meridian, Vol. VII: Archeology, Part II: The Pueblo Ruins and the Interior Tribes.* Frederick W. Putnam. Washington D.C.: U.S. Engineer Department, 1879, pp. 319-324.

Tichy, Franz. "Deutung von Orts-und Flurnetzen im Hochland von Mexiko als Kultreligiöse Reliktformen Altindianischer Besiedlung." *Erdkunde* (Bonn), 28(3):194-207, 1974.

Trombold, Charles D. "Causeways in the Context of Strategic Planning in the La Quemada Region, Zacatecas, Mexico." In *Ancient Road Networks and Settlement Hierarchies in the New World.* New York: Cambridge University Press, in press.

Trombold, Charles D. A "Reconsideration of Chronology for the La Quemada Portion of the Northern Mesoamerican Frontier." *American Antiquity,* 55(2), 1990.

Truell, Marcia. "An Examination of Small Site Diversity in Chaco Canyon in the Late A.D. 1000s and Early to Middle 1100s." *National Park Service Publications in Archaeology,* 18D, 1986. Manuscript on file, Chaco Center, Southwest Cultural Resources Center, National Park Service, Albuquerque.

Twain, Mark. *Roughing It.* Hartford: American Publishing Company, 1872.

Tyler, Hamilton A. *Pueblo Gods and Myths.* Norman: University of Oklahoma Press, 1964.

Vivian, Gordon. *The Hubbard Site and Other Tri-Wall Structures in New Mexico and Colorado.* National Park Service Archaeological Research Series No. 5. Washington D.C.: U.S. Government Printing Office, 1959.

Vivian, Gordon, R. Memorandum to Superintendent, Chaco Canyon National Monument. Subject: Prehistoric water conservation project. Date: November 20, 1964. Ms. on file, Division of Cultural Research (Chaco Center), Southwest Cultural Resources Center, National Park Service, Albuquerque.

Vivian, Gordon, and Tom W. Matthew. *Kin Kletso.* Southwest Parks and Monuments Association Technical Series, Vol. 6, Part 1. Globe, Arizona: Southwest Parks and Monuments Association, 1964.

Vivian, Gwinn. "Identifying and Interpreting Chacoan Roads: An Historical Perspective." In *Chaco Roads Project Phase I: A Reappraisal of Prehistoric Roads in the San Juan Basin.* Chris Kincaid, editor. Bureau of Land Management, Albuquerque District Office, 1983.

Vivian, Gwinn. "An Inquiry into Prehistoric Social Organization at Chaco Canyon, New Mexico." In *Reconstructing Prehistoric Pueblo Societies,* William A. Longacre, editor. Albuquerque: University of New Mexico Press, 1970, pp. 59-83.

Vivian, R. Gwinn. "Kluckhohn Reappraised: The Chacoan System as an Egalitarian Enterprise." *Journal of Anthropological Research,* University of New Mexico, 45(1), Spring 1989.

Vivian, R. Gwinn, and Robert Buettner. "Pre-Columbian Roadways in the Chaco Canyon Region, New Mexico." Paper presented to the 37th Meeting of the Society of American Archaeologists, May 1973.

Voth, H.R. "The Oraibi Powamu Ceremony." Field Columbian Museum, *Anthropological Series,* 3(2), Chicago, 1901.

Waters, Frank. *Mexico Mystique: The Coming Sixth World of Consciousness.* Newbury Park: Sage Books, 1975.

Wetherill, Lulu Wade, and Byron Cummings. "A Navajo Folk Tale of Pueblo Bonito." *Art and Archaeology,* Vol. 14, September 1922.

Wheatley, Paul. *The Pivot of the Four Quarters.* Chicago: Aldine, 1971.

Windes, Thomas C. *Investigations at the Pueblo Alto Complex, Chaco Canyon, 1975-1979,* Volume 1. Summary of Tests and Excavations at the Pueblo Alto Community, National Park Service, Santa Fe, New Mexico, 1987.

Wilcox, David R. "The Evolution of Hohokam Ceremonial Systems." In *Astronomy and Ceremony in the Prehistoric Southwest.* John B. Carlson and W. James Judge, editors. Papers of the Maxwell Museum of Anthropology, No. 2, 1987.

Williamson, Ray A., Howard J. Fisher, Abigail F. Williamson, and Clarion Cochran. "The Astronomical Record in Chaco Canyon, New Mexico." In *Archaeoastronomy in Pre-Columbian America.* Anthony F. Aveni, editor. Austin: University of Texas Press, 1975.

Williamson, Ray A., Howard J. Fisher, and Donnel O'Flynn. "Anasazi Solar Observations." In *Native American Astronomy*. Anthony F. Aveni, editor. Austin: University of Texas Press, 1977.

Williamson, Ray A. "Light and Shadow, Ritual, and Astronomy in Anasazi Structures." In *Astronomy and Ceremony in the Prehistoric Southwest*. John B. Carlson and W. James Judge, editors. Papers of the Maxwell Museum of Anthropology, No. 2, 1987.

York, Frederick. "An ethnographic survey of localities of significance to the Navajo population in the vicinity of the NMGS impact area." 1982. In New Mexico Generating Station Third-Party Environmental Impact Statement: Cultural Resources in San Juan, McKinley, and Sandoval Counties, New Mexico. Carol J. Condie, editor. *Quivera Research Center Publication,* 39:IV-186. Manuscript on file, Albuquerque District Office, Bureau of Land Management, Albuquerque.

Young, M. Jane. "The Southwest Connection: Similarities between Western Puebloan and Mesoamerican Cosmology." In *World Archaeoastronomy: Selected Papers from the 2nd Oxford International Conference of Archaeoastronomy*. Anthony F. Aveni, editor. Cambridge: Cambridge University Press, 1989.

Zeilik, Michael. "Anticipation in Ceremony: The Readiness is All." *Astronomy and Ceremony in the Prehistoric Southwest*. John B. Carlson and W. James Judge, editors. Papers of the Maxwell Museum of Anthropology, No. 2, 1987.

Zeilik, Michael, "Keeping the Sacred Connection: Archaeoastronomy in the Pueblo Southwest." *World Archaeoastronomy: Selected Papers from the 2nd Oxford International Conference of Archaeoastronomy*. Anthony F. Aveni, editor. Cambridge: Cambridge University Press, 1989.

Zolbrod, Paul G. *Diné bahane': The Navajo Creation Story*. Albuquerque: University of New Mexico Press, 1984.

Index

A Brief
Handbook
of English

with Research Paper

A Brief
Handbook
of English

with Research Paper

Hulon Willis

Bakersfield College

HARCOURT BRACE JOVANOVICH, INC.

New York / Chicago / San Francisco / Atlanta

For Sara

ISBN: 0-15-505561-5

Library of Congress Catalog Card Number: 75-35324

Printed in the United States of America

Contents

CONTENTS

SECTION SIX

THE RESEARCH PAPER 239

27 The Research Paper 241

Preface

A Brief Handbook of English is also available in a variant version that does not include the section on writing the research paper.

This text is a concise reference guide to usage and grammar for beginning writers. It is designed to help them improve the conciseness, clarity, and correctness of their writing. With the book's usefulness foremost in my mind, I have concentrated on the writing problems most troublesome to students. I have avoided subtleties such as "squinting modifiers" and disputed areas of usage such as "reason is because," and have given short explanations—rather than exhaustive analyses—of why the rules are what they are. As much as possible I have avoided discussing options in various aspects of usage, in order not to confuse students or bog them down in a consideration of exceptions. For example, I simply state the rule that a comma is used to separate independent clauses joined by a coordinating conjunction. If a student inserts such a comma in one of the rare cases when it is not needed, no error will be marked; but if the book were to give a full explanation of options, the student might become confused. For this reason I have given concise rules and instructions without splitting hairs. One of my basic assumptions in preparing this book is that in one semester an average student cannot master the basics *and also* many of the refinements of writing. I have restricted myself to the basics. The book, I hope, is not overly prescriptive, but it does take a positive stance in presenting basic rules that the student can rely on.

In so far as is possible, each section of the book is self-contained and offers a minimum of technical explanations. Still, many common grammatical terms must be used in such a reference guide. Students using the book in a non-sequential way may encounter unfamiliar terms that are not explained at that point. Since it is impractical to define terms fully each time they are used, I have included a long opening chapter that explains the basic system of English grammar as scholarly-traditional grammarians see it. I have, however, omitted aspects of grammar that do not have a bearing on the teaching of usage and composition. The book can be used with profit even if Chapter 1 is ignored altogether, but many instructors will want their students to become familiar with the organization and content of this chapter at the beginning of the composition course. The chapter is designed to be a reference book within a reference book. Students can use it easily, since the book's outside back cover indexes all the grammatical terms defined in Chapter 1. The Instructor's Manual contains some exercises on Chapter 1, so that a teacher who wishes may use Chapter 1 and the whole book as a teaching text as well as a reference text.

The Instructor's Manual also contains tests. Since virtually every school nowadays has means of quick reproduction of exercises and tests, it seemed practical to make these available in this form. Instructors may ignore the Manual or may use its materials as their own. The preface to the Manual explains its nature in detail.

Two different correction charts are provided for the teacher's use in guiding the student's revisions. One chart gives number-letter symbols according to the book's organization, with the name of the error or weakness accompanying the number-letter symbol. Teachers who use this chart will therefore make such marks as 3A, 10C, 22D, and so forth on the student's paper, and the student will know which section to refer to for guidance. This chart can also be used more generally, as when the instructor uses the number 10 to indicate an error in the use of the comma without specifying which rule has been violated.

The other chart is composed of traditional symbols, such as *agr, DM, W,* and so on, with the full name of the error following the symbol. The section of the handbook devoted to that error is identified in parentheses after the name of the error. Thus instructors who do not want to use number-letter symbols have a traditional correction chart available to them. The student will find both systems equally usable.

Except where such use would serve no purpose, I have used student writing for examples, on the theory that such examples will ring true to the student when an artificial example might not. In giving a revised version of a student sentence containing an error, I have corrected the error only and have not tried to improve the sentence in other ways. To change more than the error under discussion would, I think, distract the student. Still, the revisions are not *bad* sentences that might adversely affect the student's future writing. Every example is clearly labeled *wrong, right, poor style,* and so on, to eliminate any possibility of confusion.

Two sections of the book may be called glossaries. Section 16G is composed of homophones—such as *course* and *coarse*—and other words that are often confused in spelling but not in meaning. Section 22B is composed of words often confused in meaning—such as *infer* and *imply.* Both correction charts allow the teacher to refer the student to the glossaries.

HULON WILLIS

Introduction
to the Student

This text is a guide to usage and grammar to help you improve the conciseness, clarity, and correctness of your writing. Primarily, you will use it as a reference book. It is designed so that your teacher can refer you to particular sections that will explain an error or weakness in your writing and give you guidance in revision. You may also be given exercises and exams to test your mastery of various sections of the book. Even when you are not using the book to revise one of your papers, you may use it to look up rules of punctuation, capitalization, spelling, and so on, so that your paper will require less revision.

Explanations of various rules and instructions about writing require the use of some grammatical terms. You may not be familiar with all of them. Therefore the first chapter is a simplified explanation of the basic system of

English grammar. You will probably not be required to read this chapter all at once, but you should skim it to see what information it contains and how that information is organized. Read the sections that you think you need, and return to the chapter as necessary throughout your course. So that you may use this chapter for quick reference, the outside back cover of the book lists alphabetically, with page numbers, all the grammatical terms defined in Chapter 1. Thus if you need to find out what, say, a conjunctive adverb is, you can refer to the index on the back cover and then to the page in Chapter 1 that clearly explains what a conjunctive adverb is. This chapter avoids grammatical terms and concepts that are not useful in the teaching of usage and composition.

SECTION ONE

GRAMMAR

1

Introduction:
The Basic System
of English Grammar

Since this text is a reference book, you will not be studying or referring to its chapters in sequence. Instead, on any particular day you may refer first to, say, Chapter 24, then Chapter 3, then Chapter 12, and so on. Thus you need to know some basic grammatical terms before you begin to use this book. This introductory chapter contains simple definitions, with brief examples, of the basic terms you need to know in order to use this book with ease and profit. Probably you already know some of these terms, and maybe all of them, but here they are for your reference, review, or study, should your teacher suggest that. Think of this chapter as a reference book within a reference book. Become familiar with it now, and refer to it for help whenever problems arise in your writing. All of the important terms in it are listed alphabetically with page references on the outside back cover.

1A   PARTS OF SPEECH

Our language is composed of words, and each word is a part of speech. We recognize words as particular parts of speech by their form or their function, or both. Parts of speech have characteristic forms and functions: nouns serve as subjects and complements, adjectives modify nouns and pronouns, and so on. Yet in actual sentences, nouns and even verbs sometimes modify nouns. Thus parts of speech must be classified **by function** as well as by form. Examples:

ADJECTIVE MODIFYING NOUN: a **pretty** dress
NOUN MODIFYING NOUN: a **cotton** dress
VERB MODIFYING NOUN: a **soaking** dress
DETERMINER MODIFYING NOUN: **her** dress

Knowing that parts of speech may be classified by form and by function will help you use some chapters in this book more profitably. Further illustration of this dual classification, with names of the parts of speech by function, will be given in Section 1E.

The four parts of speech by form that carry the vast bulk of meaning in our language — **nouns, verbs, adjectives,** and **adverbs** — are known as **content words.** They will be defined next. Since these parts of speech are difficult to define, we will briefly discuss several characteristics of each. After a little practice you will come to have a natural feeling for which words are nouns, verbs, adjectives, and adverbs, if you do not already.

1A1   Nouns

One quite satisfactory definition of *noun* is that it is the name of anything that exists or that can be conceived. Thus such "names" as *chaos, time, love,* and *apple* are nouns.

Almost every noun can either be made plural or possessive or both. Examples:

> one **game**   two **games**
> one **ox**   two **oxen**
> **golf**'s contribution to the sports world
> **concentration**'s effect on the mind
> the **Harrises**' wedding anniversary

In these ways nouns can be identified by form.

Almost all nouns can be meaningfully preceded by one of the indefinite articles, *a* or *an;* or by the definite article, *the;* or by a possessive word such as *my, your,* or *John's.* Examples:

> a **drink**   the **whisky**   Fred's **pride**
> my **love**   her **hose**   Julia's **devotion**

Do not let intervening words—as in *a crisp, sweet apple*—keep you from understanding how *a, an, the, my,* and so on announce the presence of a noun.

Finally, certain word endings, or suffixes, added to other parts of speech form nouns. (Such suffixes are occasionally added to nouns also.) A knowledge of these suffixes will help you get a natural feeling for nouns. Here are the most common, with the suffixes in boldface:

> mile + **age** = mileage
> deny + **al** = denial
> appear + **ance** = appearance
> assist + **ant** = assistant
> beg + **ar** = beggar
> dull + **ard** = dullard
> purify + **cation** = purification
> secret + **cy** = secrecy
> king + **dom** = kingdom
> refer + **ee** = referee
> superintend + **ent** = superintendent
> advise + **er** = adviser
> China + **ese** = Chinese

boy + **hood** = boyhood
just + **ice** = justice
act + **ion** = action
social + **ism** = socialism
commune + **ist** = communist
labor + **ite** = laborite
active + **ity** = activity
achieve + **ment** = achievement
lovely + **ness** = loveliness
counsel + **or** = counselor
slave + **ry** = slavery
kin + **ship** = kinship
dissent + **sion** = dissension
introduce + **tion** = introduction
fail + **ure** = failure

These word endings are known as **noun-forming suffixes.**
 Knowledge of all the above characteristics of nouns will
help you in identifying this part of speech.

1A2 Verbs

Verbs are words that express an action or a state of being.
Usually, a verb gives an indication of the time of occurrence
of the action or state of being. This indication is called
tense. For example, the noun —

 a fight

expresses an action but no time of occurrence. But in —

 José **will fight** fairly

or

 Sara **fights** viciously,

the same word used as a verb specifies a time of occurrence. (Note that a verb may be one word or more than one
word. In the first sentence, "will fight" is the verb.)
 Verbs, however, are most easily identified by form. With
a very few exceptions, every verb in English has an *ing* form

and a singular, present-tense form ending in *s* or *es*. Also every verb has either a regular *(ed)* or irregular past-tense and past-participle form. Thus virtually every English verb will fit this framework (called a paradigm):

infinitive	third-person singular, present tense	present participle	past tense	past participle
to hug	hugs	hugging	hugged	hugged
to break	breaks	breaking	broke	broken

For simplicity, we can say that any word that takes, the *ing* suffix and the *s* suffix to make the singular present tense is a verb.

For proper use of this text you need to know the three categories of verbs and three of their special functions. The three categories of verbs are as follows:

a. Intransitive verbs An intransitive verb is an action verb that, in a sentence, does not have a direct object. The subject performs an action without anybody or anything receiving the action. Examples:

INTRANSITIVE VERBS: Quincy **smokes** frequently.
                    This can opener never **works.**
                    Melissa **smiled** at me.

Modifiers, such as the adverbs *frequently* and *never* and the prepositional phrase *at me,* do not prevent a verb from being intransitive. The pronoun *me* is the object of the preposition, not a direct object of the verb.

b. Transitive verbs A transitive verb is an action verb that, in a sentence, takes a direct object; that is, the action is performed on someone or something. Examples:

TRANSITIVE VERBS: Lucy **smokes** cigars.
                  Maury **beats** his wife.

Cigars and *his wife* are direct objects. Some verbs are intransitive in some sentences and transitive in others.

c. Linking verbs Linking verbs are state-of-being verbs, such as *to be, to seem, to appear, to become, to look,* *to taste, to sound, to remain.* Linking verbs are followed either by a predicate noun, which tells what the subject is or seems to be, or by a predicate adjective, which describes the subject. Examples:

LINKING VERBS: Julius **is** a weirdo.

Mr. Merle **became** dogcatcher.

Shirley **looks** pregnant.

Barry **remained** calm.

Weirdo and *dogcatcher* are predicate nouns, and *pregnant* and *calm* are predicate adjectives.

Some verbs can function as either intransitive, transitive, or linking. Examples:

INTRANSITIVE: The tree **grew** slowly. (no direct object)
TRANSITIVE: George **grew** a beard. (direct object *beard*)
LINKING: My date **grew** restless. (predicate adjective *restless*)

Linking verbs cause some special writing problems, which are covered in later chapters.

The three special functions of verbs that you need to know are the following:

d. Tense   Tense is the function of verbs that specifies time of occurrence. The tense system in English is immensely complex, but for use of this book you need to know only whether a verb form contains one of the past, present, or future tenses. Examples:

PAST TENSES: My horse **vanished** last night.

The cops **had left** before I **returned.**

PRESENT TENSES: I **am telling** you the truth.

Shelley usually **studies** after midnight.

FUTURE TENSES: Times **will get** better.

Maurice **is going to plead** guilty.

e. Voice   Voice has to do with whether a subject performs or receives an action. Only action verbs have voice. If in a sentence the subject performs the action, the verb and sentence are said to be in the **active voice.** Example:

ACTIVE VOICE: Benny **mugged** an old man for six pennies.

If the subject receives the action, the verb and sentence are said to be in the **passive voice.** Example:

PASSIVE VOICE: An old man **was mugged** for six pennies.

If the doer of the action in a passive-voice sentence is mentioned, he is named in a *by* phrase; e.g., *by Benny* could be attached to the preceding example sentence. A passive-voice verb always has a form of *to be* in it.

 f. Mood Mood is the function of a verb that expresses the speaker's attitude toward the factuality or likelihood of what he says. The **indicative mood** expresses a fact or what is believed to be a fact. Example:

INDICATIVE MOOD: Ricky **makes** more money stealing than I **do** working.

The **subjunctive mood** indicates condition contrary to fact, or doubt, potentiality, desirability, obligation, and other such nonfactual concepts. Examples:

SUBJUNCTIVE MOOD: I wish I **were** a member of the Realities.
I suggested that he **keep** quiet. (Note that *keeps* won't function here properly even though *he* is singular.)
You **should marry** a second wife.

The **imperative mood** states a request or command. Examples:

IMPERATIVE MOOD: **Get** off my back.
Scatter before we're caught.

There are other functions of verbs, but the foregoing are the ones that have to do with writing problems discussed in later chapters.

1A3 Adjectives

An adjective is a describing word; it describes (or modifies) a noun or pronoun. But other parts of speech—such as the noun *comedian* and the verb *stumbles*—also carry an element of description. Thus *adjective* is very hard to define. But an understanding of the following characteristics of adjectives will give you a feel for identifying them.

First, almost all adjectives can be **compared** with *er* (or *more*) and *est* (or *most*). Examples:

stem	*comparative form*	*superlative form*
sweet	sweeter	sweetest
beautiful	more beautiful	most beautiful

But since adverbs also can be compared, more is needed to identify adjectives by form. Thus if a word can be compared *and* (1) can have *ly* added to make an adverb *or* (2) can have *ness* added to make a noun, it is an adjective. Examples:

clear	clearer	clearest	clearly
mean	meaner	meanest	meanness

Words fitting these two requirements are always adjectives. In comparing some adjectives (or adverbs) *more* and *most* are used instead of *er* and *est* solely to make the word sound smooth rather than awkward. *Beautifulest* is awkward, while *most beautiful* is smooth. The comparative *(er)* and superlative *(est)* forms of *good* and *well* are the irregular *better* and *best;* of *bad* and *ill* they are the irregular *worse* and *worst.*

Another easy test to help you get the feel of the adjective is to see that adjectives fit this pattern (any common noun can be used instead of *student*):

That _____ student is very _____.

Examples:

> That **bright** student is very **bright.**
> That **obscene** joke is very **obscene.**

Almost always when a word fits this pattern it is an adjective by form, and almost all adjectives will fit the pattern.

Here is another easy test to identify adjectives:

> He (she, it) seems _____.

Virtually every word *except a noun* that will fit this slot is an adjective. Examples:

> He seems **up-tight.**
> She seems **virtuous.**
> It seems **dead.**

An understanding of this structural position of the adjective will improve your ability to recognize that part of speech automatically.

Finally, we use a number of suffixes to convert other parts of speech (and occasionally other adjectives) into adjectives. Here are the most common, with the suffixes in boldface:

> read + **able** = readable
> person + **al** = personal
> Africa + **an** = African
> resist + **ant** = resistant
> fortune + **ate** = fortunate
> conserve + **ative** = conservative
> exist + **ent** = existent
> sin + **ful** = sinful
> athlete + **ic** = athletic
> boy + **ish** = boyish
> assert + **ive** = assertive
> mercy + **less** = merciless
> bird + **like** = birdlike
> lone + **ly** = lonely
> prohibit + **ory** = prohibitory
> courage + **ous** = courageous
> quarrel + **some** = quarrelsome
> shine + **y** = shiny

These word endings are known as **adjective-forming suffixes.** Understanding them will help you develop a feel for identifying adjectives. Be sure to note that the suffix *ly* forms only a few adjectives; in most cases that suffix changes an adjective into an adverb. If a word ending in *ing* or *ed*—such as *interesting* and *excited*—can be modified by *very,* it is an adjective.

1A4 Adverbs

Like the adjective, the adverb is a describing word. Its most common function is to describe (or modify) a verb, telling how, when, or where. (Also, adverbs sometimes modify adjectives and other adverbs.) The so-called "pure" adverbs are those that are formed from adjectives by the addition of the suffix *ly*. Examples:

adjective	*adverb*
rapid	rapidly
sweet	sweetly
loving	lovingly
excited	excitedly

Like adjectives, such adverbs can be compared. Examples:

stem	*comparative form*	*superlative form*
bitterly	more bitterly	most bitterly
happily	more happily	most happily

This is the easy way to recognize most English adverbs, but you should be careful not to confuse the few *ly* adjectives— *kindly, lovely, friendly, timely*, and a few others—with adverbs.

The difference between adjectives and adverbs is illustrated in these two sentences:

ADJECTIVE: John looked **curious.**
ADVERB: John looked **curiously.**

The first sentence (with *looked* as a linking verb) describes the appearance of John. The second (with *looked* as an intransitive verb) tells the manner in which John looked at something.

English also has a number of so-called "flat" adverbs that do not end in *ly* but that do usually modify verbs. Most of them express either time or place. The most common ones are *soon, never, often, there, here, upward, well* (which is also an adjective), *inside, now, seldom, always, somewhere, behind, above,* and some other words like these.

A useful fact to know about adverbs is that most of them express **time, place,** or **manner** and thus can have the words *then, there,* and *thus* substituted for them. Examples:

I'll come **sometime.** = I'll come **then.**
I can't find the jam **anywhere.** = I can't find the jam **there.**
She smiled **wickedly.** = She smiled **thus.**

However, words and word groups that are not adverbs by form also modify verbs, and they may meaningfully have *then, there,* or *thus* substituted for them. Examples:

Cheryl came **home.** = there   (*Home* is a noun.)
We'll call **at ten o'clock.** = then   (*At ten o'clock* is a prepositional phrase.)
Hemingway wrote **standing.** = thus   (*Standing* is a verb.)

In Section 1E we will make modification clearer, but understanding the above characteristics of adverbs will give you a feel for identifying them. Some important writing problems are concerned with the distinction between adjectives and adverbs.

1A5   Structure Words

The vast majority of words in English are nouns, verbs, adjectives, and adverbs. As content words, they are **open classes,** which means that new words (or new definitions of old words) enter these classes frequently, thus expanding the English vocabulary. A much smaller number of words, but a larger number of parts of speech, are called **structure words.** Even though most of these words carry some meaning, their chief function is to provide a framework for arranging the many nouns, verbs, adjectives, and adverbs into meaningful sentences. The structure words all belong to **closed classes,** because new ones very rarely enter the language. There are many kinds of structure words, and there is much overlapping in the groups. (That is, one word, such as *that,* may belong to several groups.) Their grammatical behavior is complex. We will mention and briefly define only those of which you need an elementary knowledge in order to use this text as a reference handbook. What follows is only a very small part of the total grammar of structure words, the part that will be useful to you.

a. Determiners   Words that signal that a noun is coming are called determiners. They determine something about the nature of the noun that follows. Sometimes two determiners precede a noun. A few single determiners consist of two words. Here are examples of the chief determiners:

a bottle	**John's** hangover	**all** prisons
an oyster	**this** remedy	**every** chance
the grape	**no** money	**such a** pity
my beer	**some** disease	**all the** excuses

The words in boldface may be thought of as noun markers. Any **noun marker** like these is a determiner. Of course other words may come between the determiner and its noun, as in *a silly old man.*

Incidentally, the list above shows how parts of speech may be labeled differently as their functions differ. While *John's* is a determiner here, *John* is commonly a noun; *all* and *some* can be pronouns, and so on.

b. Prepositions   A preposition is a kind of connective that shows a relationship between two words. The second word is usually a noun or noun substitute which functions as the object of the preposition and helps form a prepositional phrase. (Prepositional phrases are discussed in more detail in Section 1B1.) Examples, with the prepositions in boldface and the prepositional phrases underlined:

the man **with** the hoe	different **from** mine
the time **of** day	do it **for** me
a trip **to** the islands	conducted **by** the composer

You would be very hard pressed to give a clear definition of *with, from, of,* and *for* in these constructions; they are structure, not content, words. However, most prepositions do have some meaning. In using a number of the chapters of this text you will need to recognize prepositional phrases. Here are the most common single-word prepositions:

above	besides	into	through
across	between	like	till
after	beyond	near	to
along	but	of	toward(s)
among	by	off	under
around	down	on	until
at	during	outside	upon
before	for	over	with
behind	from	past	within
below	in	save	without
beside	inside	since	

We also have compound prepositions in English, of which the following are the most common:

ahead of	contrary to	instead of
apart from	due to	on account of
as for	for the sake of	out of
as well as	in addition to	owing to
aside from	in back of	rather than
away from	in case of	together with
because of	in front of	up at
belonging to	in place of	up on
by means of	in spite of	up to
by way of	inside of	with regard to

Some of these compound prepositions—as in the construction *in addition to the money*—can be analyzed as forming two prepositional phrases rather than one phrase with a compound preposition.

   c. Verb auxiliaries Many verbs are composed of two or more words, the last word being the main verb and the others being auxiliaries that specify tense and other meanings. Examples, with the auxiliaries in boldface:

have been going   **will be** gone
could have gone   **should have been** going

The number of possible combinations of auxiliaries in English verb forms is enormous. Fortunately, in order to use this text, you need only recognize auxiliaries, not understand their complex grammar.

The verbs *to be, to do,* and *to have* have meanings in English and can function as sentence verbs. But forms of these verbs also function as auxiliaries, with their meanings being entirely different from their meanings as regular verbs. For example, in —

I **have** some beans,

have has the meaning of *possess.* But in —

I **have** roasted some beans,

have has no such meaning. It is an auxiliary verb that helps to convey tense. The case is similar with *to be* and *to do.* These forms of *to be, to do,* and *to have* function as verb auxiliaries:

to be: be, am, is, are, was, were, being, *and* been
to do: do, does, *and* did
to have: has, have, having, *and* had

Examples:

Joseph **has been** studying for an hour.
Molly **does** respect her parents.

Another group of words are called **modal auxiliaries.** Although they are used with a main verb, they carry meaning of their own. The chief modal auxiliaries are the following:

| can | may | must | shall | will |
| could | might | ought to | should | would |

Examples:

I **may** leave early, but you **ought to** help the committee.

The modals carry some tense meaning and also express subtle meanings of intent, possibility, obligation, condition, and so on.

d. Coordinating connectives   A coordinating connective joins two grammatical constructions equal in rank, such as two nouns, two prepositional phrases, or two independent clauses. Many of the chapters in this text will refer to them. Two classes of these connectives are to be identified:

Coordinating conjunctions (with two exceptions) may be used to join pairs of many kinds of constructions, from single words to independent clauses. (Clauses will be discussed more fully later in this chapter.) They are the following:

and	or	both . . . and
but	nor	not only . . . but (also)
yet	for	either . . . or
	so	neither . . . nor

For and *so* can be used to join only independent clauses. The two-part conjunctions are also called **correlatives.**

Conjunctive adverbs are coordinating connectives that join only independent clauses. They are the following:

accordingly	furthermore	otherwise
afterward(s)	hence	still
also	however	then
besides	later	therefore
consequently	moreover	thus
earlier	nevertheless	

Both kinds of coordinating connectives express such relationships as **contrast, cause-and-result, accumulation, condition,** and **time.** When a coordinating connective joins two independent clauses, each could stand by itself as a full, complete sentence, for a sentence may begin with a coordinating connective.

e. Subordinating conjunctions   A subordinating conjunction is a connective that expresses a relationship between two ideas that are not equal in rank. That is, one of the ideas can stand by itself as a sentence, but the idea introduced by the subordinating conjunction cannot. If let stand by itself, it would be a nonsentence, or a sentence fragment. Many words that are subordinating conjunctions in some sentence can be prepositions or other connectives in other sentences. You will recall that there is much over-lapping of structure words in English. For reference, here is a list of subordinating conjunctions:

after	if	since
although	in case (that)	so long as
as	in order that	so (that)
as . . . as	in that	than
as if	inasmuch as	though
as long as	less than	unless
as soon as	like	until
as though	more than	when
because	no matter how	where
before	now that	whereas
even though	once	while
fewer than	provided (that)	

The subordinating conjunctions are very important words that express such relationships as **cause-and-result, contrast, condition, manner** or **method, purpose, time,** and **place.** To use this reference handbook fully, you need a basic understanding of them.

f. Pronouns   A pronoun is defined as a word that stands for a noun, the noun being the pronoun's **antecedent.** But the English pronoun system is far more complex than that definition indicates. The pronoun system causes so many writing problems that it will be dealt with in several chapters of this book. Here, we will identify five kinds of pronouns: personal, relative, interrogative, demonstrative, and indefinite.

The **personal pronouns** have **case,** which means that they change their forms according to their use in sentences. There are three cases in English: (1) the **subjective,** (2) the **objective,** and (3) the **possessive.** Here are the case forms of the personal pronouns:

subjective case	*objective case*	*possessive case*
I	me	my, mine
you	you	your, yours
he	him	his
she	her	her, hers
it	it	its
we	us	our, ours
they	them	their, theirs

The personal pronouns also have **reflexive** forms, as follows:

myself	himself
ourselves	herself
yourself	itself
yourselves	themselves

The chief **relative pronouns** are *who* (subjective case), *whom* (objective case), *whose* (possessive case), *which,* and *that.* (These last two do not have case.) A relative pronoun is used to connect (or relate) a dependent clause to another part of a sentence. Example:

There's the cop **who** busted me.

The antecedent of *who* is *cop. Who* introduces the clause and relates it to the first part of the sentence. The relative pronouns, then, are connectives. In a complex grammatical way they join ideas to each other.

Sometimes a relative pronoun is not stated but is understood in a sentence. Example:

The course I like best is Marriage and Family Life.

The relative pronoun *that,* with *course* as its antecedent, is understood before *I.*

Who and *whom* are also **interrogative** (question-forming) pronouns. They pose a writing problem that is discussed in Section 5C.

The **demonstrative pronouns** are the "pointing" pronouns *this, that, these,* and *those.* They may be used with nouns (as determiners) or by themselves, with the nouns understood. Examples:

> **This** pornography seems mild today.
> **That** is the one I want.

In the second sentence, whatever subject is under discussion is understood after *that*.

This and *that* are also used in a more general way to refer to whole ideas. Examples:

RIGHT: I expected Professor Sneed to flunk me, and **that** is what he did.
RIGHT: We are out of cash again. **This** is getting to be a common occurrence.

In these examples, both *that* and *this* have whole ideas as their antecedents.

There is also a sizable group of words in English known as **indefinite pronouns.** They function as nouns but make indefinite reference to people or things.

one	anybody	another
no one	everybody	one another
anyone	nobody	each other
everyone	somebody	anyone else (and
someone	other	others with *else*)

g. Qualifiers   A small group of words that modify adjectives and adverbs are called qualifiers because they qualify, or limit in some way, the meaning of adjectives and adverbs. Some colloquial qualifiers, discussed in Section 20B, should be avoided in semiformal writing. (Most college writing may be classed as semiformal.) The chief qualifiers used in semiformal writing are the following:

very	somewhat	fairly	a little
rather	especially	wholly	quite

1B SENTENCES

The parts of speech defined in Section 1A are variously arranged, of course, to form sentences. Every sentence is composed of a **subject** and **predicate,** and every predicate contains a verb. A predicate may or may not contain a **complement,** which is a word or word group that completes a meaning begun in the verb.

1B1 Subjects

The **subject** of a sentence is the person, thing, or concept that performs the action stated in the verb if the verb is in the active voice or that receives the action if the verb is in the passive voice (see Section 1A2e) or that is in the state of being expressed by a linking verb (see Section 1A2c). A simple test for determining the subject of a sentence is to ask who or what about the verb. Examples:

Our team won the championship.

Who won? *Our team,* which is therefore the subject.

The championship was won by our team.

What was won? *The championship,* which is the subject.

Sally appears dazed.

Who appears? *Sally,* which is the subject.

Sometimes the subject is a noun with many modifiers. Such a noun and all of its modifiers together form the **complete subject.** Example:

Any high official of the United States government can be impeached.

Who can be impeached? *Any high official of the United States government,* which is the complete subject. The central noun (also known as the headword) in such a long subject is known as the **simple subject.** It—and it alone—controls the verb. Example:

> Any member of a nudist camp that is affiliated with other camps can have free access to those camps too.

Who can have free access? *Any member,* which is the simple subject within the complete subject. (The complete subject is all of the words preceding *can have.*)

A good point to remember is that in the vast majority of English sentences the subject precedes the verb. Two rather frequent exceptions are sentences that begin with *there* and *it* as expletives (fillers without meaning). Examples, with the complete subjects in boldface:

> There is **no way to form a compound out of helium and hydrogen.**

What is? The whole boldface construction is, with *no way* as the simple subject.

> It is true **that Doug jilted Maggie.**

What is true? The whole boldface noun clause, which is the subject. (There is no single-word simple subject in such sentences.) Some writers do at times use inverted sentence order; but usually asking who or what about the verb will tell you the subject.

1B2   Predicates

The predicate of a sentence is the verb and its complement, if it has one, plus any modifiers (see Section 1E). Examples, with the predicates in boldface:

> The bee **stung Uncle Wilhelm.**
> Pete **can run very fast.**
> The young mother **screamed at the teenagers bullying her children.**

The headword in the predicate is always the verb (which may be one or more words). The verb must be what is called

finite, that is, it must be a form that can serve as a sentence verb. Some examples of finite verbs are the following:

> Jess **has been going** to a psychiatrist for a year now.
> He **is profiting** from his treatment.
> His parents **aren't.**

Verb forms that cannot function as sentence verbs are known as **nonfinite.** Some examples are *known, been gone,* and *having escaped.* You can see that the following groups of words are not sentences:

> We known about the fire
> Shirley been gone now for two days

The addition of verb auxiliaries would make these verbs finite and make correct sentences:

> We **should have known** about the fire.
> Shirley **has been gone** now for two days.

Many predicates have **complements** of the verbs—that is, words or constructions that complete a meaning initiated in the verb. To use this book effectively, you need to understand only four kinds of complements:

a. Direct objects A direct object is the person or thing that receives the action of a transitive verb. Examples:

DIRECT OBJECTS: Jonesy lit his **cigar.**
               The transcriber omitted an **expletive.**

b. Indirect objects An indirect object normally occurs only in conjunction with a direct object. It specifies the person or thing to or for whom the action is performed. Examples:

INDIRECT OBJECTS: Hortense gave **me** a kiss.
                 The deacon told **the preacher** a lie.

Kiss and *lie* are direct objects. Indirect objects can always be converted into prepositional phrases beginning with *to* or *for.* Example:

> The deacon told a lie **to the preacher.**

In this sentence the indirect object has been replaced by a prepositional phrase.

   c. **Predicate nouns**   A predicate noun follows a linking verb and renames the subject in different terms. Examples:

PREDICATE NOUNS: Elsie remained **chairperson** of the English Department.
Susie is a **sweetheart.**

   d. **Predicate adjectives**   A predicate adjective follows a linking verb and describes the subject. Examples:

PREDICATE ADJECTIVES: The moon is **bright** tonight.
Julio became **bitter** as the interview progressed.

In all the examples given above, the complements plus the verbs and modifiers form the sentence predicates.

1B3   Kinds of Sentences

Though there seems to be an infinity of different kinds of English sentences, for simplicity we will identify four types.

   a. **A simple sentence** is one that contains only one independent clause and no dependent clause. (See Section 1D for a description of clauses.) Even though various kinds of phrases carrying additional ideas may be in such a sentence, it is still called simple. Examples:

Glass is a noncrystalline substance.
Without any hesitation, I strode into the panther's cage.

Regardless of its length, a simple sentence has only one subject and one predicate.

   b. **A compound sentence** is one composed of two or more independent clauses but no dependent clauses. Examples, with the independent clauses in boldface:

We broke the speed limit without care, but **the liquor store had already closed.**
The sun and moon appear to be about the same size; however, **they are really vastly different in size.**

A compound sentence has at least two subjects and two predicates.

c. **A complex sentence** is one with one independent clause and one or more dependent clauses. Examples, with the dependent clauses in boldface:

While Ruthie kept guard, I climbed through the transom.

I won't vote for Mr. Huston **because he slandered minority groups.**

If it rains, we'll call off our race, **since the roadway would be too slippery for our tires.**

d. **A compound-complex sentence** contains at least two independent clauses and at least one dependent clause. Examples, with the dependent clauses in boldface:

If the weather is fair, we will go on our hunting trip, and I expect us to find much game.

Since I could see his hat on the table, I knew of the intruder's presence, but I made no move **in case he had a pistol.**

This traditional four-fold classification of sentence types does not tell the whole truth about the great variety of structure in English sentences, but it is a useful starting point.

1C PHRASES

A phrase is a group of words that function as a unit but that do not have a subject and predicate. You need to understand three kinds of phrases in order to utilize this book fully.

1C1 Prepositional Phrases

A prepositional phrase begins with a preposition and closes with the object of the preposition, usually a noun or pronoun. Examples:

PREPOSITIONAL PHRASES: The girl **in the bikini** standing **by the pool's edge** was invited **as an additional guest.**

Prepositional phrases are used as modifiers, like adjectives and adverbs.

1C2   Verbal Phrases

A verbal phrase is a verb form plus various other words that go with it to form a unit. Many different verb forms can be headwords in verb phrases, but to use this book you need not know their names. You need only to recognize that a verb form is the headword of the phrase and that the phrase is a unit. Examples:

VERBAL PHRASES: The man **to see about tickets** is Scalper Joe.

Realizing we were trapped, we meekly surrendered.

Known for her generosity, Carrie was often imposed upon.

Jogging every morning helped me lose ten pounds.

Several kinds of errors in sentence structure and punctuation involve verbal phrases.

1C3   Noun Phrases

A noun phrase is composed of a noun headword plus all its modifiers. Examples:

NOUN PHRASES: **A list of students serving as student-body officers** was posted in the library.

A number of spectators at the construction site offered much advice to the workers.

The headwords in these phrases are *list* and *number;* they govern the whole phrases. You will need to understand the nature of noun phrases to deal with subject-verb agreement.

1D CLAUSES

A **clause** is a construction that has a subject and predicate (see Sections 1B1 and 1B2). Clauses are either independent or dependent.

1D1 Independent Clauses

An **independent clause** is in effect a simple sentence. It is a clause that can stand alone, beginning with a capital letter and ending with a period or question mark. The material in Sections 1B1 and 1B2 gives you information that applies to independent clauses as well as to sentences.

1D2 Dependent Clauses

Dependent clauses are like independent clauses in having a subject and a predicate containing a finite verb. They differ in that they begin with subordinating connectives, which keep them from standing alone as complete sentences. *Grammatically,* a dependent clause depends on the rest of the sentence, but, since it has a subject and predicate, it contains a full unit of meaning. There are three kinds of dependent clauses.

a. **Adjective clauses** usually begin with one of these relative pronouns, which serve as subordinating connectives: *who, whom, whose, which,* and *that.* Like adjectives, an adjective clause usually modifies a noun or pronoun. In the examples below, each adjective clause modifies the noun it follows.

ADJECTIVE CLAUSES: The guest **who arrives last** will receive a booby prize.

A man **whose wife is beautiful** is always worried.

We elected Sneedby, **who paid two dollars a vote.**

I voted for Scraggs, **to whom I owed a debt.**

The subjects and predicates of these adjective clauses are as follows:

>   who / arrives last
>   whose wife / is beautiful
>   who / paid two dollars a vote
>   I / owed a debt to whom

Occasionally an adjective clause can modify the whole idea of a sentence or word group, in which case it must begin with *which*. In this example, the adjective clause, in bold-face, modifies the whole idea of the independent clause:

> The catcher of our team batted .406 this year, **which set a new local record.**

An understanding of adjective clauses is especially important in knowing how to punctuate correctly.

   b. Adverb clauses begin with one of the subordinating conjunctions listed on page 18. The subordinating conjunction expresses a relationship between the adverb clause and, usually, some other whole idea. Examples:

ADVERB CLAUSES: **If you drink,** I will drive.
I proposed to you **because you are rich.**
You will marry me **because I am handsome.**

The subjects and predicates of these adverb clauses are as follows:

>   you / drink
>   you / are rich
>   I / am handsome

The subordinating conjunctions *if* and *because* make the clauses dependent, or keep them from standing alone as complete sentences.

   c. Noun clauses begin with *that* (a meaningless sub-ordinating connective), with *what,* with a relative pronoun, or with a subordinating conjunction. (Only a few of the sub-ordinating conjunctions can begin noun clauses.) The distinctive characteristic of noun clauses is that they function as nouns in sentences — usually as subjects or direct objects. The best way to test for a noun clause is to see that either *someone* or *something* can be substituted for it. Examples:

NOUN CLAUSES: I know **that you love me.** (I know something.)

When you leave is no concern of mine. (Something is no concern of mine.)

Whoever buys the beer chooses the music we play. (Someone chooses the music we play.)

The subjects and predicates of these noun clauses are as follows:

you / love me
you / leave
whoever / buys the beer

The *that, when,* and *whoever* prevent the clauses from standing as complete sentences.

A number of the following chapters, especially those on punctuation, will deal with dependent clauses.

1E MODIFIERS

A **modifier** is a word or word group that describes, limits, or adds to another word or word group. For example, if to the phrase *a shirt* we add the modifier *blue* to get *a blue shirt,* we have (1) described the shirt to a degree; (2) limited the shirt, since all non-blue shirts are now excluded; and (3) in a sense, added to the shirt, since we have told something about it that formerly we did not know. This all seems simple, but actually modification is one of the most complex aspects of grammar. You need to know some of the aspects of modification in order to deal with many writing problems treated in the following chapters.

There are three general kinds of modifiers. In discussing them we return to the fact that parts of speech are classified by form and by function. Thus some words may function as adjectives or adverbs even though they are classified as other parts of speech. The three general kinds of modifiers are **adjectivals, adverbials,** and **sentence modifiers.**

1E1   Adjectivals

Any word or word group that modifies a noun or pronoun is by function an adjectival. Here are examples of various kinds of adjectivals. The adjectival is in boldface and the noun it modifies is underlined:

> the **tastiest** biscuit   [*Tastiest* is an adjective.]
> This cloth feels **smooth.**   [*Smooth* is an adjective.]
> a **paper** tiger   [*Paper* is a noun functioning as an adjectival.]
> a **running** thief   [*Running* is a verb functioning as an adjectival.]
> the apartment **below**   [*Below* is an adverb functioning as an adjectival.]
> the go-go dancer **on stage in the nightclub**   [*On stage* and *in the nightclub* are prepositional phrases functioning as adjectivals.]
> the girl **not wearing a bikini**   [The verbal phrase functions as an adjectival.]
> **Being exhausted,** Joe took a nap.   [The verbal phrase functions as an adjectival.]
> Dr. Smale, **whose specialty is urology**   [The adjective clause functions as an adjectival.]
> a time **when all chickens are asleep**   [The adverb clause functions as an adjectival.]

Although most of the constructions in boldface are not adjectives, they are all adjectivals by function because they modify nouns.

1E2   Adverbials

Any word or word group that modifies a verb, adjective, or another adverb is an adverbial by function. Most adverbials answer the questions *Where? When?* or *How?* Here are examples of various kinds of adverbials. The adverbial in each instance is in boldface and the verb it modifies is underlined:

> to peer **cautiously**   [*Cautiously* is an adverb.]
>
> arrived **yesterday**   [*Yesterday* is a noun functioning as an adverbial.]
>
> If you study **long,** you study **wrong.**   [*Long* and *wrong* are adjectives functioning as adverbials.]
>
> frozen **by the north wind**   [The prepositional phrase functions as an adverbial.]
>
> to eat **standing**   [*Standing* is a verb functioning as an adverbial.]
>
> I studied hard **to improve my grades.**   [The verb phrase functions as an adverbial.]
>
> smoking **where it is forbidden**   [The adverb clause functions as an adverbial.]

All of the constructions in boldface are adverbials because they modify verbs.

1E3   Sentence Modifiers

In some sentences a modifier modifies not a single word but a whole idea. Then it is a sentence modifier. Here are examples of sentence modifiers, which are in boldface.

> **Happily,** Tweed did not die.   [*Happily* is an adverb modifying the whole sentence. Note how different in meaning this sentence is from "Tweed did not die happily," in which *happily* is an adverbial modifying *die.*]
>
> **Under the circumstances,** we should engage in plea bargaining.   [The prepositional phrase modifies the whole idea.]
>
> **Strictly speaking,** the purchase of a new car is not an investment.   [The verbal phrase modifies the whole idea.]
>
> We invested in common stock, **which is a good way to go broke fast.**   [The dependent clause modifies the first idea.]

In determining what a word or word group modifies, the best approach is to ask *what goes with what.* In sections 1E1 and 1E2, if you will ask this question about the examples, you will see that the boldface construction goes with what is underlined.

1F   APPOSITIVES

Basically, an **appositive** is a noun repeater; that is, it renames in different words the noun it is **in apposition to.** It
gives more information about that noun. An appositive may
be a single word, a phrase, or a clause. Examples of appositives, with the appositive in boldface and the noun it is
in apposition to underlined:

> Neutron stars, **heavenly bodies with a diameter of only a few
> miles,** were discovered in the 1970's. [The appositive is a
> noun phrase.]
> The British writer **John Wilson** may receive a Nobel Prize.
> [The appositive is a noun.]
> The belief **that like produces like** is an old superstition.
> [The appositive is a noun clause.]
> Her first love — **eating wild mushrooms** — was her last act.
> [The appositive is a verbal phrase.]

Sometimes an appositive is in apposition to a whole idea.
Example:

> He conceded the election, a **gesture** his backers disapproved of.

The appositive in boldface is in apposition to the underlined sentence. Occasionally appositives are introduced by
such connectives as *that is, namely,* and *or.* Example:

> *Vibrissae,* or **whiskers,** grow on the faces of all species of cats
> and seals.

Whiskers is in apposition to *vibrissae.*
     Appositives involve important aspects of punctuation
and will be considered further in Section II.

1G   COORDINATION

Coordination means the joining of two or more sentence
parts or independent clauses so that they are equal in rank.

This grammatical function, which involves problems in punctuation and sentence structure, usually calls for one of the coordinating connectives discussed in Section 1A5d. Parts are said to be **compounded** when they are coordinated; also, we speak of coordinated parts as being **items in a series.** Example of coordination:

> **Riding horses, drinking whisky,** and **writing novels** were William Faulkner's favorite pastimes.

The three phrases in boldface are equal in rank.

1H SUBORDINATION

Subordination means that one sentence part is unequal in rank to, or is placed beneath, another part. A subordinated phrase or clause is usually introduced by one of the subordinating conjunctions discussed in Section 1A5e or by a relative pronoun or by *that* or *what.* Also, any kind of sentence modifier is a subordinate construction. Example of subordination, with the subordinated clause in boldface:

> Vodka is intoxicating, **though it is free of fusel oils.**

If the *though,* which produces subordination, is changed to *but,* coordination results:

> Vodka is intoxicating, but it is free of fusel oils.

Now the clauses are equal in rank.

Coordination and subordination are involved in various aspects of sentence structure and punctuation. An understanding of coordination and subordination is important for expressing meaning precisely.

1I AMBIGUITY

An important term in grammar is **ambiguity.** This means that a sentence has two possible meanings, often without

a clue to show the reader which meaning is intended.
Examples of ambiguity:

> How would you like to see a model home?
> Bathing beauties can be fun.
> During my college career I had thirty odd teachers.
> I will lose no time in reading your manuscript.

Ambiguities can be entertaining, but usually ambiguity is a grave weakness in writing.

The foregoing are explanations of the basics of English grammar that pertain to the writing problems to be discussed in the rest of this reference handbook. You may not need to make much use of this introductory chapter, but it is here for you, and it may at times answer pressing questions or give you insights that will improve the quality of your writing.

2

Sentence Fragments

A good writer needs to have **sentence sense** to avoid writing in **sentence fragments,** or nonsentences. Sentence sense is the ability to recognize that a construction is either a complete sentence, capable of standing alone, or a sentence fragment that should not stand alone. Sentences, of course, begin with capital letters and end with marks of end punctuation. The person with sentence sense automatically composes in complete sentences, but one who does not have full sentence sense often makes serious errors in writing. These errors are discussed in this chapter and Chapter 3.

Sentence sense is largely intuitive. Many people easily develop sentence sense without fully understanding just why they have it. Some other people have much difficulty in developing it. Generally, people who study grammar, which is compactly presented in our first chapter, develop sentence sense more easily than do those who are unaware of the nature of grammar.

The whole problem of sentence sense is complex and involves oddities. For example, consider the following construction:

While the professor explained the theory of relativity

Every word (except possibly *while*) in that construction contains its own full meaning without reference to a preceding sentence; yet the construction is not a sentence and should not be entered into writing as though it were a sentence. But many constructions that people with sentence sense automatically recognize as sentences cannot, so far as *meaning* is concerned, stand alone, because they must draw meaning from previous sentences through reference. But *grammatically* they can stand alone.

Sentence sense lets us recognize the following:

1. That pronoun reference to a preceding sentence does not prevent a construction from being a sentence. Example:

SENTENCE: He gave it to them.

By itself, this sentence is far from having complete meaning, but it can stand alone.

2. That reference of a verb auxiliary to a preceding sentence does not prevent a construction from being a sentence. Example:

SENTENCE: He could if I did.

The auxiliaries *could* and *did* must draw their meaning from a preceding sentence. Still, in spite of its lack of meaning, this construction is a sentence.

3. That the reference of *so, thus, then,* and *there* to a preceding sentence does not prevent a construction from being a sentence. Example:

SENTENCE: So was Uncle John.

Both *so* and *was* must get their meaning from the preceding sentence.

4. That a construction may begin with a coordinating connective or transitional phrase and still stand alone as a sentence. Examples:

SENTENCES: But she wouldn't.
For example, alcohol can be fermented from potatoes.

Coordinating connectives and transitional phrases are frequently used to begin sentences.

On the other hand, sentence sense lets us recognize the following:

1. That a clause beginning with a subordinating connective (subordinating conjunctions, relative pronouns, and a few connectives such as *that* and *what*) is **not** a sentence. Examples:

NONSENTENCES: Although Elaine is an excellent student.
Because the hot water heater exploded.
What Glenda had in mind.

The subordinating connectives *although, because,* and *what* keep these meaningful subject-predicate combinations from being sentences.

2. That a construction without a subject and predicate is not a sentence. Examples:

NONSENTENCES: To be free. To live in peace.
Without contributing a nickel.
Mercilessly unfair to all.

Though these constructions deliver more meaning than, say, the sentence *he could,* they are not sentences because they do not have subject-predicate combinations.

If you find that you need to refer to this chapter or Chapter 3 very often, you need to work on developing your sentence sense. You should carefully study Sections 1B and 1D and perhaps all of Chapter 1.

2A   DETACHED CLAUSES AS SENTENCE FRAGMENTS

Write in complete sentences; do not let a dependent clause stand as a sentence.

A common kind of sentence fragment is a **detached dependent clause** which, instead of standing by itself with a beginning capital letter and end punctuation, should be attached to the preceding sentence, sometimes with and sometimes without a comma separating it. Examples, with the fragments italicized:

WRONG: Feel free to talk with your date. *Because if she likes your conversation she'll give you another date.*

RIGHT: Feel free to talk with your date, because if she likes your conversation she'll give you another date.

WRONG: Parents must let their children know that they love and trust them. *Since children who do not feel secure become behavior problems.*

RIGHT: Parents must let their children know that they love and trust them, since children who do not feel secure become behavior problems.

WRONG: The scoutmaster and advanced scouts went exploring. *While we tenderfeet stayed at camp to gather firewood.*

RIGHT: The scoutmaster and advanced scouts went exploring while we tenderfeet stayed at camp to gather firewood.

Subordinating connectives such as *because, since,* and *while* prevent detached dependent clauses from standing as sentences.

2B   DETACHED PHRASES AS SENTENCE FRAGMENTS

Write in complete sentences; do not let a phrase stand as a sentence.

A construction without a subject-predicate combination — that is, a phrase rather than a clause — is a fragment even if it is not introduced by a subordinating connective. Such **detached phrases** are a common source of sentence fragments. Examples, with the detached phrases italicized:

WRONG: The horse lifts his head. *His ears straight up.*
RIGHT: The horse lifts his head, his ears straight up.

WRONG: The government has many people on welfare who could work. *Instead of doing nothing.*
RIGHT: The government has many people on welfare who could work instead of doing nothing.

WRONG: If poor children do not have the things they need, they are likely to grow up evil. *Thus becoming problem adults.*
RIGHT: If poor children do not have the things they need, they are likely to grow up evil, thus becoming problem adults.

Noun, prepositional, and verbal phrases frequently are detached from the sentences they belong to, thus becoming sentence fragments. Detached clauses and phrases are usually due to the writer's lack of sentence sense.

2C SENTENCE FRAGMENTS DUE TO CONFUSED STRUCTURE

Write in complete sentences; avoid jumbled structures.

A third, but less common, kind of sentence fragment is one in which a necessary part of a sentence has been omitted or in which the sentence structure is jumbled rather than complete. Examples:

WRONG: Most teenagers who run away because their parents won't listen, which is the main reason for running away.
RIGHT: Most teenagers who run away because their parents won't listen, which is the main reason for running away, eventually return to try again to achieve a good home life.

WRONG: Parents, who should let their children go out and see the world, but they don't trust the children.
RIGHT: Parents should let their children go out and see the world, but they don't trust the children.

In the first example, the writer forgot to compose a predicate that would finish the sentence. In the second, the writer also forgot to provide a predicate for the subject *parents* and instead let the sentence become a jumbled fragment. Such fragments are often due to the writer's carelessness.

2D FRAGMENTS WITH NONFINITE VERB FORMS

Write in complete sentences; do not let a construction with a nonfinite verb form stand as a sentence.

A fourth, but not very common, type of sentence fragment is a construction with a **nonfinite verb form** rather than a finite (sentence-forming) verb form. Examples, with the nonfinite verb forms italicized:

WRONG: I finished that task and then *coming* home and *sitting* down to work.

RIGHT: I finished that task and then came home and sat down to work.

WRONG: He *should picking* a good time to ask her for a date, so that most likely she would say yes.

RIGHT: He should pick a good time to ask her for a date so that most likely she would say yes.

Many, perhaps most, such fragments are due to carelessness, but some are due to the writer's lack of sentence sense.

3

Comma Splices and Run-Together Sentences

Independent clauses are in effect simple sentences, and two of them (perhaps with other constituents) are very often joined to form compound or compound-complex sentences. But when two independent clauses have *only* a comma and *no coordinating conjunction (and, but, yet, or, nor, so, for)* between them, a **comma splice** is formed, usually indicating that the writer has imperfect sentence sense. Without a coordinating conjunction between independent clauses, either a semicolon or a period between them is required. (A semicolon has the same force as a period, but is normally used only when the independent clauses are especially closely related.) If a period is the best mark of punctuation to use, then the second sentence of course begins with a capital letter.

3A COMMA SPLICES WITHOUT CONNECTIVE WORDS

Do not use a comma to separate two independent clauses that are not joined by a coordinating conjunction.

Many times a comma only, with no connective, is placed between sentences (or independent clauses), thus incorrectly "splicing" the sentences and producing a **comma splice.** In such cases, the second sentence usually begins with some kind of word—such as *this, another, there, it,* and other pronouns—that leads the writer to believe that the sentence is continuing, when actually a new sentence has begun. Either a period or, occasionally, a semicolon must replace the comma to eliminate the comma splice. Examples:

WRONG: The truly Christian person acts morally as well as attends church, this kind of behavior in everyday affairs is what the Christian religion is all about.

RIGHT: The truly Christian person acts morally as well as attends church. This kind of behavior in everyday affairs is what the Christian religion is all about.

WRONG: One reason an eighteen-year-old man in our state should be able to buy alcohol is that he is old enough to fight for his country, another is that he can now vote and participate in other adult affairs.

RIGHT: One reason an eighteen-year-old man in our state should be able to buy alcohol is that he is old enough to fight for his country. Another is that he can now vote and participate in other adult affairs.

WRONG: Why should a person be put in jail because of a few minor mistakes, there must be a better way to handle victimless crimes.

RIGHT: Why should a person be put in jail because of a few minor mistakes? There must be a better way to handle victimless crimes.

WRONG: Little children should be praised when they behave well, this makes them want to continue to behave well.

RIGHT: Little children should be praised when they behave well; this makes them want to continue to behave well.

In the last example a period instead of a semicolon would also be correct. A semicolon calls for the same duration of voice pause that a period does. Thus where a period at the end of a sentence is correct, a semicolon normally cannot be called wrong, though it may produce awkward style.

3B COMMA SPLICES WITH CONJUNCTIVE ADVERBS

Do not use a comma to separate two independent clauses joined by a conjunctive adverb.

The conjunctive adverbs — *however, therefore, nevertheless,* and so on — are coordinating connectives frequently used to join sentences (or independent clauses), but they are not coordinating conjunctions. When a comma (instead of a period or semicolon) is used with them between sentences, a comma splice occurs. Example:

WRONG: Students deserve to have a Fairness Committee set up on this campus, however, I admit that most student complaints about teachers are not justified.

RIGHT: Students deserve to have a Fairness Committee set up on this campus; however, I admit that most student complaints about teachers are not justified.

Note several points here: (1) With a comma before and after *however,* the rapid reader might not at first know which clause the *however* goes with; quite often sentences end with a conjunctive adverb. (2) A period rather than a semicolon after *campus* would also be correct. And (3) the *however* could be shifted to the interior of the second clause, for example, after *admit.* Most of the conjunctive adverbs can be shifted to the interior of the second clause, and this fact provides you with a test for proper punctuation: if the connective can be shifted, a period or semicolon must come after the first clause.

Another example:

WRONG: Communication between parents and children is a two-way affair, therefore, children should make an effort to understand their parents, as well as the other way around.

RIGHT: Communication between parents and children is a two-way affair. Therefore, children should make an effort to understand their parents, as well as the other way around.

A semicolon after *affair* would not be wrong. The *therefore* could be shifted, as in *Children, therefore, should . . . .*
One more example:

WRONG: I got my rifle in readiness to fire instantly, then a jackrabbit jumped from right under my nose.

RIGHT: I got my rifle in readiness to fire instantly; then a jackrabbit jumped from right under my nose.

In this sentence *then* is a conjunctive adverb, not a coordinating conjunction; thus either a semicolon or a period must come after *instantly.* The *then* could be shifted to come after *jackrabbit,* but that structure might sound awkward. Nevertheless, that shift is a test that shows the necessity of a semicolon or period between the clauses.

3C   RUN-TOGETHER SENTENCES

Do not run two sentences together with no punctuation between them and no capital letter beginning the second sentence.

The error known as **run-together sentences** means that two sentences are run together with no punctuation or coordinating conjunction between them and no capital letter starting the second sentence. This error generally occurs when the second sentence starts with a word such as *this, another, there, it,* or some other pronoun, which sometimes leads the writer to believe he or she is continuing a sentence, not starting a new one. Examples:

WRONG: After college I expect to be a law-enforcement officer that is what I have dreamed of since I was a child.

RIGHT: After college I expect to be a law-enforcement officer. That is what I have dreamed of since I was a child.

WRONG: You can also learn what you want to do with your life this is a very important aspect of a college career.

RIGHT: You can also learn what you want to do with your life. This is a very important aspect of a college career.

In such run-together sentences the fact that the second sentence does not begin with a capital letter usually indicates that the writer has not been careless but lacks full sentence sense. Semicolons could be used instead of periods between such independent clauses, but periods are usually better.

If you find that you must refer to this chapter often, you probably need to study Sections 1B and 1D carefully and perhaps need to study all of Chapter 1.

Misused Modifiers

A **modifier** is a word or word group that describes, limits, or adds to another word or word group. The common misuses of modifiers are the incorrect use of an adjective for an adverb to modify a verb and the incorrect use of an adverb as a predicate adjective.

4A MISUSED ADJECTIVE FORMS

Do not use an adjective form to modify an intransitive or transitive verb.

Such a misused adjective form almost always follows the verb it modifies. To determine whether a word is modifying a verb, remember that asking *what goes with what* is a useful test. For example, consider the sentence—

Jack comes to our nightly big bashes very seldom.

Ask "What does *seldom* go with?" and your answer should be *seldom comes,* showing that *seldom* modifies (goes with) the verb of the sentence.

Here are examples of adjectives misused for adverbs, with the modified verb underlined:

WRONG: After my father inherited some money, he began to gamble *considerable.*

RIGHT: After my father inherited some money, he began to gamble **considerably.**

WRONG: At first I was nervous on my first date, but he talked very *friendly* and that put me at my ease.

RIGHT: At first I was nervous on my first date, but he talked **in a friendly way** and that put me at my ease.

In the first example the *ly* adverb form *considerably* is needed to modify the verb *to gamble.* In the second example *friendly* is one of a few adjectives (*heavenly, lovely,* and others) that end in *ly* but that almost never function as adverbs. Since the adverb form *friendlily* sounds awkward, the adverbial prepositional phrase *in a friendly way* is needed to modify the verb *talked.*

Two other examples:

WRONG: You explain it all so *clear* that I am learning more English than ever before.

RIGHT: You explain it all so **clearly** that I am learning more English than ever before.

WRONG: After we worked on him for some time, he began to breathe *normal* again.

RIGHT: After we worked on him for some time, he began to breathe **normally** again.

WRONG: Len seems to speak *different* now.

RIGHT: Len seems to speak **differently** now.

The adverb forms *clearly* and *normally* are needed to modify the verbs *explain* and *to breathe.*

A particularly sticky writing problem involves *well,* which is both an adjective and an adverb, and *good,* which is only an adjective. A writer should always use *well* to modify a verb. Here are examples, with the verbs underlined:

WRONG: I worked all day overhauling my bike and by evening had it <u>running</u> *good.*

RIGHT: I worked all day overhauling my bike and by evening had it <u>running</u> **well.**

WRONG: I went out of the exam thinking I <u>had done</u> *good.*

RIGHT: I went out of the exam thinking I <u>had done</u> **well.**

The italicized words modify the verbs *running* and *had done,* and thus the adverb *well,* not the adjective *good,* is required. Remember that you *do well, write well, play well, argue well, dress well, behave well, work well,* and so on. (You can *feel good* or *feel well,* with somewhat different meanings.)

Another adjective form sometimes misused for an adverb is *near* for *nearly.* Examples:

WRONG: My paper wasn't *near* as bad as your red marks made it seem.

RIGHT: My paper wasn't **nearly** as bad as your red marks made it seem.

WRONG: But my father, in spite of what he said, wasn't *near* as mad as my mother.

RIGHT: But my father, in spite of what he said, wasn't **nearly** as mad as my mother.

Remember that the correct phrase is *not nearly as. . . .*

4B   MISUSED ADVERB FORMS

Do not use an adverb to function as a predicate adjective after a linking verb.

After a linking verb, the correct modifier is an adjective, which describes the subject, not an adverb. The chief linking verbs are *to be, to get, to feel, to seem, to sound, to taste, to look, to remain, to become, to appear,* and a few others; but some verbs that are normally linking — such as *to feel* and *to look* — are sometimes used as intransitive or transitive verbs. It is not possible to give a complete list of linking verbs, although there are comparatively few of them, for many normally intransitive or transitive verbs occasionally function as linking. The clue is that the linking verb is followed by an adjective that modifies the subject or by a predicate noun that renames the subject. Thus such verbs as *to go, to turn, to marry, to die, to retire,* and others are normally intransitive or transitive but occasionally function as linking, being followed by predicate adjectives that describe the subjects. Examples:

> The well went **dry.**
> Billy turned **hostile.**
> Louise married **young.**
> Dave died **old.**
> Fred retired **happy.**

Since the meanings are *dry well, hostile Billy, young Louise, old Dave,* and *happy Fred,* the verbs in these instances are linking.

The most commonly misused adverb form is *badly* after the linking verb *to feel.* Examples:

WRONG: After I was caught plagiarizing, I felt very *badly.*
RIGHT: After I was caught plagiarizing, I felt very **bad.**

WRONG: When I began to see what grownups do, I didn't feel so *badly* about having shoplifted when I was in my early teens.
RIGHT: When I began to see what grownups do, I didn't feel so **bad** about having shoplifted when I was in my early teens.

WRONG: I felt *badly* when I realized how I had hurt my parents.
RIGHT: I felt **bad** when I realized how I had hurt my parents.

In these cases *feel* and *felt* are linking verbs, and therefore the adjective *bad* is needed as a predicate adjective to modify the subject *I.* Technically, *to feel badly* would mean to have a faulty sense of touch, such as being unable to tell whether a surface is smooth or rough. Also note that you would be very unlikely to say either of the following sentences:

WRONG: I feel *sadly* about your divorce.
WRONG: I feel *gladly* that you made an A.

Sad and *glad* are clearly the correct predicate adjective forms, as is *bad.*

Occasionally a writer will incorrectly use other adverb forms with linking verbs, probably because of having heard the incorrect *I feel badly* construction. Examples:

WRONG: We had to make a forced march at night in the rain, and we all felt as *miserably* as could be.
RIGHT: We had to make a forced march at night in the rain, and we all felt as **miserable** as could be.

WRONG: When I was a child I stole a watermelon from a patch, and I still remember how *unpleasantly* it tasted, because I was so scared.
RIGHT: When I was a child I stole a watermelon from a patch, and I still remember how **unpleasant** it tasted, because I was so scared.

Miserable and *unpleasant* are needed as predicate adjectives to go with the linking verbs *felt* and *tasted* and to modify the subjects *we* and *it.* In the last example, the predicate adjective precedes its linking verb and subject. This is not an especially common construction but is not rare, either.

4C DOUBLE NEGATIVES

Do not use a double negative.

A **double negative** is a construction in which two words expressing negation—such as *no* and *nothing*—are used to make one negative statement. In usage, such constructions are considered in the same unacceptable category as *ain't.* Examples, with the two negative words italicized:

WRONG: But after walking the streets for hours I could *not* make *no* sales of that soap.

RIGHT: But after walking the streets for hours I could **not** make **any** sales of that soap.

WRONG: It did*n't* mean *nothing* to us to lose that game, since we had the title cinched.

RIGHT: It did**n't** mean **anything** to us to lose that game, since we had the title cinched.

Remember that the correct constructions are *not . . . any, not . . . anything, not . . . anyone,* and *don't (doesn't) . . . any* (rather than *no*).

Another incorrect double negative involves the words *hardly* and *scarcely.* Since these words are both negatives, using another negative in a construction with one of them produces a double negative. Examples, with the double negatives italicized:

WRONG: Some parents do*n't* pay *hardly* any attention to their children as soon as they are old enough to play outside.

RIGHT: Some parents pay **hardly any** attention to their children as soon as they are old enough to play outside.

WRONG: It had*n't scarcely* begun to rain before the floor of our tent was flooded.

RIGHT: It **had scarcely** begun to rain before the floor of our tent was flooded.

Remember never to use *no* or *not* in a construction with *hardly* or *scarcely.*

Pronoun Case Forms

Case is the grammatical function that requires (though not in all instances) the change of the form of a pronoun according to its use in a sentence. The **subjective case** forms — *I, we, she,* and so on — are used as subjects and as predicate nouns, or, more exactly, predicate pronouns. The **objective case** forms — *me, us, her,* and so on — are used as objects of verbs and prepositions. And the **possessive case** forms — *my, our, her,* and so on — are used to show possession. Sometimes writers use incorrect pronoun case forms.

5A IN COMPOUND CONSTRUCTIONS

In compound constructions use subjective case forms as subjects and objective case forms as objects.

A compound construction is one in which two or more parts are coordinated, or used in a series of two or more. Very seldom does anyone use a wrong pronoun case form when a single pronoun is a subject or object. For example, you could wait for years and probably not hear such constructions as these:

WRONG: *Me* was invited to Jane's party.
WRONG: The package was for *I*.

But often when two pronouns, or a noun and a pronoun, occur in a compound construction, a faulty pronoun case form is used.

Here are examples in compound subjects, with the faulty pronoun forms italicized:

WRONG: My dad and *me* could hardly wait for our hunting trip to begin.
RIGHT: My dad and **I** could hardly wait for our hunting trip to begin.

WRONG: The teacher and *him* got into a big argument.
RIGHT: The teacher and **he** got into a big argument.

The subjective forms *I* and *he* are needed to serve as subjects of *were* and *got.* When in doubt you can test such constructions by omitting one part of the compound construction. That is, omit *dad* and *teacher* in the above examples and you will immediately see that *me could hardly wait* and *him got into an argument* are incorrect. Remember that the correct expressions are such as these: *Melissa and she arrived, José and I conferred, the Joneses and they are . . ., the Alvarados and we began . . .*, and so on.

Similarly, subjective case forms should *not* be used in compound constructions that are objects of verbs or prepositions. Examples, with the incorrect pronoun case form italicized:

WRONG: My mother told my sister and *I* that dad was on the warpath.
RIGHT: My mother told my sister and **me** that dad was on the warpath.

WRONG: The argument was just between my sister and *I*.
RIGHT: The argument was just between my sister and **me.**

Again, a simple test is to drop one part of the compound structure (*sister* in the above examples). You would not write "My mother told I . . ." or "The argument was between I. . . ." Clearly, since the pronoun is the object of the verb *told* and of the preposition *between,* the objective form — *me* — is needed. Remember that the correct expressions are such as these: *between you and me, for Tom and him, with Jack and me, overheard Mary and her, invited the Medinas and us,* and so on.

5B AFTER *TO BE*

Use subjective pronoun forms after forms of the verb *to be*.

Since the verb *to be* is a linking verb, any predicate noun or pronoun that follows a form of it renames the subject. Therefore since the subject is, obviously, in the subjective case, a predicate pronoun, which is the same as the subject, should also be in the subjective case. But in informal use nowadays objective pronoun forms are usually acceptable after forms of *to be.* Examples, with the pronouns in bold-face:

INFORMAL: It's **me.**
INFORMAL: I'm sure it was **her.**
INFORMAL: Could you have been **him?**
INFORMAL: Did you think it was **us?**

However, in semiformal and formal situations subjective pronoun case forms should follow forms of *to be.* Examples:

SEMIFORMAL: It's **I.**
SEMIFORMAL: The guilty ones were **they.**
SEMIFORMAL: I'm sure it was **she.**
SEMIFORMAL: It might be **he** who wins.

Even in informal conversation many people still prefer the subjective case forms in such constructions.

5C *WHO* AND *WHOM*

Use *who* (or *whoever*) in subject positions and *whom* (or *whomever*) in object positions.

However, it is customary nowadays in informal conversation to use *who* as an object except directly after a preposition. Examples:

INFORMAL: **Who** were you talking to? (object of *to*)
INFORMAL: I don't care **who** you invite. (object of *invite*)

But in semiformal or formal writing you should distinguish between *who* and *whom.* Examples:

RIGHT: I voted for the candidate **whom** my father voted for. (object of *voted for*)
RIGHT: It got so we were always wondering **whom** the cops would bust next. (object of *would bust*)
RIGHT: You should always vote for the candidate **who** you feel will do the best job. (subject of *will do*)
RIGHT: I was ready to give the answers to **whoever** asked me for them. (subject of *asked;* the whole noun clause *whoever asked me for them* is the object of *to*.)

Sometimes you may need to test a construction in order to choose the right form of *who.* The test is this: (1) turn a question into a simple sentence or express the part of a sentence containing a form of *who* as a simple sentence; then (2) see whether *he* or *him* fits the *who* slot in your simple sentence. If *he* fits, use *who;* if *him* fits, use *whom.* Examples:

_____ did the jury say was guilty?
(Who *or* Whom?)

The jury did say *he* was guilty. (not *him*)
Who did the jury say was guilty?

_____ was Professor Skole angry with?
(Who *or* Whom?)

Professor Skole was angry with *him.* (not *he*)
Whom was Professor Skole angry with?

We usually become fonder of someone _____
    we do a favor for.   (who *or* whom?)
We do a favor for *him*. (So use *whom* as the object of *for*, even
    though *whom* doesn't come directly after *for*.)
We usually become fonder of someone **whom** we do a favor for.

Shelley is the student _____ it seems will be
                                    (who *or* whom?)
    selected to give the graduation address.
It seems *she* will be selected. (So use *who* as the subject of
    will be selected.)
Shelley is the student **who** it seems will be selected to give the
    graduation address.

The test is simple and reliable. We should note that even in
casual conversation some people still prefer to distinguish
between *who* and *whom*.

5D   IN COMPARATIVE CONSTRUCTIONS

**After the comparative words *as* and *than* use the pronoun
case form that the understood part of the clause calls for.**

In such a sentence as—

    I gave more to charity than _____,
                                    (he *or* him?)

a part of a dependent clause is understood but not stated.
In the above sentence the understood part is *(than he) gave
to charity.* Testing such sentences by mentally supplying the
understood part of the clause will tell you the correct pronoun to use. Examples, with the understood parts in
parentheses:

RIGHT: My parents have always treated my sister better than (they
        treated) **me.**
RIGHT: Donna Smith deserved the award as much as I (deserved
        the award).
RIGHT: Bruce gave Betty more money than (he gave) **me.**
RIGHT: Bruce gave Betty more money than I (gave Betty).

As the last two examples show, the pronoun form at the end of a comparative construction sometimes determines the meaning. The test for choosing the correct form is both simple and reliable.

5E WITH VERBAL PHRASES

Use the possessive form of a pronoun (or noun) to modify an *ing* verbal phrase when the phrase refers to just one aspect of a person and not the person as a whole.

Example, with the pronoun form in boldface:

RIGHT: We all agreed with Derick, but we could see that the coach was furious at **his** not having followed orders.

Him would be incorrect, for the coach was not furious at him as a whole but only at his not having followed orders. Two more examples:

RIGHT: Jill heard **me** coming, and she did not like **my** coming on a motorcycle.
RIGHT: We were delayed by the McCombs' arriving an hour late.

The *me* is correct because it refers to the whole person, and the *my* is correct because it refers to just one action of the person. In other words, the sentence does not say that "she did not like me" but only that she did not like one of my actions. Similarly, the possessive form *McCombs'* is correct.

5F THE *WE STUDENTS-US STUDENTS* CONSTRUCTION

Use *we* or *us* in conjunction with a noun according to whether the noun functions as a subject or object.

If the noun is a subject, use *we;* if it is an object, use *us.* The very simple test that will guide you correctly in choosing *we* or *us* is to mentally omit the noun and then to use the pronoun form that sounds natural. Examples, with the noun to be mentally omitted in parentheses:

RIGHT: After three meetings, **we** (students) decided we did not want to sit on the Administrative Committee.
RIGHT: **We** (girls) in the dorm do not have as much freedom as those who live in town.
RIGHT: Then the coach gave **us** (players) the worst dressing down we had ever had.
RIGHT: The judge was simply unfair to **us** (demonstrators) who committed no violent acts.

Since no one would write such constructions as *us decided* or *to we,* this simple test is thoroughly reliable.

5G DEMONSTRATIVE PRONOUNS

Never use *them* as a demonstrative ("pointing") pronoun in place of *these* or *those.*

Examples:

WRONG: I asked for *them* books to be reserved for me.
RIGHT: I asked for **those** books to be reserved for me.

WRONG (pointing and speaking with emphasis): I want one of *them.*
RIGHT: I want one of **those** (or **these**).

When there is no pointing action, *them* is correct, as in—

I was the first to see **them.**

5H REFLEXIVE PRONOUNS

In semiformal or formal writing do not use a reflexive pronoun as a subject or object.

Examples:

WRONG: Jerry and *myself* managed to slip through the transom into our dorm's kitchen.

RIGHT: Jerry and **I** managed to slip through the transom into our dorm's kitchen.

WRONG: It turned out that the invitation was for both my brother and *myself.*

RIGHT: It turned out that the invitation was for both my brother and **me.**

An exception to this rule is the use of the reflexive pronoun as an object when it refers to the same person as the subject, as in *I cut myself.*

Also avoid these incorrect spellings of the reflexive pronouns: *hisself, theirselves,* and *its self.* The correct forms are *himself, themselves,* and *itself.*

6

Subject-Verb Agreement

The grammatical term **number** has to do, obviously, with the number of units involved. The two numbers in our grammar are the **singular** (one) and the **plural** (more than one). For writing to be correct, verbs must agree in number with their subjects. This writing problem is limited, however, because all English verbs except *to be* have singular and plural forms only in the present tense. And even then the only variation in verb form for number is that the third person singular, present tense verb form ends in *s* or *es*, as in *John walks, Shirley touches*, and so on; the other present tense form (*walk, touch*, and so on) is used with *I, you, we, they*, and plural nouns. The verb *to be* has number in the present tense *(am, is, are)* and in the past tense *(was, were)*. The auxiliaries *to have* and *to do* have number only in the present tense *(has, have* and *does, do)*. The modal auxiliaries *(can, could*, and so on) do not have number. But in spite of the limited opportunities to make errors in subject-verb agreement in English, there are a number of trouble spots, which we will cover in the following sections.

6A   NOUN PHRASES AS SUBJECTS

The verb of a sentence should agree in number with the headword of a noun-phrase subject.

Of course, many subjects are single nouns, such as a person's name. But often a noun phrase functions as a subject. The whole noun phrase is the **full subject,** and the **headword** of the noun phrase is the **simple subject.** The headword is the noun (or noun substitute, such as *many*) that governs the entire phrase; all other words and word groups in the noun phrase either modify the headword or modify other words in the phrase. The simple subject, or headword of the noun phrase, governs the verb. Thus singular headwords call for singular verbs and plural headwords call for plural verbs. Here are examples, with the headwords, or simple subjects, and the verbs in boldface:

RIGHT: A smelly **pile** of old water-soaked haystacks **was** our refuge.

RIGHT: A **man** who has a domineering wife and only daughters for children always **looks** harried.

The singular headwords (simple subjects) *pile* and *man* govern the singular verbs *was* and *looks.*

RIGHT: Several **coeds** with a lot of money but no brains **were** very popular in Las Vegas.

The plural simple subject *coeds* takes the plural verb *were.*

When the headword is followed by a prepositional phrase with the compound preposition *as well as* or *together with,* the object of the prepositional phrase does not affect the verb. Also, the prepositional phrase is often set off by commas. Examples:

WRONG: The *scoutmaster* as well as the advanced scouts *were* trying to bully us tenderfeet.

RIGHT: The **scoutmaster,** as well as the advanced scouts, **was** trying to bully us tenderfeet.

WRONG: Our club *leader,* together with three "bodyguards," *were*
         staked out in our tree house.
RIGHT: Our club **leader,** together with three "bodyguards," **was**
         staked out in our tree house.

6B INDEFINITE PRONOUNS AS SUBJECTS

The indefinite pronouns *one, each, either,* and *neither* are
singular and require singular verbs.

Examples:

WRONG: *Either* of the answers *are* correct.
RIGHT: **Either** of the answers **is** correct.
RIGHT: At least **one** of the members **is** coming.
RIGHT: **Neither is** the kind I am looking for.
RIGHT: **Each** of the twins **was** surprised to be chosen.

The indefinite pronouns *any* and *none* may correctly
take either a singular or a plural verb. Example:

RIGHT: **None** of you **are** (or **is**) to blame.
RIGHT: **Any** of the voters **is** (or **are**) entitled to challange the
         candidates.

6C RELATIVE PRONOUNS AS SUBJECTS

When a relative pronoun functions as a subject, its verb
agrees in number with the pronoun's antecedent.

This means that *who, whom, which,* and *that* are either
singular or plural according to the nouns they refer to.
Examples, with the relative pronoun, its antecedent, and the
verb in boldface:

RIGHT: I have an **uncle** in Peoria **who** still **makes** bathtub gin.
RIGHT: The **theories** of cosmogony **which** in the future **are** likely
         to be re-examined are the big-bang and steady-state
         theories.

A special subject-verb agreement problem involving relative pronouns appears in sentences with the construction *one of those* _____ *who* (or *which* or *that*). Example:

RIGHT: Steve is one of those **students who do** well in all subjects. (*Does* would be wrong.)

The point is that *students*, and not *Steve*, is the antecedent of *who*, which means that a plural verb is required. When in doubt, you can use a simple test to choose the proper verb. All such sentences as the one illustrated will undergo this transformation:

Of those **students who do** well in all subjects, Steve is one.

This test clearly shows the verb form needed.

6D COMPOUND SUBJECTS

Compound subjects consist of two or more coordinated constituents (or unified parts of a sentence).

6D1 With the Coordinating Conjunction *and*

When two (or more) subjects are joined by *and*, they form a plural subject and should take a plural verb.

Examples:

RIGHT: My uncle **and** one of my cousins **are** going to Las Vegas with me.

RIGHT: Where you go **and** whom you go with **are** none of my business.

But when two nouns or constructions joined by *and* are considered a single unit, they take a singular verb. Examples:

RIGHT: Apple pie and cheese **is** on the menu.

RIGHT: Some gas and dust actually **shows** up in photographs of interstellar space.

Apple pie and cheese is considered a single dish; *gas and dust* is considered a unified, or singular, mass of matter.

6D2   With Correlatives and *but not*

When compound subjects are joined by one of the correlatives or by *but not*, the verb agrees in number with the part of the subject closest to the verb.

The correlatives are the two-part connectives *either (neither) . . . or (nor), not only . . . but (also),* and *not . . . but.* (The correlative *both . . . and* makes compound subjects just as *and* by itself does.) Examples, with the noun governing the verb and the verb in boldface:

RIGHT: Either a wolf or small **dogs were** responsible for the kill.
RIGHT: Either small dogs or a **wolf was** responsible for the kill.

RIGHT: Not only a police sergeant but two **plainclothesmen are** assigned to this case.
RIGHT: Not only two plainclothesmen but also a police **sergeant is** assigned to this case.

RIGHT: Not a boy but several **girls are** the guilty ones.
RIGHT: Not those girls but a **boy is** the guilty one.

Sometimes the *either* of *either . . . or* and the *also* of *not only . . . but also* are omitted, but the rule for subject-verb agreement stays the same.

When two subjects are joined by the connective *but not,* the verb agrees in number with the part of the subject closest to the verb. Examples:

RIGHT: All the wives but not a single **husband was** willing to go.
RIGHT: Mr. Busbee but not his **children were** willing to go.

6E   SPECIAL NOUNS AS SUBJECTS

Three special kinds of nouns sometimes cause problems in subject-verb agreement.

6E1 Collective Nouns

Collective nouns take singular verbs unless they are used so as to mean individuals and not a group.

Collective nouns are those singular in form but plural in meaning, since they specify many individuals. Some of the most common collective nouns are *family, team, crew, series, jury, flock, student body, faculty, staff, pride* (of lions), *gaggle* (of geese), *collection,* and so on. Examples:

RIGHT: The English **staff is** holding a meeting.
RIGHT: The **jury is** deadlocked.
RIGHT: The **team is** in excellent physical shape.

When a collective noun is used so that it must be thought of as meaning separate individuals, then it takes a plural verb. Example:

RIGHT: My family **are** individualists.

Such use of collective nouns is not common.

The collective nouns *number, crowd, group,* and perhaps a few others pose a different problem. When one of these singular nouns is followed by a prepositional phrase with a plural noun object, the verb may be plural. Examples, with the simple subjects and the verbs in boldface:

RIGHT: A **number** of students **were** suspended.
RIGHT: A **crowd** of spectators **were** injured.
RIGHT: A **group** of Mohawks **were** on the prowl.

Some writers prefer singular verbs in such sentences, and that usage is of course correct. But individuals are so clearly meant in the example sentences and others like them that the plural verb must also be considered correct. Some experts prefer the plural verb.

6E2 Singular Nouns Plural in Form

Normally, nouns plural in form but singular in meaning take singular verbs.

The most common such nouns are *economics, physics, mathematics, politics, statistics, checkers, measles, mumps,* and *molasses.* Examples:

RIGHT: Physics **is** my hardest course.
RIGHT: Politics **is** a risky profession.
RIGHT: Measles **is** a serious disease.
RIGHT: Checkers **is** an intellectual game.

6E3   Nouns of Weight, Measurement, Time, and Money

A plural noun that establishes a weight or measurement or a period of time or an amount of money takes a singular verb.

Examples:

RIGHT: Two hundred and fifty pounds **is** not an unusual weight for a football player.
RIGHT: Five miles **is** a long distance to walk.
RIGHT: Two years **is** the gestation period for elephants.
RIGHT: Forty dollars **is** the least I will take for that record.

6F SUBJECTS IN INVERTED SENTENCE ORDER

When a subject follows its verb, the verb still agrees in number with the subject.

Examples, with the verbs and subjects in boldface:

RIGHT: Standing at the professor's lectern **were** two **chimpanzees.**
RIGHT: Under the rose bushes **is** a stretched-out **king snake.**

Note that the nouns *lectern* and *bushes* have no effect on the verbs.

The most common kind of inverted sentence order, however, and the one that gives most trouble in subject-verb agreement, is the sentence that begins with *there* and has its subject following the verb. The *there* is just a filler and has no meaning. The verb agrees with the subject. Examples:

WRONG: There *is* some *parents* who just won't give their children a chance to talk to them.

RIGHT: There **are** some **parents** who just won't give their children a chance to talk to them.

WRONG: There *exists* many *ways* that students use to cheat on exams.

RIGHT: There **exist** many **ways** that students use to cheat on exams.

When the opening word *there* does not mean a place, the sentence subject will follow its verb.

7

Shifts

Various kinds of inconsistencies frequently occur in writing because of **faulty shifts in grammatical constructions.** That is, a writer will begin with one kind of grammatical construction but will unnecessarily (and incorrectly) shift to a different kind of construction. Example:

INCONSISTENT: The American child is different from his European counterparts.

This writer opened with the singular *American child,* thus committing himself (or herself) to talking about children in general in the singular, which is perfectly acceptable. But then he inconsistently shifted to the plural *European counterparts.* The writer either should have continued in the singular with *European counterpart* or should have begun with the plural *American children.* Maintaining complete grammatical consistency is not an easy task even for professional writers. In this chapter we will deal briefly and simply with the six kinds of shifts that produce most inconsistencies. These are shifts in **number, person, tense, voice, mood,** and **point of view.**

7A IN NUMBER

The most common kind of faulty shift in number is from a singular noun to a plural pronoun. Examples:

INCONSISTENT: The *teacher* always thinks *they are* right because *they don't* want to admit that *they know* less than a student.

CONSISTENT: **Teachers** always think **they are** right because **they don't** want to admit that **they know** less than a student.

INCONSISTENT: I think that a college *athlete* should be paid, because *they work* just as hard as teachers do.

CONSISTENT: I think that college **athletes** should be paid, because **they work** just as hard as teachers do.

Sometimes, however, the faulty shift is from the plural to the singular. Example:

INCONSISTENT: *People* are honest most of the time only because *one doesn't* like *one's* neighbors to know that *he* or *she is* a cheater.

CONSISTENT: **People are** honest most of the time only because **they don't** like **their** neighbors to know that **they are** cheaters.

You must give thought to whether you will write in the singular or the plural in order to avoid such shifts.

7B IN PERSON

There are three **persons** in English grammar: (1) the **first person** is the person speaking *(I, me, we, us)*; (2) the **second person** is the person spoken to *(you)*; and (3) the **third person** is the person or thing spoken about *(he, him, she, her, it, they, them,* and all nouns and indefinite pronouns). The grammatical inconsistency dealt with in this section is due to our language's use of the **indefinite second person** *you* to refer to people in general. Use of the indefinite *you* is not at all improper, but it is improper to begin a passage in the third person and then to shift inconsistently to the indefinite *you*. Examples:

INCONSISTENT: College is designed to aid *those* interested in becoming educated. Without the opportunity to attend college, *you* might not receive the education *you* will need in *your* vocation.

CONSISTENT: College is designed to aid **those** interested in becoming educated. Without the opportunity to attend college, **one** might not receive the education **he** or **she** will need in a vocation.

INCONSISTENT: Most parents constantly strive to give their *children* a sense of security. If *you* grow up feeling insecure, *your* parents have failed *you*.

CONSISTENT: Most parents constantly strive to give their **children** a sense of security. If **children** grow up feeling insecure, **their** parents have failed **them.**

Note particularly in the first example the use of the indefinite third person pronoun *one* to maintain consistency in person. Very many of the improper shifts from the third person to the indefinite *you* are due to the writer's failure to understand the use of the third person *one*, which refers to people in general.

7C IN TENSE

In summarizing fiction or history, do not inconsistently shift from the past to the present tense or the present to the past tense.

There are a number of different present and past tenses, but we need not differentiate among them; just recognizing that a verb is in one of the present or one of the past tenses is enough. In summarizing events of the past we may use either the past tense or the **historical present tense,** but the writer who inconsistently shifts from one to the other is careless. Examples:

INCONSISTENT: In the story a boy named Giovanni *had gone* to Padua to study. He *rents* a room and from it he *looks* into a very weird garden.

CONSISTENT: In the story a boy named Giovanni **has gone** to Padua to study. He **rents** a room and from it he **looks** into a very weird garden.

INCONSISTENT: In the 1932 election campaign FDR *promised* to reduce taxes if he *was elected.* But in 1933 he *begins* to ask Congress for tax increases and *continues* to ask for increases every year.

CONSISTENT: In the 1932 election campaign FDR **promised** to reduce taxes if he **was elected.** But in 1933 he **began** to ask Congress for tax increases and **continued** to ask for them every year.

In each of these examples the writer began a summary in the past tense and inconsistently shifted to the historical present. In the first example we restored consistency by changing the past tense *(had gone)* to the present *(has gone).* In the second, we changed the present tense *(begins, continues)* to the past *(began, continued).* The point is to be consistent. You should *know* which tense you have chosen for a summary and should stick to it.

7D IN VOICE

Do not inconsistently shift from the active to the passive voice.

In the active voice, the subject performs the action; in the passive voice the subject receives the action. Sometimes there are good reasons for using the active voice and sometimes there are good reasons for using the passive. But once you have started describing a sequence of actions in the active voice, do not inconsistently shift to the passive.

(If you shift from the passive to the active, you should have started in the active voice to begin with.) Example:

INCONSISTENT: I first *place* the bit in the horse's mouth and *adjust* the bridle. Then the saddle blanket and saddle *are put* on. Now I *am* ready to mount.

CONSISTENT: I first **place** the bit in the horse's mouth and **adjust** the bridle. Then I **put** the saddle blanket and saddle on. Now I **am** ready to mount.

In the inconsistent passage, the first and third sentences are properly in the active voice, but the middle sentence is inconsistently in the passive voice. Since the writer is performing all the actions, there is no reason to say vaguely that they are performed.

7E IN MOOD

Do not inconsistently shift from the imperative to the subjunctive mood.

Verbs have mood. Request or command sentences are in the imperative mood, which is also often used for giving directions. That is, you might say to someone—

> First **go** to . . . . Then **take** the first left . . . . After that, **turn** at . . . .

The boldface verbs are in the imperative mood, directly telling someone to do certain things. One form of the subjunctive mood uses the modal auxiliaries *should* and *ought to* so that the writer does not tell someone to do something but rather that he or she *should* do something. In giving directions, do not inconsistently shift from the imperative to the subjunctive mood. Example:

INCONSISTENT: The first thing to do in breaking a wild mustang stallion is not to let him get close enough to kick or bite you. *Keep* him tethered and hobbled for the first few days. *Feed* him by placing grain under his head and leaving him to himself for a while. Next you *should try* just to touch him gently. After you have got him used to your presence, you *should try* getting a bridle on him, without a bit. When you do try getting the bit into his mouth, *keep* him hobbled and *keep* his head in a tight grasp so that he can't bite you.

CONSISTENT: (Simply remove the *you should*'s from sentences four and five.)

It is possible, of course, to give directions so that *essential* steps are phrased in the imperative mood and *desirable* (but not essential) steps are phrased in the subjunctive mood, but no such differentiation exists in the passage above. To be consistent, such a passage requires *keep, feed, try,* and other such verbs in the imperative mood.

7F IN POINT OF VIEW

Do not inconsistently shift the point of view when discussing or explaining someone's opinions.

Point of view refers to the source of an opinion or idea being presented. The writing should make clear whether the opinion is the writer's own or that of someone being discussed. Sentences should be composed so that the point of view does not inconsistently shift. Example:

INCONSISTENT: Everybody nowadays thinks slavery is a wholly inhumane and unacceptable institution, but Aristotle thought it was rooted in human nature and thus acceptable. Some people are born to be leaders and some to be followers or servants. Human nature can't be changed, and thus the slave class remains the slave class. Slavery is fixed in human nature.

CONSISTENT: Everybody nowadays thinks slavery is a wholly inhumane and unacceptable institution, but Aristotle thought that it was rooted in human nature and thus acceptable. **He claimed** that some people are born to be leaders and some to be followers or servants. **He maintained** that human nature can't be changed and that that is why the slave class remains the slave class. Slavery, **he argued,** is fixed in human nature.

In the inconsistent passage the writer began by stating a modern point of view and contrasting it with Aristotle's. But the passage fails to show that the last three sentences reflect Aristotle's point of view also. In the consistent passage, the *he claimed, he maintained,* and *he argued* clearly retain Aristotle's point of view and prevent inconsistency.

8

Verb Forms

Incorrect subject-verb agreement (Chapter 6) perhaps accounts for most verb problems in writing. However, occasionally wrong verb forms are used, chiefly because English has both regular and irregular verbs that sometimes cause confusion. All English verbs (with slight exceptions for *to be*) have five forms, as follows:

infinitive	*third-person singular, present tense*	*present participle*	*past tense*	*past participle*
to talk	talks	talking	talked	talked
to freeze	freezes	freezing	froze	frozen
to bring	brings	bringing	brought	brought

The present tense (except for the third person) is always the infinitive without the *to*. The first three forms of all verbs are regular; differences in some verbs appear in the last two forms. Verbs that end in *ed* in the past tense and past participle are called **regular;** others are **irregular,** sometimes with the past tense and past participle being different from each other (as with *freeze*) and sometimes identical (as with *bring*).

For your reference, here is a list of the so-called **principal parts** of the chief irregular verbs in English. The stem is the present tense, or the infinitive without the *to.*

stem	*past tense*	*past participle*
arise	arose	has arisen
bear	bore	has borne, was born
begin	began	has begun
bind	bound	has bound
blow	blew	has blown
break	broke	has broken
bring	brought	has brought
buy	bought	has bought
catch	caught	has caught
choose	chose	has chosen
come	came	has come
creep	crept	has crept
deal	dealt	has dealt
dive	dived, dove	has dived
do	did	has done
draw	drew	has drawn
drink	drank	has drunk
drive	drove	has driven
eat	ate	has eaten
fall	fell	has fallen
flee	fled	has fled
fly	flew	has flown
forbid	forbad, forbade	has forbidden
freeze	froze	has frozen
give	gave	has given
go	went	has gone
grow	grew	has grown

VERB FORMS

stem	past tense	past participle
hang	hung	has hung
hang (execution)	hanged	has hanged
know	knew	has known
lay	laid	has laid
lead	led	has led
lie	lay	has lain
lose	lost	has lost
mean	meant	has meant
ride	rode	has ridden
ring	rang	has rung
rise	rose	has risen
run	ran	has run
see	saw	has seen
seek	sought	has sought
send	sent	has sent
shake	shook	has shaken
shine	shone, shined	has shone, has shined
sing	sang	has sung
sleep	slept	has slept
speak	spoke	has spoken
spin	spun	has spun
spit	spat	has spat
spread	spread	has spread
steal	stole	has stolen
stink	stank	has stunk
swear	swore	has sworn
swim	swam	has swum
swing	swung	has swung
take	took	has taken
teach	taught	has taught
tear	tore	has torn
thrive	thrived, throve	has thrived, thriven
throw	threw	has thrown
wear	wore	has worn
weep	wept	has wept
write	wrote	has written

8A PAST-TENSE FORMS

Do not use the past participle of an irregular verb as the past-tense form, unless the two are identical.

Examples:

WRONG: When my parents *begun* to pressure me about my school work, I did even worse.

RIGHT: When my parents **began** to pressure me about my school work, I did even worse.

WRONG: I *swum* forty laps in record time.

RIGHT: I **swam** forty laps in record time.

WRONG: We *drunk* more than three cases that night at Hollis's apartment.

RIGHT: We **drank** more than three cases that night at Hollis's apartment.

8B PAST-PARTICIPLE FORMS; *COULD OF*

Do not use the past-tense form of an irregular verb as the past participle, unless the two are identical.

The past participle is always used with an auxiliary, often *has, have,* or *had* (see list above). Examples:

WRONG: I *had chose* the wrong course in math, and consequently I failed.

RIGHT: I **had chosen** the wrong course in math, and consequently I failed.

WRONG: After we *had began* our last practice session, word came that Fresno was dropping out of the tournament.

RIGHT: After we **had begun** our last practice session, word came that Fresno was dropping out of the tournament.

WRONG: I *had ran* the hundred-yard dash in ten seconds and still came in third.

RIGHT: I **had run** the hundred-yard dash in ten seconds and still came in third.

Also, do not convert an irregular verb form into an incorrect regular form.

Examples:

WRONG: The wind *blowed* all the time we were in Las Vegas.
RIGHT: The wind **blew** all the time we were in Las Vegas.

WRONG: If I *had knowed* about the importance of English, I might have studied more when I was here the first time.
RIGHT: If I **had known** about the importance of English, I might have studied more when I was here the first time.

Never use the word *of* for the contraction of *have*.

The two forms sound the same and thus the error is common. Example:

WRONG: I *could of* made the team if I had tried harder.
RIGHT: I **could've (could have)** made the team if I had tried harder.

8C   TO LIE—TO LAY; TO SIT—TO SET; TO BEAR

Do not confuse *lay* with *lie* or *set* with *sit*.

Here are the principal parts of these verbs:

present tense	present participle	past tense	past participle
lie, lies (to recline)	lying	lay	lain
lay, lays (to place or put)	laying	laid	laid
sit, sits (to be seated)	sitting	sat	sat
set, sets (to place something)	setting	set	set

To lie is an intransitive verb; virtually no one ever uses it incorrectly, that is, as a transitive verb (as in the incorrect *I will lie the book down*). Examples of its use:

RIGHT: I **lie** down when I have a headache.
RIGHT: I **lay** on the floor for hours before anyone found me.
RIGHT: I **had lain** in bed longer than usual.
RIGHT: I **had been lying** in the muck for some time.

To lay is a transitive verb and is used correctly only when it has a direct object. Examples, with the verbs and direct objects in boldface:

RIGHT: I **lay** my **gun** down whenever I hear other hunters.
RIGHT: I **laid** the **bottle** of wine slightly up-ended.
RIGHT: I **have laid** expensive **carpet** professionally for a year.
RIGHT: I **was laying** the **baby** down when the phone rang.

The errors come when forms of *lay* are used instead of forms of *lie*. Examples:

WRONG: I need to *lay* down.
RIGHT: I need to **lie** down.

WRONG: I *laid* in bed all morning.
RIGHT: I **lay** in bed all morning.

WRONG: I *had laid* under the rose bushes for an hour.
RIGHT: I **had lain** under the rose bushes for an hour.

WRONG: I *was laying* in ambush.
RIGHT: I **was lying** in ambush.

To sit is also an intransitive verb. Virtually no one ever uses it incorrectly, that is, as a transitive verb (as in the incorrect *I'll sit the table*). Examples of its use:

RIGHT: That empty bottle **sits** on the mantel as a symbol.
RIGHT: Another bottle **sat** there last year.
RIGHT: I **have sat** on antique chairs before.
RIGHT: Joe **has been sitting** in front of the TV for twelve hours.

To set is a transitive verb used correctly (except for some uncommon meanings) only when it has a direct object. Examples, with the verbs and direct objects in boldface:

RIGHT: I **will set** the **bottle** down immediately.
RIGHT: Yesterday I **set it** in a hiding place.
RIGHT: I **have set** potted **plants** all around the house.
RIGHT: I **was setting** the **plants** in their tubs when Mavis arrived.

The errors come when forms of *set* are used instead of forms of *sit*. Examples:

WRONG: Let's *set* for a spell.
RIGHT: Let's **sit** for a spell.

WRONG: Donny just *set* in his seat like a goon.
RIGHT: Donny just **sat** in his seat like a goon.

WRONG: *Has* Charlie *set* there all day?
RIGHT: **Has** Charlie **sat** there all day?

WRONG: We *were* just *setting* around talking.
RIGHT: We **were** just **sitting** around talking.

The verb *to bear* also needs mentioning. In active-voice sentences, its past participle is *borne.* Examples:

RIGHT: Elaine **has borne** six children.
RIGHT: I **have borne** all the slander I can take.

But in the passive voice, *born* is the past participle of *to bear* in the meaning of coming into the world. Example:

RIGHT: I **was born** in Muncie, Indiana.

8D SUBJUNCTIVE VERB FORMS

Do not use the indicative form of a verb when a subjunctive form is needed.

The indicative mood states facts or what are thought to be facts. The subjunctive mood states conditions contrary to fact or conveys desirability or urgency of some sort. In informal speech the indicative mood is often used for conditions contrary to fact, and so on, but in semiformal speech and writing the subjunctive mood is preferred. Examples:

INFORMAL: I wish I *was* my own boss.
SEMIFORMAL: I wish I **were** my own boss.

WRONG: We desire that this application form *is* filled out in triplicate.
RIGHT: We desire that this application form **be** filled out in triplicate.

WRONG: It is obligatory that he *is* an eagle scout.
RIGHT: It is obligatory that he **be** an eagle scout.

WRONG: We demand that she *comes* immediately.
RIGHT: We demand that she **come** immediately.

SECTION TWO

PUNCTUATION AND MECHANICS

9

End Punctuation

End punctuation occurs at the end of sentences and of some constructions that are not sentences.

9A THE PERIOD

Use a period to end a normal sentence that is not a question and is not especially emphatic.

Declarative and imperative sentences end with periods. **Declarative sentences** are those that make statements. Examples:

RIGHT: The mass of men lead lives of quiet desperation.
RIGHT: A foolish consistency is the hobgoblin of little minds.

Imperative sentences are those that issue a request or command or give directions. Examples, with the imperative verbs italicized:

RIGHT: *Direct* your eye right inward, and you'll discover a thousand regions in your mind yet undiscovered.
RIGHT: *Travel* them, and *be* expert in home-cosmography.

There are two kinds of **indirect questions:** (1) those which simply state that someone asked something and (2) those that ask for an answer but are not phrased in question form. Periods close each kind. Examples:

RIGHT: The employment agency asked whether I would take a job guarding a gaggle of geese.

RIGHT: I wonder whether you can direct me to Skid Row.

A sentence that includes an indirectly quoted question also ends with a period. An example is: ''He asked me if I would like to go swimming.'' Note that this sort of indirect question must be rephrased from its original form or else enclosed within quotation marks. Example:

WRONG: She asked did I have a few minutes to spare.

RIGHT: She asked if I had a few minutes to spare.

RIGHT: She asked me, ''Do you have a few minutes to spare?''

Courtesy questions are those in which *will you* is equivalent to *please.* They normally are closed with periods rather than question marks, though a question mark at the end of such a sentence is not wrong. Example:

RIGHT: Will you let me know whether I need to take further action.

RIGHT: Will you let me know whether I need to take further action?

(Periods used with abbreviations are illustrated in Chapter 14.)

9B THE QUESTION MARK

Use a question mark to close a question.

Examples:

RIGHT: Who but the President knows best when national security is at stake?

RIGHT: Has a turn away from open pornography begun yet?

When a question ends a quoted part of a declarative sentence, the question mark goes inside the quotation marks and no additional period is used even though the whole is a statement rather than a question. Example:

RIGHT: The vicar asked, ''Have you been playing golf for the past
    six Sundays?''

When a question in a quoted part of a sentence comes first, a question mark is put inside the quotation marks but no other mark of punctuation separates the quoted part from the remainder. A period closes the whole. Example:

RIGHT: ''What is the difference between a metaphor and a sym-
    bol?'' Luis asked.

A question mark also is used in parentheses to indicate that the immediately preceding information is not certain or is questionable. Example:

RIGHT: The altruism (?) of some tycoons makes them richer.

Information enclosed in parentheses is followed by a question mark when the information is uncertain. Example:

RIGHT: Herodotus (died 428 B.C.?) was the first great historian.

9C THE EXCLAMATION POINT

The exclamation point (or mark) is used to close sentences or nonsentence exclamations or bits of information enclosed in parentheses when the writer wants to
show strong emphasis.

Examples:

RIGHT: We will never, never yield to those insane terrorists!
RIGHT: What irony!
RIGHT: Our first week's sales of *The Reptiles* (25,000 copies!)
    broke all records for that kind of book.

The exclamation point, however, should be used only spar-
ingly, for the writer who uses the mark very frequently is like the little boy crying ''Wolf!'' In a short time no reader will believe in the force of any of the exclamation points.

10

The Comma

Aside from marks of end punctuation, the comma is by far the most commonly used mark of punctuation and, perhaps because of that, poses more writing problems than any other mark of punctuation. Since rules for punctuation in modern English are almost wholly based on sentence structure, they are mostly precise and fixed. Some options do occur, such as using or not using, according to your pleasure, a comma to separate two short independent clauses joined by a coordinating conjunction. But we will give the basic rules and not elaborate on exceptions, for it is best for you to learn the rules and follow them before you begin to exercise options. Since there are so many rules for the use of the comma, we will use not only our number-letter system of classification but will also number the rules themselves.

In grammar, a constituent is any unified part of a sentence, from single words with specific grammatical functions apart from other words to various kinds of phrases and clauses.

10A CONSTITUENTS IN A SERIES

<u>Rule 1</u>   **Use commas to separate three or more constituents in a series.**

Examples:

RIGHT: On that scavenger hunt we had to collect a frog, a corset, a bottle with a rye-whisky label, a book printed in French, and a polka-dot bow tie.

RIGHT: When Roscoe will come, what he will do, and when he will leave are questions causing us profound anxiety.

If *two* constituents in a series are not joined by a coordinating conjunction, they should be separated by a comma. Example:

RIGHT: I learned to live without working, to consume without sharing.

10B COMPOUND SENTENCES

<u>Rule 2</u>   **Use a comma to separate independent clauses joined by a coordinating conjunction to form one sentence.**

The coordinating conjunctions are *and, but, yet, or, nor, for,* and *so.* Examples, with the coordinating conjunctions italicized:

RIGHT: The work proved much harder than the ad had led us to believe, *and* after two hours on the job we walked off without uttering a word.

RIGHT: The Circle K Club ran the prettiest candidate for Homecoming Queen, *yet* she received the fewest votes.

RIGHT: Our group continued working, *for* we feared that the Inquisition would inquire into any idleness on our part.

10C INTRODUCTORY CONSTITUENTS

<u>Rule 3</u>   **Use a comma to set off an introductory constituent whose meaning exhibits some separation from the sentence subject.**

Most sentences open with their subjects, but many open with a word, phrase, or clause that is not a part of the full subject. Such introductory constituents should normally be set off by commas. Examples:

RIGHT: Above, the tree tops were filled with chirping birds.
RIGHT: Unfortunately, our plot to have the final exam canceled did not succeed.
RIGHT: Before leaving, the drugstore manager secretly hired one of the clerks to watch the assistant manager.
RIGHT: Above all, the trees must be sprayed with insecticide.
RIGHT: Please, can we discuss this calmly?
RIGHT: After the disputants both had had their say, the arbitrator retired to reflect on the evidence.
RIGHT: Wearing her wig and carrying an old-fashioned parasol, Madame Gagnon tottered across the lawn toward us.

Introductory adverb clauses and verbal phrases are almost always set off, as in the last two examples, since they are usually followed by a voice pause.

10D TERMINAL CONSTITUENTS

<u>Rule 4</u>   **Use a comma to set off a terminal constituent (one that comes at the end of a sentence) that is preceded by a distinct voice pause.**

Examples:

RIGHT: Ken is just eccentric, not crazy.
RIGHT: The bear looks for ripe berries, and leaves the unripe ones on the bushes.

RIGHT: Many teenagers are not understood by their parents, if by
       anyone.

(Sometimes terminal constituents are set off by dashes, as is explained in Chapter 11.)

10E   PARENTHETIC CONSTITUENTS

<u>Rule 5</u> **Use commas to set off parenthetic constituents within a sentence.**

A parenthetic constituent is a kind of aside. It is an expression that is not a part of the main sentence but that contains a comment or information that the writer wants to insert within the sentence. Some examples are *as the preacher said, according to my private sources, you will find out, in the first place,* and so on. Also, conjunctive adverbs and transitional phrases that come within an independent clause are considered parenthetic. They are words and phrases such as *however, moreover, for example, in fact,* and so on. Examples:

RIGHT: The highest football score ever, according to the *Guinness*
       Book of Records, was 222 to 0.
RIGHT: The Tories, you'll soon see, will get us into a depression.
RIGHT: The way to a man's heart, Cheri discovered, is not neces-
       sarily through his stomach.
RIGHT: The moral thing to do, nevertheless, is to reveal the whole
       truth.
RIGHT: The evidence of demonic possession, on the other hand,
       may be mere misinterpretation of cause and effect.

Of course some introductory and terminal constituents, as shown in Sections 10C and 10D, are by nature parenthetic, but here we are considering only internal parenthetic constituents. Sometimes parenthetic constituents are set off with dashes or parentheses (see Chapter 11).

10F ESSENTIAL AND NONESSENTIAL CONSTITUENTS

<u>Rule 6</u>   Use a comma or commas to set off a nonessential constituent.

A nonessential constituent, though it may be set off in the same way that a parenthetic constituent is, is not parenthetic but is in the writer's view an essential part of the meaning of the sentence. The grammatical label *nonessential* simply means that if the constituent is removed, the remaining sentence will still be complete and meaningful even though it lacks information the writer wants in it. When an *essential* constituent is removed, the sentence no longer is fully clear and meaningful. Most essential and nonessential constituents are phrases or clauses that modify nouns or are appositives. The key to understanding the difference between them is that an essential constituent is necessary to complete the identification of the noun it is associated with (and thus is not set off with commas) and that a nonessential constituent merely gives additional information about an already-identified noun (and thus requires commas).

The recognition of essential and nonessential constituents poses perhaps the most difficult aspect of English punctuation, and thus further explanations and illustrations are needed. First consider this sentence:

West Point cadets *who break the honor code* are expelled.

The italicized adjective clause is an essential constituent modifying the compound noun *West Point cadets.* It is essential because if it were removed, the noun would not be fully identified, for certainly it is senseless to say *West Point cadets are expelled.* The clause is needed to identify *which* West Point cadets are meant. Thus no commas are called for. Now consider this sentence:

The Commander of West Point, *who personally investigated the cheating scandal,* urged leniency.

The italicized adjective clause modifies *The Commander of West Point,* but that noun phrase carries its own full identification (there is only one Commander of West Point), and thus the adjective clause, which gives additional and not essential information, could be removed and still leave a fully meaningful sentence. The clause, then, is nonessential and is therefore set off with commas.

The ability to punctuate essential and nonessential constituents correctly is especially important because the presence or absence of commas can alter meaning. Two versions of the same sentence, one with commas and one without, can have quite different meanings. For example, consider these sentences:

The slide rule, which you showed me how to use, has been a help in this course.

The slide rule which you showed me how to use has been a help in this course.

In the first sentence the writer refers to the slide rule as a tool and does not mean any particular slide rule. The clause within commas simply adds nonessential information. In the second sentence the absence of commas shows that the meaning is "this particular slide rule—the one which you showed me how to use." In the millions of sentences you read, it will at times be important for you to interpret punctuation correctly to distinguish such meanings.

Most essential and nonessential constituents are either adjective clauses, adjective phrases, verb phrases, or appositives. Here are further examples, with explanations. The essential or nonessential constituents are italicized.

WRONG: Our Dean of Instruction *who was not appointed President when a vacancy occurred* decided to resign as an administrator.

RIGHT: Our Dean of Instruction, *who was not appointed President when a vacancy occurred,* decided to resign as an administrator.

Dean of Instruction is fully identified by *our,* and thus the adjective clause is nonessential and is set off by commas.

As we have noted, some sentences may be correctly punctuated with or without commas around a clause, depending upon the meaning that is intended or is conveyed by the rest of the passage.

RIGHT: The students *who did most of the work building the float* were intensely pro-fraternity.

If the adjective clause is necessary to identify which students are meant, it is essential and thus not set off.

However, if *students* has been fully identified in a previous sentence, its modifier in this sentence is nonessential and thus set off. Example:

RIGHT: We were surrounded by a group of students who were regaling us with odd stories about college homecomings. The students, who did most of the work building the float, were intensely pro-fraternity.

The students are fully identified in the first sentence. This identification carries over into the second sentence so that the adjective clause is nonessential and thus set off. However, this kind of construction is not very common, and therefore we will continue to illustrate with single sentences.

More examples, with adjective phrases italicized:

RIGHT (essential): The wife *happy with her lot in life* is the envy of many of her sisters.
RIGHT (nonessential): Mrs. Wurryfree, *happy with her lot in life,* is puzzled by the high divorce rate.

In the first sentence the phrase is necessary to identify which wife is being discussed. In the second, Mrs. Wurryfree is identified by name and therefore the modifying phrase simply gives additional information.

More examples, with appositives italicized:

WRONG: Raul's wife *Conchita* is president of the local Red Cross chapter.
RIGHT: Raul's wife, *Conchita,* is president of the local Red Cross chapter.

In the wrong sentence, *Conchita* is made essential, thus identifying which of Raul's wives is being mentioned. But since (presumably) Raul has only one wife, *Raul's wife* identifies her, and her name is nonessential information.

WRONG: The German writer, *Hermann Hesse,* is a favorite with college students.

RIGHT: The German writer *Hermann Hesse* is a favorite with college students.

Since Germany has more than one writer, the name is essential to identify which one is under discussion.

RIGHT (if Morley has written only one novel): Richard Morley's novel, *Rotten in Denmark,* has sold only two hundred copies.

RIGHT (if Morley has written more than one novel): Richard Morley's novel *Rotten in Denmark* has sold only two hundred copies.

Further typical examples of incorrectly punctuated sentences from student writing:

WRONG: Emily Dickinson wrote mostly about nature *which she felt had God-like qualities.*

WRONG: I took the case to my counselor *who backed the teacher and gave me no help at all.*

WRONG: We owe many duties to our parents *who nourish and care for us from birth until we can be self-supporting.*

WRONG: We came to the conclusion, *that it takes money to make money.*

Nature, my counselor, and *our parents* are fully identified without the italicized adjective clauses; thus the clauses, being nonessential, must be set off with commas. In the last sentence, the clause is essential to identify *conclusion* and thus the comma should *not* precede it.

Nonessential constituents may also be set off with dashes (see Chapter 11).

10G COORDINATE ADJECTIVES

<u>Rule 7</u>   **Use a comma to separate coordinate adjectives which come in front of a noun and are not joined by *and*.**

The best definition of coordinate adjectives is that they are two adjectives that would sound natural if joined by *and*. If two modifiers in front of a noun will not sound natural when joined by *and*, they are not coordinate. Examples, with the adjectival modifiers italicized:

SOUNDS UNNATURAL: a *white* and *frame* house
SOUNDS UNNATURAL: a *silly* and *old* man
SOUNDS UNNATURAL: a *purple* and *wool* shawl

Since the adjectives do not sound natural with *and* joining them, they are not coordinate. With the *and* removed they would not be separated by commas. Examples:

RIGHT: a white frame house
RIGHT: a silly old man
RIGHT: a purple wool shawl

Examples of adjectives that do sound natural joined by *and:*

SOUNDS NATURAL: a *well-read* and *intelligent* woman
SOUNDS NATURAL: a *malicious* and *vengeful* old man

These adjectives are coordinate and thus the normal and correct punctuation would be as follows:

RIGHT: a well-read, intelligent woman
RIGHT: a malicious, vengeful old man

Of course more than two coordinate adjectives can occur in front of a noun, in which case all of them would be separated by commas, as in—

RIGHT: a malicious, vengeful, greedy, stubborn, dishonest old man

But in actuality writers do not often use more than two coordinate adjectives in front of a noun.

10H ADVERB CLAUSES

<u>Rule 8</u> Use a comma or commas to set off an internal or terminal adverb clause when it is separated from the rest of the sentence by a distinct voice pause or pauses.

Since adverb clauses, which are introduced by subordinating conjunctions, cannot be clearly classified as essential or nonessential (except in the case of *when* and *where* clauses), no rule more definitive than that above can be given for punctuating them. Quite often an internal adverb clause will need to be set off because it requires distinct voice pauses. Examples:

RIGHT: George, since he had a preference for big cars, bought a used Cadillac rather than a new Vega.

RIGHT: The top of the pine tree, after the wind died down, again became a roosting place for a multitude of birds.

A terminal adverb clause may or may not have a voice pause preceding it. In this aspect of punctuation, writers are mostly on their own with no precise rules to guide them. Example:

RIGHT: I refused to pay the repair bill, since my car had been damaged rather than repaired.

But change the *since* to *because* and many professional writers would feel no need for a comma. The subtleties of this aspect of punctuation are too great to be covered in a brief, elementary discussion.

Introductory adverb clauses are normally set off by commas, as rule 3 in Section 10C directs.

10I DATES AND ADDRESSES

<u>Rule 9</u> In dates use a comma to separate the name of a day from the month and the date of the month from the year.

Examples:

RIGHT: I predict that an earthquake will occur in San Francisco on Monday, May 5, 1980.
RIGHT: We made a date for Saturday, December 5, 1981, to celebrate our narrow escape from marriage.

When only a month and year are given, no punctuation is necessary. Example:

RIGHT: I can find the proof I want in the June 1974 issue of *Scientific American.*

Some writers like to set off 1974 in such a construction, but the commas serve no useful purpose.

Rule 10 In addresses use commas to separate the name of a person or establishment from the street address, the street address from the city, and the city from the state.

Examples:

RIGHT: The fire started at Murphy's Drive-In, 1923 Seventh Street, La Canada, California, and spread throughout a broad area.
RIGHT: At 236 La Cross Avenue, Lureville, New York, is a branch of the infamous Anti-Media Charter Group.

10J MISUSED COMMAS

Do NOT enter an obstructive comma into any part of a sentence.

Rule 11 Do NOT separate a subject from its verb with a single comma.

Examples:

WRONG: The bill I support, is the one to make all beaches public property.
RIGHT: The bill I support is the one to make all beaches public property.

WRONG: That we were unwelcome, was evident.
RIGHT: That we were unwelcome was evident.

Of course a parenthetic or nonessential constituent set off on both sides may come between a subject and its verb.

<u>Rule 12</u>   Do NOT separate a verb from its complement (direct object and so on) with a single comma.

Example:

WRONG: The cause of our breakdown was, that some vandal had put oil in the magneto.
RIGHT: The cause of our breakdown was that some vandal had put oil in the magneto.

Of course a constituent set off on both sides can come between a verb and its complement.

<u>Rule 13</u>   Do NOT separate noncoordinate adjectives with a comma.

Examples:

WRONG: Mr. Scearce is an energetic, Baptist preacher.
RIGHT: Mr. Scearce is an energetic Baptist preacher.

WRONG: We saw the suspects in an old, blue Chevrolet.
RIGHT: We saw the suspects in an old blue Chevrolet.

Energetic and Baptist and *old and blue* would not sound natural, and thus in each instance the two modifiers are not coordinate.

<u>Rule 14</u>   Do NOT separate two constituents in a series joined by a coordinating conjunction.

Example:

WRONG: My only obligation is to follow my conscience, and to help the unfortunate.
RIGHT: My only obligation is to follow my conscience and to help the unfortunate.

11

The Dash; Parentheses; Brackets; the Colon

11A USES OF THE DASH

As a mark of punctuation, the dash has uses similar to some uses of the comma. Generally it is used when, for emphasis, the writer wants a pause slightly longer than a comma calls for or when other commas in the sentence make dashes necessary for clarity. On the typewriter a dash is made with two hyphens (--). In a sentence no space is left before or after a dash.

Rule 1   Use dashes to set off a parenthetic comment that is very long or that is a complete sentence itself.

Examples:

RIGHT: You may say many wise things—you who have lived past your allotted three score years and ten—, but we young will continue to listen to our own inner voices.

RIGHT: I wrote these words—I was completely isolated at the time—when my pessimism had reached its greatest depth.

In the first example, the comma after the second dash is also correct, for it would be needed if the whole parenthetic constituent were removed (see 10B). Parentheses instead of dashes would be wrong because the writers want the interpolated comments to stand out boldly rather than having something of the nature of a footnote. Commas instead of dashes would be correct in the first example but would not provide the emphasis that the dashes do.

Rule 2   Use a dash or dashes to set off a nonessential constituent that is especially emphatic or that contains commas of its own.

Examples:

RIGHT: The nation's most popular sport━bowling!━now attracts more than thirty percent of the population.

RIGHT: Our leader's coded message━written in blood━had us all wild with curiosity.

In these cases the writers wanted to add emphasis to their nonessential constituents and thus used dashes instead of commas to set them off.

RIGHT: All of the humanities━literature, philosophy, drama, art history, rhetoric, and the fine arts━are experiencing increasing enrollments.

Since the nonessential appositive has commas of its own, commas to set it off would cause confusion. Dashes provide clarity.

Rule 3   Use a dash to give emphasis to a constituent that would not normally be set off at all.

Example:

RIGHT: Those corrupt politicians deserve credit for giving Americans an overdue━and much-needed━civics lesson.

And much-needed need not be set off at all, but the writer set it off with dashes in order to emphasize it. Commas would provide some emphasis but not as much as dashes.

Rule 4   Use a dash to set off a terminal constituent that is an explanation of a preceding constituent or that is a very distinct afterthought.

Examples:

RIGHT: Strawn resorted to his only hope—plea bargaining.
RIGHT: The best way to settle an argument is to speak softly—or buy drinks all around.

In the first example, a colon after *hope* would also be correct but more formal. In the second example, only a dash will produce the delayed-afterthought effect the writer wanted.

Rule 5   Use a dash to set off an initial series of constituents which is then summarized by a noun or pronoun that serves as the sentence subject.

Examples:

RIGHT: Federalists, Whigs, Know-Nothings, Dixiecrats, Bull Moosers, Progressives—all are vanished political labels.
RIGHT: Tax reform, environmental clean-up, more federal aid to education, revision of welfare laws, reduction in armaments, lower unemployment—these changes were the candidate's stated goals.

The pronouns *all* and *these* are used to summarize the initial constituents in order to emphasize them.

Caution: Do *not* use dashes instead of periods as end punctuation.

11B   USES OF PARENTHESES

The word *parentheses* is plural, meaning both the curved marks that go by that name (*parenthesis* is the singular). A space is used outside a parenthesis unless another mark of punctuation follows it, but no space is used on the inside of a parenthesis. If an entire sentence following a mark of end punctuation is enclosed in parentheses, the period to close the sentence goes inside the final parenthesis. If only the terminal part of a sentence is enclosed in parentheses, the period closing the sentence goes outside the parenthesis. If a complete sentence enclosed in parentheses does not come after a mark of end punctuation, the period closing the entire sentence goes outside the parenthesis.

<u>Rule 6</u>   Use parentheses to enclose any kind of parenthetic or nonessential constituent—even a sentence or group of sentences—when such a constituent has a tone of isolation from the main sentence and is intended to be an aside.

Examples:

RIGHT: We continued to frolic with carefree abandon (later we would learn that we had troubles).

The writer does not intend to discuss the troubles at this point; hence the parenthetic comment is in parentheses, which isolate it more than a dash would. Note that even though the enclosed construction is a complete sentence, the period closing the whole sentence goes outside the parenthesis because the nonenclosed sentence does not have end punctuation. Another correct way of punctuating this construction is this:

RIGHT: We continued to frolic with careless abandon. (Later we would learn that we had troubles.)

RIGHT: In 1933 Norris Baxter (later to become a movie star) attracted much attention with his theory of orgones.

Parentheses rather than dashes or commas set off this constituent because it has a tone of isolation, or something of the nature of a footnote.

RIGHT: Both Turner and Avinger were refusing to sign contracts. (Grady and Towle had signed as early as February, but they were hardly star players. Tooey had signed, too, but he alone could not constitute a pitching staff.) Not only were they asking for huge salary increases but also for other concessions. . . .

The enclosed two sentences are an aside, not directly a part of the discussion of Turner and Avinger. Note that the *they* of the last sentence refers to Turner and Avinger, not to the names within the parentheses. Also note that the period goes inside the parentheses because complete sentences are enclosed.

Rule 7   Use parentheses to enclose numerals used to number items in a series.

Example:

RIGHT: The five most useful spelling rules are **(1)** the doubling-of-the-final-consonant rule, **(2)** the dropping-of-the-silent e rule, **(3)** the retention-of-the-silent e rule, **(4)** the y-to-i rule, and **(5)** the ie-ei rule.

Note that the conjunction *and* precedes the parentheses that enclose the last item.

Rule 8   Use parentheses to enclose cross references and bits of information inserted so as not to be a part of the grammatical structure of the sentence.

Example:

RIGHT: Deism **(**see also Natural Religion**)** was most vigorously promoted by Thomas Paine **(**1737–1809**)**.

The first enclosure is a cross reference. The second enclosure is information — birth and death dates — that the writer wanted to insert without composing another sentence or large constituent in order to do so.

11C   USES OF BRACKETS

Square brackets [like the ones enclosing this phrase] should not be confused with parentheses.

Rule 9   Use brackets to enclose nonquoted material inserted into a direct quotation for the purpose of clarification.

Example:

RIGHT: "She [Maria Wilson] was found guilty as an accomplice in the murder and received a fifteen-year sentence."

The writer wished to use a direct quotation, but the readers would not have known the reference of the pronoun *she.* Therefore the reference is given in brackets for clarification.

Rule 10   Use brackets to enclose comments inserted into direct quotations.

Such insertions may be information included to make a quotation intelligible or personal comments. Examples:

RIGHT: "I got into English 50 because my consalar [sic] advised me to take it."

The word *sic* means *thus* and is used by the writer to indicate that the error was in the original quotation.

RIGHT: "I have endeavored to cooperate in every way possible [a gross overstatement] with the committee."

Here the writer wanted to insert a personal comment at the appropriate place rather than to delay the comment until the quotation was ended.

11D   USES OF THE COLON

The colon is a mark of punctuation used to introduce various kinds of constituents or longer passages of discourse.

Rule 11   Use a colon after the salutation in a formal letter.

Examples:

FORMAL: Dear Professor Burnsides:
INFORMAL: Dear Millie,

Rule 12   Use a colon after an introductory label.

Examples:

INCORRECT: Peel them potatoes.
CORRECT: Peel those potatoes.

<u>Rule 13</u> Use a colon to introduce a series which is prepared for in the main clause of a sentence.

Example:

RIGHT: My deductions were as follows: the student has a photographic memory; she had read the chapter carefully; in her term paper she unconsciously used the wording of the original as though it were her own.

<u>Rule 14</u> A colon may be used after a sentence that introduces a direct quotation.

Example:

RIGHT: It was William James who said: "To *know* is one thing, and to know for certain *that* we know is another. One may hold to the first being possible without the second."

<u>Rule 15</u> A colon may be used to introduce a terminal constituent that is an explanation.

Example:

RIGHT: I was left with but one desire: an hour of solitude.

A dash after *desire* would also be correct, though more informal.

<u>Rule 16</u> Do NOT use a colon directly after the verbs *are* and *were.*

Instead, use no punctuation at all, or use such a word as *these* or *the following* after *are* or *were* and before the colon. Examples:

POOR STYLE: The facts in the case were: the defendant had not been advised of his rights; the arresting officer has used unnecessary force; and the crime violated a law that had not been invoked for over fifty years.

PROPER STYLE: The facts in the case were the following: the defendant had not been advised of his rights; the arresting officer had used unnecessary force; and the crime violated a law that had not been invoked for over fifty years.

WRONG: The most distant planets are: Uranus, Neptune, and Pluto.
RIGHT: The most distant planets are Uranus, Neptune, and Pluto.

12

The Semicolon

A general rule is that semicolons are used to separate only coordinate, not noncoordinate, constituents. The semicolon calls for a voice pause as long as that of a period, but it is used only as internal punctuation.

12 A COMPOUND SENTENCES WITHOUT CONNECTIVES

<u>Rule 1</u> Use a semicolon to separate two independent clauses that form a compound sentence but that do not have a connective word between them.

Examples:

RIGHT: My losses mounted steadily; I began to fear that my roulette system had a flaw of some sort.

RIGHT: The jet was hardly above tree-top level; its deafening scream added to the fright of the neighborhood's residents.

Writers use such compound sentences because they do not want to separate such closely related clauses into separate sentences. Note particularly that semicolons are required between the clauses; commas would produce comma splices (see Chapter 3).

12B COMPOUND SENTENCES WITH CONNECTIVES

Rule 2 Use a semicolon to separate two independent clauses joined by a connective other than a coordinating conjunction.

When independent clauses are joined by a coordinating conjunction, they usually need only a comma between them. When they are connected by a conjunctive adverb or a transitional phrase, they must be separated by a semicolon unless they are punctuated as separate sentences. Sometimes the conjunctive adverb or transitional phrase is shifted to the interior of the second clause. Examples:

RIGHT: The Purple Frogs failed to show up for their scheduled rock concert; however, a local group, the Flat Tires, substituted.
RIGHT: Our college always offers a course for far-out students; for example, last semester the Biology Department offered a course in exobiology, the study of life on other planets.
RIGHT: We learned that the rapids were very swift; several of us, however, got into the boats.

The semicolons in these examples are necessary, unless each example were punctuated as two sentences. Commas in place of the semicolons would produce comma splices (see Chapter 3).

12C CONSTITUENTS IN A SERIES

Rule 3 Use semicolons to separate constituents in a series when the constituents have internal punctuation of their own or when they are especially long.

Examples:

RIGHT: We were directed to separate the debris into three piles:
(1) cans, bottles, and plastic containers; (2) scrap metal,
rubber, and sheet plastic; and (3) stucco, bricks, mortar,
and concrete.

Since each of the three parts of the series has commas of
its own, semicolons clarify the structure. Note that the semicolons still separate coordinate constituents. Also note that
this example illustrates one use of the colon and one use of
parentheses.

RIGHT: Professor Means's study showed that American Indians
from reservations made lower average scores on standardized tests than Indians living off reservations; that Indians
who live in a stable community scored higher than those
who are migrant; and that Indians tested in their own
languages scored higher on I.Q. tests than Indians tested in
English.

Because the constituents in a series in this example are so
long, the semicolons make the sentence structure clearer
than commas would, though commas would be acceptable.

12D MISUSED SEMICOLONS

<u>Rule 4</u> Do NOT use a semicolon between noncoordinate
constituents.

Example:

WRONG: Because of the heavy freeze, our water pipes had burst;
the main valve not having been shut off the night before.
RIGHT: Because of the heavy freeze, our water pipes had burst,
the main valve . . .

A comma should replace the semicolon since the second
constituent is not an independent clause and thus is not
coordinate with the constituent that precedes the semicolon.

Rule 5 Do NOT use a semicolon after the connective *such as.*

Example:

WRONG: We chose several kinds of books, such as; fiction, travel
        books, psychology texts, and *Playboy* joke books.
RIGHT: We chose several kinds of books, such as fiction, travel
        books . . .

Rule 6 Do NOT use a semicolon in place of a dash or colon.

Examples:

WRONG: Just one thing kept me from carrying out my plan; lack of
        money.
RIGHT: Just one thing kept me from carrying out my plan—lack
        of money.

WRONG: On this particular job I had four duties; to open the store
        in the morning and prepare for customers, to restock the
        shelves, to carry empty boxes and such to the outside
        trash bins, and occasionally to wait on customers when
        everybody else was busy.
RIGHT: On this particular job I had four duties: to open the
        store . . .

13

Quotation Marks

DIRECT QUOTATIONS

<u>Rule 1</u> Enclose direct quotations in quotation marks.

Examples:

RIGHT: Feuer maintained that "a minority of students are turning to shallow faculties on the outskirts of the universities where a variety of [charlatans] . . . offer courses in which they provide answers as well as questions."

This is the kind of direct quotation that might appear in a term paper. (Note that square brackets enclose material not in the direct quotation but entered by the writer for clarification. Also note that three spaced periods indicate ellipsis, or omission of part of the quotation.)

RIGHT: He maintained that children are "credulous" and "unresistant to indoctrination."

111

When such a connective as *and* joins two quoted units, as in the above example, each quoted unit is enclosed in quotation marks but the unquoted connective word is not.

RIGHT: Rodney asked, "Will you join the organization?"
"No."
"Then you must not repeat anything you have heard tonight."

This is an example of direct quotations as they are used in dialogue in fiction.

13B QUOTATIONS WITHIN QUOTATIONS

<u>Rule 2</u> **When a direct quotation is used within a direct quotation, enclose the internal quotation in single quotation marks and the whole quotation in regular quotation marks.**

Example:

RIGHT: The commencement speaker said: "In Ecclesiastes we read that 'In much wisdom is much grief, and he who increaseth knowledge increaseth sorrow,' but we must still pursue knowledge for the fulfillment of God's will."

Also the constituents covered in rules 3, 4, 5, and 6 in Sections 13C and 13D should be enclosed in single quotation marks if they appear within a direct quotation.

13C TITLES

<u>Rule 3</u> **Use quotation marks to enclose the quoted titles of short stories, short poems, one-act plays, essays, chapters, and other literary works of less than book or three-act-play length.**

Examples:

RIGHT: E. A. Robinson's poem "Mr. Flood's Party" is about an old man who has outlived his time.

RIGHT: "The Capital of the World" is one of Hemingway's best stories.

RIGHT: The third chapter of *The Scarlet Letter* is entitled "The Recognition."

RIGHT: Professor Lucy Phurr distinctly said, "Read Melville's short story 'Bartleby the Scrivener' by tomorrow."

Note the single quotation marks enclosing the title in the last example.

Titles of book-length literary works are underlined in longhand and italicized in print (see Section 14B). No title should ever be both underlined and enclosed in quotation marks.

Rule 4   **Do NOT put quotation marks around a title used as the heading of a theme or essay.**

Of course if a quoted unit is included in the title, that unit is enclosed in quotation marks. Examples:

TITLE AS HEADING: How Nellie Paid the Mortgage on the Farm

TITLE AS HEADING: A Study of Christian Symbols in Steinbeck's "The Flight"

If the second title appeared in a paragraph, the whole title would be in regular quotation marks and the title of the story in single quotation marks.

13D   SPECIAL CONSTITUENTS

Rule 5   **A word used as a word and not for its meaning may be enclosed in quotation marks.**

Examples:

RIGHT: Both "tomato" and "tart" are commonly used as slang terms.

RIGHT: Ling Chan's proposal contained too many "if's."

Also, words used as words may be underlined in longhand and italicized in print (see Section 14B), but never are they both underlined and put in quotation marks.

<u>Rule 6</u> Use quotation marks to enclose a word or phrase used in a special or ironical sense.

Examples:

RIGHT: Mona feels that she must belong to the "right set."
RIGHT: The "justice" of the verdict was enough to make me cry.

In the first example, the quotation marks mean that the writer's concept of what is the right set is different from Mona's—that is, that Mona only thinks that the set she belongs to is special or worthy of praise. In the second example, the quotation marks mean that the writer did not think the verdict represented justice at all.

You should avoid enclosing slang terms in quotation marks as an apology for their use. Example:

POOR USAGE: Claudette has a "hang-up" about rich boys trying to date her.
BETTER: Claudette has a hang-up about rich boys trying to date her.

If a slang term is worth using, use it without apology.

13E WITH OTHER MARKS OF PUNCTUATION

<u>Rule 7</u> Always put periods and commas inside rather than outside quotation marks, regardless of whether the period or comma belongs to the quoted unit.

Examples:

RIGHT: I decided to entitle my paper "Existentialism in *Moby-Dick.*"
RIGHT: Although our preacher says "The way of the transgressor is hard," I notice that our local crooks have an easy time of it.

Neither the period in the first example nor the comma in the second belongs to the quoted unit, but each is correctly placed within the quotation marks.

<u>Rule 8</u> Marks of punctuation other than the period and the comma are placed inside quotation marks when they are a part of the quoted unit and outside the quotation marks when they are not a part of the quoted unit.

Examples:

RIGHT: Did Professor Gallegos say "to chapter ten" or "through chapter ten"?

Since the question mark does not belong to the quoted unit, it is placed outside the quotation marks.

RIGHT: Ann Landers was heard to utter, "Why am I so lonely?"

Since the question mark belongs to the quoted unit, it is placed inside the quotation marks. Note also that no additional period is used even though the whole sentence is a statement and not a question.

RIGHT: Franklin said, "He who hesitates is lost"; he also said, "Look before you leap."

The semicolon is not a part of the quoted unit and thus is placed outside the quotation marks.

14

Mechanics

14A MANUSCRIPT FORM

14A1 For Handwritten Papers

Observe the following directions in preparing handwritten papers:

1. Use blue or black ink, if possible. Never use red or reddish ink.
2. Write on lined 8½ x 11 notebook paper.
3. Do not skip every other line unless the notepaper is narrow-spaced. Avoid narrow-spaced paper, if possible.
4. Write on one side of the paper only.
5. Compose a title (not just a statement of the topic) for your paper. Skip a line between the title and the first line of your paper.

6. Do *not* enclose your title in quotation marks and do *not* underline it. A unit within the title, such as the title of a short story or a word used in a special sense (see Section 13D), should be enclosed in quotation marks. The title of a book within your paper's title should be underlined.

7. Do not write outside the left-hand margin line (usually in red, if there is one), except to put numbers of questions if you are writing a test.

8. Leave at least a half-inch margin on the right-hand side of your notebook paper; do not crowd the right-hand side nor write down the right-hand margin. Also do not leave an excessively wide right-hand margin.

9. Use a hyphen to divide a word at the end of a line and divide *only* between syllables. Do *not* divide a one-syllable word, such as *twel-ve* or *walk-ed*. Do *not* divide a word so that a single letter is set apart, such as *a-bove* or *pun-y*. Consult a dictionary, if necessary, for syllabication.

10. Never let a mark of end punctuation, a comma, a semi-colon, or a colon begin a line of your paper. Never end a line with the first of a set of quotation marks, parentheses, or brackets.

11. Indent each paragraph about one inch.

12. Make corrections neatly. Do not leave errors enclosed in parentheses. Try to make every physical aspect of your paper neat. Proofread carefully.

13. Follow your instructor's directions for folding your paper and entering your name and other information on it.

14A2   For Typewritten Papers

Observe the following directions in preparing typewritten papers:

1. Use unruled 8½ x 11 bond paper, if possible. Do not use onionskin paper.

2. Avoid using a red-ink ribbon. Type on one side of the paper only.
3. For your title, follow directions 5 and 6 in Section 14A1.
4. Double space between the lines of your paper (except for inset quotations and footnotes in a term paper).
5. Double space horizontally (that is, use two typewriter spaces instead of one) after all marks of end punctuation and colons.
6. Single space after commas, semicolons, parentheses, and brackets.
7. Make a dash with two hyphens (--) and leave no space before or after a dash.
8. When underlining to show italics, underline the spaces between words too, unless your instructor gives you different instructions.
9. To make the numeral 1, use the small letter l on the keyboard, *not* the capital i.
10. Use Arabic numerals (1, 2, 3, 4, and so on) rather than Roman numerals (I, II, III, IV, and so on) to number pages.
11. Follow direction 9 in Section 14A1 for dividing words at the end of a line.
12. Maintain a 1½-inch margin on the left-hand side of each page and about a one-inch margin on the other three sides. Of course the right-hand ends of lines in typewriting, as in longhand, will be uneven.
13. Indent paragraphs five spaces.
14. Keep your paper neat and proofread it carefully.
15. Follow your instructor's directions for folding your paper and entering your name and other information on it.

14B UNDERLINING AND QUOTATION MARKS

Underlining in longhand or typing is equivalent to italics in print. Underlining and quotation marks are linked in certain ways.

14B1 Underlining

Rule 1 Underline titles of book-length literary works, newspapers, magazines, musical compositions, works of art, and names of ships and aircraft.

Examples:

RIGHT: Mark Twain's <u>Tom Sawyer</u>
Shakespeare's <u>Romeo and Juliet</u>
Milton's <u>Paradise Lost</u>
<u>Harper's</u> magazine (Only the name of the magazine is under-lined.)
the Los Angeles <u>Times</u> (The city is not usually underlined.)
Handel's <u>The Messiah</u> (a musical composition)
Degas' <u>The Dancer and the Bouquet</u> (a painting)
the <u>Titanic</u> (a ship)
<u>Air Force One</u> (an individual aircraft)

Rule 2 Underline foreign words and phrases that have not been fully Anglicized.

Consult a dictionary if necessary. Examples:

RIGHT: The <u>sine qua non</u> of science is accuracy.
RIGHT: The <u>raison d'être</u> of freshman composition is employment for English teachers.

Rule 3 Words or phrases used as words or phrases and not for their meaning may be underlined.

Examples:

RIGHT: The slang phrase <u>out of sight</u> originated in the nineteenth century.
RIGHT: Professor Stone's inaccurate use of <u>epistemology</u> confused his students.

Words used as words may be enclosed in quotation marks, but they are never both underlined and enclosed in quotation marks.

Rule 4 Words or phrases may be underlined for emphasis.

Examples:

RIGHT: I kept quiet precisely because I <u>didn't</u> want the defendant found not guilty.

RIGHT: For human survival we must discontinue <u>all arms manufacturing</u>.

Single words or short phrases, such as *not,* may be capitalized, instead of underlined, for emphasis. However, underlining or capitalization for emphasis should be used judiciously, for overuse will cause readers to lose faith in the need for emphasis.

14B2   Quotation Marks

The use of quotation marks for enclosing direct quotations is covered in Chapter 13. Here we discuss these marks only as they are related to underlining (italics). Periods and commas are always put inside quotation marks, even when they are not a part of the quoted unit. Other marks of punctuation are put inside quotation marks when they are part of the quoted unit and outside when they are not part of the quoted unit. See Section 13E for examples.

<u>Rule 5</u>   Use quotation marks to enclose titles of short stories, short poems, one-act plays, essays, chapters, and other literary works of less than book or three-act-play length.

Examples:

RIGHT: Frost's poem "Birches"
       Faulkner's short story "That Evening Sun"
       Fred Jacobs's short play "Golden Land"
       Thoreau's essay "Civil Disobedience"
       Chapter 14 is entitled "The Campaign of '48."

No title is ever both underlined and enclosed in quotation marks.

<u>Rule 6</u>   **Do not put a title used as a heading in quotation marks.**

Units within the title as heading may, however, be enclosed in quotation marks. Examples:

TITLE AS HEADING: Abroad with Two Yanks
TITLE AS HEADING: The History of "Gab" as Slang

<u>Rule 7</u>   **A word or phrase used as a word or phrase and not for its meaning may be enclosed in quotation marks.**

Examples:

RIGHT: "Biddable" is one of the most euphonious words in English.
RIGHT: The expression "rattle your cage" is a merging of two slang terms.

Also, words used as words may be underlined, but never both underlined and enclosed in quotation marks.

<u>Rule 8</u>   **Use quotation marks to enclose a word or phrase used in a special ironic sense.**

Example:

RIGHT: Bernie likes to think he is a member of the "literary" set.

The quotation marks mean that the writer does not think Bernie's set has real literary attributes.

14C ABBREVIATIONS

Rules for using abbreviations vary considerably, as you will observe in your reading. The rules given here are an acceptable guide for the sort of writing done in English composition courses. They do not apply to such writing as addresses on envelopes, lists, technical data, and other special forms of composition.

14C1   **Abbreviations Acceptable in All Kinds of Writing**

<u>Rule 9</u>   Use the following abbreviations designating individuals:

Mr.	Mmes. (plural of Mrs.)
Mrs.	St. (Saint)
Ms. (any female)	Sr.
Messrs. (plural of Mr.)	Jr.

<u>Rule 10</u>   Use abbreviations to designate any earned or honorary degree or special awards.

Examples:

DEGREES: A.B.
          B.A.
          M.A.
          M.D. (medical doctor)
          Ph.D. (doctor of philosophy)
          Ed.D. (doctor of education)
          D.D.S. (doctor of dental science)
          D.D. (doctor of divinity)
          J.D. (doctor of jurisprudence)
          D.V.M. (doctor of veterinary medicine)
          D.Lit. *or* D.Litt. (doctor of literature)
          LL.D. (doctor of laws)
          D.H.L. (doctor of Hebrew literature)

SPECIAL AWARDS: O.M. (Order of Merit: English)
                 D.S.C. (Distinguished Service Cross)
                 D.S.M. (Distinguished Service Medal)

<u>Rule 11</u>   Use the following abbreviations designating time:

1800 B.C. (before Christ)
A.D. 1462 (in the year of our Lord)
DST, PST (daylight saving time, Pacific standard time, and so on)
4:12 A.M. *or* 4:12 a.m.
3:30 P.M. *or* 3:30 p.m.

<u>Rule 12</u> Use abbreviations to designate well-known agencies, organizations, and unions, either governmental or private.

Examples:

UN	CIA
UNESCO	VA
WHO	VFW
CARE	ILGWU
CAB	UAW

While such abbreviations usually appear with no periods, you may use periods if you wish. The important thing is to be consistent and to make sure your usage will be clear to the reader.

<u>Rule 13</u> Frequently-used technical terms may be abbreviated.

Examples:

mpg (miles per gallon)	rpm (revolutions per minute)
mph (miles per hour)	BTU (British thermal unit)

<u>Rule 14</u> The abbreviations *no., nos.,* and $ are acceptable when used with numerals.

Examples:

RIGHT: The winner was no. 4238.
RIGHT: Please pay particular attention to nos. 2, 6, 9, and 13.
RIGHT: My plumbing bill was $1239.62.

<u>Rule 15</u> The following abbreviations of standard foreign phrases may be used. They normally are italicized.

i.e. (that is)	*viz.* (namely)
e.g. (for example)	*cf.* (compare with)
c. (*circa:* about)	

<u>Rule 16</u> In purely technical writing abbreviations of technical terms are acceptable.

Examples:

cc. (cubic centimeter)   gm. (gram)
cm. (centimeter)   in. (inch)

The examples in the above eight rules are representative. Other abbreviations of the same sort are acceptable. When in doubt, consult a dictionary.

14C2   Abbreviations to Be Avoided in Semiformal Writing

<u>Rule 17</u> **Avoid abbreviating titles of individuals** (except as specified in Section 14C1, Rule 9).

Examples:

WRONG: The *Pres.* will hold a press conference today.
RIGHT: The **President** will hold a press conference today.

WRONG: The committee includes *Prof.* Dingbat and *Sen.* Jonas.
RIGHT: The committee includes **Professor** Dingbat and **Senator** Jonas.

<u>Rule 18</u> **Avoid abbreviating first names.**

Examples:

WRONG: Benj.   Geo.   Jas.   Theo.

<u>Rule 19</u> **Avoid abbreviating the names of states, provinces, and countries.**

Examples:

WRONG: The Holdens went to *N. Y.* for their vacation.
RIGHT: The Holdens went to **New York** for their vacation.

WRONG: Professor Ainsley spent her sabbatical in *Eng.*
RIGHT: Professor Ainsley spent her sabbatical in **England.**

<u>Rule 20</u> **Avoid abbreviating the names of days, months, and seasons.**

Examples:

WRONG: The last day of *Feb.* falls on a *Thurs.* this year.
RIGHT: The last day of **February** falls on a **Thursday** this year.

Rule 21   Avoid abbreviating names of streets, avenues, boulevards, and courts.

Examples:

WRONG: Phil just bought a house on Baylor *St.*
RIGHT: Phil just bought a house on Baylor **Street.**

Rule 22   Avoid abbreviating the word *company* and avoid the ampersand (&), unless it is part of the name of a firm.

Examples:

WRONG: the Johnsons & the Smollets
RIGHT: the Johnsons **and** the Smollets

WRONG: T. L. Floyd *& Co.* is an equal-opportunity employer.
RIGHT: T. L. Floyd **& Company** is an equal-opportunity employer.

Rule 23   Avoid the abbreviation Xmas.

Rule 24   Avoid abbreviating weights and measurements.

Examples:

WRONG: oz.   RIGHT: ounces
        lbs.   pounds
        ft.   foot *or* feet
        yds.   yards

Rule 25   Avoid abbreviating common words.

Examples:

WRONG: yrs.   RIGHT: years *or* yours
        bldg.   building
        sch.   school
        Rom. C.   Roman Catholic
        con't.   continued
        gov't.   government

14D NUMERALS

Although usage varies, the following rules for the use of numerals and spelled-out numbers are a satisfactory guide.

<u>Rule 26</u>   **For random figures, spell out numbers that require no more than two words; use numerals for numbers that would require more than two words if spelled out.**

Examples:

PREFERRED: There are **five thousand** students in our college, but only **thirty-three** are taking calculus.
PREFERRED: The *Times* estimated that **three million** voters would go to the polls; the exact figure was **3,002,473.**
PREFERRED: This year we had **174** school days.

In the second example, note the use of commas without spaces in the large figure written in numerals.

<u>Rule 27</u>   **In a sentence or passage that contains a series of figures, use numerals for all of them.**

Example:

PREFERRED: My unit sales for each of my first seven work days were **9, 22, 8, 101, 61, 3,** and **102.**

Note that the word *seven* is written out, since it is not part of the series.

<u>Rule 28</u>   **Use numerals in dates, addresses, and time when accompanied by A.M. or P.M.**

Examples:

RIGHT: July **11, 1922** *or* (military and technical style) **11** July **1922.**
RIGHT: **242** Columbus Street, Apartment **3B**
RIGHT: Room **701,** Hotel Padre
RIGHT: **8:22** A.M.

On checks and other such writing, dates may be written in this way: 7-11-22 *or* 7/11/22.

<u>Rule 29</u> Use numerals to state measurements, page numbers, and money used with $.

Examples:

RIGHT: Professor Mole's research notes are all on **4″ x 6″** index cards.
RIGHT: That high school basketball center is **6′ 11″** tall.
RIGHT: The information is on pages **3** and **26** of the *World Almanac.*
RIGHT: Our surplus was **$26.13.**

But when simple, nonfractional numbers are involved, they may be spelled out. Examples:

RIGHT: Our rival's center is nearly **seven** feet tall.
RIGHT: We expect **twenty dollars** to be sufficient.

<u>Rule 30</u> When decimals or fractions are involved, use numerals.

Examples:

RIGHT: My average weight loss was **2.65** pounds per day for a week.
RIGHT: No longer can one borrow money at **5 3/4** percent interest.

<u>Rule 31</u> Use numerals for code numbers, such as Social Security numbers, air flight numbers, and telephone numbers.

Examples:

RIGHT: My Army serial number was **34571285.**
RIGHT: You may reach me by phone at **871-7120,** extension **242.**
RIGHT: United's Flight **23** was delayed an hour.

<u>Rule 32</u> To prevent misreading when two numbers appear consecutively, spell out the first one and use numerals for the other.

Example:

RIGHT: I caught **six 8-inch** trout.

<u>Rule 33</u> Except in purely technical writing, do not open a sentence with numerals.

Examples:

POOR STYLE: *1250* partisan voters attended the rally.
PREFERRED: **Twelve hundred and fifty** partisan voters attended the rally.

<u>Rule 34</u>   Except in legal and commercial writing, it is not good style to enter numerals in parentheses after a spelled-out number.

Example:

INAPPROPRIATE STYLE: I purchased *twenty-five (25)* paperback books at the College Bookstore's recent sale.
BETTER: I purchased **twenty-five** paperback books . . .

14E   CONTRACTIONS

Nowadays, contractions such as *won't, doesn't, shouldn't,* and so on appear in semiformal writing in such magazines as *Harper's, Consumer Reports, Science News,* and so on and in many books of nonfiction. Opinion among English teachers, however, is divided as to whether contractions should be allowed in writing assigned in college composition courses. You should ascertain your instructor's preference and follow it.

SECTION THREE

SPELLING

15

Spelling Rules

English spelling is, as everyone knows, full of irregularities which make spelling a difficult subject. But there is much regularity in our spelling system, too, and the irregularities are for the most part rather narrowly limited. For example, the sound /f/ is not always spelled *f*, but it is always spelled either *f* (as in *fit*), *ff* (as in *buff*), *ph* (as in *photo*), or *gh* (as in *laugh*) and so has a degree of regularity. Thus, though English spelling is hard and most people have trouble with it, an understanding of its regularities can improve anyone's spelling. There are several spelling rules that are highly useful to everyone who masters them, for they give much insight into the regularities of English spelling. (There are spelling rules other than those that follow, but they are so riddled with exceptions and so hard to remember that they are not very useful.)

15A THE DOUBLING-OF-THE-FINAL-CONSONANT RULE

The doubling-of-the-final-consonant rule is complex but applies to a great many common words. The rule:

<u>Rule 1</u> When adding a suffix beginning with a vowel to a word which is accented on the last syllable and which ends in a single consonant preceded by a single vowel, double the final consonant.

The accented or stressed syllable is the one spoken with most force. For example, we accent the last syllable of *re-FER,* but we accent the first syllable of *SUF-fer.*

This complicated rule is based on an important phonetic principle in English spelling called the long-vowel, short-vowel principle, which has two parts. First, in a vowel-consonant-vowel sequence the first vowel, *if it is in an accented syllable,* is long. Thus in *debate* the a-t-e sequence in the accented syllable causes the *a* to be long. Second, in a vowel-final consonant sequence or a vowel-consonant-consonant sequence, the vowel is short. Thus in *bat* the a-t sequence at the end makes the *a* short; also in *batted* the a-t-t sequence keeps the *a* short. There are, inevitably in English, many exceptions to this principle, but it is regular enough to be highly useful, both in understanding the doubling-of-the-final-consonant rule (which is almost always regular) and in understanding many other words. For example a great many people misspell *occasion* by using two *s*'s instead of one, which misspelling would give the pronunciation *o-KASS-yun* instead of the correct *o-KAY-zyun.* Understanding the long-vowel, short-vowel principle prevents such mistakes.

Here are some more examples of the principle at work:

long vowels	*short vowels*
rate	rat
Pete	pet
bite	bit
rote	rot
cure	cur

In the first column the silent *e*'s—forming a vowel-consonant-vowel sequence—make the first vowel long. In the second column the vowels are short because the second consonant ends the word. The whole purpose of the doubling-of-the-final-consonant rule is to preserve the short vowel sound in such words as *dis-BAR*, *re-FER*, *ad-MIT* and *dot* when a suffix beginning with a vowel is added to them. (The letters *a* and *e* have more than one short-vowel sound so far as this rule is concerned.)

Since the rule is complex, here again are the three main parts of it:

1. The suffix added must begin with a vowel. Such suffixes are *ing*, *ed*, *er*, *est*, *able*, *y*, and so on.
2. The word to which the suffix is added must be accented on the last syllable. All one-syllable words and such words as *pre-FER*, *oc-CUR*, and *com-PEL* are examples.
3. The word to which the suffix is added must end in a single consonant preceded by a single vowel. *Admit*, *repel*, and *slap* are examples. *Equip* and *quit* are examples too, since the *qu* really stands for the consonant sound *kw*, leaving the single vowel *i* before the final consonant.

When the above three conditions are present, the final consonant is doubled and the short vowel sound is retained.

Here are some doubling-of-the-final-consonant words that are frequently misspelled:

> admit + ed = admi**tt**ed
> begin + er = begi**nn**er
> begin + ing = begi**nn**ing
> brag + ing = bra**gg**ing
> confer + ed = confe**rr**ed
> defer + ed = defe**rr**ed
> equip + ed = equi**pp**ed
> expel + ed = expe**ll**ed
> fad + ism = fa**dd**ism
> fog + y = fo**gg**y
> jog + ing = jo**gg**ing
> lag + ing = la**gg**ing

man + ish = ma**nn**ish
occur + ed = occu**rr**ed
occur + ence = occu**rr**ence
omit + ed = omi**tt**ed
rebel + ing = rebe**ll**ing
red + est = re**dd**est
refer + ed = refe**rr**ed
regret + ed = regre**tt**ed
star + ing = sta**rr**ing
swim + ing = swi**mm**ing
transfer + ed = transfe**rr**ed
(un)forget + able = unforge**tt**able

Two notes of caution: (1) If the last syllable of a word is not accented, its final consonant is not doubled when a suffix beginning with a vowel is added. Examples:

aBANdon + ed = abandoned   BENefit + ed = benefited
BANter + ing = bantering   proHIBit + ing = prohibiting

(2) When a suffix is added to a word ending in a silent *e*, the consonant preceding the *e* is *never* doubled. Examples:

come + ing = coming   shine + ing = shining
dine + ing = dining   write + ing = writing
interfere + ed = interfered

These five words are very frequently misspelled because the consonants preceding the silent *e*'s are incorrectly doubled.

15B THE DROPPING-OF-THE-SILENT-E RULE

A great many words in English end in a silent *e*. When suffixes are added to these words, sometimes the *e* is dropped and sometimes it is retained. In this section we will consider the rule calling for the dropping of the silent *e*, and in the next, the rules calling for retention of the silent *e*. The basic silent *e* rule is this:

<u>Rule 2</u>   When adding a suffix beginning with a vowel to a word ending in a silent *e*, drop the silent *e*.

One of the rules in the following section is an important exception to this basic rule, but we must explain the rules separately.

The dropping-of-the-silent e rule is also due to the long-vowel, short-vowel principle discussed in the preceding section. Though there are exceptions, most terminal silent e's are doing the job of making the preceding vowel long. That is, if the silent e is dropped, the preceding vowel becomes short. Examples:

> hate (long *a*)   hat (short *a*)
> dine (long *i*)   din (short *i*)

Thus the terminal silent e is usually at work. However, because of the long-vowel, short-vowel principle *any* vowel will do the work of the silent e, for a vowel-consonant-vowel sequence would still be maintained, making the first vowel long if it is in an accented syllable. Thus when a suffix beginning with a vowel is added to a word ending in a silent e, the silent e is no longer needed because the vowel of the suffix will do the work of the silent e, which therefore can be dropped. Hence we have the basic silent e rule.

Here are examples of the rule in action:

> dine + ing = dining   shine + ing = shining
> write + ing = writing   interfere + ed = interfered
> guide + ance = guidance   create + ive = creative
> mange + y = mangy   shine + y = shiny
> condole + ence = condolence   fame + ous = famous
> bite + ing = biting   confuse + ing = confusing

In words like these the long-vowel sound is preserved because a vowel-consonant-vowel sequence is maintained.

Some words in English, however, end in silent e's that do no work, but the rule still applies to them. Examples:

> come + ing = coming   imagine + ative = imaginative
> hypocrite + ical = hypocritical   pursue + ing = pursuing

The silent e's in these words do not make the preceding vowels long; they are just part of the many irregularities in English spelling. Still, the basic rule applies to them.

15C   THE RETENTION-OF-THE-SILENT-E RULES

There are two rules for retaining silent *e*'s when suffixes are added. The first is an important exception to the basic rule in the previous section.

<u>Rule 3</u>   When adding the suffix *able, ous,* or *ance* to a word that ends in a silent e preceded by a c or g, retain the silent e.

This rule, too, is based on important phonetic principles in English spelling. Both the *c* and the *g* are used for spelling two entirely different sounds.* First we will consider the *c*, which (with a few exceptions) is pronounced either as an *s*, as in *city*, or as a *k*, as in *cable*. The *c* pronounced as an *s* is called a soft *c*, and the *c* pronounced as a *k* is called a hard *c*. A *c* is almost always soft when it is followed by an *e, i,* or *y*, and it is almost always hard when it is followed by an *a, o,* or *u* or when it is the last letter of a word or syllable. Thus when a word ends in a silent *e* preceded by a *c*, the silent *e* is doing the job of making the *c* soft. For example, the *c* is soft in *service*, but if the silent *e* is dropped, we would pronounce the remainder *ser-vik*. Similarly, if when adding the suffix *able* to *service* we dropped the silent *e*, the *c* would be followed by an *a*, thus becoming hard, and we would have the pronunciation *ser-vik-able*. Since we want the pronunciation *ser-viss-able*, we retain the silent *e* so that the *c* will remain soft.

For convenience, here is a repetition of this part of the general rule:

When adding *able* to a word that ends in a silent e preceded by a c, retain the silent e to preserve the soft c sound.

---

* In addition the *c* has a *ch* sound in some imported words, such as *cello* and *concerto*, and is silent in some other words, such as *indict* and *muscle*. *Ch* is a single sound unlike the usual sounds *c* stands for. Also, there are some complex aspects of *g* that we will not explain, for they are not involved in the rule we are discussing.

Here are typical examples:

replace + able = replaceable	notice + able = noticeable
trace + able = traceable	peace + able = peaceable
splice + able = spliceable	embrace + able = embraceable

Another rule involving the hard *c* is this:

When adding the suffix *y* or a suffix beginning with *e* or *i* to a word that ends in *c*, add a *k* in order to preserve the hard *c* sound.

For example, if the suffix *ed* were added to the verb *panic*, the *c* would become soft and produce the pronunciation *pan-iced.* So we add a *k* to preserve the hard *c* sound. Here are examples of the main words involved in this minor rule:

panic + ed = panicked	picnic + ing = picnicking
panic + y = panicky	politic + ing = politicking
picnic + er = picnicker	traffic + ing = trafficking

Many of our words already have the *k*, such as *kick* and *pick*.

Now we will consider the *g*. The hard *g* is pronounced *guh*, as in *got* and *begin*. The soft *g* is pronounced as a *j*, as in *gin* and *gyp*. The two sounds of *g* do not follow regular phonetic principles to the extent that the two sounds of *c* do, for the *g* is sometimes soft and sometimes hard when followed by *e* or *i*. However, the *g* is virtually always soft when followed by a silent *e* and virtually always hard when followed by *a, o,* or *u* or when it is the final letter of a word. Thus we have this part of the general rule:

When adding *able, ous,* or *ance* to a word ending in a silent *e* preceded by a *g*, retain the silent *e* to preserve the soft *g* sound.

For example, *arrange* has a soft *g*. But if when adding *able* to *arrange* we dropped the silent *e*, the pronunciation would be *ar-rang-able.* Thus we keep the silent *e* to preserve the soft *g* sound: *ar-range-able.* Here are other examples:

courage + ous = courageous	stage + able = stageable
outrage + ous = outrageous	charge + able = chargeable
advantage + ous = advantageous	change + able = changeable

Now the second rule for retention of the silent *e:*

Rule 4   When adding a suffix beginning with a consonant to a word ending in a silent e, retain the silent e.

The long-vowel, short-vowel principle makes this rule necessary. For example, the silent *e* in *fate* makes the *a* long. If the silent *e* were dropped when the suffix *ful* is added, the pronunciation would be *fat-ful*. Here are other examples of the rule in action:

like + ness = likeness   hate + ful = hateful
late + ly = lately   safe + ty = safety
complete + ly = completely   care + less = careless

The *e* must be retained to prevent such pronunciations as *lik-ness* and *lat-ly*.

Sometimes the final silent *e* does not make the preceding vowel long, but the rule still holds. Examples:

immediate + ly = immediately
appropriate + ly = appropriately
approximate + ly = approximately
delicate + ly = delicately

Misspellings due to the dropping of the silent *e* when adding *ly* are quite common.

There are a few exceptions to the above rule. Here are the main ones:

whole + ly = wholly   argue + ment = argument
true + ly = truly   judge + ment = judgment
awe + ful = awful

In these words the silent *e* is dropped even though the suffix added begins with a consonant.

15D   THE *Y-TO-I* RULE

Rule 5   When adding a suffix to a word ending in y preceded by a consonant, change the y to i. If the y is preceded by a vowel, do not change the y to i.

When adding the suffix *s* to make the plural of a noun that ends in *y* preceded by a consonant or when adding the suffix *s* to a verb that ends in *y* preceded by a consonant, change the *y* to *i* and add *es*. Examples:

ally + s = allies	try + s = tries
reply + s = replies	deny + s = denies
harpy + s = harpies	defy + s = defies

The rule also operates with many other suffixes. Examples:

comply + ance = compliance	mercy + ful = merciful
cry + er = crier	easy + ly = easily
dry + est = driest	lonely + ness = loneliness

The rule does not apply when the suffix is *ing* or *ist*. Examples:

study + ing = studying	worry + ing = worrying
hurry + ing = hurrying	copy + ist = copyist

In these words the *y* is *never* dropped; misspellings such as *studing* for *studying* are common.

There are a number of exceptions to the rule, all of them involving one-syllable words. Here are the main exceptions:

shyness	slyly	dryness
shyly	wryness	dryly
slyness	wryly	dryer (the machine)

A minor rule the reverse of the *y*-to-*i* rule is this:

When adding *ing* to a verb ending in *ie*, change the *ie* to *y*.

Examples:

die + ing = dying	tie + ing = tying
lie + ing = lying	vie + ing = vying

For convenience, here is a repetition of the second part of the y-to-i rule:

When adding a suffix to a word ending in *y* preceded by a vowel, do not change the *y* to *i*.

Examples:

annoy + s = annoys	valley + s = valleys
convey + ed = conveyed	alley + s = alleys
stay + ed = stayed	donkey + s = donkeys
coy + ly = coyly	boy + hood = boyhood

There are a few common exceptions to this part of the rule:

lay + ed = laid	day + ly = daily
pay + ed = paid	gay + ly = gaily
say + ed = said	

In these words the *y* is changed to *i* even though the *y* is preceded by a vowel.

The y-to-i rule does not apply in spelling the plural of proper names nor the possessive form of any noun ending in *y*. Examples:

the Bradys	Betty's car
the Kennedys	one ally's advantage
several Sallys	the company's president

15E THE *IE/EI* RULES

The *ie/ei* rules do not cover many words, but they do cover common words that are frequently misspelled.

<u>Rule 6</u>   Place *i* before *e* when pronounced as *ee* except after *c*. Place *e* before *i* after *c*.

Most Important: This rule covers only *ie* or *ei* combinations that are pronounced as the single long *e* sound. That is, the rule does not apply to such words as *science* and *atheist,* in which the *i*'s and *e*'s are pronounced in separate syllables, or to such words as *foreign* and *friend,* in which the combination is not pronounced as a long *e*.

To spell correctly with this rule you must know everything about a word except whether it has an *ie* or *ei* combination. For example, if you don't know that *receipt* has a silent *p*, you can apply the rule correctly and still misspell the word. Here are some common words covered by the rule:

believe	receive
chief	deceive
achieve	deceit
priest	conceive
thief	conceit
brief	receipt
relieve	ceiling
yield	perceive
niece	
tier	
mien	

There are a number of exceptions to this rule, but the only ones that give any trouble can be mastered by memorizing this nonsense sentence:

Neither sheik seized weird leisure.

All five of these exceptions have an *ei* combination pronounced as a long *e* but not preceded by a *c*. (In some dialects *neither* is pronounced with a long *i* sound and *leisure* with an *eh* sound.)

Rule 7   Place e before i when pronounced as a long a.

Of course there are various ways of spelling the long *a* sound, but if the word has either an *ie* or *ei* combination, then the writer can know that it is *ei* if the pronunciation is a long *a*. Examples:

freight	reins
weight	vein
neighbor	neigh
sleigh	reign
heinous	deign

The words *their* and *heir* may also be put in this group, though the vowel sound in them is not exactly a long *a* in many people's dialects.

16

Spelling Lists

DOUBLE-CONSONANT WORDS

The following words are often misspelled because one consonant of a double consonant is omitted. The double consonants are in boldface.

accidental	beginner	embarrass
accommodate	beginning	equipped
accomplish	biggest	exaggerate
accurate	committee	excellent
aggressive	communist	generally
annual	controlled	immediately
apparatus	curriculum	immense
apparent	different	intelligence
applies	disappear	intelligent
appreciate	disappoint	interrupt
appropriate	dissatisfied	irritable
approximate	disservice	manner
attitude	drunkenness	misspelled

narrative	planned	success
necessary	possess	summed
occurred	possession	supposed
occurrence	possible	suppress
opponent	preferred	surrounding
opportunity	roommate	swimming
opposite	stubborn	unnecessary

16B SINGLE-CONSONANT WORDS

The following words are often misspelled because a single consonant is incorrectly doubled. The single consonant is in boldface.

abandoned	disappoint
academic	during
across	eliminate
already	fulfill
among	holiday
amount	imagine
analyze	interfered
another	later
apartment	necessary
apology	occasion
becoming	omitted
benefited	operate
biting	opinion
calendar	parallel
career	primitive
column	profession
coming	professor
confused	quarrel
define	relative
definitely	shining
definition	tomorrow
dining	writing
disappear	

16C DE AND DI WORDS

The following words are often misspelled because an *e* is substituted for an *i* or an *i* for an *e*. The *de*'s and *di*'s are in boldface.

descend	**di**gest
describe	**di**gress
description	**di**lemma
despair	**di**lute
despise	**di**sastrous
despite	**di**sciple
destroy	**di**sease
destruction	**di**vide
device	**di**vine
devise	**di**vorce

16D OMITTED LETTERS

The following words are often misspelled because of the omission of one or more letters. The letters that are often omitted are in boldface.

accident**all**y	chara**c**teristics	family
accompan**y**ing	(two) communist**s**	fas**c**inate
a**c**quire	compe**t**ition	f**ou**rth
advertis**e**ment	complet**e**ly	gover**n**ment
appropriat**e**ly	(it) consist**s**	hero**e**s
approximat**e**ly	criti**c**ism	hop**e**less
asp**i**rin	crow**d**ed	hypocrit**e**
ath**e**ist	d**e**alt	imagin**e**
barg**ai**n	defin**i**tely	immedi**a**tely
befor**e**	dis**c**ipline	int**e**rest
boundar**y**	envir**o**nment	knowled**ge**
car**e**less	ever**y**thing	lab**o**ratory
carr**y**ing	experi**e**nce	lik**e**ly
chang**e**able	extrem**e**ly	liter**a**ture

144

loneliness
lonely
luxury
magazine
mathematics
meant
medical
medicine
Negroes
ninety
noticeable
nowadays
numerous
particular

(be) prejudiced
primitive
privilege
probably
quantity
realize
remember
rhythm
safety
(two) scientists
shepherd
sincerely
sophomore
stretch

studying
supposed (to)
temperament
temperature
therefore
thorough
undoubtedly
used (to)
useful
valuable
various
where
whether
whose

16E ADDED LETTERS

The following words are often misspelled because of the addition of a letter. The incorrect letters that are often added are in parentheses. (Also see Section 16B.)

among (no *u* after *o*)
argument (no *e* after *u*)
athlete (no *e* after *h*)
attack (no *t* after *k*)
awful (no *e* after *w*)
chosen (no *oo*)
disastrous (no *e* after *t*)
drowned (no *d* after *n*)
equipment (no *t* after *p*)
exercise (no *c* after *x*)
existent (no *h* after *x*)
explanation (no *i* after *la*)
final (no *i* after *n*)
forty (no *u* after *o*)
forward (no *e* after *r*)
genius (no *o* after *i*)
grievous (no *i* after *v*)

height (no *h* after *t*)
Henry (no *e* after *n*)
hindrance (no *e* after *d*)
jewelry (no *e* after *l*)
judgment (no *e* after *g*)
laundry (no *e* after *d*)
led (no *a* after *e*)
lose (no *oo*)
mischievous (no *i* after *v*)
ninth (no *e* after *in*)
pamphlet (no *e* after *h*)
personal (no *i* after *n*)
privilege (no *d* after *le*)
procedure (no *ee*)
remembrance (no *e* after *b*)
similar (no *i* after *l*)
truly (no *e* after *u*)

16F ANT-ANCE AND ENT-ENCE WORDS

abundant	resistant	existence
abundance	resistance	experience
acquaintance	servant	independent
admittance	warrant	independence
appearance		ingredient
assistant	absent	insistent
assistance	absence	insistence
attendant	adolescent	intelligent
attendance	adolescence	intelligence
brilliant	apparent	magnificent
brilliance	coherent	magnificence
constant	coherence	occurrence
dominant	competent	opponent
dominance	competence	permanent
guidance	confident	permanence
hindrance	confidence	persistent
ignorant	consistent	persistence
ignorance	consistence	present
important	convenient	presence
importance	convenience	prominent
inhabitant	dependent	prominence
pleasant	dependence	reverent
predominant	different	reverence
redundant	difference	sufficient
redundance	excellent	sufficience
relevant	excellence	superintendent
relevance	existent	superintendence

16G HOMOPHONES AND CONFUSED WORDS

Homophones are words that are pronounced alike but that have different spellings and meanings, such as *course* and *coarse*. The following list consists of homophones that cause frequent misspellings and also other pairs of words which are so similar that the spelling of one is often confused with the spelling of the other. Information about the words is also included. The abbreviations used have the following meanings: n. = noun; v. = verb; adj. = adjective; adv. = adverb; pro. = pronoun; prep. = preposition; conj. = conjunction; poss. = possessive; contr. = contraction; sing. = singular; and pl. = plural.

accept: (v.) to receive
except: (prep.) not included

access: (n.) a way of approach or entrance
assess: (v.) to estimate the value of

adapt: (v.) to adjust to a situation
adopt: (v.) to take in or take a course of action

advice: (n.) counsel, information, or suggestions given
advise: (v.) to give advice or counsel

affect: (v.) to influence or have an effect on
effect: (n.) the result of an action
effect: (v.) to accomplish or execute

aisle: (n.) a corridor or passageway
isle: (n.) an island

all ready: (n. + adj.) everyone is prepared
already: (adv.) at or before this time; previously

all together: (n. + adj.) all in one place
altogether: (adv.) completely; wholly

allude: (v.) to refer to
elude: (v.) to evade or escape

allusion: (n.) a reference
illusion: (n.) a false impression

aloud: (adv.) audibly or loudly
allowed: (v.) permitted

altar: (n.) an elevated place for religious services
alter: (v.) to change

always: (adv.) constantly; all the time
all ways: (determiner + n.) in every way

anecdote: (n.) a little story
antidote: (n.) something that counteracts a poison

angel: (n.) a heavenly being
angle: (n.) figure formed by the divergence of two straight lines from a common point

arc: (n.) a part of a circle
arch: (n.) a curved part of a building

ascend: (v.) to rise or go up
ascent: (n.) a movement upward
assent: (v.) to agree
assent: (n.) an agreement

assistance: (n.) help given
assistants: (n. pl.) helpers

band: (n.) a group
banned: (v.) excluded or prohibited

beside: (prep.) by the side of
besides: (adv. *and* prep.) in addition to

boar: (n.) a male hog
bore: (n.) someone who tires you

boarder: (n.) one who pays for room and meals
border: (n.) a boundary

born: (v.) given birth to (always in the passive voice)
borne: (v.) given birth to (always in the active voice); carried

brake: (n.) a mechanism to stop a vehicle
break: (v.) to cause to fall into two or more pieces

breath: (n.) air inhaled and exhaled
breathe: (v.) to take in breaths and let them out

canvas: (n.) a kind of coarse cloth
canvass: (v.) to search or examine or solicit

capital: (n.) a city that is a seat of government
capitol: (n.) a building occupied by a legislature

censor: (v.) to prohibit publication
censor: (n.) one who prohibits publication
censure: (v.) to reprimand or disapprove of
censure: (n.) disapproval

choose: (v.) to select (present tense)
chose: (v.) selected (past tense)
chosen: (v.) selected (past participle)

cite: (v.) to quote; to charge with breaking a law
site: (n.) a location

coarse: (adj.) rough; unrefined
course: (n.) school subject; a way or path

complement: (n.) items which complete
compliment: (n.) a statement of praise

conscience: (n.) what tells you right from wrong
conscious: (adj.) awake; alert

council: (n.) a group that deliberates
counsel: (v.) to give advice
counsel: (n.) advice given

descent: (n.) a going down
dissent: (v.) to disagree
dissent: (n.) disagreement

desert: (n.) a geographical area
desert: (v.) to abandon
dessert: (n.) food

device: (n.) a contrivance
devise: (v.) to prepare a method or contrivance

do: (v.) to perform
due: (adj.) used with *to* to specify the cause of something; owing

dual: (adj.) twofold
duel: (n.) a fight between two

eminent: (adj.) famous
imminent: (adj.) likely to occur soon

envelop: (v.) to cover or enclose
envelope: (n.) an enclosure used for mailing

extant: (adj.) still existing
extent: (n.) the degree of something

formally: (adj.) in a formal manner
formerly: (adv.) at an earlier time

forth: (n.) forward; onward; out
fourth: (n.) the one after the third

human: (adj.) pertaining to people
humane: (adj.) pertaining to compassion or kindness

its: (poss. pro.) belonging to it
it's: (contr.) it is *or* it has

later: (adj.) after a specified time
latter: (n.) the last one mentioned

lead: (v.; pronounced *leed*) to conduct
lead: (n.; pronounced *led*) the metal
led: (v.) past tense and past participle of the verb *lead*

loose: (adj.) not tight
lose: (v.) to misplace; to be defeated

marital: (adj.) pertaining to marriage
martial: (adj.) military

maybe: (adv.) perhaps
may be: (v.) possibly may occur

meant: (v.) past tense and past participle of the verb
    mean
ment: not a word

passed: (v.) past tense and past participle of the verb
    pass
past: (n.) an earlier time

patience: (sing. n.) calm endurance
patients: (pl. n.) those under medical care

peace: (n.) not war
piece: (n.) a part of

personal: (adj.) pertaining to oneself
personnel: (n.) the employees of a company or organization

principal: (n.) head of a school; money owned
principal: (adj.) chief; most important
principle: (n.) a rule or doctrine

prophecy: (n.) a prediction
prophesy: (v.) to make a prediction

quiet: (adj.) not noisy
quite: (adv.) completely or almost completely

sense: (n.) ability to think well; meaning
since: (prep. *and* conj.) before this time; because

stationary: (adj.) in a fixed position
stationery: (n.) paper to write on

than: (conj.) used to compare things
then: (n. or adv.) indicating time

their: (poss. pro.) belonging to them
there: (adv.) a place; also used as an expletive to begin sentences
they're: (contr.) they are

to: (prep.) generally indicating direction
too: (adv.) excessively; overmuch
two: (n.) the number

trail: (n.) a rough path
trial: (n.) experimental action, or examination before a court

vice: (n.) immorality
vise: (n.) a device for holding

weather: (n.) the state of the atmosphere
whether: (conj.) expressing alternatives

whose: (poss. pro.) belonging to whom
who's: (contr.) who is *or* who has

your: (poss. pro.) belonging to you
you're: (contr.) you are

16H OTHER TROUBLESOME WORDS

The following common words, not included in the preceding sections, are also often misspelled.

a lot	doesn't	marriage	ridiculous
actually	eighth	minute	sacrifice
against	endeavor	nickel	schedule
amateur	familiar	optimism	separate
amount	favorite	ours	sergeant
article	February	paid	source
battalion	foreign	peculiar	speech
beauty	grammar	perspiration	surprise
breathe	guarantee	practical	technique
bulletin	height	precede	themselves
buried	hers	preparation	theirs
category	hundred	prescription	tragedy
children	inevitable	prestige	Tuesday
comparative	interpretation	proceed	until
condemn	involve	psychology	Wednesday
counselor	January	pursue	(one) woman
courtesy	library	repetition	yours

Note: A proper name ending in y is made plural by the addition of s (the Darbys) and a name ending in s is made plural by the addition of es, with no apostrophe (the Davises).

17

Capitalization

Although practices in capitalization do vary, the following specific rules are adhered to by almost all writers. The name commonly used for small letters is **lower case.**

17A RULES OF CAPITALIZATION

For convenience, we will not only use our number-letter system of classification but also will number the rules.

17A1 The Basics

<u>Rule 1</u> Capitalize the first word of each sentence, the pronoun *I*, and the interjection *O*, but not other interjections unless one opens a sentence. In using direct quotations, follow the capitalization of the original author exactly.

17A2   Titles of Literary Works

Rule 2   In a title or chapter heading, capitalize the first word and all other words except articles, short prepositions, and coordinating conjunctions.

Examples:

TITLE OF A BOOK: *The Decline and Fall of the Roman Empire*
TITLE OF A SHORT STORY: "The Capital of the World"
TITLE OF A POEM: "The Death of the Hired Man"
CHAPTER HEADING: The Debate Between Skinner and Foster

17A3   Specific School Courses

Rule 3   Capitalize the name of a specific school course but not the name of a general subject-matter area, unless it is a proper name.

Examples:

I am taking History 17A and American Literature Since 1865, but I would rather be taking courses in chemistry and math.

17A4   Proper Nouns and Proper Adjectives

Rule 4   Capitalize all proper nouns and adjectives formed from proper nouns, unless the proper adjective — such as *venetian red* — is commonly spelled with a lower-case letter.

Consult a dictionary if necessary. A proper noun is the name of an individual of some sort, animate or inanimate. Examples:

Sweden	John Doe	Oriental
Swedish	New Yorker	Arabian
English	Hollywoodish	San Franciscan
French	Platonism	Newtonian
Yosemite	Mount Rushmore	Statue of Liberty

17A5   **Religions and Related Topics**

<u>Rule 5</u>   Capitalize references to the Deity or Deities in all recognized religions, the names of religions, religious sects, divine books, and adjectives formed from these.

Examples:

God	**C**atholic	**J**ewish
our **L**ord	**P**rotestant	**M**ormonism
Christ	the **B**ible	**H**induism
Allah	**B**iblical	the **N**ew **T**estament
Christian	**B**aptist	the **U**panishads

17A6   **Relatives**

<u>Rule 6</u>   Capitalize the titles of relatives when used with the person's name or as a substitute for the name, but not when the term designating the relationship is used with a possessive pronoun, such as *my*.

Examples:

> The caller was **A**unt **H**elen.
> The caller was my **a**unt **H**elen.
> My **m**other is a nurse.
> We see **G**randfather **B**rown playing golf daily.

Usage varies with terms of relationship used as names in direct address.

> "Thanks for the help, **s**on (*or* **S**on)."
> "Oh, **F**ather (*or* **f**ather), hurry over here."

17A7   **Officials**

<u>Rule 7</u>   Capitalize the titles of important officials when used with their names. Capitalize a title used in place of a name to designate a particular individual. Do not capitalize a title that designates an office but not a particular individual.

Examples:

> Vice-President Forbes
> Senator Javits
> Colonel Wetzler
> Reverend Puder
> The Congressman will not be in today. (A specific congressman is understood.)
> The Dean left instructions for preparing the memo. (A specific dean is understood.)
> A college president does not have an enviable job. (No specific president is meant.)
> The office of mayor is vacant.

17A8   Days, Months, and Holidays

<u>Rule 8</u>   **Capitalize the days of the week, the months of the year, and official holidays. Do not capitalize the names of the seasons.**

Examples:

Wednesday	Veterans Day
February	Admission Day
Christmas	winter

17A9   Specific Geographic Locations

<u>Rule 9</u>   **Capitalize the names of nations, states, provinces, continents, oceans, lakes, rivers, mountains, cities, streets, parks, and specific geographic regions. Do not capitalize the names of directions.**

Examples:

Uganda	Lake Louise	Jefferson Park
Alabama	the Red River	the West Coast
Alberta	Deer Mountain	the South
Asia	Baltimore	the Near East
the Pacific Ocean	Tenth Street	Walk east two blocks.

17A10 Buildings

Rule 10 Capitalize the names of specific buildings.

Examples:

the Haberfeld Building   the Palace Theater
the Pentagon   the Language Arts Building

17A11 Private and Governmental Organizations

Rule 11 Capitalize the names of private and governmental organizations.

Examples:

the Elks Club   the Veterans Administration
the American Legion   the Peace Corps
Rotary   the State Department

17A12 Historical Documents, Events, and Eras

Rule 12 Capitalize the names of historical documents, events, and eras.

Examples:

the Bill of Rights   World War II
the Atlantic Charter   the Battle of Midway
Public Law 16   the Middle Ages
the Diet of Worms   the Renaissance

17A13 Brand Names

Rule 13 Capitalize brand names but not the name of the product.

Examples:

a Ford car   Dial soap
Arco gasoline   Mum deodorant

17A14   Outline Headings

Rule 14   Capitalize the first word of an outline heading.

Examples:

 I. Uses of the dictionary
  A. To determine multiple definitions of a particular word
   1. Methods of ordering definitions
    a. By frequency of use

17A15   Celestial Bodies

Rule 15   Capitalize the names of celestial bodies and of geographic regions of the moon.

Do not capitalize the words *earth, world, universe, galaxy, moon,* and *sun.* Examples:

Arcturus (a star)	Venus
Halley's Comet	the Crab Nebula
the Sea of Rains (on the moon)	Phobos (a moon of Mars)

Exception: When named as a planet among other planets, *earth* is generally capitalized.

 In the solar system Earth is between Venus and Mars.

17A16   Abbreviations

Rule 16   Capitalize abbreviations when the whole word or phrase would be capitalized.

See Section 14C for other aspects of the capitalization of abbreviations and also for punctuation in abbreviations. Examples:

the UN	the U.S. Army
the NAACP	b. 1891 (born)
CORE	120 h.p. (horsepower)
Oct.	gloss. (glossary)

17B MANDATORY LOWER-CASE LETTERS

17B1 Centuries

<u>Rule 17</u> Do not capitalize the names of centuries unless a century is being mentioned as a specific historical era.

Examples:

> It was my destiny to be born in the twentieth century.
> The Age of the Enlightenment is sometimes called simply the Eighteenth Century.

17B2 Common Animate and Inanimate Objects

<u>Rule 18</u> Do not capitalize the names of foods, games, chemical compounds, general geographical formations, animals, plants, or musical instruments unless they designate specific individuals or kinds.

Sometimes, however, a proper noun, which is capitalized, is a part of the name of a species. Examples:

rice	escarpment	violoncello
spaghetti	trout	Thompson's gazelle
golf	robin	a Canary pine
bridge	collie	a Baltimore oriole
sulfur dioxide	maple	a game of Scrabble
schist	rose	our cat, Princess
canyon	piano	Lady Baltimore cake

17B3 Occupations

<u>Rule 19</u> Do not capitalize the names of occupations.

Examples:

> engineer
> doctor
> professor

17B4   Diseases

<u>Rule 20</u>   Do not capitalize the names of diseases.

Sometimes, however, a proper noun, which is capitalized, is part of the name of the disease. Examples:

mumps
gastritis
Hodgkin's disease

18

The Apostrophe

The apostrophe is a mark used in spelling, not a mark of punctuation. Marks of punctuation clarify sentence structure, whereas apostrophes clarify word form.

THE APOSTROPHE IN POSSESSIVE CONSTRUCTIONS

Use an apostrophe with a noun in a possessive construction.

There are two ways of expressing possession in English (aside from simply saying *I own something*). The first and most common is with the so-called **possessive construction,** in which the person or thing doing the possessing comes in front of the thing possessed, as in *Estella's good looks* and *the President's power*. The possessive construction calls for an apostrophe *only* if a noun does the possessing, *never* when a personal possessive pronoun, such as *his* or *your,* expresses the possession. The use of the apostrophe for possessive spellings poses two problems: (1) whether or not an apostrophe is needed, and (2) if so, where it should be placed.

The second way of expressing possession in English helps solve both of the writing problems just mentioned. This second way makes use of a *belonging to* or *of* phrase. For example, *good looks belonging to Estella* and *power of the President* have exactly the same meanings as the two possessive constructions in the previous paragraph. Thus any possessive construction will **transform** into a *belonging to* or *of* phrase meaning the same thing as the possessive construction. The *belonging to* or *of* transformation may sound much more awkward than the possessive construction, but it nevertheless will be meaningful English. For example, *Julie's first date* sounds more natural and smooth than *the first date of Julie* or *the first date belonging to Julie,* but the latter are meaningful English. The transformation proves that the former is a possessive construction and thus requires an apostrophe.

When a construction will transform into a *belonging to* or *of* phrase with the same meaning, it is always a possessive construction and requires an apostrophe (that is, when a noun does the possessing). Thus if you have trouble recognizing possessive constructions, with a consequent writing problem in using the apostrophe, learn to test for the transformation. If the construction you are not sure of will transform into a *belonging to* or *of* phrase, you need to use an apostrophe; if a construction will not transform in that manner, it cannot be a possessive construction and thus must not take an apostrophe.

Here are some examples, with the apostrophes required for the possessive constructions omitted.

    Garys hang-up = hang-up belonging to Gary
    the Ferrises bankruptcy = bankruptcy of the Ferrises
    The Ferrises came. = (no transformation possible)

Since the first two constructions transform, they are possessive and require apostrophes in the spelling of *Gary's* and *Ferrises'*. Since the last construction will not transform, it cannot be possessive, and thus *Ferrises* must be spelled without an apostrophe. The test for the transformation is simple, and anyone who masters it should have no trouble knowing when an apostrophe is needed.

The transformation not only shows that an apostrophe is needed but also tells where to place it. (Remember, an apostrophe never belongs directly above an *s*, but either before or after the *s*.) At the end of the *belonging to* or *of* phrase is the **base noun** that will be made possessive and thus will require an apostrophe. Examples, with the base nouns italicized:

> a Christian's faith = faith of a *Christian*
> Lois's GPA = GPA belonging to *Lois*
> the Arabs' oil = oil belonging to the *Arabs*
> the children's misbehavior = misbehavior of the *children*
> The Harrises stayed. = (no transformation possible)

For the four possessive constructions, the base nouns are *Christian, Lois, Arabs,* and *children,* which, in the possessive constructions, must take apostrophes.

In determining where to place the apostrophe in a possessive spelling, you are not interested in whether the base noun is singular or plural, but only whether it does or does not end in *s*. The simple rule is that if the base noun does not end in *s*, in the possessive construction an *'s* is added. But if the base noun does end in *s*, then in the possessive construction an apostrophe after the *s* gives a correct spelling. Examples:

> Bettys new stereo = new stereo belonging to *Betty*

The base noun *Betty* does not end in *s;* therefore the correct possessive spelling is *Betty's new stereo.*

> the Crosses delinquent son = delinquent son of the *Crosses*

The base noun *Crosses* ends in *s;* therefore the correct possessive spelling is *the Crosses' delinquent son.*

In some nouns ending in *s* pronunciation requires the addition of a syllable (es) that is not shown in the written form of the noun. That syllable for pronunciation is shown in brackets below.

Luis[es] importance = the importance of *Luis*
Iris[es] stagefright = the stagefright of *Iris*

The base nouns *Luis* and *Iris* end in *s;* therefore a correct possessive spelling is *Luis'* and *Iris'*.

There is one alternate possessive spelling that we must mention. If the base noun ends in *s* and is singular, its spelling in the possessive construction may not match its pronunciation. For example, the name in the phrase *Thomas' secret deal* is spelled with two syllables but is pronounced in three syllables (Thom-as-es). In such cases the writer has the option of adding an *s* after the apostrophe (Thomas's). Some people prefer the added *s* because it suits the pronunciation better. Either form is correct. Examples:

RIGHT: Mavis' inheritance *or* Mavis's inheritance

This alternate spelling applies only to singular nouns ending in *s*. If the base noun ends in *s* and is plural, the only correct possessive spelling is an apostrophe after the *s*. Example:

RIGHT: the Lewises' squalling brats = squalling brats of the *Lewises*

Caution: An *es* is often added to a noun to make it plural, and the plural noun can then be made possessive by the addition of an apostrophe; but an *es* is *never* added to a noun to make it possessive. Example:

WRONG: Jameses date
RIGHT: James' date *or* James's date

18A1   Possessive Proper Nouns

Use an apostrophe with a proper noun in a possessive construction.

A proper noun is the name of a unique individual or thing and is capitalized. A proper noun in a possessive construction must be spelled with an apostrophe. If the proper noun to be made possessive does not end in *s*, in the possessive spelling an apostrophe goes before the *s*. Examples:

RIGHT: Sally's motives for running away are unknown.
We were eager to see Mr. Foster's fifth wife.
Mount Whitney's elevation is 14,495 feet.

If the proper noun to be made possessive ends in *s*, adding an apostrophe after the *s* is correct; but if the noun is also singular, another *s* may be added after the apostrophe. Examples:

RIGHT: The Gonzaleses' in-laws are very proud of Ray.
You should have heard Phillis' (*or* Phyllis's) argument with the Dean.
The auditors found Mr. Bass' (*or* Bass's) mistake.

Sometimes a possessive noun ends a sentence with the thing possessed being understood. Such a possessive noun takes an apostrophe. Examples:

RIGHT: Carol's baby is heavier than Jane's.
This stamp collection is worth more than Mr. Foss's (*or* Foss').

Baby and *stamp collection* are understood after *Jane's* and *Mr. Foss's,* and thus those names are possessive.

Caution: Never use an apostrophe in spelling the plural of a last name when the name is not also possessive. Examples:

WRONG: The Alvarados' are our neighbors.
RIGHT: The Alvarados are our neighbors.
RIGHT: The Gillises won't speak to the Hargises.

One way to test for the correct spelling is to see what pronoun would be substituted for the last name. If *they* or *them* will substitute, the name is not possessive and must not take an apostrophe. If *their* will substitute, the name is possessive and must take an apostrophe after the *s.*

18A2   Possessive Common Nouns

Use an apostrophe with a common noun in a possessive construction.

A common noun is most easily defined as one that is not capitalized because it is not the name of a unique individual or thing. A common noun in a possessive construction must be spelled with an apostrophe. If the common noun to be made possessive does not end in *s*, in the possessive construction an apostrophe is placed before the *s*. Examples:

RIGHT: The children's toys are being used as real weapons.
A teacher's work doesn't end at 3:00 each day.
It required six sheep's fleece to make that robe.

If the common noun to be made possessive ends in *s*, adding an apostrophe after the *s* is correct; but if the noun is also singular, another *s* may be added after the apostrophe. Examples:

RIGHT: Those roses' odor is somewhat like a crocus's (*or* crocus').
We trapped two lionesses' cubs on our first safari.
A lioness' (*or* lioness's) cubs are playful and unafraid of humans.
My boss' (*or* boss's) temper tantrums keep us all quiet.

18A3   Possessive Indefinite Pronouns

Use an apostrophe with an indefinite pronoun in a possessive construction.

A group of words called **indefinite pronouns** function as nouns and may be called noun substitutes. The chief ones that can be made possessive are *one, no one, someone, anyone, everyone, somebody, anybody, everybody, nobody, other, another, one another,* and *each other.* Also the *one* and *body* words are often used with *else,* as in *somebody else.* When one of these words is in a possessive construction, it requires an apostrophe and an *s.* Since none of these words ends in *s*, the apostrophe will always come before the *s*. Examples:

RIGHT: Somebody's nose is going to be bloodied if it gets closer to me.

I couldn't think of anyone's phone number.

Everybody else's habits need reforming.

We should all be concerned with each other's welfare.

You can put it into your mind that anytime you hear the *s* on one of the *one* or *body* words (except *one* itself) or on the *else*, the spelling will virtually always be *'s*.

18A4   Periods of Time and Sums of Money

Use an apostrophe to show a possessive construction with a period of time or a sum of money.

Words that name periods of time are frequently used in possessive construction in English, and they take apostrophes just as any other nouns do. Examples:

RIGHT: One month's vacation is preferable to two months' salary.

Today's crisis is no worse than yesterday's.

February's weather made me think the year's death was occurring.

An hour's value nowadays seems to be $14, at least for plumbers.

Words that name sums of money are also used in the possessive construction in English and require apostrophes just as other nouns do. Examples:

RIGHT: One dollar's worth of steak won't register on the scales.

I prefer a quarter's worth of gin to two dollars' worth of cola.

There wasn't a nickel's difference in our tallies.

Your two cents' worth will get you nowhere.

18B THE APOSTROPHE IN CONTRACTIONS

Use an apostrophe in a contraction.

In contractions, enter an apostrophe where one or more letters have been omitted. Examples:

don't	shouldn't
doesn't	o'clock
we've	I'm
you'll	Henry's here.
they're	Everybody's gone.

Do *not* confuse contractions with personal possessive pronouns. The possessive pronouns are already possessive, and so nothing else — not even an apostrophe — is needed to make them possessive. Examples:

possessive pronouns	*pronoun contractions*
its (belonging to it)	it's (it is *or* it has)
whose (belonging to whom)	who's (who is *or* who has)
your (belonging to you)	you're (you are)
their (belonging to them)	they're (they are)

Also, *never* put an apostrophe in one of these possessive pronouns:

yours	ours
hers	theirs

These words are already possessive, as *his* and *mine* are, and must not take an apostrophe.

18C THE APOSTROPHE IN PLURAL SPELLINGS

Use apostrophes in certain plural spellings.

Use an 's to form the plural of words used as words, of letters of the alphabet, of abbreviations, of numerals, and of symbols. Examples:

RIGHT: Don't put too many *if*'**s** in your proposal.

There are four *s*'**s** and four *i*'**s** in *Mississippi*.

Professor Smelly'**s** capital C'**s** look like his 9'**s**.

Joey is more concerned with rpm'**s** than with his girl friend.

The 1700'**s** were good years for aristocrats.

You have too many +'**s** in your equation.

The apostrophes in these plurals make for clarity. When there is no chance of the reader's being momentarily confused, some writers omit apostrophes in some of these special plural spellings.

Caution: Never spell the ordinary nonpossessive plural of a noun with an apostrophe. Examples:

WRONG: Too many cook's spoil the broth.

WRONG: Many cooks' are unsanitary.

RIGHT: Too many cooks spoil the broth.

RIGHT: Many cooks are unsanitary.

19

The Hyphen

Like the apostrophe, the hyphen is a mark used in spelling, not a mark of punctuation. It should not be confused with the dash, which is a mark of punctuation twice as long as the hyphen.

19A WORD DIVISION AT THE END OF A LINE

<u>Rule 1</u> **When dividing a word at the end of a line, use a hyphen and divide only between syllables.**

Never divide a one-syllable word, such as *tw-elve* and *len-gth*. Do not divide a word so that a single letter is left at the end of one line or the beginning of another, such as *a-muse* and *shin-y*. When necessary, consult a dictionary for proper syllabication.

19B COMPOUND NUMBERS AND FRACTIONS

<u>Rule 2</u> **Hyphenate spelled-out compound numbers (twenty-one through ninety-nine) and spelled-out fractions.**

If a fraction is unambiguously used with the indefinite article *a* or *an,* do not hyphenate it. Examples:

thirty-eight wins	two-fifths of my whisky
ninety-two losses	one-half of a loaf
our fifty-seventh anniversary	a third of the profits

Caution: Do *not* hyphenate noncompound numbers. Examples:

WRONG: one-hundred, three-thousand
RIGHT: one hundred, three thousand

Note that *twenty-four* really means twenty plus four but that *one hundred* does not mean one plus a hundred. It simply tells how many hundreds are involved.

19C COMPOUND NOUNS

<u>Rule 3</u> **Hyphenate compound nouns when hyphenation contributes to clarity.**

A compound noun is composed of two or more words that function as one noun. A few compound nouns—such as *son-in-law* and *self-control*—are always hyphenated, and some—such as *the White House* and *cooking apples*—never are. When necessary, consult a dictionary. Here are a few of the hyphenated compound nouns that appeared in one issue of a national magazine:

job-hunting	shadow-boxing
self-interest	kilowatt-hours
dry-goods	globe-trotters
well-being	by-product
Europe-firsters	passers-by

19D PREFIXES AND SUFFIXES

<u>Rule 4</u>   Use a hyphen to separate the following prefixes and suffix from their root words: *self*, *all*, *ex* (meaning former), and *elect*.

Examples:

> self-government for Togo
> an all-American quarterback
> an ex-mayor of Atlanta
> the governor-elect of Texas

Use a good dictionary to guide you in the use of such prefixes as *anti, co, non, pro, pseudo, quasi,* and *ultra.*

<u>Rule 5</u>   Use a hyphen to separate a prefix when its last letter and the first letter of the root word are the same.

Examples:

> anti-industrial   de-emphasize
> re-echo   pro-organization

Some common words, such as *cooperate,* do not now follow that rule. When necessary, consult a dictionary.

<u>Rule 6</u>   Use a hyphen to separate a prefix when nonhyphenation might be ambiguous.

Examples:

> a *co-op* and a *coop*
> to *re-collect* the equipment and to *recollect* a story
> to *re-cover* a sofa and to *recover* from an illness
> to *re-act* a scene and to *react* to a stimulant

<u>Rule 7</u>   Use a hyphen to separate a prefix when the root word is capitalized.

Examples:

> non-Christian   mid-August
> un-American   anti-Kennedy

19E COMPOUND ADJECTIVALS

<u>Rule 8</u> Hyphenate two or more words that serve as a single adjectival in front of a noun.

An adjectival is a modifier of a noun, and all kinds of English words can be combined to function as a single adjectival. Failure to hyphenate such adjectivals will often make a reader stumble momentarily or perhaps waste time figuring out word relationships. For example, this phrase appeared in a national advertisement:

the new embedded in plastic printed wiring circuit

Probably most readers had to pause to think out the word relationships, whereas if the writer had followed the above rule (plus the rule for separating coordinate adjectives) the meaning would have been immediately clear:

the new embedded-in-plastic, printed-wiring circuit

Rule no. 8 above is especially important for maintaining clarity in writing.

Here are some examples of rule no. 8 taken from one issue of a national magazine:

cradle-to-grave needs	law-school faculty
two-fisted gesture	civil-rights battle
double-parked car	a soft-spoken type
all-too-human attributes	cigar-making firm
long-term outlay	an eight-year-old girl
state-supported schools	high-pressure steam

Long compound adjectivals should be hyphenated rather than enclosed in quotation marks. Example:

RIGHT: He took an I-won't-budge-an-inch-if-I-die attitude.

Note: When the words which form the adjectival follow the noun, they are not normally hyphenated. Examples:

the faculty of a law school	a girl eight years old
attributes that are all too human	a battle for civil rights

Rule 9   When a conjunction is entered into a compound adjectival so that two or more adjectivals are intended, leave a space before and after the conjunction but put a hyphen after the word or words that precede the conjunction.

Examples:

all third- and fourth-grade pupils
all first-, second-, and third-ranked candidates

SECTION FOUR

DICTION

20

Appropriate Word Choice

Since writing takes many forms and fulfills many purposes, the words a writer chooses should be appropriate to the purpose. A great deal of slang might be appropriate in a friendly letter from one college student to another but quite inappropriate in a letter of application to be read by some unknown personnel officer. In discussing word choice (which is diction) in this chapter, we are limiting ourselves to the kind of writing usually called for in college—themes, essay exams, reports, and term papers.

Words wholly suitable for such kinds of writing may be classified into two groups: (1) **general-purpose words** and (2) **semiformal words.** General-purpose words are suitable for any writing situation and make up the bulk of most kinds of writing. They include virtually all the structure words, such as *no, some, about, such, however,* and so on, and a great many common content words, such as *house, dress, sentence, hungry, good, common,* and so on and on. Semiformal words are not commonly used in the casual conversation of people of moderate education, but they do occur frequently in semiformal or formal writing. Some examples are *disburse* (for *pay out*), *tortuous* (for *winding* or *twisting*), *subsequent* (for *coming after*), *rectitude* (for *moral behavior*), *rectify* (for *make right*), *altruistic* (for *selfless* or *charitable*), and so on. Your college writing need not be limited exclusively to general-purpose and semiformal words, but you should be cautious in departing from these categories. The following sections give advice about appropriate word choice.

20A SLANG

Avoid using slang expressions unless you feel that they enrich your writing rather than detract from its effectiveness.

Slang is language that seems to sprout from nowhere for the purpose of providing lively (and usually young) people with irreverent, racy, pungent, and sometimes off-color words and expressions to use instead of words that they consider stale or stuffy or inappropriate for their social situations. A typical example is *stop bugging me* for *stop annoying me.* Volumes could be written about slang, but the following points are sufficient for this chapter: (1) Slang is not bad language *per se;* it can be very good language when appropriately used. (2) The traditional four-letter obscenities and nonstandard words or constructions, such as *ain't got no,* are not slang. (3) A word—for example, *boogie-woogie*—is not slang unless it has a higher level counterpart in the language. (4) The distribution of slang terms both regionally and socially is extremely complex. (5) Some slang terms, such as *hang-up* and *burn artist,* are admirably effective coinages, but others, such as *lousy* and *peachy keen,* are so limp and colorless as to be offensive to anyone who loves language. (6) Most slang terms are new applications of established words, such as *burned out* for *exhausted,* but a few, such as *floozy* and *snafu,* are completely new coinages. (7) Most slang terms are short-lived, for new generations are constantly rejecting some of the language of older people and inventing new slang terms for their own use. (8) Many slang terms, however, rise to the level of standard diction and thus enrich our vocabulary. *Freshman, tidy* (for *neat*), *club, tantrum, mob,* and many other common words were once scorned as mere slang. And (9) a few slang terms, such as *gab* (idle talk) and *broad* (a woman), linger on as slang for centuries.

To repeat, the advice in this section is for you to avoid slang in your college writing unless you consciously think that a pungent slang term will make a sentence more effective than an ordinary, perhaps staid, term with the same meaning. Examples from student writing, with the slang terms in italics:

POOR STYLE: The preacher acted *real cool* when I told him how *I blew the job,* and I began to feel that I could keep from being *popped* If I confessed everything.

EFFECTIVE USE OF SLANG: Within a day after agreeing to the partnership with Marlin, I realized I had a *pencilneck* on my hands and that the background in mechanics he boasted about was sheer *plastic.*

Of course, the ineffectiveness or effectiveness of a slang term can best be judged in the context of a whole paragraph or paper rather than in one sentence. But in general, slang — which appears occasionally in such high-level magazines as *Harper's* and *The Atlantic* — is most effective when it is sparingly used in conjunction with diction of a generally high level.

20B COLLOQUIALISMS

Though you need not avoid colloquial diction in your college writing altogether, you should use it sparingly. Make an effort to choose some semiformal words, especially when you realize that you had first intended to use words on a low colloquial level.

The word *colloquial* has nothing to do with *local* but comes from a Latin word meaning "conversation." Thus originally, colloquial diction was considered suitable for informal conversation but not for writing. One might say *I have a bone to pick with you* in conversation but would write *I have a disagreement to settle with you.* But nowadays *colloquial* means informal in both speech and writing. All but one of the good collegiate dictionaries use either the label *informal* or *colloquial* to indicate that a word, or one of its definitions, is considered on a level below the semi-formal. However, we need to make two points here: (1) Colloquial words are in no way tainted and are not to be avoided unless a writing or speaking situation is important enough to call for a higher level of diction. For example, a bathrobe is eminently suitable clothing to wear in a bedroom but would be out of place at a formal banquet. Similarly, *let's do away with these grandaddy by-laws* might be wholly acceptable in one situation, whereas *let's rescind these outdated by-laws* might be the kind of phrasing most appropriate for another situation. The point is that levels of diction (excluding general-purpose words) do exist, just as different modes of behavior exist in society (compare a stag party for executives with a business meeting to determine company policy). As a writer you want to choose words which will do most to improve the quality of your writing. For college writing that means using colloquial diction judiciously and striving to use a desirable amount of semi-formal diction along with the many general-purpose words you must use.

And (2) there is not only one narrowly-bound level of colloquial diction but a very broad level, stretching from almost-slang to almost-semiformal. For example, *to butter up* (to flatter) is barely above the slang level and normally would be inappropriate in semiformal writing; but *to needle* (to goad or provoke) is close enough to the general-purpose category to pass without question in, say, an article in a serious journal. Thus much colloquial diction should be avoided in any writing of importance and much other colloquial diction often has a secure place even in writing as formal as, say, that of a textbook. As students mature educationally, they become more and more able to judge the levels of diction.

Here are some examples of colloquial diction in student writing, with semiformal revisions:

COLLOQUIAL: In algebra I was able to catch on without beating my brains out, and that made me feel a lot better about trying to go on in college.

SEMIFORMAL: I was able to understand algebra with ease, and that encouraged me to continue my college studies.

COLLOQUIAL: When I thought she was giving me the eye, I got carried away and made a fool of myself by trying some shenanigans in the pool with her.

SEMIFORMAL: When I thought she was showing some interest in me, I responded over-enthusiastically and must have appeared foolish when I tried to be intimate with her in the pool.

COLLOQUIAL: The boys thought they could get away with it by claiming over and over that they had told everything, but they couldn't bring it off.

SEMIFORMAL: The boys seemed to assume that they could avoid the appearance of guilt by repeatedly claiming innocence, but they did not succeed in their effort.

The colloquial sentences in these examples are *not* incorrect or even bad writing. However, the person whose writing vocabulary is limited to such a colloquial level will not be able to compose business letters, memos, reports, and so on of the quality demanded in well-paying jobs of importance. So, though colloquial phrasing is respectable, do not let it dominate your writing.

We should make two more points about colloquial diction. First, much colloquial diction in English consists of phrases that have single-word equivalents above the colloquial level. Here are a few examples:

down in the mouth—glum	put up with—tolerate
make a go of it—succeed	catch up with—overtake
give in—acquiesce	get on with it—continue

If you will *think* about your word choice, you will often find that you can improve a sentence by substituting a single-word equivalent for a colloquial phrase.

Second, we frequently use as modifiers of adjectives and adverbs a class of words known as qualifiers. The ones most commonly used in semiformal writing are these:

GOOD STYLE:	**very** irritable	**fairly** expensive
	quite incomprehensible	**wholly** incorrect
	rather staid	**especially** convincing
	somewhat embarrassed	**a little** disturbed

Avoid the following colloquial qualifiers:

POOR STYLE:	*real* intelligent	*sort of* peculiar
	sure pretty	*kind of* sad
	plenty excited	*awfully* conceited
	awful bad	*pretty* imaginative

Again, these constructions are not out-and-out errors, but they do produce poor style.

20C JARGON

Avoid jargon in your writing.

The word *jargon* has several definitions, but it is most commonly used to mean writing that is so full of pretentious diction and abstract and technical terms that it is almost incomprehensible, even to an educated person. Here is an example of jargon from a textbook on language:

> Discussions on the possibility of a universal base (as distinct from claims about universal constraints on the form of the base component) have mainly been concerned with whether the elements specified in the rules of a universal base — if there is one — are sequential or not.

Perhaps your teacher can give you an understandable revision of this passage. This writer on language doesn't know what that writer on language meant.

In much writing, technical terms cannot be avoided, and certainly words on a semiformal level should not be avoided (see the second paragraph of this chapter). But a writer on any subject can try to make the meaning clear rather than obscure it with jargon. In your writing you should strive to use a college-level vocabulary, but you should avoid pretentious diction, for that contributes to jargon. Happily, not many college freshmen indulge in jargon, though many graduate students do.

20D CLICHÉS

Avoid clichés in your writing.

A cliché is an expression that, because of long and thoughtless use, is trite, stale, worn out, and lacking in originality. For example, many people who use the phrase "feed at the public trough" don't even know that, when pigpens were common, they contained troughs to hold food for the greedy pigs, and thus many users of the phrase are unaware of its origin. Clichés are very common and have long lives because most people are too lazy or unimaginative to try to form their thoughts in their own language rather than in hackneyed phrases that are used over and over.

Here are a few examples of clichés:

ice water in his veins	a tower of strength
the acid test	the crack of dawn
the irony of fate	life is what you make it
take the bull by the horns	drunk as a lord
hard as nails	sober as a judge
a chip off the old block	a hasty retreat
straight from the shoulder	the calm before the storm
sneaking suspicion	better late than never
a crying shame	the last straw
off the beaten track	green with envy

As you write, *think* about your word choice and choose words more appropriate for your purpose than clichés.

21

Exact Word Choice

21A PRECISENESS OF MEANING

Choose words that express your meaning precisely rather than approximately.

The English vocabulary is probably larger than that of any other language, and consequently it has many synonyms (words very similar in meaning) and very many near-synonyms. Good writers try to choose words that say precisely what they mean, whereas careless writers are content with any approximation. Some examples from student writing, with the inexact words italicized:

INEXACT: Tom Paine was *suspicious* of the *foundations* of Christianity.

EXACT: Tom Paine was **skeptical** of the **theological doctrines** of Christianity.

There is some overlapping of meaning between *suspicious* and *skeptical*, but *skeptical* much more precisely expresses

Paine's attitude. Also, *foundations* is a vague and inexact word for the sentence.

INEXACT: As senator, he *achieved* more good laws than any other legislator in this century, but all he got was *slander* from the press.

EXACT: As senator, he **was responsible for the passage** of more good laws than any other legislator in this century, but in turn he was **libeled** by the press.

One does not really achieve a law but sponsors it or supports it or passes it, and so on. Also, though the point is very minor, *slander* implies oral and *libel* means written or pictorial defamation of character. Consulting a good dictionary is a great aid in learning to choose words with the exact meanings you want.

Finally, here is an example that is not easily revised:

INEXACT: Life itself is based on *productivity* and *advancement,* and without this there would be no *status quo.*

What the student meant is not very clear. Perhaps by *productivity* she meant *achievement,* for the former implies material goods and the latter accomplishments of any sort. By *advancement* she perhaps meant *progress,* but either term contradicts *status-quo,* which implies things as they are without change. More careful thought on the part of the student would probably have produced a more exact sentence with, perhaps, important and interesting meaning.

We should say, however, that it is better for you to make mistakes in using the new words you learn than to timidly avoid using a college-level vocabulary for fear of making a mistake. Many students learn a great deal about writing because they *do* make mistakes and then know not to make them again.

21B   SPECIFIC AND GENERAL WORDS

Make an effort to use words as specific as your meaning calls for.

The more specific a word is, the fewer objects or concepts it applies to if it is a noun, the fewer actions or states of being it expresses if it is a verb, and the fewer qualities it signifies if it is an adjective or adverb. Of course a general word is just the opposite. For example, note how specificity increases as you pass from the very general first word to the other words in each of the following lists.

animal	talk	contented
quadruped	discuss	happy
mammal	disagree	cheerful
canine	argue	overjoyed
dog	dispute	ecstatic
mongrel	quarrel	euphoric

Animal can refer to thousands of species—millions, if insects are included—, but *mongrel* refers to just one type of one species. *Talk* can apply to dozens of types of oral communication, but *quarrel* specifies a narrow range. *Contented* can apply to numerous mental states, but *euphoric* means only the ultimate in emotional happiness. General words are very important in our vocabulary; quite often a writer wants such a general word as *animal* and no other. But the more you can choose specific words, the clearer your meaning and the better your style will be.

Here are some examples from student writing of weak use of general words, with the general words italicized:

GENERAL: Emily Dickinson thought of death as a *good thing*.
SPECIFIC: Emily Dickinson thought of death as a **desirable step into immortality.**

GENERAL: Emily Dickinson is popular because of her *sound* way of *looking* at life.
SPECIFIC: Emily Dickinson is popular because of her **realistic** way of **describing** life.

GENERAL: Now the *course* has been *improved.*
SPECIFIC: Now the **course content better suits the students' needs.**

GENERAL: Letting eighteen-year-olds drink alcohol *causes problems.*
SPECIFIC: Letting eighteen-year-olds drink alcohol **increases
traffic accidents and fights among youths.**

Choosing specific diction calls for thought. The tendency of
beginning writers is to use the first words that come into
their heads, but more experienced writers *think* in order to
make their word choice more specific.

We should add, however, that often a writer deliberately
chooses a general word with the intent of following it up
with specifics. For instance, in the last example above the
writer could have used the general word *problems* because
he then intended to specify what the problems are. (But he
didn't.)

21C CONCRETE AND ABSTRACT WORDS

As much as possible, try to choose concrete words for
your writing.

Technically, a concrete word is one that names an object
that can be seen or touched, such as *book* or *kitten.* An
abstract word is one that names a concept, such as *socialism* or *devotion,* or a quality apart from the object that can
possess it, such as *beauty* or *gracefulness.* All concrete
words can form images in the mind; that is, if you hear or
read the word *horse* you have no trouble visualizing one in
your mind's eye. An abstract word cannot directly form an
image in one's mind. For example, the word *communism,*
not being the name of a tangible object, cannot form an
image directly; whatever images come into your mind when
you read the word are due to associations you have made
with the word. Thus an abstraction can form images in
readers' minds. For example, such words as *leer, smile,
pretty, smooth, kind, song,* and so on are abstractions when

they are used apart from the person or thing that can wear a smile or be pretty. But they have much of the image-forming effect of such concrete words as *snake, houseboat, lake, owl,* and so on. The advice for you in this section is to choose, as much as possible, concrete words or nonconcrete words that have strong image-forming qualities.

Here are some examples of sentences full of abstractions, with revisions for concrete diction:

ABSTRACT: The modifications that were effected in the subject's orientation to societal mores transformed the approaches and tendencies of her existence.
CONCRETE: The changes brought about in the woman's behavior altered the color and direction of her life.

ABSTRACT: Cooper observed the large majority of all phenomena with conspicuous nonsuccess in apprehending the nature of reality.
CONCRETE: Cooper saw nearly all things as through a glass eye, darkly.

ABSTRACT: Let us render inoperable those invidious machinations that endeavor to legalize the destruction of our movement.
CONCRETE: Let's defeat the legislative bills that would outlaw our political party.

Abstractions, such as the words *modifications, mores, apprehending, invidious,* and so on in the above example sentences, need not be avoided *per se.* Individually they are good words, and we must use abstractions like them. However, when a sentence is little more than an accumulation of abstractions, it is usually not good writing. Concrete and image-forming diction generally improves clarity and style.

21D EUPHEMISMS

Avoid overuse of euphemisms in your writing.

A euphemism is a mild or roundabout word or expression used instead of a more direct word or expression to make one's language delicate and inoffensive even to a squeamish person. Probably the most frequently-used euphemism is *passed away* for *died.* The areas that demand euphemisms change over the decades. The Victorians, for example, found it convenient to employ euphemisms for bodily functions and parts of the body that might suggest sex. Even later than 1900 a great many genteel people would not use the words *leg* and *arm* because of their sexual suggestibility and talked instead about a person's *limbs.* For one satirist, *toes* became *twigs.* In our time we seem to need euphemisms for the areas of social and economic standing and war. For example, the poor nowadays are usually referred to, at least in public documents, as the *disadvantaged* or *underprivileged;* the very dull student as *educationally handicapped;* the crazy person as *emotionally disturbed;* old people as *senior citizens;* the sacking of a village in war as *pacification;* retreat in war as *planned withdrawal:* lies as *inoperative statements;* and so on.

No doubt many euphemisms do no harm and are actually useful to keep from upsetting sensitive people. But they can also be harmful in that in politics and war they can be deceptive. All writers and readers should at least know what euphemisms are and not be deceived by them. Most of us, no doubt, would rather hear the phrase *nasal discharge* than *snot,* and we can be amused at the phrase *mature entertainment;* but we should be wary of political euphemisms, so that we don't accept *bring order back to the government* for what it says when it really means *establish a dictatorship.*

21E WORDINESS

Avoid wordiness in your writing.

Good writing should be concise as well as precise — that is, it should not be rambling and wordy. Sometimes a sentence or passage is wordy because the writer rambles around without trying to make economical use of words. An example from student writing:

WORDY: Faulkner put the ditch in "That Evening Sun" so that when it is crossed, as it is several times, the reader can get the understanding that what is on one side of it is completely separated from what is on the other side. What is on one side is the world of the white people and what is on the other side is the world of the black people.

CONCISE: The ditch in Faulkner's "That Evening Sun," crossed several times by some of the characters, is a symbol of the immense gap between the white and black worlds.

Sometimes wordiness is due to the use of an unnecessarily long sentence constituent. Example:

WORDY: The rock group which was brought to play in the pasture of Mr. Hollis were half-stoned by the time they got there.

CONCISE: The rock group brought to play in Mr. Hollis's pasture showed up half-stoned.

The concise sentence uses constituents identical in meaning but shorter and thus more concise than some of the constituents in the wordy sentence. The clause beginning with *which was* is longer than the equally clear phrase *brought to play; Mr. Hollis's pasture* is less wordy than *the pasture of Mr. Hollis;* and *showed up* is much more concise than *by the time they got there.* It takes thought and revision to compose unwordy sentences, for the human mind seems naturally to indulge in wordiness.

Other kinds of wordiness are known as **deadwood** and **redundancy,** in which the elimination of wordiness usually calls not for a recasting of the sentence but simply for the omission of unneeded words. *Redundancy* means saying the same thing twice, such as *audible to the ear. To the ear* adds no meaning and is redundant because the word *audible* means "capable of being heard by the ear" (some sounds can be heard by machines but not by ears; they are not audible). Here are some examples of student sentences with deadwood or redundancy:

WORDY: I liked the biographical information *about Hardy's life* better than his *fictitious* novels.

CONCISE: I liked Hardy's biography better than his novels.

WORDY: The foreign language department has established a *new* innovation *the purpose of which is* to reduce the time we have to study written material *in the textbooks.*

CONCISE: The foreign language department has established an innovation to reduce the time we have to study written material.

WORDY: A metaphor is one kind of figure of speech *that is not literal* because the two *different* parts of the comparison are *completely* dissimilar *to each other.*

CONCISE: A metaphor is one kind of figure of speech because the two parts of the comparison are dissimilar.

The concise revisions in these examples could be written better, but their aim is to show that deadwood—needless words—can often just be omitted, with a consequent improvement in the quality of the writing.

22

Correct Word Choice

In Chapter 21 we discussed the value of choosing words for the exact meaning you want, rather than words that only approximately express your meaning. In this chapter we will deal with the choice of wrong words—words which, if taken literally, do not even approximately express your meaning. For example, if you ask someone for change for a dollar and receive nineteen nickels, your request will have been approximately met; but if instead you receive a handful of pebbles, your dollar's change is not even approximately right but wholly incorrect.

22A MALAPROPISMS

Consult a dictionary, if necessary, to prevent use of malapropisms.

A malapropism, named after a character in an eighteenth-century play who mangled the language in almost every speech, is simply a word wholly incorrect for the meaning intended but usually having some sort of humorous application, such as some similarity in sound. A couple of examples are *a shrewd awakening* for *a rude awakening* and *you lead and we'll precede* for *you lead and we'll proceed (behind you).*

Here are some examples of student malapropisms, with the malapropisms italicized:

MALAPROPISM: The fans were now supporting our team *voraciously.*
RIGHT: The fans were now supporting our team **vociferously.**

MALAPROPISM: Then I pour the *bladder* on the waffle iron and wait for the golden brown waffles.
RIGHT: Then I pour the **batter** on the waffle iron and wait for the golden brown waffles.

MALAPROPISM: Next in the church service we recited the *B attitudes.*
RIGHT: Next in the church service we recited the **Beatitudes.**

MALAPROPISM: Emerson's was a *neo-Plutonic* philosophy.
RIGHT: Emerson's was a **neo-Platonic** philosophy.

MALAPROPISM: I have been absent for the last week because I am going to get married and have been to San Francisco to get my *torso* ready.
RIGHT: I have been absent for the last week because I am going to get married and have been to San Francisco to get my **trousseau** ready.

Such boners are fairly common because young people often misinterpret the sounds they hear and give no thought to the real meanings of the words they misuse. The most common malapropism, perhaps, is *take it for granite* instead of *take it for granted.* But perhaps the funniest of all is the Sunday school child's singing about *the cross-eyed bear* when the hymn "Gladly the Cross I'd Bear" was sung. The dictionary cannot help you avoid such malapropisms as those, but it can keep you from confusing such words as, say, *tortuous* and *torturous.* The value of your dictionary can't be overemphasized.

22B   CONFUSED WORDS

Do not confuse a word with one similar to it in sound or meaning or spelling.

There are a number of pairs or trios of words in English that are so commonly confused that they cannot be labeled malapropisms, which are seldom recurring. Some of these words are listed in Section 16G for spelling purposes. Here is a brief list of the words most often confused, thus producing incorrect rather than inappropriate word choice.

> **accept** is a verb meaning "to receive."
> **except** is a preposition meaning "not included."
>
> **all ready** is an indefinite pronoun plus adjective meaning "everyone or everything is prepared."
> **already** is an adverb meaning "at or before this time."
>
> **all together** is an indefinite pronoun plus adjective meaning "everyone in unison."
> **altogether** is an adverb meaning "completely."
>
> **allude** is a verb meaning "to mention indirectly." *Allusion* is the noun.
> **refer** is a verb meaning "to mention directly." *Reference* is the noun.
>
> **anyway** is an adverb meaning "in any case."
> **any way** is a noun phrase meaning "whatever way possible."
>
> **beside** is a preposition meaning "at the side of."
> **besides** is a preposition or adverb meaning "in addition to."
>
> **broadcast** is a verb with the principal parts *broadcast, broadcast, broadcast. Broadcasted* is nonstandard.
>
> **burst** is a verb with the principal parts *burst, burst, burst. Bust* and *busted* are nonstandard for *burst.* (*Busted* is also a slang word for arrested.)

cite is a verb meaning "to mention or refer to."
site is a noun meaning "a place."

colloquialism is a noun meaning "a word or phrase suitable for informal use."
localism is a noun meaning "a word or expression used only in one locality or region."

complement is a noun (and verb) meaning "something that completes or makes a whole."
compliment is a noun (and verb) meaning "praise given."

conscience is a noun meaning "a feeling of right and wrong."
conscious is an adjective meaning "awake or alert."

could of, would of are nonstandard spellings of "could've (have)" and "would've (have)."

council is a noun meaning "an official, deliberative group."
counsel is a verb (and noun) meaning "to give advice." *Counselor* comes from *counsel.*

credible is an adjective meaning "believable."
creditable is an adjective meaning "worthy of praise."
credulous is an adjective meaning "willing to believe readily or easily imposed upon."

delusion is a noun meaning "a false belief."
illusion is a noun meaning "a deceptive appearance or false impression."

disinterested is an adjective meaning "impartial or having no personal interest."
uninterested is an adjective meaning "not interested."

farther is an adverb pertaining to physical distance.
further is an adverb pertaining to degree of advancement in ideas, concepts, and so on.

forecast is a verb with the principal parts *forecast, forecast, forecast. Forecasted* is nonstandard.

hanged is the past tense and past participle of the verb *hang* when it means execution.

hung is the past tense and past participle of the verb *hang* for all other meanings.

imply is a verb meaning "to suggest or hint."

infer is a verb meaning "to draw a conclusion or inference about."

inside of is colloquial for *within.*

irregardless is nonstandard. Use *regardless.*

kind of, sort of are colloquial phrases for *rather* or *somewhat.*

later is an adverb or adjective meaning "at a time after a specified time."

latter is an adjective (and noun) meaning "nearest the end or the last mentioned."

liable is an adjective meaning "responsible or legally bound or likely to occur."

libel is a verb meaning "to slander in print" and a noun meaning "slanderous articles."

lie, lay See Section 8C.

loose is an adjective meaning "not tight."

lose is a verb meaning "to mislay or be deprived of."

marital is an adjective meaning "pertaining to marriage."

martial is an adjective meaning "pertaining to military operations."

maybe is an adverb meaning "perhaps or possibly."

may be is a verb form indicating possibility.

moral is an adjective meaning "right or ethical."

morale is a noun meaning "a mental attitude or condition."

nohow is nonstandard for *anyway.*

oral means "spoken." It is preferable in that sense to *verbal,* which refers to both oral and written language.

passed is the past tense and past participle of the verb *to pass.*

past is a noun meaning "of a former time" and a preposition meaning "passing beside."

persecute is a verb meaning "to harass cruelly or annoy persistently."

prosecute is a verb meaning "to bring suit against."

principal is an adjective meaning "chief or most important" and a noun meaning "head of a school" or "money used as capital."

principle is a noun meaning "a rule or doctrine."

quiet is an adjective meaning "not noisy."

quite is a qualifier meaning "entirely or almost entirely."

sensual is an adjective meaning "lewd or carnal."

sensuous is an adjective meaning "characterized by sense impressions."

set, sit See Section 8C.

than is a subordinating conjunction used in a comparison.

then is an adverb of time or a conjunctive adverb meaning "therefore."

For words not on this list, consult your dictionary. Form the habit of relying on your dictionary and not just guessing.

22C INCORRECT IDIOMS

Avoid incorrect idioms in your writing.

Strictly defined, an idiom is a construction "peculiar" to a language, not understandable from the meanings of the individual words in it, and not literally translatable into another language. For example, *ran across* is a common English verb followed by a common preposition and will make such ordinary sentences as *the football player ran across the field* and *the fire truck ran across the water hose.* But consider *I ran across an old friend.* Here neither the verb nor the preposition has its regular meaning, and the whole would probably produce a hilarious construction if translated literally into another language. In this use, *ran across* is an English idiom.

More loosely defined, idiomatic English is any English phrasing that is natural and normal and clearly understandable to a native speaker of English. However, we normally think of English idioms as containing at least one preposition, or a word that looks like a preposition, and that is the way we will consider idioms in this chapter on correct word choice. Thus if (as once happened) a student should write *this contradicts with my opinion,* we would say the idiom was faulty, for native speakers would write *this contradicts my opinion.* English contains countless true idioms.

Faulty idioms are far more common in writing than in conversation, possibly because the writers are striving hard to express their thoughts in writing and make errors *because* they are striving so hard. Here are some faulty idioms from student papers.

FAULTY IDIOM: Poe has been acclaimed by many *of being* a great writer.

RIGHT: Poe has been acclaimed by many **to be** a great writer.

FAULTY IDIOM: Poe is *attributed to being* the originator of the detective story.

RIGHT: Poe is **considered** the originator of the detective story.

FAULTY IDIOM: Military service should not be *likened with* a prison sentence.

RIGHT: Military service should not be **likened to** a prison sentence.

FAULTY IDIOM: Thoreau would have died for the ideals *for which he was so radically supporting.*

RIGHT: Thoreau would have died for the ideals **which he so radically supported.**

Since faulty idioms are usually nonrecurring (except for some in nonstandard English, such as *listen at me* rather than *listen to me*), no rules can be given to keep you from writing them occasionally. The best advice is for you to think calmly and not be in a panic when you write and to proofread your work carefully. Then you are likely to write idiomatic English, for it is truly native to you (unless English is not your native language).

22D OMITTED WORDS

Do not carelessly omit a needed word.

Examples:

OMITTED WORD: The man bought the car from me was too naive to check it thoroughly.

RIGHT: The man **who** bought the car from me was too naive to check it thoroughly.

OMITTED WORD: Jane was happy about the outcome but my parents bitter about it.

RIGHT: Jane was happy about the outcome but my parents **were** bitter about it.

In the correct sentences the boldface words are needed.

SECTION FIVE

EFFECTIVE SENTENCES

23

Faulty Sentence Structure

Good writing is a complex mixture of many components, but at its heart is the sentence. The great English statesman and writer Sir Winston Churchill called the English sentence "a noble thing," and it is a truism that anyone who can write really good sentences can write longer passages well too. Sentences, however, are so complex that many things can go wrong with them. But students can learn to write sentences without faulty structure, and thus we have this chapter on the main kinds of errors in sentence structure.

23A MIXED SENTENCE STRUCTURE

Do not inconsistently shift structure in the middle of a sentence.

Mixed sentence structure usually occurs when a writer begins a sentence with one kind of structure, forgets that structure somewhere along the way, and completes the sentence with a different, incompatible kind of structure. Here is an example from a student paper:

MIXED STRUCTURE: Just loving someone is a one-way affair and has to have someone love you in return.

The shift in structure which produced this mixed sentence comes after the conjunction *and,* which indicates that either a second independent clause or another predicate parallel with *is a one-way affair* is to follow. But the writer lost his way and either did not bother to proofread carefully or else did not have sufficient sentence sense (see Chapter 2) to see that the result was a nonsentence. A unified structure might have been maintained in either of these ways:

RIGHT: Just loving someone is a one-way affair, and for happiness your loved one must love you too.

RIGHT: Just loving someone is a one-way affair and doesn't mean that you are loved in return.

The first revision has two independent clauses and the second two predicates with one subject. Both represent standard sentence structure, though not necessarily excellent writing.

Here are other examples from student writing of mixed sentence structure, with revisions:

MIXED STRUCTURE: A student who is capable of finding a job and succeeding gives him a satisfaction toward his parents.

RIGHT: A student who is capable of finding a job and succeeding in it feels grateful toward his parents.

In the mixed sentence the writer composed the long but satisfactory subject *a student . . . succeeding* but then failed to provide a predicate with a verb that fits the subject. The revision provides a suitable predicate (although, of course, it may not express exactly what the student meant).

MIXED STRUCTURE: All of these facts boil down to that science is playing a major role in our lives.

RIGHT: All of these facts mean that science is playing a major role in our lives.

In the mixed sentence the student writer failed to compose a subject and verb combination that would take the noun clause *that . . . lives* as a direct object. The revision provides a suitable subject and verb.

MIXED STRUCTURE: Those writers that Poe predicted would never make it, we have never even heard their names in our time.
RIGHT: Those writers that Poe predicted would never make it have never been heard of in our time.

In the mixed sentence the student writer composed the long but satisfactory subject *Those . . . it* and then, instead of providing a predicate for the subject, inconsistently continued with a complete independent clause. The revision changes the independent clause into a predicate that fits the subject.

23B FAULTY PREDICATION

In your independent clauses, be sure that your subject and predicate are compatible.

The grammatical term *predication* means the fitting of a predicate to a subject to make an independent clause (or sentence), such as —

The horsy set in our town / snubs people with little money.

The slash (/) separates the subject from the predicate.

When a subject and predicate are not compatible, the error known as faulty predication occurs. For example,

Courageously / is a time of happiness

is obviously a nonsentence because its predication is faulty; the adverb *courageously* cannot serve as the subject of the predicate *is a time of happiness* — or, for that matter, as the subject of any predicate. Equally a nonsentence is this student's creation:

FAULTY PREDICATION: Through God's creation alone / is the only concept of God that man has.

The prepositional phrase *through God's creation alone* will not function as the subject of the predicate that follows. The student may have meant to say something like this:

RIGHT: The only concept of God that man can have / lies in God's creation of the universe.

However, as is often the case in sentences with faulty predication, what the writer meant to say is not entirely clear.

Here are some other examples from student writing of faulty predication, with revisions:

FAULTY PREDICATION: Financial security and social standing / are arguments presented in favor of parent-arranged marriages.

Since financial security and social standing are not arguments, the compound subject does not fit its predicate. The sentence should read something like this:

RIGHT: Many people / argue that parent-arranged marriages provide financial security and social standing.

Another example:

FAULTY PREDICATION: My reaction to being in a large English class / seemed a little strange and different.

The predication is faulty because it was the class and not the student's reaction that seemed strange and different. A better version:

RIGHT: I felt that the large English class / was a little strange and different.

Two other examples:

FAULTY PREDICATION: Another misconception / is when we try to visualize God.

FAULTY PREDICATION: Characterization / is where I think Faulkner succeeded best.

These are examples of the faulty *is when* and *is where* kinds of sentences. Do not use the *is when* construction unless your subject specifies a time, and do not use the *is where* construction unless your subject specifies a place. Otherwise, such sentences have faulty predication. Better versions:

RIGHT: Another misconception / is that human beings can actually visualize God.

RIGHT: Faulkner's characterization / is the best aspect of his fiction.

Now *misconception* and *characterization* are said to be things that they can be, and the predication is sound.

23C FAULTY PARALLELISM

Make sure that the constituents in any series in your sentences are parallel in structure.

In sentence structure, parallelism means the use of two or more similar constituents in a series, usually with a coordinating connective between the last two constituents. For example:

RIGHT: **Having no money** but **wanting to attend the festival,** I considered selling my typewriter.

The two boldface constituents are parallel in structure because they function identically and are similar in form.

When two or more *dissimilar* constituents are in a series, faulty parallelism results. An example from student writing, with the constituents in faulty parallelism italicized:

FAULTY PARALLELISM: *If a man is brilliant in a specific field* but *he does not have general knowledge,* he may be useless.

Here a dependent clause and an independent clause are joined by *but,* with faulty parallelism the result. The sentence should read like this:

RIGHT: If a man **is brilliant in a specific field** but **does not have general knowledge,** he may be useless.

Now two predicates (with the subject *man*) are in correct parallelism.

Other examples from student work:

FAULTY PARALLELISM: When we entertain *friends, parents*, and *behave ourselves*, we are praised.

RIGHT: When we **entertain friends and parents** and **behave ourselves**, we are praised.

The incorrect sentence has two nouns and one predicate in faulty parallelism. Two proper sets of parallel constituents are in the correct sentence: the boldface predicates and the two nouns *friends* and *parents* in the first predicate.

FAULTY PARALLELISM: Local color was flourishing, *with Harte writing about California* and *Cable wrote about Louisiana*.

RIGHT: Local color was flourishing, with **Harte writing about California** and **Cable writing about Louisiana.**

The incorrect sentence has a prepositional phrase and an independent clause in faulty parallelism. The correct sentence has two objects of the preposition *with* in proper parallel structure.

23D DANGLING MODIFIERS

Do not let an introductory or terminal constituent dangle with no word or word group to modify.

Usually when a sentence opens with an introductory constituent that is not the subject, the constituent modifies the subject that follows. Example:

RIGHT: Having no sixth sense, I was forced to guess at the right answers.

The *having no sixth sense* constituent modifies the subject *I*, and the sentence meaning is fully clear. But suppose the sentence were written in this way:

DANGLING MODIFIER: *Having no sixth sense*, the answers had to be guessed at.

Now the sentence seems to say that the answers had no sixth sense. Since the *having no sixth sense* constituent has no word to modify, it dangles, and the sentence structure is faulty.

Here, from student writing, are other examples of dangling modifiers, with the danglers italicized:

DANGLING MODIFIER: *By bringing children up together in schools of equal opportunity,* they will become friendly.

The children (*they*) are not doing the bringing up, and thus the phrase dangles. Revision:

RIGHT: By bringing children up together in schools of equal opportunity, we allow them to become friendly.

Now the sentence has *we* for the introductory phrase to modify.

DANGLING MODIFIER: *Besides being a thing of security for active people,* shut-ins and hospital patients get pleasure from personal-advice columns.

The shut-ins and patients are not a thing of security, and thus the phrase dangles. Revision:

RIGHT: Besides being a thing of security for active people, personal-advice columns give pleasure to shut-ins and hospital patients.

Now the introductory phrase properly modifies *personal-advice columns.*

DANGLING MODIFIER: The church is a good place to go, *when unsettled in mind.*

The sentence seems to say that the church is unsettled in mind, and thus the terminal constituent dangles. Here is a revision:

RIGHT: The church is a good place to go when you are unsettled in mind.

In this revision the dangler has been altered in structure so that it no longer dangles but delivers clear meaning.

23E MISPLACED MODIFIERS

Always place a modifier in a sentence so that the word or word group it modifies is immediately clear.

Most sentences in good writing have a number of modifiers, and the good writer must give thought to the placement of modifiers if the meaning is to be immediately clear. For example, consider this sentence from a news report:

MISPLACED MODIFIER: Collins was told that his services would no longer be needed *by the personnel officer.*

When the sentence is considered in isolation, it seems clear that the personnel officer will no longer need Collins's services (though others in the company may). But the whole report made it clear that the personnel officer was firing Collins. Thus the writer misplaced the modifier *by the personnel officer* and no doubt momentarily confused thousands of readers. The italicized phrase should have been placed after *told.*

Here are some other examples of misplaced modifiers, with the modifiers italicized:

MISPLACED MODIFIER: Your interesting letter regarding the honors program *of December 2* reached me today.

Of December 2 should come directly after *letter,* for the writer was specifying the date of the letter, not of the honors program.

MISPLACED MODIFIER: They can easily destroy this magnificent creation, which represents 3000 years of careful work *with the press of a button.*

The work was not done with the press of a button. For immediate clarity, the italicized phrase should come after *destroy* or at the very beginning of the sentence.

MISPLACED MODIFIER: I feel that I am going to succeed in all my future goals *today.*

For instant clarity, *today* should come directly after *feel* or at the beginning of the sentence.

MISPLACED MODIFIER: Dickinson says that earth's heaven is nature *in her work.*

The sentence makes no sense unless the italicized phrase is placed after *says* or at the beginning of the sentence.

24

Pronoun Reference

A pronoun gets its meaning through reference to some other word or word group, which is known as the pronoun's **antecedent.** Since the pronoun does not have meaning of its own, its reference—or antecedent—must be unmistakably clear if the sentence is to deliver clear meaning. Furthermore, even when its meaning is clear, a pronoun must be properly used if the sentence is to be effective and stylistically acceptable. Sentence effectiveness is easily diminished by faulty pronoun reference.

24A REFERENCE TO TITLES

Do not use a pronoun in the opening sentence of a paper to refer to the title or a noun in the title, unless such use is deliberately intended to achieve a desired stylistic effect.

Though themes, essays, and term papers should have suitable titles, almost always a paper should be opened as though the title were not stated. Here, from a student's work, is an illustration of how *not* to use pronoun reference to a title:

TOPIC: Write an essay about one of your favorite pastimes.
TITLE: Creating Designs on Ceramics
IMPROPER REFERENCE IN OPENING SENTENCE: When you learn the technique of applying design material to *them,* you are ready to work on your artistry.

The *them* in the opening sentence, referring to *ceramics* (or does it refer to *designs?*) in the title, produces a particularly ineffective sentence and theme introduction. Almost always you should avoid referring to your title in your opening sentence.

Sometimes a careless student will even choose a topic from several written on a blackboard or handout sheet, not compose a title at all, and then begin the paper with a reference to the topic, while the teacher does not know which topic has been picked. For example, after being handed a list of seven topics to choose from, one student once opened a titleless paper with this sentence:

IMPROPER REFERENCE IN OPENING SENTENCE: First, I think *it* should be discussed more before *they* make a decision.

The *it* and *they* in the opening sentence ruined the theme at the outset.

24B AMBIGUOUS REFERENCE

Do not use a pronoun so that it can meaningfully refer to either of two nouns or word groups.

Ambiguity means having two possible meanings, and pronoun reference is ambiguous when there is more than one clearly possible antecedent for the pronoun. Example from a student paper:

AMBIGUOUS REFERENCE: I happened to walk into Professor Howard's office when he was bawling a student out. *He* appeared unruffled, but I could tell *he* was angry.

Do the *he*'s refer to the professor or the student? Later sentences made the reference clear, but it was at first ambiguous and thus destroyed sentence effectiveness. A revision:

CLEAR REFERENCE: I happened to walk into Professor Howard's office when he was bawling a student out. **The student** appeared unruffled, but I could tell that he was angry.

The two *he*'s in these sentences are unmistakably clear in their reference.

Sometimes ambiguous reference occurs when a pronoun is only understood and not stated. Example from an advertisement, with the understood pronoun in brackets:

AMBIGUOUS REFERENCE: The trunk on a Dart is actually bigger than the one on many full-sized cars. And a family of five fits inside [it] nicely.

The ad writer intended the understood *it* to refer to *Dart* but it seems to refer to *trunk.* The writer should have put *the car* after *inside.* Also note the inconsistency of specifying *one* trunk for *many* full-sized cars.

24C FAULTY BROAD REFERENCE

Avoid using *this, that, which,* and *it* with vague, indefinite, or ambiguous reference.

Broad reference means that a pronoun does not refer to an individual noun but to a whole idea expressed in an independent clause or word group. Broad reference is completely acceptable when it is clear, and, indeed, it is very common. Examples:

CLEAR BROAD REFERENCE: I made an A in American Literature, **which** is hard to do when Professor Fleenor is the teacher.

CLEAR BROAD REFERENCE: We must rewrite our Student Body Constitution. **This** is the only way we can avoid the disintegration of our student government.

CLEAR BROAD REFERENCE: I studied without a break until 1:00 A.M., but **it** did me no good on the exam.

The *which, this,* and *it* clearly refer to whole ideas, not individual nouns, and the broad reference is acceptable, or even desirable.

Often, however, broad reference is vague, indefinite, or ambiguous, and then it destroys sentence effectiveness. First, here is an example from a nationally-circulated advertisement:

FAULTY BROAD REFERENCE: Any food you buy that you do not like or use reduces the amount of your savings, *which* after all is the main purpose of our plan.

The *which* seems to refer to the idea of *reducing the amount of your savings,* whereas obviously the writer had in mind *increasing the amount of your savings.* The common remark "You know what I mean" is no excuse for such bad writing.

Here is an example, taken from a magazine, of faulty broad reference of *it:*

FAULTY BROAD REFERENCE: The odds are that such youngsters will drop out of school eight or ten years later with little to show for *it* but the experience of failure.

The *it* seems to refer to the idea of *dropping out of school,* but the writer really meant the pronoun to refer to *attending school.* The faulty reference destroys the effectiveness of the sentence.

The pronoun *this* seems to be most misused in broad reference in student writing. Example:

FAULTY BROAD REFERENCE: Take for example the TV ad wherein they shave off the sand from a piece of sandpaper. How do we know whether *that* is true? Many people, however, never give *this* a second thought.

The *that* is much too vague in its reference, and the *this* is hopelessly indefinite. A revision:

CLEAR MEANING: Take for example the TV ad in which sand is shaved off a piece of sandpaper. How do we know the shaving is not faked? Many people, however, never give a second thought to the truthfulness of TV ads.

Another example:

FAULTY BROAD REFERENCE: I will not try to convince you that all television programs are worthwhile. *This* is a fallacy.

If a reader pauses to think out the meaning, he will understand that the writer means that the idea that all television programs are worthwhile is a fallacy. But the faulty use of *this* destroys the effectiveness of the passage.

Another:

FAULTY BROAD REFERENCE: *Time* magazine says that it has been said that the generation of the 1970's is degenerate. *This* is not true.

What is not true: attributing the statement to *Time* or *Time*'s reporting or the alleged degeneracy of the generation of the 1970's? The ambiguity of the broad-reference *this* defeats the writer's purpose.

One more example:

FAULTY BROAD REFERENCE: When someone mentions voter apathy, most people think of minority groups. *This* is not true.

The *this* is so indefinitely used that the reader must supply a sentence or two of his own to see that the writer means that voter apathy is not limited to minority groups.

So, take great care with your use of the broad-reference *this,* and also of the broad-reference *that, which,* and *it.*

24D REMOTE REFERENCE

Avoid using a pronoun so far removed from its antecedent that the reader has to pause to determine its meaning.

Example from student writing:

REMOTE REFERENCE: On the first mild day of spring we decided to go sailing. At the lake we found that some vandals had damaged our boathouse and some gear, but we were able to make quick repairs and thus were not disappointed in our first sail on *it* for the year.

The *it* is so far removed from its antecedent, *lake,* that the reader momentarily stumbles and must reread to be sure of the meaning.

And here is an example from a cookbook:

REMOTE REFERENCE: To enhance the flavor of roast chicken, spill a glass of white wine and sprinkle parsley over *it* while roasting.

Aside from the fact that the sentence seems to imply that the wine may be spilled on the floor and that the cook is roasting, the *it* is too far removed from its antecedent, *roast chicken,* for clear reference.

24E IMPLIED ANTECEDENTS

Do not use a pronoun with an implied antecedent.

Pronouns may refer to whole ideas but, in good writing at least, they should not refer to adjectives or to antecedents implied and not stated. Example:

IMPLIED ANTECEDENT: Professor Stansbury is humorous and *it* makes her classes popular.

Though the meaning of the sentence is not obscured, *it* refers to the adjective *humorous,* a stylistically undesirable technique in English, and thus the effectiveness of the sentence is diminished. The reader really is forced to mentally supply the noun *humor* for *it* to have an antecedent. A revision:

BETTER STYLE: The humor Professor Stansbury displays in her classes makes them popular.

Another example:

IMPLIED ANTECEDENT: I liked Hawaii partly because *they* were all so friendly.

The absence of *Hawaiians* as an antecedent for *they* creates a poor sentence.

Two more examples:

IMPLIED ANTECEDENT: "The Second Choice" was about a young girl who fell in love and then lost *him*.

IMPLIED ANTECEDENT: In "The Grass So Little Has to Do" Dickinson seems to envy the simplicity of nature and expresses *it* in the last line of the poem.

In the first sentence, *him* is meant to refer to *lover*, who is not mentioned. The *it* in the second sentence has no noun to refer to. Presumably the writer intended it to mean "envy," but the *envy* used in the sentence is a verb. A pronoun cannot refer to a verb. The sentence can be corrected by substituting "that envy" for *it*.

24F *WHAT* AS A PRONOUN

Do not use *what* as a substitute for the pronouns *who* and *that*.

Example:

WRONG: The guy *what* sold me that car was a crook.
RIGHT: The guy **who** sold me that car was a crook.

25

Faulty Comparisons

Comparisons, which must consist of at least two constituents even if one is understood, occur frequently in our language, and three kinds of errors are common in their use. (See Section 5D for pronoun forms used in comparative constructions.) These errors diminish sentence effectiveness considerably.

25A INCOMPLETE COMPARISONS

Avoid incomplete comparisons that in effect make nonsensical sentences.

Aside from the conjunctions *than, as,* and *like* and the prepositions *like* and *from* used to form comparisons, two other words—*other* and *else*—frequently help form comparisons. These comparative words should not be omitted so as to make an incomplete or nonsensical sentence.

True, in advertising copy the *than* part of a comparison is often omitted. Example:

INCOMPLETE COMPARISON: El Ropos smoke more smoothly.

The reader might well ask, "More smoothly than what?" Of course the ad writer intends the reader to understand *than other cigars,* and the reader does understand that. Such incomplete comparisons, however, should be avoided in college writing. For example, don't write such a sentence as —

INCOMPLETE COMPARISON: Attending a private college is different

without specifying what it is different from.

A second kind of incomplete comparison is perhaps even less acceptable because it forms a nonsensical (even though understandable) sentence. This is the kind of comparison that says that one thing is longer or kinder or more extensive, and so on than itself. Example from student writing:

INCOMPLETE COMPARISON: Nixon traveled to more foreign countries than any president.

Since Nixon was a president, the sentence literally says that Nixon traveled to more foreign countries than Nixon, which, if we apply rigorous logic, is nonsense. True, the reader understands the meaning intended, but how much more effective the sentence would have been if written in this way:

COMPLETE COMPARISON: Nixon traveled to more foreign countries than any **other** president.

The *other,* a comparison-completing word, makes a great deal of stylistic difference.

Another example:

INCOMPLETE COMPARISON: My father has captured more mountain lions than anybody in our county.

The student's father presumably lives in "our county." Thus the sentence says her father has captured more mountain lions than her father, which is logical nonsense. The comparison-completing word *else* makes the sentence much more effective:

COMPLETE COMPARISON: My father has captured more mountain lions than anybody **else** in our county.

Now the comparison is complete and the sentence much improved.

Remember not to omit the words *other* and *else* in comparisons that call for one or the other of them.

25B FALSE COMPARISONS

Do not compose sentences that express false comparisons.

A comparison says that one thing is similar to, greater or lesser than, or different from another. But when the two parts of the comparison are incompatible for comparative purposes, a false comparison occurs and produces a bad sentence. Example:

FALSE COMPARISON: I was searching for a tent like the American Indian.

The sentence is literally comparing a tent with a human being, an absurdity that destroys the effectiveness of the sentence completely. The writer really meant this:

TRUE COMPARISON: I was searching for a tent like the American Indian's.

The American Indian probably had many kinds of tents, but at least now the sentence compares a tent to a tent (*tent* is understood after *American Indian's*) and the false comparison is eliminated.

Here are some other examples:

FALSE COMPARISON: We were searching for a painting more like Van Gogh.

FALSE COMPARISON: My uncle farms like the nineteenth century.
FALSE COMPARISON: Today's students' behavior is just like their parents.

Was Van Gogh a painting? Did the nineteenth century farm? Is behavior a parent? No. The sentences should express true comparisons:

TRUE COMPARISON: We were searching for a painting more like Van Gogh's.
TRUE COMPARISON: My uncle farms as farmers did in the nineteenth century.
TRUE COMPARISON: Today's students' behavior is just like their parents'.

In the first sentence, *paintings* is understood after *Van Gogh's;* in the third, *behavior* is understood after *parents'.* All three of these true comparisons have eliminated the illogicality of the three faulty sentences.

25C OMITTED COMPARATIVE WORDS

In a double comparison, do not omit a needed comparative word, such as *than* or *as.*

Sometimes a double comparison calls for two different comparative words, and careless writers often omit one of the two. Example from a student paper:

OMITTED COMPARATIVE WORD: Professor Tilley is as helpful to us students or maybe more helpful than any of the counselors.

One part of the double comparison is intended to say that Professor Tilley is *as helpful as* and the other part *more helpful than.* But the student carelessly omitted the needed second *as.* Revision:

COMPLETE DOUBLE COMPARISON: Professor Tilley is as helpful to us students **as,** or maybe more helpful than, any of the counselors.

The *as* provides the needed completion. Another example:

OMITTED COMPARATIVE WORD: Sara is more beautiful, or at least as beautiful as, the Homecoming Queen.

COMPLETE DOUBLE COMPARISON: Sara is more beautiful **than,** or at least as beautiful as, the Homecoming Queen.

In the revision the needed comparative word *than* is added and the effectiveness of the sentence restored.

26

Mature
and Well-Formed
Sentences

Avoiding errors and weaknesses in writing is important, but such successful avoidance does not guarantee good writing. Various positive qualities in a writer's sentences are also needed if the writing is to be of good quality. Our point here can be made clearer by drawing a comparison with marriage. In marriage, it is desirable for the partners to avoid quarrels, fights, and other conflicts. But does such avoidance guarantee a happy marriage? No. In addition to avoiding, as much as possible, various conflicts, the partners need to show affection for each other, to love, to share, to be delighted, at least part of the time, with each other's company. The positive and the negative: both are important in many aspects of human behavior. In this chapter we will discuss the sentence from various positive points of view.

26A SENTENCE EXPANSIONS

Strive to achieve maturity of sentence structure; avoid excessive use of short, simple sentences.

Though short, simple sentences have their place in good writing and are often needed for the writer to achieve a desired effect, most sentences in good writing are composed of more than one simple independent clause. Various kinds of sentence expansions (large sentence constituents) allow us to express two or more full ideas in one well-composed sentence. Little children write mostly in run-on simple sentences, but mature adults do not, for their command of language—including sentence structure—grows as they grow out of childhood. For example, a child might write—

> I found a nickel and I kept it and I went as soon as I could to the store and bought some candy and I didn't want to lose that nickel.

But a person who has matured in his language usage would try to *compose* a sentence with various sentence expansions attached to one or two independent clauses. Example:

> Having decided to keep the nickel I found, I rushed to the store to buy some candy, taking care not to lose the nickel myself.

The foregoing is an extremely simple illustration, but it expresses an important point. Good writers give attention to composing mature sentences with various kinds of sentence expansions, or large constituents. It is *not* necessary for a writer to know the grammatical names of large sentence constituents in order to use them well. No one thinks about grammatical labels while writing, though one may write better because of having thought about (studied) grammar in the process of achieving mature language usage. Nevertheless, we need to label the sentence expansions, or large constituents, that we will briefly discuss.

26A1   Compound Structures

One of the simplest methods of achieving mature sentence structure is to use compound structures, which means using two or more similar constituents in a series. Almost any kind of sentence constituent can be compounded. For example, often one subject will serve two predicates, allowing the writer not to repeat the subject. Example:

SIMPLE SENTENCES: The fish inspected the bait. The fish decided not to accept it.

COMPOUND PREDICATE: The fish **inspected the bait** and **decided not to accept it.**

The two boldface predicates are served by one subject, *the fish.* Other sentence parts may be compounded too, as these sentences illustrate:

COMPOUND SUBJECT: **The Queen** and **the Prime Minister** attended the launching.

COMPOUND OBJECT: In a rage Ned kicked first **the sofa** and then **the cat.**

You perhaps miss more opportunities than you realize to tighten your style through use of more compound structures.

26A2   Appositives

An appositive is essentially a noun-repeater, though in its totality as a grammatical construction it can exhibit many complex features. It is a noun-repeater in that it defines or explains a noun that it is said to be in apposition to. In spite of the fact that the appositive usually (but not always) is in apposition to an individual noun, it expresses a full idea. Example:

SIMPLE SENTENCES: A black hole is an astronomical body of such mass that not even light can escape from its gravitational pull. It is composed of matter so dense that a thimbleful of it would weigh tens of millions of tons on earth.

APPOSITIVE: A black hole, **an astronomical body of such mass that not even light can escape from its gravitational pull,** is composed of matter so dense that a thimbleful of it would weigh tens of millions of tons on earth.

Chances are that you can improve the quality of your writing considerably by using appositives more frequently.

26A3 Adjective Clauses

An adjective clause is introduced by one of the relative pronouns (*who, whom, whose, which,* and *that*), which usually has a noun antecedent in another part of the full sentence. Since it contains a subject and predicate, the adjective clause expresses a full idea, but one that is subordinated to an independent clause or a part of the main sentence. Like all the constituents we are illustrating in Section 26A, the adjective clause allows us to *expand* a simple sentence and thus achieve more mature sentence structure. Example:

SIMPLE SENTENCES: The Dean introduced the main speaker. The main speaker was to address us on choosing marriage partners wisely.

ADJECTIVE CLAUSE: The Dean introduced the main speaker, **who was to address us on choosing marriage partners wisely.**

The superiority of the structure of the second version is plain.

26A4 Adjective Phrases

An adjective phrase is composed of an adjective functioning as a headword, with modifiers clustering around it. Although, since it is a phrase, it does not have a subject and predicate, the adjective phrase, as a sentence expansion, expresses a full idea. Example:

SIMPLE SENTENCES: Otto Knutt was extremely unhappy with his recently-purchased used car. He prepared to palm it off on an unsuspecting friend.

ADJECTIVE PHRASE: Otto Knutt, **extremely unhappy with his recently-purchased used car,** prepared to palm it off on an unsuspecting friend.

Such constituents draw meaning (*Otto Knutt was* in this
case) from other parts of the sentence and thus express full
ideas.

26A5 Adverb Clauses

An adverb clause is introduced by one of the subordinating
conjunctions—*because, since, unless, if, though,* and many
others. These subordinating conjunctions express such relationships as cause-and-result, contrast, condition, time,
and so on between the idea in the adverb clause and the independent clause or a part of the main sentence. Example:

SIMPLE SENTENCES: The ballot boxes had been stuffed. The student
body had to conduct another election.
ADVERB CLAUSE: **Because the ballot boxes had been stuffed,** the
student body had to conduct another election.

The adverb clause not only has a subject and predicate,
which perforce means that it contains a full idea, but also a
subordinating conjunction (*because*) to express the proper
relationship between ideas.

26A6 Noun Clauses

Noun clauses usually do not function as sentence expansions but as subjects or direct objects in independent
clauses. However, as appositives they can, and often do,
function as expansions. Example:

SIMPLE SENTENCES: The Yazidis' basic belief is that the world is at
this time controlled by the devil. This belief derives from their
observation of the horrendous state of the world.
NOUN CLAUSE: The basic belief of the Yazidis—**that the world is at
this time controlled by the devil**—derives from their observation of the horrendous state of the world.

The use of the noun clause as an appositive produces superior sentence structure. In the first of the simple sentences, the noun clause *that the world is at this time controlled by the devil* functions as a predicate noun and is thus not a sentence expansion.

26A7 Prepositional Phrases

Often a prepositional phrase with a complex structure functions as a sentence modifier, and as such it expresses a full idea and is a sentence expansion. Example:

SIMPLE SENTENCES: The college president did not have any idea of how he would quell the disturbance. He walked into the midst of the disputants.

PREPOSITIONAL PHRASE: **Without any idea of how he would quell the disturbance,** the college president walked into the midst of the disputants.

Note that the relationship between the ideas in the simple sentences is not expressed, whereas the sentence with the prepositional phrase does express that relationship.

26A8 Verbal Phrases

Various kinds of verbal phrases (the technical names of which you don't need to know) serve as sentence expansions. Examples:

SIMPLE SENTENCES: Iva Notion did not agree with either the Republican or the Democratic policies. She joined the American Freedom Party.

VERBAL PHRASE: **Not agreeing with either the Republican or Democratic policies,** Iva Notion joined the American Freedom Party.

Two points are to be noted here. First, the verbal phrase draws meaning from the other part of the sentence and thus expresses a full idea. Second, though it does not have a connective word to express it, the verbal phrase does express the relationship of cause-and-result between the two full ideas — the disagreeing is the cause and the joining is the result.

SIMPLE SENTENCES: Basil Metabolism wanted to get admitted to the med school of his choice. He devoted enough time to his studies to be elected Phi Beta Kappa at UCLA.

VERBAL PHRASE: **To get admitted to the med school of his choice,** Basil Metabolism devoted enough time to his studies to be elected Phi Beta Kappa at UCLA.

Note again that even without a connective word (such as *because*), the verb phrase expresses a cause-and-result relationship between the two full ideas.

26A9   Absolute Phrases

An absolute phrase is a construction that has a subject with a nonfinite verb form (that is, a verb form that cannot serve as a sentence verb). Naturally such a phrase contains a full idea. Example:

SIMPLE SENTENCES: The chances of a stock market crash were high. I sold my hundred shares of Snake Oil Laboratories and put the money in a savings account.

ABSOLUTE PHRASE: **The chances of a stock market crash being high,** I sold my hundred shares of Snake Oil Laboratories and put the money in a savings account.

As in all our illustrations in Section 26A, the *maturity* of the structure of the single sentence, as opposed to the simple sentences, should be clear to you.

26A10   Complex Sentences in General

As we said, no writer thinks about grammatical labels as he or she writes, but the good writer does think about composing sentences of mature structure, even though they may frequently be short, simple sentences. All of the sentence expansions we have illustrated can be combined in an infinity of ways to produce an infinity of different, but well-formed, English sentences. An example, chosen within two seconds from an issue of *Harper's* magazine:

COMPLEX SENTENCE: When, like today, something moves me to get on the Fifth Avenue bus, my eyes invariably fall on one woman who seems, at least to me, the quintessential East Side woman, and her Martian differences quicken in me a sense of myself, a pang of self-recognition.

Though this complex sentence cannot really be called a typical sentence from *Harper's,* it is by no means unusual, and any page from that magazine or any other of good quality will contain several or many sentences of as much complexity. Good readers expect such sentences in their good reading material. In addition to two independent clauses, the sentence contains one adverb clause, one adjective clause, two prepositional-phrase sentence modifiers, and one appositive as sentence expansions.

26B EFFECTIVE SUBORDINATION

Avoid weak coordination of independent clauses; achieve effective subordination.

Sometimes two full ideas in one sentence are of equal importance and deserve equal emphasis, in which case they are usually coordinated. Examples, with the coordinated constituents in boldface:

PROPER COORDINATION: **At the beginning of the year I considered myself a staunch Republican,** but **later events caused me to adopt the label Independent.**

PROPER COORDINATION: **Being disillusioned by the scandals** but still **approving of conservative policies,** I decided to give up the man but not the Party.

In the first sentence two independent clauses are coordinated with the coordinating conjunction *but* joining them. In the second, two verbal phrases are coordinated. In each case the ideas, for effective sentence structure, deserve to be coordinated, or placed in equal rank.

Sometimes, however, one idea should, for effective sentence structure, be subordinated to another, for coordination of them makes the sentence sound childish. Examples:

WEAK COORDINATION: Personnel policies are administered in a haphazard way, and inequities result.

PROPER SUBORDINATION: **Because personnel policies are administered in a haphazard way,** inequities result.

WEAK COORDINATION: The field was not dry, and the game couldn't start.

PROPER SUBORDINATION: **Until the field dried,** the game couldn't start.

The sentences of weak coordination don't sound right because the two full ideas in each are not of coordinate importance. In the sentences of proper subordination, the boldface adverb clauses carry important meaning, but their subordination to the main clauses makes the sentences sound right—that is, makes them more effective.

26C EMPHASIS

Compose sentences so that the most important ideas in them receive the most emphasis. Cultivate the active voice.

Emphasis is achieved chiefly by choosing the most effective words to express an idea (see Chapters 20 and 21) and by placing the parts of the sentence so that the most important ideas receive most prominence. Example, from student writing:

UNEMPHATIC: Teenagers often have disagreements with their parents and the main reason is that the parents are afraid that their children will behave as *they* did when young and they therefore unreasonably restrict their children's behavior.

This sentence has an interesting idea but its parts are strung out in such a way that no peak of emphasis emerges. A revision:

EMPHATIC: Since many parents are afraid that their teenage children will behave as *they* did in their teens, they unreasonably restrict their children's behavior, thereby causing disagreements.

Now all three main ideas in the sentence are adequately emphasized, with the independent clause placed to receive most prominence.

Another example:

UNEMPHATIC: We won the game by a point, though with six minutes left we were down twelve points and down sixteen at half time.

The sentence is unemphatic because it winds down and ends with the least important information. A revision:

EMPHATIC: At half time we were down sixteen points and with only six minutes left still down twelve, but we won the game by a point.

Now the parts are placed so that the sentence rises to a proper peak of emphasis.

Though there are numerous reasons for many sentences to be written in the passive voice, the active voice will provide more emphasis if there is no special reason to use the passive voice. Example:

UNEMPHATIC: Our canoe was capsized by our rivals and so the race was won by them.

EMPHATIC: Our rivals capsized our canoe and so won the race.

The passive voice weakens the first sentence, but the active voice in the revision produces proper emphasis.

You can learn to compose sentences for better emphasis by listening to your sentences with your mind's ear. Listen, and *think* about how your sentences sound.

26D CLARITY

Above all, be sure that what you have written will be clear to the reader.

In many sections of this book we have discussed writing problems that diminish clarity, and we will not discuss those writing problems a second time. However, this is a section of the book your instructor can refer you to when you have not been fully clear in your writing but have not made one of the specific errors explained in other sections of this book. Here is one example of lack of clarity, taken from a nationally-circulated magazine:

LACK OF CLARITY: Every animal has its place and role in nature's grand design, including the predator. Ecological balance is one of nature's laws. Occasional loss of livestock must be weighed against the good *these animals* [italics supplied] do.

Most readers would be at least momentarily confused when they reached *these animals.* At first a reader may think the phrase refers to *livestock,* but that makes no sense. Eventually, it becomes clear that the phrase refers to *the predator,* but the damage of unclear writing has already been done. Besides, *predator* is singular and *these animals* plural, an inconsistency that contributes to the lack of clarity.

26E VARIETY

For more effectiveness in your writing, vary your sentence structure as you compose your paragraphs.

A series of sentences similar in structure, particularly if they are all short, produces monotonous writing. Thus you should not continue one kind of sentence pattern through a series of sentences. Sentence patterns can be varied by changing length, by varying the kinds of sentence expansions used (see Section 26A), by beginning some with the subject and others with introductory constituents, and by occasionally using inverted sentence order (that is, by putting the verb before the subject). Here is an example of a passage with little variety of sentence structure. A revision follows.

MONOTONOUS SENTENCE STRUCTURE: My father was most disturbed by my brief period of experimenting with drugs. He thinks all drugs are bad. He doesn't understand why young people want to experiment. He doesn't remember the pleasure of getting high once in a while. He took me to our doctor to discuss the problem. The doctor came to the conclusion that I had no problem now. My father accepted the doctor's conclusion.

VARIETY IN SENTENCE STRUCTURE: Though I gave him concern about various of my activities, my father was most disturbed by my experimenting with drugs, especially since he thinks all drugs are bad. He is old enough now not to understand why young people want to experiment, and he evidently has forgotten the pleasure (which I am sure he experienced) of getting high once in a while. Because of his concern about my brief use of drugs, he went with me to discuss the problem with our family doctor. The doctor, having a much better knowledge of young people than my father, quickly explained that I now had no problem that should worry my father. Upon hearing this, my father breathed a sigh of relief and showed his old trust in me.

The monotony of the original is eliminated by the variety of sentence structure in the revision.

26F TRANSITIONS AND COHERENCE

Use connectives effectively both within and between sentences.

Essentially, writing consists of strings of ideas, and relationships exist between these ideas. Often there is no word between sentences or parts of a sentence to express a relationship; the relationship is clear simply because of the nature of the writing. Example:

Growing weary with his team's many mistakes, the coach called off the practice session.

The cause-and-result relationship between the two sentence parts is fully clear even though the sentence has no specific word to express the relationship: the growing weary is the cause and the calling off is the result.

However, our language has many connective words (coordinating conjunctions, subordinating conjunctions, and conjunctive adverbs) and transitional phrases (*for example, in addition, on the other hand,* and so on) that are used to make clear the relationships between parts of sentences and between sentences. Good writers are aware of the connectives and use them wisely and liberally in order to make their writing as clear as possible. The great English writer Samuel Taylor Coleridge said, "A good writer may be known by his pertinent use of connectives." And another great English writer, Thomas de Quincy, said, "All fluent and effective composition depends on the connectives." So be aware of connectives and use them effectively. Connectives provide **transition** between ideas, which in turn helps produce **coherence** in writing. Coherence means that all parts of each sentence and all sentences in a passage stick together, making the writing clear, intelligible, and smooth.

Some examples from student writing:

POOR TRANSITION: The world has much good in it. If I were given the ability to make it better, I would take three steps.

CLEAR TRANSITION: The world has much good in it, **but** if I were given the ability to make it better, I would take three steps.

CLEAR TRANSITION: **Though** the world has much good in it, it could be better, **and** if I were given the ability to make it better, I would take three steps.

POOR TRANSITION: Today's world is moving at a tremendous pace. There are many ways to relieve the pressures of everyday living.

CLEAR TRANSITION: **Though** today's world produces tensions **because** it is moving at a tremendous pace, there are many ways to relieve the pressures of everyday living.

POOR TRANSITION: For a change of pace, a person can read the sports page. The rest of the paper should not be ignored.

CLEAR TRANSITION: For a change of pace, a person can read the sports page, **but** one should not ignore the rest of the paper.

CLEAR TRANSITION: **Though** reading the sports page can give a person a change of pace, one should not ignore the rest of the paper.

The boldface connective words in the sentences labeled *clear transition* express the relationships between ideas, relationships that are not expressed in the sentences labeled *poor transition.* Achieving clear transition through proper use of connectives is one way good writers make their writing coherent, which means that the sentences and parts of sentences flow smoothly together.

26G LOGICAL THINKING

Avoid sweeping generalizations; strive for logical thinking.

Of course people are entitled to their own opinions (at least as long as they do not let them harm others), and a composition teacher certainly should not grade a paper down because he or she disagrees with the ideas in it. However, human beings by nature often fall into illogical thinking, and thus when you have written an illogical sentence or passage, your teacher should mark the faulty logic.

The most common kind of illogical statement that appears in themes is the **sweeping generalization,** a gross overstatement of the truth of whatever idea is under discussion. Example:

SWEEPING GENERALIZATION: All students everywhere today are again giving serious attention to their studies and avoiding political activism.

That might seem to be an innocent-enough sentence to appear in a theme, but its logic is faulty because the statement is too broad. It includes all students everywhere, and surely there are many students who are not giving serious attention to their studies and surely there are still many students active politically. Such sweeping generalizations need **qualification,** which means that they should be expressed so as not to overstate the case, or include everybody when everybody should not be included. A revision:

QUALIFIED GENERALIZATION: **A great many** students today in **most parts of the country** are again giving serious attention to their studies and avoiding political activism.

Now the qualifying words *a great many* and *most* take the statement out of the sweeping generalization category. Generalizations are *not* out of place in college writing, but you should always be aware of the need to qualify generalizations that might otherwise be so overbroad as to be illogical.

There are many other kinds of illogic which we do not have space to treat in this book. But in general you should try to use sound reasoning in all your writing. For example, here is a typical bit of illogic from a student paper:

ILLOGICAL: The press should not have treated the Republicans so harshly, because the Democrats were up to just as many dirty tricks.

Now even if the second part of the sentence is true, the whole is still illogical because one group's wrongdoing does not justify another group's wrongdoing. If the Democrats were guilty of crimes during the period the student referred to, they too should have been prosecuted and punished for their wrongdoing. The student would have been much more logical had he written his sentence in this way:

LOGICAL: Though the wrongdoings of the Republicans cannot be condoned, there is evidence of Democratic wrongdoing at the same time, and the Democrats certainly should have been castigated for their crimes too. It is not right for the press to turn all its attention to the crimes of just one party.

Human beings are very prone to illogical thinking, but you can make the content of your papers sounder if you give thought to the logic of the statements you make.

THE
RESEARCH
PAPER

27

The Research Paper

THE NATURE OF THE RESEARCH PAPER

Term papers are routinely assigned in many college courses, for studying a limited topic in depth is an especially valuable educational experience. In most colleges, the freshman course in composition has traditionally been the place to teach students the standardized, step-by-step techniques of preparing a research paper—techniques that are applicable to the various kinds of term papers assigned in more advanced college courses. In preparing a research paper, you will do practical research in a library, not original research, for you will be expected to seek out recorded knowledge, not to establish new knowledge. (Most new knowledge is established by highly trained researchers in universities, in government, and in industry.)

Yet a research paper should be original in the sense that it puts together pieces of information from various sources in order to present a new view of a topic. For example, most people know that Roman Catholics in general oppose abortion on demand and that Protestants are split on the issue. But what is the view of Orthodox Jewish rabbis? Are they in general agreement, and if so, on which side? Or is there controversy among them on the issue of abortion? Perhaps no one has written an article detailing the Jewish position on abortion, and thus the topic might be a good one for a research paper. The writer of the paper would gather information from many sources and organize it into a research paper that would, in a sense, be new and original even though it used only recorded information.

27B   SELECTING A LIMITED RESEARCH-PAPER TOPIC

A freshman research paper normally runs between 2000 and 3000 words, and thus its topic must be rather narrowly limited, for a broad or general topic cannot be well developed in so few words. Students who try to write papers on such topics as "Scandals in the Nixon Administration," "The Vietnam War," "Shakespeare's Tragedies," and so on, are hopelessly lost at the beginning. After you decide on the general subject you want to write about, you must go through a process of reducing and reducing that subject until you reach a properly limited topic.

Often, reading an article or news story about the general subject you are interested in will lead you to a narrow topic. For example, one student who wanted to write about music came across just one sentence that said there is a relationship between certain kinds of religious music and jazz. Thus the student chose the good topic "The Role of Religious Music in the Development of Jazz." Another student, after reading a news article about Uri Geller, an Israeli who claims to have various psychic powers, decided she wanted to write her paper on some aspect of psychic phenomena. She realized that such topics as "Extrasensory Perception" and "Psychokinesis" were much too broad. She considered "Scientific Experiments in Extrasensory Perception," but also rejected that topic as too broad. Then a minor comment in the news article led her to the properly limited topic "Controls Used to Prevent Fraud in Experiments in Extrasensory Perception." You must, then, proceed from a general subject to a narrow aspect of it in order to select a properly limited research-paper topic.

But a narrowly limited topic is not necessarily a good research-paper topic, for a good research paper must bring together information from at least eight or ten sources. *Thus any topic for which you can find sufficient materials in only one, two, or three sources is not an acceptable research-paper topic.*

Some good research-paper topics call only for the presentation of factual, noncontroversial information; others are on controversial issues. If, for example, you are interested in mental illness and choose the topic "Some Rare Types of Mental Illness," you would gather factual information and present it in an orderly and interesting fashion. But if you should choose the topic "The Use of Chemical Therapy in Minor Cases of Mental Illness," you would find much disagreement among the experts as to whether, or how much, chemical therapy should be used to treat minor mental illnesses. You would, in effect, have a controversial topic. After studying the evidence, you would put your own conclusions in your paper, even though those conclusions would be opinions and not facts.

After you have a suitable topic, you should, before compiling a working bibliography (see Section 27D), try to decide what the main points of your paper will be. The more clearly you perceive your topic before beginning your research, the easier your research will be and the less time you will waste. Of course, before beginning your research you may know very little about your topic, but if you can establish the main questions your paper will answer, you will have a good head start.

Suppose, for example, you chose the topic "The Use of Hypnosis as an Anesthetic." You would probably look for answers to these questions: How widespread is the use of hypnosis as an anesthetic? On what kinds of patients and for what kinds of surgery is it used? How much success do the doctors who use it claim? Is there much professional opposition to its use? With these few questions in mind (they would become main headings in your outline), you would have a great advantage in beginning and pursuing your research.

27C RESEARCH MATERIALS IN THE LIBRARY

After you have selected a good topic and, if possible, derived from it the few general questions your paper will answer, your next step is to compile a working bibliography. This is a list of sources (books, magazine articles, news reports, and so on) that you expect to provide all the information you will need to write your paper. To compile a working bibliography, you must know what source materials are available and how to use them. Thus in the following sections we will classify the chief library research materials, so that you will be equipped to compile a working bibliography. Every good library has at least one reference librarian on duty whenever the library is open, and you should not hesitate to call on the reference librarian for help. Also, your composition instructor may take his or her class on a tour of your library.

27C1 General and Special Encyclopedias and Reference Books

Every library of any size has many general and specialized reference works, which are kept on open shelves in the library's reference room. Since these reference works are themselves the product of research, they alone cannot supply you with all the information you need for a good research paper. Remember, especially when contemplating the use of a general encyclopedia, that when one source supplies you with all the information you need for your research paper, you do not have a suitable topic. Nevertheless, the various reference works often supply researchers with useful bits of information, and you should consult them as necessary. For example, if you should choose the topic "Critical Reception of Mark Twain's Satires on Religion," *The Dictionary of American Biography* might provide you with some useful bits of background information about Mark Twain, though it could by no means supply you with sufficient materials to write the whole paper.

The two most important general encyclopedias are the *Encyclopedia Americana* and the *Encyclopaedia Britannica.* (An article in these works is sometimes followed by a bibliography, which may list useful sources.) Listed below, by subject, are the most widely used specialized reference works. Your library will probably have most of these, in addition to many lesser known reference books that there is not space to list here.

Agriculture
Encyclopedia of American Agriculture, 4 vols.

Art and Architecture
Cyclopedia of Painters and Paintings, 4 vols.
Encyclopedia of World Art
A History of Architecture

Biography
American Men and Women of Science, 11 vols.
Contemporary Authors, 52 vols.
Current Biography, 34 vols.
Dictionary of American Biography, 20 vols. and supplements
Dictionary of National Biography (British), 22 vols. and supplements
Who's Who (British)
Who's Who in America

Business
> *Economic Almanac,* 34 vols.
> *Encyclopedia of Banking and Finance*

Education
> *Cyclopedia of Education,* 5 vols.
> *Education Index,* monthly, with annual cumulations
> *Encyclopedia of Educational Research*

History
> *Cambridge Ancient History,* 12 vols.
> *Cambridge Modern History,* 13 vols.
> *Dictionary of American History,* 6 vols.
> *An Encyclopedia of World History*
> *Shorter Cambridge Medieval History,* 2 vols.

Literature
> *Cambridge History of American Literature,* 4 vols.
> *Cambridge History of English Literature,* 15 vols.
> *Cassell's Encyclopedia of World Literature,* 2 vols.
> *Encyclopedia of Classical Mythology*
> *Granger's Index to Poetry*
> *Mythology of All Races,* 13 vols.
> *Oxford Companion to American Literature*
> *Oxford Companion to Classical Literature*
> *Oxford Companion to English Literature*

Music
> *Grove's Dictionary of Music and Musicians,* 9 vols. and supplement
> *Musician's Guide,* 3 vols.

Political Science
> *Cyclopedia of American Government,* 3 vols.
> *Dictionary of Political Science*
> *Palgrave's Dictionary of Political Economy,* 3 vols.

Religion
> *Encyclopedia of Religion and Ethics,* 13 vols.
> *Encyclopedia of the Jewish Religion*
> *Interpreter's Dictionary of the Bible,* 4 vols.
> *New Catholic Encyclopedia,* 14 vols.

Science

> *The Harper Encyclopedia of Science*
> *Hutchinson's Technical and Scientific Encyclopedia,*
>   4 vols.
> *McGraw-Hill Encyclopedia of Science and Technology,*
>   15 vols.

Social Science

> *Dictionary of Philosophy and Psychology,* 3 vols.
> *Encyclopedia of Psychology*
> *Encyclopedia of the Social Sciences,* 15 vols.

Yearbooks

> *The Americana Annual*
> *The Britannica Book of the Year*
> *Statesman's Yearbook*
> *United Nations Yearbook*
> *World Almanac*

Don't hesitate to use any of these or other reference works to obtain useful bits of information and to verify facts, but *do not* expect to write a research paper using only reference works of this sort.

27C2   The Card Catalogue

A library's card catalogue lists, alphabetically, all the books and pamphlets in the library's holdings. To facilitate research, each book is listed at least three times: (1) under the author's name; (2) under its title; and (3) under one or more subject headings. Occasionally a college researcher will know the name of an author who has written on the researcher's topic but will not remember any of that author's titles. And occasionally the researcher may remember a title but not its author. Thus the listings by author and title can be useful. But most researchers rely mainly on subject headings to guide them to useful books and pamphlets.

Here is a reproduction of a card entered in the card catalogue by subject heading:

---

② Walking

① ③
796.5 **Sussman, Aaron.**
SUS
    ④ The magic of walking, by Aaron Sussman and Ruth
    Goode. New York, Simon and Schuster [1967]
    ⑧ 410 p. 25 cm. ⑤   ⑥   ⑦

    ⑨ "The company of walkers, a peripatetic ramble through the litera-
    ture of walking" consists of an anthology compiled by the authors.

    ⑩ Bibliography : p. 389–400.

          ⑪
      1. Walking

    G504.S9   796.5′1   67—25376

      Library of Congress   [68f5]

The encircled numbers do not appear on the card in its file. They correspond to the following explanations:

① Library call number   ⑦ Date of publication

② Subject heading   ⑧ Length and size of book

③ Author   ⑨ Statement by author

④ Title   ⑩ 11-page bibliography in book

⑤ Place of publication   ⑪ Subject heading

⑥ Publisher

The above book, with the same information about it, is also entered in the card catalogue under "Sussman, Aaron" and "The Magic of Walking," the latter being alphabetized under the M's.

27C3 Cross-References

Even after you understand how books are entered three times in the card catalogue, you may still feel insecure in doing research. You may not know any authors or titles that will provide you with useful information, and you may not know what subject heading to look under. Suppose, for example, you had seen the recent headline "Why 26,000,000 Johnnies Can't Read" and had become curious as to why so many Americans are functionally illiterate. You might eventually decide on the topic "Some Controversial Methods of Teaching First-Graders to Read." What subject heading would you look under? You might well feel baffled and frustrated. But the standardized techniques of library research come to your aid.

First you canvass your mind for subject headings that might possibly be in the card catalogue and jot them down: "Reading," "Teaching Reading," "Teaching Methods" or "Methodology," "Phonics," "Look-Say Method," "Progressive Education," "Elementary Education," "Reading Readiness," and so on. Chances are high that at least one subject heading you thought of will be in the card catalogue. Then cross-references will come to your rescue. Most subject headings have a cross-reference card which lists various related headings. These cross-reference cards come *after* all the cards listing books under a particular subject heading, and they begin with "See also." For example, in one card catalogue, after a large number of books having the subject heading "Political Science," there are twelve cross-reference cards listing about one hundred subject headings, ranging from 'Administrative Law" to "World Politics." Some subjects will have many cross-references; some may have very few. But learning to use cross-references is an essential part of learning to write research papers. We will return to this point in Section 27D, Compiling a Working Bibliography, where you will see how using cross-references will aid you in compiling a preliminary bibliography.

27C4   The Periodical Indexes

Periodical literature is that which is published at regular intervals: daily, weekly, biweekly, monthly, and so on. The hundreds and hundreds of reputable magazines and learned journals that have been published in the past (such as *Life* and *Look*) or that are still being published are rich sources of information for writers of research papers. In fact, many topics—especially ones on contemporary issues or events—will send the researcher only to magazine articles, rather than to reference works and the card catalogue. To facilitate a researcher's use of the various magazines, all good libraries purchase cumulative periodical indexes, which list articles that have appeared in all the periodicals that any one index chooses as its domain. Articles are listed twice: by author and by subject heading.

For the freshman composition student who is learning to prepare a research paper, the most useful periodical index, by far, is *The Reader's Guide to Periodical Literature,* which lists articles from about 200 widely circulated magazines. The *Guide* begins at 1900 and covers many good magazines now defunct. About every ten to twelve weeks a small volume of the *Guide* appears, and the small volumes are then combined into large volumes that list articles for one or two years. All the volumes of the *Guide* are always kept on open shelves in a library's reference room.

The list on the facing page is a sample of listings from *The Reader's Guide,* with an explanation of the first entry. The first word of each author's name and the subject headings are in boldface capitals. The title of each article is given in full. All abbreviations are clearly explained in the preface of each volume of the *Guide.* The first entry in the sample on page 251 refers to an illustrated article in *Popular Science,* volume 206, pages 108-10 and continued, February 1975.

Cross-references (such as that under "Sole") are as important in *The Reader's Guide* as they are in the card catalogue. For example, there are twenty-six cross-references for the subject heading "Literature" in one volume of the *Guide*, ranging from "Authorship" to "Symbolism in Literature." Remember, cross-references are extremely important to researchers.

"illustrated"   volume   pages   month and year

SOLAR heating
   How to trap solar heat with your windows.
      E. Allen. il Pop Sci 206:108-10+ F '75
   Now you buy solar heating equipment for
      your home. R. Stepler. il Pop Sci 206:74-
      7+ Mr '75
   Solar heating study. il Chemistry 48:4 F
      '75
   Sun power. P. Gwynne. il Newsweek 85:50+
      F 24 '75
SOLAR-MEC (Munters environmental control)
   unit. See Air conditioning equipment
SOLAR observatories. See Astronomical ob-
   servatories
SOLAR radiation
   Variable star. Sci Am 232:49 Mr '75
      See also
   Solar heating
   Solar wind
SOLAR system
   Most primitive objects in the solar system;
      carbonaceous chondrites. L. Grossman. il
      Sci Am 232:30-8 bibl(p 114) F '75
   Rubidium-87/strontium-87 age of Juvinas ba-
      saltic achondrite and early igneous activity
      in the solar system. C. J. Allègre and oth-
      ers. bibl il Science 187:436-8 F 7 '75
   Velikovsky: paradigms in collision. G. Kolo-
      dity. bibl il Bull Atom Sci 31:36-8 F '75
         See also
   Planets
SOLAR wind
   Electron microscopy of irradiation effects in
      space. M. Maurette and P. B. Price. bibl il
      Science 187:121-9 Ja 17 '75
   Solar nitrogen: evidence for a secular in-
      crease in the ratio of nitrogen-15 to nitro-
      gen-14. J. F. Kerridge. bibl il Science 188:
      162-4 Ap 11 '75
SOLE (fish)
      See also
   Cookery—Fish
SOLETA, Justin A.
   Education of the Amish. Educ Digest 40:48-50
      Ja '75
SOLID wastes. See Refuse and refuse disposal
SOLLID, John
   East Sequim bay; poem. Nation 220:473 Ap
      19 '75
SOLOMON, Goody L.
   Help for house hazards. Read Digest 106:
      177-8+ Mr '75
SOLOMON, Leslie
   Power surges and semiconductors. Pop Electr
      7:42 F '75
SOLTI, Sir Georg
   Americanization of Sir Georg Solti. R. C.
      Marsh. il Sat R 2:38-40+ Ap 19 '75 •
SOLVENTS
      See also
   Cleaning compositions
SOLZHENITSYN, Aleksandr Isaevich
   Memoir of repression. por Time 105:47 Mr 3
      '75 •

Other periodical indexes sometimes of use to beginning researchers are the following:

Art Index (from 1929)

Biography Index (from 1946)

Biological and Agricultural Index (includes books, pamphlets, and articles, from 1916)

Book Review Digest (lists book reviews by author, title, and subject, from 1905)

Dramatic Index (American and British, from 1909)

Education Index (includes books, pamphlets, and articles, from 1929)

Engineering Index (from 1884)

Index to Legal Periodicals (from 1926)

Industrial Arts Index (from 1913)

Poole's Index to Periodical Literature (covers American and British periodicals, most now defunct, from 1802 to 1906)

Public Affairs Information Service (covers books, periodicals, and pamphlets in economics, government, and public affairs, from 1915)

Quarterly Cumulative Index Medicus (covers medical literature, from 1927)

Social Science and Humanities Index (covers American and foreign periodicals, from 1907)

United States Government Publications (from 1895)

Most large libraries will have most of these indexes.

One other index that often is very useful is the *New York Times Index*, published monthly with annual volumes since 1913. It indexes all important news stories, editorials, and feature articles that appear in the *New York Times*, giving not only the location of the article but also a brief summary of it. Thus if your topic is one that at some time has been newsworthy—such as "The Entrapment of the Egyptian Third Army in the Yom Kippur War"—you can look in the

New York Times Index for 1973 and find the location and brief summaries of news reports that will furnish useful information. Even if your library does not have copies of past issues of the *New York Times,* the *Index* is still helpful, for other daily newspapers would be likely to have had news stories similar to those in the *New York Times* published on the same day.

27C5 The Periodical Card File

The periodical indexes are useful to you, of course, only when your library has a copy of the magazine you want. So that researchers can quickly find out whether particular issues of particular magazines are available, most large libraries have a periodical card file, which is located in the reference room and which lists the issues of all magazines the library has in its holdings. Smaller libraries sometimes enter the periodical cards alphabetically in the card catalogue, and some keep at the reference desk or check-out counter a typed list of all magazines in their holdings. Usually the magazines themselves are bound in volumes of six issues or more, with the inclusive dates printed on the spines, and are shelved alphabetically in the reference room. Libraries with large holdings often have old issues of magazines in storage and will make them available on request.

27D COMPILING A WORKING BIBLIOGRAPHY

A bibliography is a list of books, articles, and perhaps other source materials, such as television tapes, on a particular topic such as "Shakespeare" or "Shakespeare's Comedies" or "Shakespeare's *Twelfth Night*." The bibliography of your research paper will be a list of all the sources you used in preparing your paper. A working bibliography is a preliminary list of sources that you *hope* will provide you with useful information. It is standard practice for a researcher to compile as complete a working bibliography as possible *before* he or she begins reading sources and taking notes. Four points are of especial importance here: (1) If you have been able to derive from your topic the few general questions you expect your paper to answer (see Section 27B), you will be much less likely to enter useless sources in your working bibliography. (2) If a useful book listed in the card catalogue contains a bibliography (see Section 27C2), it is helpful to check that book out at once and use its bibliography. (3) Be especially careful to make full use of cross-references in both the card catalogue and *The Reader's Guide.* And (4) after you have compiled a working bibliography and have begun reading and taking notes, watch for other sources that you can add to your working bibliography. Thus the working bibliography is fluid, not static. You will probably drop from it sources that turn out not to be useful, and you will probably add to it after you begin reading your source materials.

Standard procedure calls for listing bibliographic entries on 3″ x 5″ cards. You *never* enter more than one item on one card. In the upper right-hand corners, number each card consecutively; having the cards numbered will let you identify the sources of your notes (see Section 27F1) by number rather than by authors and titles. Be certain to enter on each bibliography card all essential information about the book or article; failure to enter complete information will cost you much wasted time in rechecking when you are ready to obtain materials from the library and when you write footnotes and prepare the formal bibliography for your paper.

Put on each bibliography card all the following items of information that are applicable (some apply only to books; some only to magazine articles):

  (1) the library call number of a book or periodical
  (2) the full name of the author
  (3) the exact title of the item

(4) the date and place of publication and the publisher of a book

(5) the exact name of a magazine

(6) the date and volume number (if any) of a magazine and the pages on which the article appears

(7) the name and volume number of any reference work, the title of the article, and the pages on which the article appears

(8) a note as to whether the item has a bibliography of its own or some other feature, such as illustrations, that may be useful to you

All this information (except 7) can be obtained from the card catalogue or *The Reader's Guide;* you need not check out materials from the library to compile a working bibliography. *The value of following this standard procedure cannot be overemphasized.*

Here is a sample bibliography card:

403.8
B43   3

Brown, Roger. <u>Words and Things;</u>
an <u>Introduction to Language</u>. New York:
the Free Press, 1958

(Has bibliography)

A bibliography card with complete information will allow you to write footnotes and the entry in the formal bibliography without consulting the card catalogue or *The Reader's Guide* again. Also, numbering the cards 1, 2, 3, and so on, will let you indicate on your note cards where your information came from without having to write the title and author on the note card itself.

27E OUTLINING: PRELIMINARY AND FORMAL

27E1 Preliminary Outlining

The next step after compiling a working bibliography is to make, as best you can, a preliminary, scratch outline of the main points (Roman-numeral headings) of your paper. If, as you were advised to do in Section 27B, you have derived from your topic the few general questions you expect your paper to answer, you can make a serviceable preliminary outline. For example, if you should select the topic "Charles Dickens's Reactions to America and Americans," you might begin with this preliminary outline:

I. The number of and reasons for Dickens's trips to America
II. His reactions to the social structure of America
III. His reactions to the geography and climate of America
IV. His contacts with and reactions to notable American writers

Even with this slight preliminary outline, your task of scanning and reading your source materials for useful information will be far easier than if you begin reading and taking notes with no plan in mind. Also, with such a preliminary outline you can indicate by Roman numerals on your note cards where the information on them will fit in your paper.

As you read and take notes, you should revise your preliminary outline as seems appropriate, perhaps adding subheadings.

27E2   Formal Outlining

A preliminary, or scratch, outline, which need not observe all the principles of formal outlining, is for the writer's use; but a formal outline is for the reader. Your instructor may require you to submit a formal outline with your research paper, and he or she may specify either a topic outline, in which the headings are phrases, or a sentence outline. Example:

TOPIC OUTLINE: Faulkner's association with Sherwood Anderson in New Orleans

SENTENCE OUTLINE: Faulkner associated with Sherwood Anderson in New Orleans.

In the rest of this section, illustrations will be of the topic-outline kind.

Your formal outline should observe the following six principles of good outlining: (1) Your outline should be properly balanced. It should not consist only of a few Roman-numeral headings, and it probably should not have headings below the third level. For a 2500-word paper, an outline usually should consist of only two or three levels. Don't make outline headings out of specific details.

(2) Make your outline headings meaningful. Example:

MEANINGLESS HEADINGS: I. Introduction
                       II. Newspaper work

MEANINGFUL HEADINGS: I. Mark Twain's arrival in Nevada
                      II. His first full-time job as a newspaper reporter

In a scratch outline, headings need only be meaningful to the writer, but a formal outline should tell all readers quickly the main points of the paper.

(3) Be sure your headings are parallel in content. All the Roman-numeral headings should be divisions of the title or topic; all the capital-letter headings should be divisions of Roman-numeral headings; and so on. Example:

FAULTY PARALLELISM   I. Patton's sensational behavior
OF CONTENT: A. His slapping a soldier
                B. His leaking security information to the press
          II. His attempt to start a war with Russia

For parallelism of content, Roman numeral II should be C under Roman numeral I, for it is a division of that heading, not of the topic.

(4) Keep your headings parallel in structure. In a sentence outline no problem exists, but in a topic outline all the headings in any one division and level should have the same grammatical structure. Example:

FAULTY PARALLELISM   I. The critics' first reaction to *The Waste*
OF STRUCTURE: *Land*
          II. Coming to understand its symbolic meaning

A noun phrase and a verb phrase are in faulty parallelism. For proper parallelism of structure, Roman numeral II should be a noun phrase too:

PROPER PARALLELISM: II. The critics' later recognition of the symbolic meaning of *The Waste Land*

(5) Do not use single subheadings except to list examples. Example:

WRONG: I. Emerson's reaction to Whitman's poetry
        A. Favorably impressed
    II. James Russell Lowell's reaction to Whitman's poetry

The heading A should simply be incorporated into Roman numeral I, perhaps as "Emerson's favorable reaction to Whitman's poetry."

RIGHT: I. The initial success of the Head Start program
       A. Example: Results in the Grace Bird Elementary
         School
     II. The first expansion of the Head Start program

(6) Whatever your method of punctuation and of numbering headings, be consistent.

27F NOTE-TAKING AND SOME RELATED PROBLEMS

After you have compiled a working bibliography and have prepared as much of a preliminary outline as you can, your next step is to begin reading or scanning your sources to find information useful for your paper. Since you cannot remember all that you read, you must take notes, which should be written on 4″ x 6″ cards. Using your preliminary outline, you should arrange your bibliography cards in what seems to you to be the best order for investigating your sources, but of course you often must guess which book or article to read or scan next. If your topic is on a controversial issue, evaluate your sources as best you can for reliability and completeness of information. Avoid articles that have a strong ring of propaganda to them, such as one that labels a respectable politician as either a communist or fascist. As you take notes, try to digest and assimilate your materials in order to understand your topic well; do not transfer information from a source to a note card without letting it pass through and make an impression on your mind.

27F1 Techniques of Note-taking

Follow these directions in taking notes: (1) Identify the source of your information with the number of its bibliography card. This will help you avoid repeated copying of titles and authors. (2) Enter on each note card the exact page numbers from which its information comes. This will prevent your having to recheck page numbers in case you need to footnote the information. (3) Using your preliminary outline, avoid putting on one note card two or more pieces of information that will fall under different Roman-numeral headings. As your preliminary outline develops, try to indicate on each card just which part of your paper the information on the card belongs in. (4) Never put information from two sources on one note card; each card should have just one bibliography-card number. (5) Learn to scan articles and chapters from books so that you can quickly tell whether a source has useful information for you. The fuller your preliminary outline, the more effectively you can scan for useful information. When you see that a source has information important to your paper, stop scanning and read carefully in order to take usable notes. (6) Take condensed or verbatim notes according to directions given in Sections 27F2 and 27F3.

Here is a sample note card, written for a paper entitled "The Purchase of Russian America":

I   5

Quite clear why Russia wanted to sell Russian America. The territory was a burden. Produced no net income. Russian American Company bankrupt, wanting subsidies. Territory too far from seat of Russia's government. On verge of war with England and feared England might capture the territory. Needed money and felt it best to sell rather than risk total loss.

                                                         pp. 21-22

The Arabic numeral 5 is the number of the bibliography card listing the source. The information, which is condensed, came from pages 21–22 of the source. The Roman numeral I indicates that this information belongs to the first main point of the paper.

27F2   Direct Quotations

Direct quotations have four uses in research papers: (1) to give the exact words of an authority to lend weight to a point of view; (2) to present original evidence as proof of a point; (3) to emphasize a fact or opinion; and (4) to share with the reader a passage that is striking because of its excellent style, wit, or some other feature. You should *not* use a direct quotation unless it clearly fulfills one of these purposes; do not aimlessly scatter quotations throughout your paper.

Quotations that occupy five or fewer lines of a typed paper should be incorporated into the paper with quotation marks. Longer quotations, called insets, are indented five spaces, are singled spaced, and are *not* enclosed in quotation marks. Both of these methods are illustrated in Section 27H. Three spaced periods (. . .), called an ellipsis, indicate that part of a direct quotation has been omitted.

When, in taking notes, you think a passage might serve well in your paper as a direct quotation, put it on your note card verbatim and clearly indicate with quotation marks that it is the exact wording of the original. You may, of course, decide later not to use such a passage as a direct quotation. Don't overuse direct quotations.

When entering a direct quotation into your paper, lead smoothly into it with an introductory phrase or sentence that announces that a quotation is coming and indicates its purpose. For example, such a simple phrase as "According to the well-known cosmologist Fred Hoyle, . . ." can serve to introduce a quotation and tell the reader that an authority is being cited. Don't just use a direct quotation abruptly; announce it in some way.

27F3   Paraphrasing and Plagiarism

Since only a small part of your research paper will consist of direct quotations, most of your note-taking should not be verbatim but should be a condensed version of the information you expect to use. Thus as you take notes, use your own words as much as possible and compress the information so that you can re-expand it in your own words when you enter it into your paper. The process of using your own words instead of a direct quotation to incorporate source materials into your paper is known as paraphrasing. That is, you do not change the information but you do change the wording so that it is in your style and not the original author's. If you take condensed notes, paraphrasing will be much easier for you.

Failure to paraphrase is one of the deadly sins in research-paper writing, for it leads to plagiarism, which is literary theft, or pretending someone else's writing is yours. Many teachers fail research papers for plagiarism alone. Of course, since you are gathering your information from written sources, you must use some of the wording of the original, but you must not quote whole sentences and then, by not using quotation marks, pretend that you composed them. Your research paper, for the most part, must be of your own composition. Technical terms, statistics, and some phrasing must be as they are in the original source; the structure of the sentences and much of the vocabulary must be yours. As a rough guide, try never to have in one sentence more than five consecutive words exactly as they appear in the original source (except, of course, for direct quotations).

27G   DOCUMENTATION

Documentation in a research paper is the acknowledgment of the sources used. It includes footnotes and the formal bibliography.

27G1   Uses of Footnotes

In research papers, footnotes are used (1) to acknowledge the sources of direct quotations; (2) to acknowledge the sources of important paraphrased information that might be subject to question or that the reader might want to pursue further; and (3) to enter explanatory comments that would be out of place in the text of the paper. This third use is rare in freshman research papers.

Do *not* footnote (1) well-known quotations (such as those from the Bible); (2) ordinary dictionary definitions, unless one has some special purpose such as refuting widely accepted information; (3) simple and easily ascertainable facts, such as birth and death dates of a famous person; and (4) paraphrased information that a critical reader will accept without question and that is not of considerable importance to the main point of your paper.

27G2   Location of Footnotes

Some instructors prefer footnotes to be at the bottom of pages that have sources acknowledged, and some instructors prefer all the footnotes to be on a separate page, or pages, at the end of the research paper, but before the formal bibliography. The latter method is much the easier for students who type their papers, but in Section 27H the bottom-of-the-page method is illustrated.

Follow these directions in entering footnotes in your paper: (1) In the text of your paper, put the footnote number immediately after the final quotation marks for a short quotation, at the end of an inset quotation, and at the end of a paraphrased passage of which you are acknowledging the source. (2) If an author's full name has been used in a footnoted passage, omit the name in the footnote if the footnote is at the bottom of the page. (3) Use raised numbers, not numbers followed by periods, in both the text of your paper and with the footnotes themselves. (4) Number footnotes consecutively. (5) Indent each footnote as though it began a paragraph. (6) Single space each footnote, but double space between footnotes. (7) When putting footnotes at the bottom of a page, draw or type a two- or three-inch line between the text and the footnotes; leave a double space above and below the line. And (8) be sure that each footnote has marks of punctuation and underlining exactly as the forms in Section 27G3 specify.

27G3   Footnote Forms

Following are footnote forms for every kind of source material you are likely to use in preparing your research paper. Some rare forms, such as one for a book with unnumbered pages, are omitted. These forms follow *The MLA Style Sheet,* a publication of the Modern Language Association of America. The use of italics is equivalent to underlining in hand- or typewriting. The abbreviations *p.* and *pp.* mean, of course, "page" and "pages." Should you need them, which is unlikely, the abbreviations *n.d., n.p.,* and *n.pag.* mean "no date," "no publisher," and "no page." Within the parentheses are the place of publication, the publisher, and the date of publication.

A book with one author:

[1]James Work, *Boswell's Youth* (New York: Vintage Press, 1972), p. 71.

A book with two or more authors:

[2]Rachel Foreman, Clive Sims, and Earl Bates, *English Politics in the 1780's* (Chicago: The Univ. of Chicago Press, 1974), pp. 204–05.

(**Note:** If there are more than three authors, name the first and add *et al.* in this manner: "George Witter et al., ..." *Et al.* means "and others.")

An edited collection, the editor being cited:

[3]Norman Thomas, ed., *Essays on the Enlightenment* (Oxford: Clarendon Press, 1975), p. ix.

An edited work, the original author being cited:

⁴James Boswell, *Journal of a Tour to the Hebrides,* ed. Thomas Parnell (Cambridge: Belknap Press, 1969), p. 108.

An edited collection, one of the authors being cited:

⁵Edward Hooker, "Boswell's Phobias," in *Neoclassical Studies,* ed. John Putt (Los Angeles: Clark Press, 1962), pp. 116–17.

A work in several volumes:

⁶Samuel Monk, *Johnson's Circle* (New York: Norton, 1971), II, 312.

(**Note:** When page numbers follow a volume number, the abbreviation *p.* or *pp.* is omitted.)

A translated work:

⁷Klaus Brindle, *Political Poetry,* trans. H. T. More (New York: Random House, 1952), p. 92.

A later or revised edition:

⁸W. A. Tuttle, *Boswell in Holland,* 2nd ed. (New York: Viking Press, 1973), p. 84.

A reference work:

⁹"Boswell, James," *The Dictionary of National Biography* (London: Oxford Univ. Press, 1917), II, 896.

An anonymous pamphlet:

¹⁰*Preparing Your Dissertation for Microfilming* (Ann Arbor, Mich.: University Microfilms, n.d.), p. 4.

(**Note:** Signed pamphlets are footnoted just as books are.)

An article from a learned journal:

¹¹Michael Abrams, "Dr. Johnson's Poetry," *College English,* 30 (Jan. 1969), 267–68.

(**Note:** The 30 is the volume number.)

An article in a monthly magazine:

¹²Gary Puttle, "Boswell and Louisa," *The Atlantic,* Sept. 1968, pp. 90–92.

An article in a weekly magazine:

[13]Norman Uncles, "Mr. Boswell and Dr. Johnson," *Saturday Review,* 26 July 1969, pp. 21–22.

An unsigned article in a weekly magazine:

[14]"New Dirt on Boswell," *Time,* 4 July 1969, p. 32.

Articles in newspapers:

[15]Robert Kirsh, "New Material on Boswell," *The Los Angeles Times,* 9 Nov. 1974, pt. III, p. 26, cols. 2–4.

[16]"A New Boswell Scandal," *The Spokesman Review* (Spokane, Wash.), 8 Jan. 1975, p. 12, col. 3.

Subsequent references:

Once a work has been footnoted, subsequent references to it may be short forms. If a reference is identical to the immediately preceding reference except for page number, the abbreviation *Ibid.,* meaning "in the same place or work," may be used. If the page number is also the same, then *Ibid.* alone suffices.

[17]James Work, *Boswell as Lawyer* (New York: Norton, 1975), p. 121.

[18]Ibid.

[19]Ibid., p. 146.

If an author has only one work cited, just the last name and the page number make a short form. (Of course, if two authors with the same last name have been cited, then a full name is needed in a short form.) If an author has more than one work cited, then the short form must be the last name of the author, the title (shortened, if convenient), and the page number. If a subsequent reference is to an anonymous work, the title and page number make a short form.

[20]Thomas, p. xi.

[21]Work, *Boswell as Lawyer,* p. 106.

[22]"New Dirt on Boswell," p. 33.

27G4 Bibliographic Forms

At the end of your research paper you present a formal bibliography of the sources you have used. All bibliographic entries should be in one alphabetized list of authors' names.

If a work is anonymous, alphabetize it by the title, but ignore *a, an,* and *the* as initial words. Authors' last names come first in bibliographic entries. If you list two or more entries for the same author, you may substitute a long dash (————) for the name after its first use. Bibliographic entries are indented just the opposite of footnotes: the first line is flush left; the next line is indented. Single space each bibliographic entry but double space between entries. Do not number entries. Use the heading "Bibliography" and start your bibliography at the top of a new page, regardless of how much space is left on the preceding page. The following forms are modeled on those of *The MLA Style Sheet:*

A book:

Foreman, Rachel, and Clive Sims. *Boswell's Politics.* New York: Harcourt Brace Jovanovich, 1971.

(**Note:** If there is more than one author only the first author's name is inverted.)

Edited books:

Essays on the Enlightenment. Ed. Norman Thomas. Oxford: Clarendon Press, 1975.
Boswell, James, *Journal of a Tour to the Hebrides.* Ed. Thomas Parnell. Cambridge: Belknap Press, 1969.

A work in several volumes:

Parker, W. O. *Boswell: A Biography.* 2 vols. New York: Holt, Rinehart and Winston, 1973.

A translated work:

Brindle, Klaus, *Political Poetry.* Trans. H. T. More. New York: Random House, 1952.

A later or revised edition:

Tuttle, W. A. *Boswell in Holland.* 2nd ed. New York: Viking Press, 1973.

A reference work:

"Boswell, James," *The Dictionary of National Biography.* London: Oxford Univ. Press, 1917. II, 893–900.

An anonymous pamphlet:

English Political Morality. London: The Society of Friends, 1968.

An article in a learned journal:

Hogg, Jonathan. "The Sources of *Rasselas.*" *New England Quarterly,* 27 (Summer 1954), 278–91.

An article in a monthly magazine:

Puttle, Gary. "Boswell's Medical History." *Harper's,* Oct. 1972, pp. 42–52.

An article in a weekly magazine:

Uncles, Norman. "Mr. Boswell and Dr. Johnson." *Saturday Review,* 26 July 1969, pp. 20–25.

An unsigned article in a weekly magazine:

"New Dirt on Boswell." *Time,* 4 July 1969, pp. 32–33.

Articles in newspapers:

Kirsh, Robert. "New Material on Boswell." *The Los Angeles Times,* 9 Nov. 1974, pt. III, p. 26, cols. 2–4.
"A New Boswell Scandal." *The Spokesman Review* (Spokane, Wash.), 8 Jan. 1975, p. 12, col. 3.

27H SAMPLE PAGES FROM A RESEARCH PAPER

In preparing and submitting your research paper, follow your instructor's directions as to (1) the kind of folder, if any, to contain the paper; (2) the kind of paper to use and the method of typing; (3) the width of margins; (4) the kind of title page to prepare; (5) the kind of outline, if any, to prepare; (6) the location of footnotes; and (7) the method of entering charts, graphs, appendixes, and so on.

The following two sample pages of a research paper illustrate (1) the introductory paragraph of a research paper; (2) the introduction to and method of entering a short quotation; (3) the introduction to and method of entering a long (inset) quotation; and (4) the placement of footnotes at the bottom of a page.

EDUCATIONAL REFORM IN SOVIET RUSSIA IN 1968

The communist leaders of the Soviet Union have always maintained that among their greatest achievements is the constitutional
right of the Soviet citizens to free public education. The right
to ten years of education has always existed in Soviet Russia, but
the country's educational system has undergone many revisions over
the decades. A close inquiry into the causes of these revisions sheds
much light on the progress of the communist experiment. One American expert on Soviet education maintains that "the Soviet leaders
. . . claim that they revise and update their educational system
to meet the changing needs and goals of their regime, but much
evidence indicates that educational changes are made chiefly for
purposes of political indoctrination."[1] It may be, according to
Skolny, that it is becoming increasingly difficult for Russian
youth to be indoctrinated. The extensive educational reform in
Russia in 1968 seems to substantiate that conclusion.

A chief goal of Soviet education has consistently been to
abolish the social and economic distinctions between manual and

---

[1]Nicholas Skolny, Education in the U.S.S.R. (New York: The
New Press, 1972), p. 4.

-2-

mental labor, and of course this goal is political and need not
necessarily pertain to the quality of education.[2] Thus it
behooves the careful student of communism to examine closely the
details of any extensive reform in the educational system. The
details of the 1968 reform centered around the polytechnization of
all the schools.

In order to further merge the images of manual and mental
labor, the schools set about to create in Russian minds an association of productive labor with theoretical learning. After
witnessing first-hand many of the educational changes begun in
late 1967 and pressed vigorously in 1968, educational expert
Ina Kovarsky reported that

> The intent to associate learning with productivity
> begins in the first grade as pupils learn that recognizing
> words can be useful, in getting into the right room, for
> example, as well as just intellectually stimulating. As
> soon as pupils begin to learn some general physics, their
> learning is associated with vocational training and not just
> theory. Grades that older students receive for learning
> theory are openly compared with their productivity in their
> part-time jobs. A bright student but poor producer is not
> praised. No method seems to be spared to erase from the
> students' minds any idea that intellectuality is superior
> to physical productivity.[3]

Ina Kovarsky goes on to evaluate the quality of Soviet teaching and
comes to some conclusions unflattering to the communists.

---

[2]James Boroday, "Report from Russia," New Republic, 27 June
1969, p. 32.

[3]Quality of Instruction in Soviet Education (New York: Ross
and Schoenstein, 1970), pp. 8-9.

Index

A   5
B   6
C   7
D   8
E   9
F   0
G   1
H   2
I   3
J   4

CORRECTION CHART

ab	improper abbreviation (14C)
agr	faulty subject-verb agreement (6A-F)
apos	omitted or misused apostrophe (18A-C)
cap	capital letter needed (17A)
cl	lack of clarity (26D)
coh	lack of coherence (26F)
com	omitted or misused comma (10A-J)
comp	incomplete or false comparison (25A-C)
CS	comma splice or run-together sentence (3A-C)
D	faulty diction (20A-D; 21A-D; 22A-D)
DM	dangling modifier (23D)
DN	double negative (4C)
frag	sentence fragment (2A-D)
glos	glossaries (16G; 22B)
hyp	omitted or misused hyphen (19A-E)
id	faulty idiom (22C)
ital	omitted or misused underlining (14B)
K	awkward construction
lc	lower-case letter needed (17B)
log	faulty logic (26G)
man	incorrect manuscript form (14A)
MM	misplaced modifier (23E)
mod	misused modifier (4A-C)